INFINITE DIVISIONS

An Anthology of Chicana Literature

EDITED BY

Tey Diana Rebolledo
Eliana S. Rivero

The University of Arizona Press / Tucson

The University of Arizona Press
Copyright © 1993
Arizona Board of Regents
All Rights Reserved

⊛ This book is printed on acid-free, archival-quality paper.
Manufactured in the United States of America.

06 05   9 8 7 6 5

Library of Congress Cataloging-in-Publication Data

Infinite divisions : an anthology of Chicana literature / [compiled
   by] Tey Diana Rebolledo, Eliana S. Rivero.
      p.   cm.
   Includes bibliographical references.
   ISBN 0-8165-1252-3 (acid-free paper). —
   ISBN 0-8165-1384-8 (pbk. : acid-free paper)
      1. American literature—Mexican American authors.   2. Mexican
American women—Literary collections.   3. Mexican Americans—
Literary collections.   4. American literature—Women authors.
   I. Rebolledo, Tey Diana, 1937–   .   II. Rivero, Eliana S. (Eliana
Suárez), 1940–   .
   PS508.M4154   1993   92-45101
   810.8'09287–dc20

The preparation of this volume was made possible in part by grants from the
Division of Research programs of the National Endowment for the Humani-
ties, an independent federal agency; the Center for Regional Studies at the
University of New Mexico; the Graduate School at the University of Nevada-
Reno; and with the help of The Southwest Institute for Research on Women
at the University of Arizona. Partial funding was also provided by the Arizona
Commission on the Arts through appropriations from the Arizona State
Legislature and grants from the National Endowment for the Arts.

For Our Daughters
Tey Marianna Nunn
Elisabet Rivero

Contents

3   Self and Others

5   Myths and Archetypes

Preface

When we first started this project in 1984 with a grant from the National Endowment for the Humanities, we did not know that we would produce an anthology. Initially, the project was to compile an intellectual/critical history of Chicana literature dating from the 1960s. Once we found texts, which in those days were hard to come by, we intended to write a critical volume examining the vision that Chicana writers had and how they expressed it. Tey Diana Rebolledo traveled over the West and Southwest visiting libraries and archives searching for chapbooks, journals, magazines, and publications from small presses that would document Chicanas' writing. We both read the books that were barely beginning to be published by Arte Público, Bilingual Review/Press, and Third Woman Press, to name a few, and we listened and talked to the writers. Often they sent us their unpublished materials. The surprise was to see how many women were writing, even if they were not published in mainstream publications that were easy to access. What we had originally thought to be a scarcity of material turned out to be thousands of creative texts. Both of us poured over these texts, hunting for common denominators: themes, language, attitudes, perceptions. And as the critical book began to take shape, it became clear that we would be talking about many texts that the general reader would not have access to. It also became clear that many of the texts that we had so painstakingly hunted down would be lost if they were not preserved in a larger context. Thus the idea of an anthology of Chicana literature became a reality.

Anthologies are always difficult, however. The questions and problems that the compilers face are sometimes unresolvable. Whom are we going to include? What will be the underlying vision of the anthology? Will we choose only the "best" texts from the "best" authors, or will we include texts that also have cultural and historical significance? Who are the "best" authors—what criteria will we use for the selections? Will including some authors and not others create a sort of "canon" of Chicana literature, and is that desirable?

Although when we began this project Chicana literature was still developing, in the ensuing years it has blossomed into a rich and complex body of work. And, as Chicana writers begin to enjoy more mainstream attention, there is also some suspicion ascribed to the anthologizer. Are we appropriating the writers? We also asked ourselves that question; but still the collective vision won out. As editors we felt it important that we document our literary and cultural history: that the visions of writers less well known should be represented along with the better known ones. As the project continued and we unearthed more and more early writers, the frontiers of its early history began expanding backward into time until we were in the early 1880s. This inclusion of early writers has begun to foment another project by Rebolledo that will extend to the late sixteenth century.

In answer to some of the questions posited here, we began to organize the writings we had collected into thematic areas. It was certain that a major area of concern was that of the struggle to define oneself, as a woman and as a member of an ethnic minority group. We wanted to know how these things shape Chicanas' lives: how they relate to language, what language writers choose to speak in, whether women writers write differently from men, how women feel about being writers, why there are so many texts about growing up, who the role models in the stories are, who the symbolic figures are and why they were chosen.

Once major areas of emphasis were decided upon we tried to group texts by specific subjects, rather than placing all works by one author together. We found that interesting dialogues emerged among the texts. The perspectives on mothers or on la Malinche seem to talk to one another.

Deciding on the criteria for the text selection itself was also difficult. At first we thought we should only include authors that had already produced a published body of work. But we had difficulty defining a "published body of work" for the minority writer. A published body of work could mean books published by established publishing houses or in reputable journals and literary magazines. But this definition didn't take into account published works appearing in small local or regional presses (Mango) and magazines (*Caracol*) or those works that had been self-published. The amount of significant work in these publications obviously needed to be included. As the anthology took shape it also became obvious that sometimes a single piece of work was so important to the metadialogue taking place within Chicano writing that it needed to be included, as in the case of "La Loca de la Raza Cósmica" of La Chrisx, a female answer to "Yo soy Joaquín."

Early on we made a decision to search out those wonderful texts that could be called feminist, that is, that showed women's strengths. Those texts, we thought, inquired about how women came into their own, and how they survived difficult, often violent situations and relationships. It also encompassed how they had achieved power, how the community recognized their power, and from where they derived their strength and their survival skills. We wanted to show how these writers used humor in adversity, tenderness and sympathy in times of need. We also wanted to emphasize their celebrations and their concern for community.

Because Chicana writers have created their texts in Spanish, English, and a mixture of both languages, we had to consider linguistic questions from the onset. We decided that we would publish works in both Spanish and English, and, if a text had originally been published in Spanish with no translation, we would reproduce the original and add a translation. Where the text was in English but with a great deal of Spanish idiomatic expressions we would add footnotes for the sake of English readers. When the Spanish seemed to be easily understood, or referred to general concepts made clear later in the text, we did not footnote. In order to preserve the flavor of the writings, as well as the authors' intentions, we have left the Spanish as it appears in the original text.

Many of the texts written early in the Chicano Renaissance (in the sixties and early seventies) were poetic; today we have many more narrative pieces. Because we included many texts for their historic as well as literary significance, there are many more poems included in this anthology than narratives.

The anthology has both a historical framework and an internal logic. It begins with a chapter which includes some of the early lives of women in the oral tradition, such as the stories found in the California narratives in the WPA Archives in New Mexico. In an attempt to begin to elaborate a heritage of both the oral and the written traditions, this chapter also includes texts from women writing before the Chicano Renaissance. Chapter 2 contains many texts dealing with personal identity, as Chicana writers tried to define their multi-faceted lives. Chapter 3 contains texts exploring the complex relationships writers have with friends and family. Although most of these texts concern relationships with women, the last section also illustrates the plurality of Chicana relationships with men. Chapter 4 examines the shifting spaces of Chicana reality, from private spaces of the house to public spaces, such as the city, and it describes how Chicanas feel about such spaces. In Chapter 5 the texts center around myths and archetypes central to Chicana writing: from Doña Marina /

La Malinche and La Llorona to the curandera, as well as to some more contemporary heroines. Chapter 6 explores why writers write and what they write about, as well as the process of writing itself. These texts discuss creativity and the difficulties of writing when work and household tasks demand one's time. Chapter 7 contains a series of growing up texts, where writers examine how societal and cultural factors influenced them to become the persons they are. Finally, Chapter 8 envisions the multiple empowering factors and celebrations in Chicanas' lives. Thus the pieces that comprise the anthology are 173 creative texts and 5 texts from the oral tradition; there are 52 authors and 4 storytellers. What becomes evident in this volume and in the process of compiling it is that many important works have already been written; other works are underway even now, exploring the condition of being a writer and of being a Chicana. This anthology is only a beginning in the enormous task of documenting our social and cultural history.

In particular we would like to thank some friends who were there with advice and support when the going got rough. Their collective strength and wisdom were extremely nourishing: Sandra Cisneros, Margarita Cota-Cárdenas, Erlinda Gonzales-Berry, and Pat Mora. Y como siempre a Mikko.

Tey Diana Rebolledo
Eliana S. Rivero

Photographic Images

Some of the Contributors

EULALIA PERZ 139 YEARS OF AGE

Eulalia Pérez, c 1880. *Courtesy Bancroft Library, University of California, Berkeley.*

Cleofas Jaramillo, c 1898–1900.
Courtesy Museum of New Mexico.

Nina Otero-Warren (center), c 1920. *Courtesy New Mexico State Records Center and Archives.*

María Esperanza López de Padilla, 1941. *Courtesy of author.*

Carmen Celia Beltrán.
Courtesy of author.

Esther Vernon Galindo (left) and cousin **Ella Galindo,** c 1920. *Courtesy of daughter.*

Estela Portillo Trambley. *Courtesy of author.*

Cordelia Candelaria. *Courtesy of author.*

Gloria Anzaldúa. *Courtesy of Aunt Lute Books.*

Ana Castillo. *Photo credit Barbara Seyda. Courtesy of author.*

Lucha Corpi. *Photo credit Carolina Juárez. Courtesy of author.*

Inés Hernández. *Photo credit Juan A. Avila Hernández. Courtesy of author.*

Cherríe Moraga. *Photo credit © Lily Dong, 1989. Courtesy of author.*

Pat Mora. *Courtesy of author.*

Evangelina Vigil-Piñón. *Courtesy of author.*

Margarita Cota-Cárdenas.
Courtesy of author.

Antonia Quintana Pigno. *Courtesy of author.*

Gina Valdés. *Courtesy of author.*

María Herrera-Sobek. *Courtesy of author.*

Alma Villanueva. *Courtesy of author.*

Patricia Santana-Béjar.
Courtesy of author.

Mary Helen Ponce. *Courtesy of author.*

Beverly Sánchez-Padilla.
Courtesy of author.

Left to right: **Tey Diana Rebolledo, Demetria Martínez, Erlinda Gonzales-Berry, Denise Chávez.** *Photo credit Cynthia Farah. Courtesy Cynthia Farah.*

Miriam Bornstein. *Courtesy of author.*

Adaljiza Sosa Riddell.
Courtesy of author.

Marina Rivera, 1992. *Photo credit Merrill the Muralist. Courtesy of author.*

Sandra Cisneros. *Photo credit Rubén Guzmán. 1992. Courtesy of author.*

Carmen Tafolla. *Courtesy of author.*

Patricia Preciado Martin, 1992. *Courtesy of author.*

Infinite Divisions

Introduction

You insult me
When you say I'm
Schizophrenic.
My *divisions are*
Infinite.
BERNICE ZAMORA

Life for Mexican American[1] women in the United States has always been complex. Yet, as women, they have been portrayed in literature, the movies, and television of the United States, particularly in the West, as "Chile Queens"—the spicy Mexican women of the saloon—or as enduring, suffering mothers. Reality, as Bernice Zamora indicates, is far different. However, until the Chicano Renaissance of the 1960s Mexican American women in their totality were unrecognized from the outside. Certainly they wrote little about their own experiences, and what they wrote was generally unknown. In the years since 1960, however, Chicanas have been writing their experiences—as this anthology clearly shows. In fact, Chicana literature is still an emerging literature. Each year adds to the outpouring of new creative literature and essays enriching the known corpus of Chicano literature. With the growing number of Chicana scholars,[2] literary archaeologists concerned with tracing Chicana social and

---

1. Many terms are used to define the Mexican/Chicano experience. Here, when talking about the colonial Southwestern experience, the women are referred to as Spanish/Mexicanas or as Hispanas. After the Mexican National Period they are known as Mexicanas, and after 1848 as Mexicanas, Mexican American, or are identified by the regions in which they lived: Californias, Tejanas, Nuevo Mexicanas. After 1960 we refer to the women as Chicanas. This nomenclature, albeit complex, is an attempt to be historically accurate, as well as to define identity as the women would have defined it themselves.

2. Here we do not necessarily just mean women scholars, but all those scholars who study Chicanas.

literary history have also become increasingly aware of earlier testimonies and writings of Hispanas/Mexicanas in the West and Southwest which enhance our knowledge of the lives of these women. Information from California narratives in the Bancroft Library, the Public Works Administration files and stories, and other oral and written information that has been passed from generation to generation suggests the rich creative life Hispanic women in the West lived. Nevertheless, the information on the struggles, lives, and dreams of Hispanic women in the West from 1580 to 1940 is just beginning to be pieced together.

LAS POBLADORAS (THE COLONIZERS)

After the conquest of Mexico by Hernán Cortés in 1521, the Spaniards continued to look for riches in these new lands. Because Mexico was so rich in material goods and people, the Spaniards believed other places in the unexplored territories would surely yield similar treasures. Early explorers searched for the mythic land of origin of the Aztecs—Aztlán—said to be in the North (Chávez, 8–13). Some searched for the Fountain of Youth. Other myths, such as that of the fabulous seven cities of Cíbola, attracted treasure seekers. Even after these myths were dispelled, the pressure of expansion and the desire of colonists to seek their own land pushed families out from Mexico in successive waves onto the northern frontier.

Although the exploration and colonization of the northern frontier has been attributed to military men and priests, shortly after the first explorations the areas were settled by colonists: families that included a goodly number of women. Indeed, in the early expeditions to New Mexico, which was the first area beyond what we now know as Mexico to be colonized, there was at least one woman who accompanied the soldiers. In the Espejo expedition of 1582, Casilda de Anaya and her three sons accompanied her husband Miguel Sánchez Valenciano. We know she became pregnant on the journey (Hammond, Rey, 1). In the Juan de Oñate expedition of 1598, forty-seven wives accompanied the soldiers. Settlement efforts were important to the Spanish government, so women were recruited, and they traveled to what for them were unknown frontiers. They often walked from up to ten miles a day and had little food and water, and, because their husbands were military men, many soon became widows.[3]

Life was hard for these women even after they had settled. Ranches and

---

3. Because church marriage records were meticulously kept, those desiring to enter into matrimony had to declare whether they had been previously married, to whom, and what happened to them. Much information about life on the frontiers has been retrieved from these records.

farms were scattered along rivers. They had to build houses, run households, care for children, nurse the sick, plant, and take care of livestock. Life in the small towns was often no easier. It has been pointed out by scholars that life in the provincial frontiers controlled by Spain was very different from the individualistic frontier that is portrayed in the literature of the United States. Individuals and families were allowed to migrate to the provinces only by permission of the crown and were not generally free to come and go as they pleased. Thus the early settlers came in groups sponsored by the government or by private individuals, were granted land on which to live, but could not simply settle anywhere without permission. Colonization on the northern outposts of New Spain was a group effort with carefully established rules and regulations. It is true that women were granted special rights under Spanish law that later immigrants under the Anglo tradition did not have: under the Spanish crown women had the right to inherit and own property under their own name and separately from their husbands, and they had the right to litigate in court and often did. It is from these court, property, and church records that we are able to obtain much of the information we have about Spanish/Mexicana women during the colonial period.

Of course the settlers in New Mexico, as later in California and Texas, did not settle a wilderness. They came across established social orders of native peoples. Indeed they often lived near them because the native peoples generally settled near water and fertile lands. The Spanish/Mexicanos would use the native peoples, if they could, as a source of labor, and they felt it part of their responsibility to Christianize them. Their relationships with the native population were always a gradual process of racial, cultural, and social interplay. At best the interplay was beneficial and peaceful. More often, however, the Spanish/Mexicanos subjugated and oppressed the natives. And while we have some information about social interchange among Mexicanos and Indians as a whole, as yet the relationships of Hispanas with Native American women have not been carefully studied.

It is also clear that the military men and female and male settlers who arrived in New Mexico were a mixed group of people. Hispanas, mestizas, mexicanas, blacks, mulatas, lobas, and persons of varying degrees of mixed blood mingled with the native peoples. The racial composition of the women on the frontier continued to be complex. New terms evolved to explain racial composition: *coyota/coyote*, which originally was the term for the mixture between Indios and Mestizos, in New Mexico evolved in the nineteenth and twentieth centuries to describe a person of Mexican and other (mostly Anglo) ancestry.

The frontier was a place of great hardship for the settlers. The early colonists often took grain, food, and other goods from the Indians, leaving many "Indian women stark naked, holding their babies to their breasts" (Hernández, 41). In 1680, after almost one hundred years of settlement, the Indians in New Mexico finally rebelled against the often harsh treatment and injustices by the Spanish/Mexicanos. Known as the Pueblo Revolt, the rebellion affected the lives of the more than 2,400 settlers living in the area. Four hundred Hispanos died, survived by 2,000 others, mostly women and children. Many women were killed during the Pueblo Revolt; some of the women were captured. Records in the colonial archives before 1680 were destroyed so what little we know about the lives of women and their cultural and intellectual interests until the end of the colonial period generally comes from records and written sources after 1692. With the De Vargas resettlement effort in that year Hispano women and children returned to their homes in New Mexico. New settlers also were recruited. Among the women there were many widows and single female heads of households. They again included Mexican Indians, New Mexican Indians, blacks, mulattas, lobas, coyotas, and mestizas (Hernández, 87). They were strong independent women, and they came from all social classes.

During the seventeenth and eighteenth centuries the lives of Hispanic women in New Mexico continued to be difficult; survival was the primary concern. They built homes and ranches, cared for children and families, nurtured plants and animals. There were few doctors in the region, and women with knowledge of medicinal herbs and curing techniques were highly sought after. Illnesses and childbirth were important events in these isolated areas. Since there was little effective birth control, there are records of women having eleven, twelve, thirteen children, but little is known about how many of them survived.

Recently, scholarship has begun to focus more closely on women's lives and concerns during the colonial period, particularly as it can be traced through court documents. Ramón Gutiérrez, for example, showed how a 1702 court case on seduction and marital impediment, due to a previous promise of betrothal, not only illuminates cultural issues and the relationship between the sexes but documents the voice and predicament of a young woman (Gutiérrez, "Marriage," 447–58). Juana Luján had been seduced by Bentura de Esquibel, who promised to marry her. But Juana was not of the same social class: Bentura's father felt that "Juana Luján [was] not Bentura's equal in honor or racial status" (Gutiérrez, 452). Bentura's parent, wishing to stop the marriage, sent him away. Apparently, this tactic was effective, for when he returned to Santa Fe, he soon became betrothed to another. Juana Luján, now pregnant, asked the court to impede the marriage since she had a prior claim. During the court testimony Bentura, trying to show Juana lacked sexual integrity, sought to sully Juana's name by claiming that she was not a virgin when he seduced her, and moreover that a Mateo Márquez (who turned out to be her cousin) often frequented her home. Juana speaks out in her defense, as Gutiérrez points out, "acidly."

> How can Bentura say I was not a virgin when he himself saw the evident sign of my virginity which was the blood that was left stamped on his shirt from our act. That same blood which I tried to wash out of the shirt because of my great remorse. And while washing the shirt at the river my cousin Phelipa Mansanares saw me and asked what blood that was, and I told her what happened the night before. She saw me burn it so that it would not serve as a testament and remainder of my frailty. . . . That Bentura has had a change of heart and now wants to marry Bernardina Lucero saying that she is honorable and Spanish, I only say that I cannot dispute that Bernardina is indeed from a very honorable family; but that she is better than me in racial status is disputable, for I am as good as she. And finally, Reverend Father, I am forced, and will drop my impediment so that Bentura can marry whomever he wishes. For what kind of life would I have to endure if you forced him to marry me? And besides, the governor has threatened me, saying that he will stymie my request by whatever means are necessary. I am helpless against the sinister violence of such a formidable adversary. (Gutiérrez, "Marriage," 454–55)

Bentura was ordered to pay Juana 200 pesos as indemnity. These incidences of life, honor, and its importance to women in the colonial period are illustrated here. Moreover, Juana's independent resolve in standing up for herself and her family name is remarkable. Also, Juana sees clearly her social and political situation as she accedes to reality.

By 1770, the northern region of Mexico was a land marked by scattered small settlements, the settlement pattern being marked by gradual movement from central Mexico to the northern outposts and then to the frontier. There were three major north-south areas and routes that were composed of the following cities linking the centers with the frontier: (1) Durango, Chihuahua, and New Mexico (The Santa Fe Trail); (2) Sinaloa, Sonora, Baja California, Alta California; (3) Coahuila, Tamaulipas, Texas.

The settlement of Baja and Alta California was similar to that of New Mexico. Life for women followed many of the patterns characteristic of New Mexico. They were later settlements since Los Angeles was not established until 1781. The Spanish/Mexicano settler population was composed primarily of vaqueros and presidio soldiers and their families (Ríos Bustamante, Castillo, 2). In 1790 the census count for Los Angeles showed men and women in equal numbers. Of the native population, most of the Indians in California were moved early on to presidios where they were Christianized and supervised by the mission priests. As far as we know, the women who settled these regions left no written accounts of their lives. Yet further researchers may discover, archived in Mexico and Spain, the poems, their stories, their letters put into trunks and carefully saved.

Our stories in this anthology begin with an example of the oral narratives given to Herbert Bancroft in the 1870s by Hispanic women in California, as he was researching his monumental histories. Although not written by them, their authorship shows because of the careful recording done by Thomas Savage, Bancroft's assistant. Often these narratives concern their fathers, and other male family members, yet many of these women also spoke of the part they had played in the colonization of California. A distinct female voice is clear in these women's narrations. Granted, it is at times a muted voice, but when one reads accounts like the following excerpt from the memoirs of Doña Inocencia Pico, dictated in 1878, the complex dimension of women's experience on the northern Mexican frontier emerges.

> At the school they taught us to read and to write, and the four rules of arithmetic in whole numbers. Many girls did not finish even these few studies because their mothers took them out of school, almost always for the purpose of marrying them off, for there existed the evil custom of marrying off girls at a very tender age, whenever they were sought in matrimony. I was in the school only to the age of fourteen years, when my mother took me out to the rancho to teach me how to work and at the age of fifteen years and eight months, I married. (Pico, 5)

She married Miguel Avila in 1826 and had fifteen children. One of the more interesting anecdotes she tells in her reminiscences is an account of the California revolutions in the 1830s. Accused of raising secret funds to finance a revolution against General Micheltorena, her husband Avila is captured. They take him away at midnight and threaten to execute him. Pico says:

> At dawn I sent out to enquire what was going on. A Sr. Araujo sent me a letter saying that he had not made up his mind to anything definite, but that my husband would be tried at Pismo. I quickly had a great supply of provisions gotten together for the general and his officers, such as chicken, mutton, cakes, cheese, enchiladas, good wine, excellent whiskey etc. All this, richly decorated, along with fine napkins, etc., I dispatched loaded upon two mules. I also secretly sent for aid for my husband. By the same man who took the provisions the general sent me a letter telling me that I should have no fears concerning my husband and that he would return him to me from Santa Inez. Micheltorena was true to his word, setting my husband free at Santa Inez and returning to me all the horses which they had taken. These horses, however, all came back without ears or tails. This

did not matter to me—my husband was free. They had not summarily executed him, but, on the contrary, treated him well. The general thanked me for the provisions which he said had been very useful to them. (Pico, 6)

In the narrative of Doña Eulalia Pérez, we glimpse some facets of working class women's life during the colonization period. Her account of how she won the "cooking contest" and became the housekeeper of the mission is exemplary of the work women contributed to the establishment of the colony. The voices that come to us from these California narratives not only cement the place of women in the population of the new frontier, but also show us the ingenuity and survival skills of these women in difficult times. Although the family was generally the major foci for most women, it did not prevent them from exercising a strong role in their own self-definition, whether it was within or without the family.

THE MEXICAN NATIONAL YEARS TO 1848

From 1810 to 1825 Mexico, like most of Spain's colonies in the Americas, freed itself from Spanish domination. The immediate effect of the fall of Spanish rule over the Mexican provinces to the North was a laxity of control, as well as of neglect, by Mexico. Power struggles in Mexico itself virtually left the frontier helpless and unsupervised. Gradually, as the missions were secularized in the 1830s, the Spanish priests serving in the missions were sent back to Spain, and the Indians under the protection of the friars were left to fend for themselves. In some areas their land was taken by settlers as the missions deteriorated. In other areas (New Mexico, Texas, Arizona) the Navajo, Apache, and Ute tribes, in particular, were much feared by the Hispanic settlers, because their homes and ranches were regularly raided by the tribes for livestock and crops. Settlers in rural areas were greatly affected by the nonfunctioning of the presidios and military outposts. The Indian depredations became a dreaded reality as Native American tribes reacted to the pressures from Anglos pushing West, the loss of their native hunting grounds and lands, and other threats to their economic survival. Often Mexican women and children were captured by the raiders. Some were later ransomed; some were never seen again. Many women feared capture by Indians, and such captivities occurred frequently enough to give their fears a basis in reality. In fact, it was often a reality. Of course, Native peoples had also suffered captivity and enslavement by the Spanish/Mexicanos. Since colonial days the Mexicanos had used them as labor, with women often serving as domestic servants. Baptismal records and oral accounts show that Native children were often "Christianized" and then supposedly "adopted" into Mexicano families. In some instances this may have been so, but in general, at least for the first generation, the women and children served as slave labor and were sometimes even traded and sold among their owners. (This can be seen in the account of Señá Martina, as told by Fabiola Cabeza de Baca.)

During the Mexican national years the frontier provinces were cut off from virtually all legally supplied trade goods (Ríos-Bustamante, Castillo, 59). The people living in the affected areas suffered from the lack of supplies and turned to creative methods of obtaining necessities. In rural areas people were even more dependent on locally made goods—mostly produced by women. In more populated areas like California, and on the coast, the residents turned to smugglers. These smugglers were often Yankee and French traders who filled the trade void without fearing sanctions from Spanish or later Mexican officials.

The provinces were thus left pretty much to themselves. Local authorities were given, and took, much more control over local matters. Gradually, there began to be more citizen participation. The missions were secularized, and, as a result, particularly in California, there was more intermixing of the Natives with the Mexican population. The provinces also had to deal with serious famine, drought, and epidemics. Los Angeles suffered a serious plague and Tucson an intense cholera epidemic. There was a lack of formally trained medical personnel during this time, and, as a result, women served as the primary "physicians" and nurses.

Nevertheless, during the colonial and Mexican periods women of all classes, rural and urban, were survivors. In fact, Hispanas/Mexicanas were often likely to have other occupations besides caring for home and children. Many paid occupations for women were listed in the census: servants, bakers, weavers, gold panners, shepherds, laundresses, stocking-knitters, healers, midwives, ironers, and prostitutes (Lecompte, 74). And in the literature of the times we see women as innkeepers, vendors, ranchers, and farmers.

With the weakening of Mexican power, the defense of their lands by Native peoples, and the push of Yankee immigrants (as well as the threat of other foreign invasions into the land) the people of the provinces of the North were buffeted by times of change. The loss of Texas in 1836, the annexation of one-third of the territory of Mexico by the United States in 1848, and the California Gold Rush in 1849 altered the lives of indigenous peoples and Mexicanos in the West and Southwest. As more and more Anglo settlers entered the Southwest, there were often racial as well as economic antagonisms (Camarillo, 15–32). While the white settlers saw the territories as empty lands to be possessed, hunted, and worked, the now native populations began to see themselves dispossessed of lands that in some instances they had considered theirs for several hundred years. This pressure and pull greatly influenced the women already living in the territories.

1848 AND BEYOND: ACCOMMODATION, ASSIMILATION, AND SURVIVAL

The Treaty of Guadalupe Hidalgo in 1848,[4] changed forever the lives of Hispanos living in the United States. With the tremendous migration of Yankees into the territories, the widespread social, economic, and political change that took place within the next forty years significantly affected the lives of women of all social classes. Over a period of time, Mexicanos became a landless and impoverished people who were exploited economically and politically. Society became two-tiered, and racial and religious prejudice were evident. Mirandé and Enríquez state, "If the achievements of Hispanic women are difficult to document during the colonial period, they prove to be even more elusive after the American takeover of the Southwest. The Anglo conquest transformed Mexicans from a colonizing to a colonized people and brought about the almost total disruption of life" (Mirandé, Enríquez, 68). In fact, Janet Lecompte has gone so far as to comment:

> The extraordinary independence of New Mexico women, in full flower during the Republican period, came to an end in 1846 when New Mexico was invaded by United States soldiers, convinced of their own superiority and disdainful of the natives. . . . Only fifteen years after the American conquest, the New Mexican woman had all but abandoned her easy, graceful costume and was yielding to the fashionable tyranny of corsets, hoopskirts, and bonnets. Her fandangos were corrupted beyond recognition by strong American whiskey and rough American frontiersmen. Her legal rights upheld in alcalde courts were curtailed in American courts. Her Sunday merriment became a private thing, as foreign priests swept fandango music and gaiety out of the churches, and American officials banned other Sabbath activities. As years went by, ethnic discrimination denied her husband political power and jobs, her children were forbidden to speak Spanish in school, and her folk festivals and folk art were scorned. (Lecompte, 87–88)

The period immediately after the annexation was one of tremendous shifting and mobility in social, political, and cultural patterns. The effects on

---

4. The Treaty of Guadalupe Hidalgo was the treaty that signaled the end to the Mexican American War. Approximately one third of Mexican territory was ceded to the United States. However, Mexican citizens could choose to become American citizens with the same guarantees that American citizens, with property rights protected. The reality was to prove quite different.

women are difficult to pinpoint because of the amount of diversity that existed among Hispanic societies in the different areas affected: California, Arizona, Texas, and New Mexico. Various regions and the amount of recent versus past immigration were to impose differing attitudes and perspectives upon the women who lived there. Those areas where immigration took place during the Spanish period (up to 1821) tended to have long-rooted feelings about their Spanish ancestry and the soil. Those regions where more recent immigrations took place tended to be more allied with Mexico and to understand better their mestizaje. All regions felt the oppression after the Anglo domination: all were effectively silenced during long periods of time. Hispanic women especially suffered under the negative perceptions held by both Anglo men and women. They were Catholic, dark-skinned, wore loose clothing, smoked, and gambled. In general Anglos' early negative perceptions of the Hispanas/Mexicanas continued to hold forth.[5]

Life during the middle and last part of the nineteenth century was characterized by all sorts of conflict. Ethnic antagonisms, discrimination, and economic disparities existed in the midst of interdependence. While the new Anglo immigrants created trade opportunities and economic progress (mostly for themselves) and the arrival of the railroads brought in more goods and inhabitants, the Hispanos began to experience the loss of their land due to new American laws, legal and taxation systems they did not understand, intermarriage, and outright chicanery. The loss of economic and political hegemony was reflected in women's lives. One aspect that very much affected the lives of women, particularly of elite women, was the growing intermarriage that took place between Anglo men and Hispanic women from 1850 to 1910. It was a fairly widespread phenomenon that took place in all regions. After 1848 Anglo men typically arrived in the former Mexican provinces without wives or children. They were traders, military men, scouts, politicians, surveyors, real estate speculators, and ranchers. Some historians have seen the intermarriages as a strategy for Anglos to acquire large landed estates, since Hispanas/Mexicanas were able to inherit and own property. Others have stated that Hispanas were valued by the men they married as wives and companions. However, given the attitudes of racial superiority that many Anglo men brought with them, it must have impacted attitudes at times. In any event cross-cultural marriages, historians have said, accelerated the acculturation process and required difficult adjustments for the Hispanas who were involved. As Darlis Miller states, "Women who married Anglo men typically were forced to adjust to changing environments,

---

5. There has been much written about this; see Castañeda, "The Political Economy," 213–36; Crumm, ed., *Down the Santa Fe Trail*; Gregg, *Commerce of the Prairies*.

primarily because exogenous marriages disrupted primary group relationships and thus undermined the cohesiveness of Hispanic society" (Miller, 96).

Intermarriage seems to have been particularly frequent among women from elite families; for example, in New Mexico there were the Jaramillo sisters, who married scout Kit Carson and Governor Charles Brent; in California María Amparo Ruiz married Charles Burton, and Teresa de la Guerra married William Hartnell. While it has been contended that the children of these marriages comprised a sort of new elite that bridged two cultures, wealth on the Hispanic side and power on the Anglo side, others claim that sometimes the children assimilated into the Mexicano rather than the Anglo culture. It is not clear what the mechanism of ethnic survival in these families was. Did the women in the family take on the public aspects of Anglo culture, while speaking Spanish and preserving Spanish traditions in the home? Or, as Miller asserts, did some wives adopt "an Anglo mode of living but retained Spanish customs, becoming bicultural in the process" (Miller, 110)?

There are two pieces of literature (one early and one newer piece) that document the processes of cross-cultural marriages and the impact on the children. María Amparo Ruiz de Burton, in her novel *The Squatter and the Don* (1875), shows the loss of land in California to squatters. The main character in the novel is an Anglo, Mary Moreneau, married to William Darrell. She has a strong sense of social (and economic) justice, particularly when it has to do with the squatters (portrayed as a crass and vulgar group of men) who want to take away the land of Don Mariano Alamar, the owner of an original Spanish land grant. Ruiz de Burton documents the clash of two different legal systems and two different cultural ways of doing business. While the courteous Don Mariano tries to accommodate and find ways of negotiating so that all can work together, the squatters are portrayed as scheming greedy men, unwilling to work for a living.

Also involved in the characterization is a romance between Clarence Darrell, Mary's son, and young Mercedes, the daughter of Don Mariano. It is through this romance that we see the political and social ambiguities of these cross-cultural relationships. Clarence, influenced by his mother, shows himself to be a moral and thoughtful man, aware of the injustices done to the Californios. He says to Don Mariano:

> My father is a blind worshiper of the Congress of these United States and consequently it is difficult to persuade him that our legislators might possibly do wrong. He believes that Congress has the right to declare all California open to pre-emption, and all American citizens free to choose any land not already patented. Thus, he thinks he has the right to locate on your land (according to law, mind you), because he believes your title has been

rejected. But as my faith in our lawgivers is not so blind, my belief is that Congress had no more right to pass any law which could give an excuse to trespass upon your property, than to pass a law inviting people to your table. I feel a sort of impatience to think that in our country could exist a law which is so outrageously unjust. . . . I only wish I could wipe out those stains on our national honor, by repealing at once laws so discreditable to us. Yes, the more so, as they bear directly upon the most defenseless, the most powerless of our citizens—the orphaned Spano-Americans (sic). So then, I hope you will help me to avoid this American shame, by permitting me to pay for our land whatever price you think just. (Ruiz de Burton, 68)

Although patronizing in tone, "poor orphaned Spano-Americans," the ideas expressed in this passage were precisely what many Californios espoused. After many struggles in this romanticized story, Clarence finally marries Mercedes, but Don Mariano dies in the effort to maintain his land and in the ensuing ethnic antagonisms. Even as love prevails, the hero of the novel, Clarence, not only wins the heroine but also the land.

Another narrative, *The Beautiful Cruel Country* (1988, but written about the 1920s), by Eva Antonia Wilbur-Cruce, written long after Ruiz de Burton's novel, nevertheless continues many of the ideas and ambivalences that the earlier novel conveys. *The Beautiful Cruel Country* is the creation of an Arizona woman whose father, Agustine Wilbur (son of a Mexicana), was married to Ramona Vilducea, of Italian and Mexican origin. Since her grandparents were all homesteaders in Arizona, she came from a different class background than Ruiz de Burton. The autobiography is about her childhood in Arizona around the turn of the century. The Wilbur children learned to read and write in Spanish and then English. And the picture that emerges from Wilbur's narration is of a harsh and stern father and a silenced mother. Even the father's ethnic identity shifts back and forth:

"Everything," my grandfather used to say, "is a change. Life is a change. You have to accept it or you can't live." At that time my father was more Anglo than the Anglos. And he never spoke to me in Spanish; he spoke to me in English. And when I came back my father met me speaking with a strong Spanish accent . . . I wasn't used to it! And I said, "What's the matter with my Papa?" And he said, "Well, I have ten Mexican families here and that's all I speak. . . . And when I came back from Los Angeles, I used to have an English accent! Talk about a change! My mother spoke mostly Spanish, but she spoke English too—it was mixed from beginning to end. So we spoke Spanish and English and both were wrong!

What I speak is a dialect—a corral dialect—a Wilbur dialect! In fact, my brother Henry told me when I went to see him in Los Angeles, "When

I came here Eva—would you believe me that nobody understood me, except William, my brother!" Of course I believed him![6]

Although the intervening time frame between the two narratives is different, there are many similarities to be found in examining the impact of cross-cultural relationships as they are carried out in ensuing generations.

During this time frame, 1880–1920, other voices of women from the territorial and early statehood period of New Mexico begin to emerge. A 10,000-item collection of papers of the Amador family in Las Cruces, New Mexico, documents not only family history, but in particular the perspectives of the women in this family (Stephens, 257–77). The women represented are the mother Doña Refugio, and her five daughters, Emilia, María, Clotilde, Julieta, and Corina. Unusual as it is to have such a large collection of letters written by women, the letters are also of interest because the family was connected to prominent families in Mexico, thus spanning the cultural and social borders between the two countries in times of transition and change. The letters of the women were not only concerned with the financial fortunes of the family but with education and social matters as well. Sandra L. Stephens is particularly impressed with the concern over personal health matters as the women reported their problems to each other "with a startling candor" (Stephens, 266). Among these problems were a large number of miscarriages and infant deaths. With further study and analysis this collection will yield new information about the complex inter-familial relationships among women in the family. In addition, Stephens states:

> The letters of the women clearly demonstrate values consistent with both Mexican and American upperclass society in the Victorian and Progressive eras, and their papers reflect shifts in attitude and behavior demanded by changing patterns of agricultural development after the Mexican Revolution and the Great Depression. Future research in the Amador Collection will result in a more detailed picture of this unique, yet representative, family, and will provide further insights into the changing fortunes and responses of Hispanic women of the upper classes. (Stephens, 273)

Most women, however, particularly poor women, did not write letters, because schooling for women was late to come. Public schools were not universal until the 1920s. Well-to-do young women were educated at home or sent to convent schools. Those who had no money were not educated except for what was necessary. Many women on early documents could not even sign their names. But education and intelligence are not necessarily connected. The women have left their legacy in the stories they told, in their beautiful embroidery and sew-

---

6. From *Songs My Mother Sang to Me*, edited by Patricia Preciado Martin (University of Arizona Press, 1992).

ing, pottery, and crafts. By 1880 we begin to have a better glimpse of what women's lives in the territories may have been like.

One important source for the voices of women in this period is found in the Federal Writers' Project collections from Arizona and from New Mexico. These folklore projects collected the stories of "old-timers," and since women have always been valued storytellers, their voices and their creativity show through. One of the collections is entitled *Some New Mexican Grandmothers*. Most of the women who tell stories were in their seventies and eighties at the time of telling. These tales often have women as their heroines in dramatic situations that contribute to some understanding of the symbolic role that women played during these times. Some of these stories, like "Las Tres Gangozas," aim at regulating female behavior; others show women challenging traditional norms. Still others are about witches (*brujas*) who are also healers (*curanderas*) (see the story entitled "Quiteria Outwits the Witch Nurse"). They are strong women who exercise power over and within their world. These *cuentos* are full of details and descriptions of places and people. As Genaro Padilla has pointed out, a colonized people needs to remember the details of their domination, in order to redeem their life before the domination. These cuentos accomplish this on a symbolic as well as realistic level (Padilla, "Imprisoned Narrative?" 43–44).

Between 1880 and 1920, there was great change in Mexicano families as well as in Mexicano culture. As Richard Griswold del Castillo states:

> Struggle and decline were the dominant pattern of the economic life for most Mexican-Americans in Los Angeles. But it would be wrong to conclude that they were completely submerged—economic oppression was the substratum out of which the pobladores forged new social and cultural patterns of survival within the family and community.
>
> Changes in the size and composition of the family indicated something of the rate of modernization. The traditional extended family gave way to more fluid arrangements. Increasing numbers of women entered into common-law unions, intermarried with Anglo-Americans, found themselves as sole heads of households, became wage-earners and received a formal education. Women married later and had fewer children. By 1880 the nuclear family dominated the domestic arrangements of the Spanish-speaking. The family and the Church ceased to be the main institutions for the socialization of La Raza. Many Mexican-Americans sent their children to English-language public schools to study new secular subjects. More and more Mexican-Americans learned to read and write, due less to public instruction than to increased Mexican immigration and private schooling. (Griswold del Castillo, 197)

The coming of the railroads brought an influx of migrant labor into the West and Southwest, and this immigration from Mexico often strengthened Mexican folk traditions, as well as the Spanish language. It also signaled increased racial prejudice. In some places, the native Spanish population tried to distance itself from the newly arriving Mexicans by calling themselves "Spanish Americans" and emphasizing their Spanish heritage rather than their Mexican and Indian heritage. For others, the prejudice served to strengthen their ethnic identity and ties.

As more and more people began to be geographically and occupationally mobile, as more Mexicanos moved from rural to urban settings, cultural and language breakdown began. Segregation began to occur as Mexicanos lived together in barrios. At the same time mechanisms of ethnic survival were in place. One of these mechanisms was the Spanish language press, which in some cities sprang up where there had been no press, during the colonial and Mexican national periods. Literacy was increasing as was growing awareness of ethnic identification. Community groups began to organize along ethnic lines. Among these groups were the formal *mutualista* organizations that banded together to help each other in times of need. There were also literary clubs, music clubs, and theater clubs. And, of course, they had their women's auxiliaries. The population centers of the cities began to grow rapidly; for example, between 1900 and 1910, the population of Los Angeles tripled, from 102,479 to 319,198 (Ríos-Bustamante, Castillo, 107). Many of those who lived in the inner Western cities were of Mexican descent. All of this spelled the necessity for survival skills for those women living in the barrios.

The Mexican Revolution of 1910, which lasted for approximately fourteen years, also impacted the West and Southwest. Many families fled Mexico for the relative safety of the United States, and they encountered the stratified, prejudiced society that had become the norm in the United States (see Pat Mora's poem "1910"). Some radical Mexican intellectuals came to the United States and wrote articles on social justice in Spanish language newspapers. Among these were many women interested in social justice and revolutionary causes: Teresa and Andrea Villarreal, Sara Estela Ramírez, Leonor Villegas de Magnón, and Jovita Idar. Many of them participated in producing a radical newspaper, *Regeneración,* as well as other newspapers, which helped politicize Mexican women in the Southwest. As Emma Pérez points out, however, the revolutionary ideology was in general male-oriented, mainly serving a nationalist cause—the Mexican Revolution—rather than one to enhance any true equality for women. Nonetheless, many of these female journalists challenged the male ideology about women, both supporting the revolution *and* women's rights (Pérez, "A la mujer," 471). Recent research by Clara Lomas has begun to point out the importance of the writing of these women as role models for the community at large.

As mentioned, the Spanish language press was active throughout the West and Southwest. Many of these newspapers carried a literary page or cultural supplement that contained poetry, short stories, and "serial" novels. While well-known writers from Latin America and Spain were published on these pages, original work was also solicited. Juanita Lawhn has studied *La Prensa*, a San Antonio Spanish language newspaper, between 1913 and 1920 and discovered that many women writers were published in the paper; in their poetry, narratives, and essays, they engaged in lively polemics on women's rights. Nevertheless, Lawhn also reaches the conclusion that many of the editorial opinions expressed were very male-oriented, and the indoctrination of male norms and male expectations prevailed through the issues of this newspaper (Lawhn, 12).

A writer nourished by roots in the Spanish language press, Arizona's Carmen Celia Beltrán notes that the early 1900s were very difficult years for women. Her family had fled Mexico during the revolution. Thus:

> Mexican-American women had nothing to look forward to except being wives and mothers. They could not vote and they were not considered to be important enough to have a say so in the community or family. She, though, aspired to be a poet and writer. Shortly after her arrival in San Antonio she became totally immersed in learning the new language. For her being a woman was not the only hardship she encountered. Her family was large, and her father was not around very often; so she, as the oldest child, had to go out and earn a living. She was a quick learner. (Tinajero, 22)

Beltrán held a variety of jobs, including court reporter, actress in national radio shows, and writer for periodicals. Many of her poems are occasion poems that specifically direct themselves to Mexican themes: the 12th of October (El día de la Raza), the 15th of September (Mexican Independence Day), poems to the Virgen Morena (The Virgen of Guadalupe), Mexico's patron saint. Because she wrote in Spanish and devoted a large part of her work to patriotic Mexican themes, Beltrán is one of those writers involved in what Ríos-Bustamante and Castillo call cultural self-defense—a stance among Mexicanos that evolved from 1920 on, and reflected the need for cultural and ethnic survival on the part of Mexicanos in the face of prejudice and Anglo hegemony.

THE 1920S—1950S: FLOWERING OF A LITERATURE
OF RESISTANCE

After the tumultuous upheavals of the Mexican Revolution and the First World War, the late 1920s and 1930s were difficult years for Mexican Americans. Social conditions became worse as immigration continued and social services could not keep up with demands. The Great Depression affected all Americans, but those at the lower poverty levels struggled harder to meet daily demands. Many Mexican nationals returned home or were deported. Many Mexican Americans tried to assimilate into Anglo society by suppressing their language and acquiring an education. Often Mexican Americans, unable to deal with this society, turned inward to their families and their barrios and adopted a politics of survival. However, the economic hardships of Mexicano families often forced women out of the home and into jobs in the public sector, which, of course, changed their perspectives. In 1936 one third of all Mexican women in Los Angeles worked outside the home—more than 85 percent in unskilled jobs (Ríos-Bustamante, Castillo, 145).

In the 1930s the international arts and crafts revival, with its interest in folklore, emerged in a worldwide context that was to profoundly influence contemporary Chicano art and literature. In New Mexico, influenced by the New Deal and the Federal Writers' Project, three New Mexican women began to write about their lives and their cultural heritage: they were Cleofas Jaramillo, Fabiola Cabeza de Baca Gilbert, and Nina Otero-Warren, all of whom are included in this volume. Along with Jovita Gonzales, who was collecting Texas folklore in the 1920s and 1930s, these women felt the need to document what they saw as a vanishing cultural heritage: their sense that their identity was being assimilated through history and cultural domination. This generation of writers document the time when land and society were shifting from Hispanic to Anglo control. Although their writing presents the perspective of a landed society, they nevertheless cultivate the seeds of cultural resistance to Anglo hegemony that had been planted before, as we have seen, in the California narratives.[7] Close readings of the texts written by these women show that landscape is one symbolic icon for describing the loss of land. In both *We Fed Them Cactus* (Cabeza de Baca) and *Romance of a Little Village Girl* (Jaramillo) the landscape at the beginning of the narration is a verdant paradise and at the end a windswept purgatory.[8]

In the writing of Jaramillo, Cabeza de Baca Gilbert, and Otero-Warren we can discern the rumblings of dissent, narrative strategies of resistance that show their writers' discontent. Among the strategies are the following:

1. A sense of colonized identity and the naming of that identity by detailing the cultural signs embedded in it, such as Hispano topography, endless

---

7. The literature of resistance had already been seen in the writings by men in the late 1800s. Certainly the corrido shows this resistance in the oral tradition, even as early as 1800. However, it is not so apparent in the literature written by women.

8. For a detailed analysis of the symbolic function of landscape in Chicana literature see Rebolledo, "Tradition and Mythology," 96–124.

accounting of family names, and friends' family names. On the one hand the repetitive naming slows the narrative down and distracts the reader; on the other hand, the attention to detail serves as a resistance to a present filled with the loss of those names and places. The narrative function of this strategy is to completely fill the physical and psychological space of the book with the historical imprint of cultural hegemony from the past as a recall of cultural memory to the Anglo cultural hegemony of the present. Again the books are filled with long accounts of cultural resistance, such as stories of social banditry (indeed, admiration for the social bandits such as Vicente Silva).

2. A sentimental recall of the past, generally expressed in nostalgic Edenic terms. It is nevertheless a past that questions present authority. The past is seen in the context of the community, rather than the individual. This sense of community includes the past as center, the present as margin.

3. The blending or blurring of various forms: the oral with the written, history with creative autobiography, recipes and narrative, family history and romance. The mixing of genre (recipes with fiction, autobiography with poetry) was seen by these writers as acceptable because it was a *recuerdo*, a remembering, and because all the narration was underscored by the *cuento* storytelling tradition. In Hispanic storytelling the mixtures of genres with strong attention to personal detail was acceptable, even expected. As Padilla argues, the recuerdo does not take on the direct authority of an autobiography because it would be a collective, not an individual memory (Padilla, "The Recovery," 287). Thus the personal subjectivity incorporates all the discourses of history, sociology, psychology, and geography, but it is the personal storytelling that binds it together.

4. Because it was acceptable for women to be the storytellers, although not the story writers, and because the passing on of recipes and traditions was "women's work," these strategies could also include a highly feminine voice. One example is the narration about Señá Martina, the curandera in the tale by Fabiola Cabeza de Baca in this anthology.

5. Implicit in all of the above is the "translation" from Spanish into English. In the translation there exists a critique of Anglo culture, of Anglo's understanding of Hispanic culture and the imposition of the spirituality of Hispanic culture. The Hispano generally comes across as a superior being; the Anglo is often ridiculed. For example, Nina Otero-Warren in *Old Spain in Our Southwest* profiles the growing tensions between Anglos and Hispanos as Anglos entered the territory and populated the state in ever larger numbers.

"Strangers do not understand our hospitality," said Don Antonio's brother-in-law. "A young attorney from the States came to the hacienda a short time ago on business. He brought his wife. My señora received her guest in her usual courteous manner. The shutters of the guest room had been opened, the room well aired, the sun allowed to look through the deep windows. The high bed, with its feather mattress, was made ready. A silver basket, filled with fruit, was placed beside the candle on the bedside table. On retiring for the night, my wife told the American lady: 'My house, all that it contains, is yours.' She did not know that this phrase, perfectly sincere, is our way of making a guest feel at ease. One hardly accepts a house and its belongings! My señora had left a set of jewelry, a brooch, bracelet and earrings on the dresser of the guest room. The American lady took these away with her, thinking it was a gift to her. It was her understanding of our hospitality, 'My house is yours.'" (Otero-Warren, 33)[9]

This description of cultural misunderstanding is amusing to Hispanos and is certainly part of a cultural "translation."

THE SECOND WORLD WAR

As a result of U.S. involvement in World War II life changed for Mexicans in the United States as it did for everyone. The employment situation improved and jobs became easier to find. Mexican women began to work in ever increasing numbers; many were able to enter semi-skilled and even skilled occupations. (Ríos-Bustamante, Castillo, 157). The long history of participation in labor struggles among Mexicanas was to extend into a political and social struggle as well.[10] Many young men and women from Mexican American communities everywhere joined the armed forces and made personal sacrifices for their country. These sacrifices, however, did not alter the social biases against them. In many places in the country schools and eating places were still segregated, Spanish was forbidden, and students' names were anglicized. Among the most notorious examples of racial prejudice were the Zootsuit riots that arose from the Sleepy Lagoon Case of 1942.[11] The fights between Anglo servicemen and "draped" Mexican youngsters were escalated by the press into what was labeled

---

9. For more details on these women and their strategies see Rebolledo, "Narrative Strategies of Resistance," 134–46. On the writers in general, see Rebolledo, "Las Escritoras," 199–214.

10. There has been much research done on the participation of Chicana in the labor movement and in labor struggles. See the following: Calderón and Zamora, "Manuela Solis Sager and Emma B. Tenayuca," 269–80; Argüelles, "Undocumented Female Labor," 299–312; Ruiz, *Cannery Women*, 1987.

11. In 1942 a group of Mexican teenagers were arrested in the midst of media coverage about Pachucos. They were accused of murdering another Mexican teenager in a fight. The trial caused a sensation and became a cause for Mexicans in Los Angeles. The teenagers were convicted but later acquitted in 1944. This incident has been dramatized in Luis Valdez's play *Zoot Suit*. See also Mazón, *The Zoot-Suit Riots*.

"Pachuco Terrorism." The language the teenagers used to try to create their own cultural identity is now a widely accepted cultural idiom. It was not only young men who distinguished themselves by their flamboyant dress, exaggerated mannerism, and tough dialectical street talk; young women also adapted a style identified by pompadours, tight short skirts, and a brassy "with it" dialect. This pachuca style has been captured in Chicana literature as the streetwise, tough "ruca" seen sometimes in poems by Inés Hernández and Evangelina Vigil, as well as in stories by Mary Helen Ponce.

As Mexican Americans returned from the war, they faced unique challenges. More young people enrolled in colleges and universities than ever before. They looked around and saw the social and political realities. A number of organizations were formed in order to combat discrimination in all areas. These were organizations such as the Unity Leagues, the Community Service Organization formed to help the Mexican American masses achieve full citizenship through Americanization Programs; and the G.I. Forum, formed to help secure civil rights (Chávez, 123). As usual, these organizations were aided by their women's auxiliaries.

As historians point out, Mexicanos often found themselves in the 1950s and 1960s caught between opposing cultural messages:

> On the one hand, Spanish-language popular culture implied that they were part of a unique cultural tradition distinct from white America. On the other hand, the English-language educational system told Mexicans that they had best become something altogether different from their ancestors. Throughout that decade and into the 1960s, individuals diligently tried to balance Spanish-language newspapers, magazine, movies, live performances, radio programs, and television with a school experience that sought to envelop them in an English-speaking, Anglo-defined mainstream. (Ríos-Bustamante, Castillo, 170)

The response to these mixed messages was varied and complex. Some manifested it in the nostalgic denial of language (see "Refugee Ship" by Lorna Dee Cervantes), some in denial of ethnicity. Still others began organizing on many different levels, seeking support in numbers. With the impetus of the Black civil rights movement and the growing feminist movement, a new social consciousness began, particularly among Mexican American youth. The Mexicano community was also growing rapidly throughout the country. Largely working class, this group also had its share of artists and intellectuals. On campuses across the country students, both men and women, began to organize and demand rights. The long debate about the Vietnam War further served to exacerbate the protests. The United Farmworkers Movement, 1965, the National Chicano Moratorium, and the founding of the Raza Unida Party, 1970, all contributed to an awakening of what is now known as the Chicano Movement. Although speaking of Los Angeles, Ríos-Bustamante and Castillo's comments also apply to the experience of Chicanos throughout the West and Southwest:

> In hindsight, the Chicano movement can be seen to have served as a social catalyst within the city's larger Spanish-speaking community. By 1970, many young Mexicans had already guessed what the Anglo establishment would leave for them. In every way possible, they turned their backs on it. In that turnabout, young Chicanos motivated a large percentage of their community to present a stronger public presence. In effect, they demanded that society at large receive a new message about what it was to be Mexican. They also generated support for educational, political and economic advancement. Public officials began addressing issues of concern to Mexicans in a serious, more respectful manner. Finally, and perhaps most important, the Chicano movement facilitated certain concessions from the Anglo mainstream. These concessions—bilingual education, Chicano Studies Programs, and affirmative action employment practices—created a setting from which a viable Mexican middle class could rise to local prominence. (Ríos-Bustamante, Castillo, 182)

THE CHICANO/CHICANA RENAISSANCE

The late 1960s and the 1970s saw a flowering of artistic and literary creativity that arose from the questioning, turmoil, and energy of social and political movements. Some important literary forerunners had begun to establish a new kind of literature that examined the Chicano experience. By 1958 Américo Paredes published *With His Pistol in His Hand*, exploring the importance of the Mexican *corrido*, and also several short stories; José Antonio Villarreal published *Pocho* in 1959; and the Teatro Campesino was active in 1965, with many Chicanas taking an active part in the creation of, as well as the acting in, the productions.[12] Quinto Sol published *El Espejo / The Mirror: Selected Chicano Literature* (1969), the first anthology of Chicano literature published by Chicanos. Included among the writers were Estela Portillo, Raquel Moreno, and Georgia Cobos. The editors proclaimed that the material was not just writing reactive to Anglo-American society, but "rather a literature that is recreating its own legends, its myths" (Romano-V, Ríos, xiii). In addition they said it was "coupled with a strong demand by the Chicano community for works by Chicano authors that reflect Chicano experiences from a Chicano perspective" (Romano-V., Ríos, xiv).

---

12. Yolanda Broyles Gonzáles has written extensively on this aspect of the Teatro Campesino. See "Toward a Re-Vision of Chicano Theatre History," 209–38; "Women in El Teatro Campesino," 162–82.

Although some women were included among the first writers to be published, it was the male authors who made the initial inroads, were most easily and frequently published, and were the most recognized: Alurista, Oscar Acosta, Rudolfo Anaya, Tomás Rivera, and Rolando Hinojosa to name but a few. These authors became a canonical liturgy for Chicano writing. Indeed, early writing by many Chicanas emphasized their sense of being marginalized by the Chicanos themselves, their sense of being left behind. Margarita Cota-Cárdenas wrote:

> he's very much aware now
>   and makes fervent Revolution
>   so his children
>   and the masses
>   will be free
> but his woman
>   in every language
>   has only begun to ask
>   —y yo querido viejo
>   and ME? (Cota-Cárdenas, in *La Palabra*, 40)

And Lorna Dee Cervantes reiterated:

> you speak of the new way,
> a new life . . .
> Pero your voice is lost to me carnal,
> in the wail of tus hijos,
> in the clatter of dishes,
> and the pucker of beans upon the stove.
> Your conversations come to me
> de la sala where you sit,
> spreading your dream to brothers. (Cervantes in Fisher, 381–82)

The fact that many Chicana texts were not published until the mid 1970s, and the great onset of Chicana publications does not begin until the 1980s, does not belie the fact that Chicanas were writing during this early period. They *were* writing, but, having been silenced for long periods of time, the authors found breaking that silence into a public act difficult. As Gloria Anzaldúa states:

> For silence to transform into speech, sounds and words, it must first traverse through our female bodies. For the body to give birth to utterance, the human entity must recognize itself as carnal—skin, muscles, entrails, brain, belly. Because our bodies have been stolen, brutalized or numbed, it is difficult to speak from/through them. No hables de esas cosas, de eso

no se habla (Don't talk about those things, don't talk about that) . . . when she transforms silence into language a woman transgresses. (Anzaldúa, *Making Face,* xxii)

One of the first anthologies of Chicana texts appeared in September 1973, *Chicanas en la literature y el arte: El Grito,* edited by Estela Portillo Trambley. Soon after, Chicanas began to publish poetry, novels, and essays. A few of the books were from regional publishing houses; more of the publications were in literary magazines, chapbooks. Even as late as 1985 María Herrera-Sobek stated that the previous ten years had witnessed "a modest but encouraging number of works of fiction" by Chicanas, and Rosaura Sánchez noted that "what distinguished Chicana writers from their male counterparts was their relative 'invisibility' presenting "a compelling case for the reexamining of Chicano *machismo* and short sighted discriminatory practices visited upon Chicanas by members of their own group" (Herrera-Sobek, *Beyond Stereotypes,* 11). Yet Chicanas continued to write and to publish with or without support. And their writing displayed a wide range of concerns and perceptions. In the main, the Chicanas' concerns for and about political and social oppression, arising from long years of communal experience, are, according to Herrera-Sobek "primary vectors structuring many of their works. This does not detract from the beauty of the work, but in fact invigorates and transforms it into a powerful work of art" (Herrera-Sobek, Viramontes, *Chicana Creativity,* 10). Gloria Anzaldúa agrees and says that "art is about identity, among other things and her creativity is politics. Creative acts are forms of political activism employing definite aesthetic strategies for resisting dominant cultural norms and are not merely aesthetic exercises. We build culture as we inscribe in these various forms" (*Making Face,* xxiv).

There is a powerful dialogue that continues between Chicanas and community. Norma Alarcón sees that the rigid gender determination in Mexican American society often produced "a crisis in those recalcitrant Chicanas who question their overly restricted position in the symbolic contract. It is this crisis which erupts into creative explorations of the self, her sexuality, and intra and inter-sexual relationships" (Herrera-Sobek, Viramontes, *Chicana Creativity,* 35).

As the numbers of published texts increased, critics began to analyze their contents. This anthology and its thematic divisions illustrate some of the main concerns of the writers: Who am I? How did I become the person that I am? What are my historical and cultural antecedents, my racial characteristics, and how do these factors define my place in society? Some of these questions focused on the role of female models. What has been the influence of my mother, my abuelita, and extended female family on my life? Indeed one central aspect of Chicana writing is the need to explore and explode the stereotypes given to

Chicanas—they have done this by emphasizing the realities of Chicana existence and the plurality of Chicana personalities. In terms of an internal mythology, Chicanas have looked to their cultural heritage to find myths and archetypes that form a paradigm to their own lived experience and have consciously designed and re-designed myths and archetypes not to their liking (see the chapter on literary role models). Thus, Malinche is an archetype redeemed and changed through Chicana literary discourse. And the Virgin of Guadalupe acquires tennis shoes, a sewing machine, a suitcase, and whatever other implements she needs to increase her activism. These myths and archetypes are in no way static—rather they derive from an ever-changing reflection of Chicana ideology, ideals, and desires.

Chicanas in the 1980s wrote *Bildungs* texts, explored the social and the political, looked for role models in their literary heritage, fought back at what they saw as an oppressive dominant society, and came together as a consciously awakened group of women. As Marta Sánchez points out:

> The Chicanas of this particular generation . . . faced a double set of social restrictions. Primarily related to ethnicity and gender, these restrictions operated inside and outside their Chicano communities. Like Chicanos, Chicanas experienced racial discrimination in the large society; like white women, they also experienced sexual discrimination. Chicanas thus had reason to identify with both communities. They drew strength from both cultural environments, profiting from their participation in the racial struggles that united them with Chicanos as well as from the visibility of the Anglo women's movement which focused attention on women's issues. Significantly this double identification was characterized by a double ambivalence. As Chicanas, they supported Chicanos in a struggle for racial equality, but Chicanos were also their sexual oppressors. As women, their ethnic position as Chicanas precluded a smooth interaction with white women's groups. (Sánchez, 5)

This dilemma often placed Chicanas in a tenuous position between Anglo feminists and their male Chicano colleagues. It put an additional strain on the Chicana lesbian feminists who felt, moreover, that their heterosexually oriented sisters did not fully support them. These issues raised in Chicana literature are still in a state of dialogue between the various perspectives as writers struggle with issues of unity versus separatism.

Throughout the 1980s, it is safe to say, Chicana literature was in a state of process. This could be seen by the titles given to critical works about the literature: Rebolledo, "Chicana Poetry: The Quiet Revolution"; Sánchez, *A Critical Approach to an Emerging Literature*; Herrera-Sobek, *Beyond Stereotypes* and

Charting New Frontiers in American Literature. Often the literature was seen as being a literature "between," a concept that would blossom more fully in the latter part of the decade. Writers saw themselves as "writing from the margins." Margarita Cota-Cárdenas declared that it was precisely that sense of alienation that engendered the creative process. Anzaldúa felt Chicanas were "speaking from cracked spaces," their wounds spilling over into language. This would develop more fully into a "mestiza consciousness" and is explored in the next section.

CONTEMPORARY TRENDS IN CHICANA LITERATURE

As the decade of the 1990s begins one would like to think that Chicana writers have become mainstreamed, but this is still not so. They are, however, enjoying more success. And in the plethora of publishing, writing, and examination that is being seen currently, there are important developments and trends.

The first area of development is the growth of the personal essay by Chicana writers. In the early days of Chicano literature, during and immediately after the Chicano Renaissance of the 1968 movimiento, most of the introspection, the political examination, and the outright reflection of "quién soy" were embedded in creative texts; that is, what could be discerned about the intellectual formation of the Chicana writers had to be inferred from what was hinted at in the texts themselves. One could never really be sure because it was, after all, a creative text, and critics were taught to separate the creative poem or narrative from the "real text" of the author's life. That was also the heyday of structuralist criticism that regarded the text as an autonomous entity and separate, although surely influenced by the author. What has changed in the meantime is the writing of deliberately conscious essays in which the author more directly states what is on her mind. The subjects range from taboo issues of sexuality to identity, to a coming of consciousness, to reflection on gender and ethnicity. In a 1990 *Glamour* article, Sandra Cisneros identifies her father with what she calls "the public majority. A public who is disinterested in reading, and yet one whom I am writing about and for, and privately trying to woo." She says:

> Once, several years ago, when I was just starting out my writing career, I was asked to write my own contributor's note for an anthology I was part of. I wrote: "I am the only daughter in a family of six sons. *That explains everything.*"
>
> Well, I've thought about that ever since and yes, it explains a lot to me, but for the reader's sake I should have written: "I am the only daughter in a Mexican family of six sons." Or even: "I am the only daughter of a Mexican father and a Mexican-American mother." Or, "I am the only daughter of a

working-class family of nine." All of these had everything to do with who I am today. (November 1990, 256)

In her 1984 essay "Literary Wetback," Alicia Gaspar de Alba tried to determine how she became a "Chicana" writer from a family background that treasured its ties to Mexico. What Pat Mora had examined in her poem "Legal Alien," where she writes "an American to Mexicans / A Mexican to Americans / a handy token / sliding back and forth," Gaspar de Alba sees as cultural schizophrenia:

> At home I was pura Mejicana. At school I was an American citizen. Neither place validated the idea of the Mexican-American. Actually, I grew up believing that Mexican-Americans, or Pochos, as my family preferred to call them, were stupid. Not only could they not even speak their own language correctly (meaning Spanish), but their dark coloring denounced them as ignorant. ("Literary Wetback")

Her slipping and sliding between two worlds forces her to try to bridge the gap by creating something new, in this case her writing and her interest in language: "My brother and I used to sneak conversations in English, even swear words, behind my Grandma's back. I would write hour after hour in my journal/portable confessional, playing with the forbidden words and sentences as if they were a hieroglyphics that only I could read."

In her essay, "Searching for a Voice," Erlinda Gonzales-Berry also examines what effect graduate training and patriarchal language have on her persona:

> The fact that I was bilingual by historical accident and by academic training raised the first obstacle in my quest for voice. In which language would my voice speak? While I am certainly English dominant in the social domain, my formal experiences in Spanish outnumber those in English. I lecture daily in Spanish and I have read more literature in that language than in English. I have done some acting in Spanish, but never in English. On stage Spanish offers me an immediate persona. My Spanish persona has a certain flair, it's a risk taker, is a game player, is witty. The English me, on the other hand, is more conservative, insecure, highly self-conscious. In Spanish I always felt loved and accepted. In English I always felt . . . spied upon, on the verge of being judged: Did I, or didn't I, measure up?

Emma Pérez in "Sexuality and Discourse: Notes from a Chicana Survivor," says: "We have not had our own language and voice in history. We have been spoken about, written about, spoken at but never spoken with or listened to" (Pérez, "Sexuality," 175). In her essay Pérez insists on imposing boundaries between herself and those who hold sociosexual racial power as a form of survival. "I think of myself as one who must separate to my space and language of women to revitalize, to nurture and be nurtured" (Pérez, "Sexuality," 178).

What is different about these essays from those written in the late sixties is the personal tone, the direct voice of the author, questioning herself and society. They explore the problematics of socialsexual and racial ideology in a compelling way. All power relationships are questioned in a search for an understanding of how Chicanas came to be as they are and for a new way of being. In the early days of the Chicana Renaissance the tone was more socially directed, more angry toward Chicano males who the women felt were silencing them.

The second area of growth is the redemption of the male relationships in the lives of Chicanas, particularly the father-daughter relationship. When they first began to write, Chicanas had been so overwhelmed for such a long time by a dominant, patriarchal society that most of the male figures, especially the fathers, were either present in their writing as violent characters or were absent from it altogether. Tired of long-standing gender stereotypes, women wrote to demythologize the male figure, to challenge him, to make fun of him. Their main focus was in rescuing the female maternal figures from oblivion and from silence. Thus the figures of the mother, or, in particular the grandmother, took on singular importance. Also in the forefront were other females who had figured prominently in the writers' lives: sisters, friends, and teachers. More recent writing has allowed Chicana writers time and perspective to reevaluate these male figures. While we still see sexual abuse, physical abuse, and desertion, these figures appear to be more complex than before. We also see the emergence of a more sympathetic male parent; one such example is Sandra Cisneros' constant reexamination of her relationship with her father, as he becomes more open to the person that she has become. Perhaps part of the explanation for this is that Chicanos have evolved culturally over the last twenty years, opening themselves to change, new perspectives, and new behaviors; or perhaps it is the women who have decided to set the rules and limits for how much male behavior and vision will impact their lives. It also may simply be the change in times, perspective, and age. In any event, the vision of men in the lives of Chicanas is changing.

The third new area of growth in Chicana literature involves dealing more openly with sexuality. The 1989 issue of *Third Woman* on *The Sexuality of Latinas* is perhaps the culmination of this trend. As the editors say in the introduction to this volume, "In 1984 *Third Woman* decided to pursue the publication of a Chicana-Latina lesbian issue. However, such an issue has yet to materialize. In part this is due to the fact that very few professional writers—be they creative or critical—have actively pursued a lesbian political identity. . . . As a result we made the decision to forego a special lesbian issue and instead present her voice as an integral part of the Latina experience—from the actively heterosexual, to the celibate, to the secretly sexual, to the politically visible lesbian" (Alarcón, Castillo, Moraga, 8).

This volume of *Third Woman* sold out, and a new edition was prepared. The volume contains many audacious and even outrageous texts. It is a clear declaration that taboos are being tossed aside and that Chicana desire and sexuality will be articulated from various perspectives. In 1991, notwithstanding the cautions expressed in *The Sexuality of Latinas,* the long-awaited volume on Chicana lesbian sexuality appeared. *Chicana Lesbians: The Girls Our Mothers Warned Us About* continued the elaboration of lesbian issues, of articulating lesbian identity. As the editor Carla Trujillo emphasized, "The Chicana lesbian is similar to any other Chicana, or any other lesbian, yet her own experience is usually that of attempting to fit into two worlds, neither of which is readily accepting" (Trujillo, ix). Trujillo talks about the difficulties heterosexual Chicanas and Chicanos have in accepting lesbian sexuality, in part because participants in the lesbian experience "give validation to the sexuality of another woman as well" (Trujillo, x). Chicana lesbians in their writing address the particularly difficult problems not only of expressing their perspective but also in altering traditional roles and institutions that are antithetical or resistant to their experience. Trujillo acknowledges that while it was fathers who tried to impose sexual conformity, "it was usually our mothers who actually whispered the warnings, raised the eyebrows, or covertly transmitted to us the 'taboo nature' of same sex relationships" (Trujillo, x). But the expression and writing about lesbian and heterosexual sexuality, as both these volumes will attest, have risen above the whispers, above the taboos. They are dispelling the myth of the unknown. As Carmen Abrego states:

> the truth of the matter is that you know
> nothing about me or of me.
> i like the samba . . .
> but much more i
> like to dance it with that woman from
> brazil.
>
> (Trujillo, 10)

Within the general topic of sexuality the writers take on tradition, society, violence, myths, and all the secret thoughts that revolve around sexual behavior. The women who emerge from these pages are women who are taking control of their lives and of their sexuality. In a story by Carmen Tafolla, "Federico y Elfiria," Tafolla tells the story from the point of view of Federico, a young man imbued with all the stereotypes of women, especially the sexual ones. A woman is virgin or puta, and his wife is a good girl. After the birth of their first child, Elfiria comes to him "real suavecito" and says:

Hace mucho tiempo. I'm healed now, tú sabes, down there . . ." Federico was touched, but, muy caballero, comforts, "That's O.K. honey. I don't need it. I can wait some more." The dam burst, and Elfiria, tired and glad the baby was finally asleep, burst too. "But I need it! I can't wait some more!"

Federico was stunned. " . . . But you hombre! I always thought you were . . ." he gulped and said it directo, " . . . a good girl."

"Ya para con estas tonterías! Of course I'm a good girl! I'm more than that! Soy una madre—the mother of our child y soy tu esposa—wife, you know. Like married?"

Federico had never thought of it that way. He had always heard of pos, tú sabes—desas, bad girls, y también of course de good girls—but of someone being a good girl plus more? Maybe that explained it. Maybe eso de ser mother and wife let her do these kinds of things plus be a good girl. He hadn't figured it out completely, pero Elfiria interrupted him and said, "¡Ya olvídate de esas cosas! Let's go to bed" And they did, and pos, tú sabes, a man can only do so much all by himself. (In Alarcón, III)

The other face of sexuality fulfilled is sexuality violated. The volume contains poignant first-person narratives of men's violence against women, of incest and wife beating; the discovery of becoming a woman in a world that finds sexuality dirty, secret, that does not talk about it; the discovery that comes as a shock to young women who are not prepared; the anguish of lesbians who are not accepted by their families, who feel at the margins of society. Yet the love of and between women is also declared, "suavemente, dulcemente." Adela Alonso says, "mis manos descubren tus pechos / se deslizan por las pesadas curvas / que como frutas maduras / coronan tu esbelto cuerpo / y ahí como lo esperaba / a flor de piel / anidado entre tus pechos / tiento un durazno colorado / blandito / y dulce" (in Alarcón, 15).[13] What comes forth clearly in this volume, and in other new writing about sexuality by Chicanas, is the acceptance of female desire by all the writers, the acceptance of being a woman with all its joys and travails.

One strategy of Chicana writing that has always been unique has been the sense of humor and irony that lies lightly beneath its surface. Humor helps dissipate anger and taboos when writing about sensitive subjects. This strategy is often seen when dealing with sexuality. Denise Chávez, who captures the orality of women's voices (and the humor in them), does it once again when a grandmother admonishes her granddaughter against sex.

---

13. my hands discover your breasts / they slide along their heavy curves / which like ripe fruit / crown your slender body / and there as I expected / on the skin's surface / nestled between your breasts / I feel a reddish peach / soft and sweet.

Mama Lupita wanted one of her grandchildren to become a nun. Priests in the family are a dime a dozen. . . . What this family needs is a nun. Women's prayers, anyone knows, are more powerful. Any man can give up sex for four years, especially if they get them before they know what to do with that thing between their skirts. Cassocks that's what they call them. After that, you know what happens. When a woman gives up sex, it's final. Try and sneak sex on a woman, see what happens. Nine months later there's everlasting hell to pay. . . . Think about it. You like to read. Nuns read all the time and no one interrupts them. They can be quiet and have no one belch out loud and scratch themselves or make pedos you know, on the way to the you know what, the excusado . . . men can't be trained. They're wild bulls, or changos, monkeys. I don't know which. And that's not all. They shed. I could never keep a clean tub. . . . So think about it. I mean, becoming a nun. Your mother's childhood friend, Estella Fuentes, became a nun. She's now Sister Mary Margaret Marie of the Holy Magdalenes. She don't have no wrinkles. Her face smooth like a baby's nalgas. (Alarcón, 69–70)

And Sandra Cisneros shatters all taboos with her poem "Down There." In particular when she equates sexuality with writing, and desire with expression, she joins a long line of women who believed that writing, the pen, is not the penis, rather the body the clitoris, creativity the uterus. She says:

In fact,
I'd like to dab my fingers
or a swab of tampax
in my inkwell
and write a poem across the wall.
"A Poem of Womanhood"
Now wouldn't that be something?
(Alarcón, 23)

All these transgressions on cultural taboos constitute a sort of guerrilla warfare. The new sexuality is definitely a political ideology on the part of Chicana writers: an ideology that shreds the silences and arrives at a new openness.

The final trend is the concern that Chicanas have always had about borders. Fluidity, translations, multiplicities, limits, complications, alienations, the other, the outsider, the insider, the center, the margin. And, although the concern has always been there, it has become more clearly articulated, more explicit, more prevalent. It is a concern that derives from the triple and more cultures that must be explained, understood, constantly translated. Chicanas are Malinches all. It was Malinche, after all, who is understood symbolically to be the first indigenous woman to speak in tongues, that is, she spoke more than one indigenous language. Because she was an intelligent woman she rapidly, legend tells, learned Spanish. She was then able to use words to communicate culture, to betray culture, to assimilate, to not assimilate, to start a new race and a new culture. History is not clear whether she spoke with an accent, whether her translations were accurate, whether she resisted. She is the first translator of the foreign male/mail (see Cervantes "Beneath the Shadow of the Freeway") and as such has remained a problematic figure to both Mexican and Chicano literary critics, as the long history of observations on her as a symbolic figure will attest.

Malinche/Doña Marina has taken a beating from many critics and writers. She is the betrayer of her culture, of her race; she is la Chingada, the forced one, the violated one. She is violated sexually as well as in and by language. She did not deny language; she used, assimilated language, and through language and her body she accepted the foreigner. Through her body she created a child, a male child to be sure, who denied her in turn. One wonders how Malinche's daughter would have fared.

It is this problematic that Chicana writers find so attractive. Through myriad texts they explore the ambiguities, the complications, the implications that exist in La Malinche. For they, too, are translators. They shift from one culture to another, from one perspective to another, from a private space which may be Spanish-centered, to a public space that is English-centered. At home, as we have seen from Gaspar de Alba's text, they may feel centered, but outside that space they may feel slightly uncomfortable, no matter how assimilated they are. Or they may try to imprint their own identity on the public space. Certainly, the Chicano movement strived toward imprinting and asserting Chicano on Anglo culture. And, additionally, Chicanas must imprint themselves on Chicano culture. As Ramón Saldívar has noted, the question of identity reveals multiple and contradictory answers (Saldívar, 205–18). This might be a problem to those who saw reality as fixed all along and are just recently awakening to change. But for those who have lived the Chicana experience, living in contradictory and multiple realities has required the negotiation of many survival techniques. Indeed they find themselves the richer for it. So, the translations, the slipping and sliding continue.

The crossing of cultural and historic borders is not a new phenomenon. In the 1930s Cleofas Jaramillo wrote an autobiography published in English in 1955, *Romance of a Little Village Girl,* where she tried to understand all the changes that had come about during her lifetime in New Mexico. She stated, "Forgive me for my want of expression." After having been at boarding school (and speaking always in English), on her way home she exclaimed, "I had chattered all the way home in my fond Spanish" (Jaramillo, *Romance,* 41–42). Jaramillo created a world she wanted to reconstruct in English, but throughout the autobiography she was jarred by the inconsistencies, the feeling of alienation. Lorna Dee Cervantes clearly stated the same feeling in "Beneath the Shadow of the Freeway." The freeway—being the line that delineates one space from another—may be the contemporary analogy to "across the railroad tracks." Since many freeways in large urban areas were built in the barrios, the freeways often run along Chicano residential areas. In addition, they may have also destroyed much of the older sections of the barrios, thus destroying traditions. In any event, the line, the boundaries that Cervantes sees clearly in this poem are not only ones of Chicano (specifically Chicana) space between dominant and minority cultures, but they are also generational borders. It is the narrator and the abuelita connecting, across borders. The narrator clearly sees herself as the link between that private space of her grandmother and the public space. "I am the translator of foreign mail," she declares. In other texts Cervantes decried the fact that she was brought up with "no language," meaning she had lost her Spanish/Indian roots. And while clearly she is often at the center of the culture since she has come to a "consciousness about her culture," she knows where her heart lies, she understands clearly her cultural boundaries, and she is in the process of participating in the "new" culture. Nevertheless, at crucial moments in Cervantes' poetry, ambiguity strikes. She may be independent, she may build her own house by herself like her grandmother did, she may be the translator, but she is, nevertheless, wounded; "my own days bring me slaps on the face. Every day I am deluged with reminders / that this is not / my land" (Cervantes, *Emplumada*, 36).

Pat Mora, too, has articulated the complications of living in multiple cultures. In her book *Borders* (1988), she examined the relationship between men and women—"the side by side translations were the easy ones" (Mora, *Borders*, 9). She also is acutely conscious of class differences. She, the American Mexican, sits having coffee while the Mexicana Mexicans are working in the kitchen. The soft voices of these women speak to Mora in whispers. She recognizes their exclusion, she wonders about their secrets, she dreams their dreams. These women from "over the border" place the speaker of her poems in opposition to them, yet they are the same. In the world in which she lives the poetic speaker is not quite at home; there is always a pea under the mattress, a cactus thorn in the flesh. Nonetheless, these voices of Mora's form the background for a new order the poet would like to create: a place where these women would feel secure, could realize their dreams, could bloom. Mora's landscapes are harsh ones, richly reflective of an alien environment. The sun beats down fiercely on these borderlands and there is little water. Mora's comparisons of Chicanas to cacti shows these women's survival skills, their ability to adapt in hostile environments. Oppression, pain, disappointment are born, at first, in silence, then in language and eventually in writing.

Gloria Anzaldúa has also participated in the articulation of the frontier woman, the border woman, by defining and opening up the limits and boundaries of mestizaje, sexuality, and myth. She calls the U.S.–Mexican border "una herida abierta where the Third World grated against the first and bleeds. And before a scab forms it hemorrhages again, the lifeblood of two worlds merging to form a third country—a border culture. Borders are set up to define the places that are safe and unsafe, to distinguish us from them. A border is a dividing line, a narrow strip along a steep edge. A borderland is a vague and undetermined place created by the emotional residue of an unnatural boundary. It is in a constant state of transition. The prohibited and forbidden are its inhabitants" (Anzaldúa, *Borderlands*, 3).

Thus, while for some borders are limiting devices, Anzaldúa and other Chicanas find the state of being "mitá y mitá" (half and half), in whatever form you prefer to define it, as being a powerful state. This state can be the state of being lesbian, Mexican American, or any of the other border states in which we find ourselves. It is no longer a "duel between the oppressor and oppressed," it is a search for a new consciousness. For Anzaldúa that means that we must be on "both shores of the border at once, and see at the same time through both eagle and the serpents' eyes" (Anzaldúa, *Borderlands,* 78). While the clash of cultures may at times result in states of perplexity, more concisely expressed in the early days of Chicana literature, at the same time these multiple cultures, multiple states, multiple languages allow them to pick their survival strategies. Just as writing their silence is a sensuous act, it allows them to endure, to create their own images, their own souls. For Anzaldúa, coming into a new sense of Chicana consciousness, collective yet at the same time individual, signals the transformation of the border state into something powerfully positive. It is a sentiment echoed by Chicana writers everywhere. As Alicia Gaspar de Alba states in this anthology:

> The Chicana writer, like the curandera or the bruja, is the keeper of the culture, keeper of the memories, the rituals, the stories, the superstitions, the language, the imagery of her Mexican heritage. She is also the one who changes the culture, the one who breeds a new language and a new lifestyle, new values, new images and rhythms, new dreams and conflicts into that heritage, making of all of this brouhaha and cultural schizophrenia a new legacy for those who have still to squeeze into legitimacy as human beings and American citizens. (This vol., 291)

So writing has become the symbolic border that writers cross at will. They have conquered the linguistic oppressions that kept women silenced for so long; they have also learned the survival skills to opt for their cultures and more. This anthology gives witness to this learning, this crossing, and it celebrates their triumphs.

Foremothers

The memory of my grandfather and
grandmother and many of my aunts is
also the memory of old-time customs
and ways of living.

CLEOFAS M. JARAMILLO

The collection of texts from Mexican American women writing in the United States between 1848 and 1960 is, at this point, very slim. In the early years, many women were unable to read or write unless their families were wealthy. Formal education for women was not considered a prime necessity, particularly in pioneer days; later, Spanish-speaking women who immigrated from Mexico were often poor women who needed to earn a living, leaving little leisure time for reading and writing. Of those who did write, much of their writing was preserved within the family, unpublished, and undisseminated. What has remained of the early culture of women is to be found mainly in the oral tradition. Examples in this anthology come from two primary sources: the California narratives and the New Mexico Federal Writers' Project. Still there were women who wrote: they published poetry in Spanish language newspapers, they collected recipes and wrote narratives about folklore and traditions, romantic novels, and stories. In the 1930s and 1940s, sparked by the Federal Writers' Project, there was a great deal of interest in gathering oral histories and trying to preserve the history and culture of the "old-timers" in the Southwest. From all of these sources we are able to piece together the lives of women and writers of the past (see Introduction).

As mentioned, between 1930 and 1940, the Federal Writers' Project took oral histories of pioneer and early settlers of New Mexico and Arizona. Many who were interviewed were Hispanics in their sixties and seventies, people who had populated the Southwest in the late nineteenth century. From these short histories we are able to discover a little about their education, their occupations, and their lives. In Arizona some of the more interesting interviews of women were carried out by Romelia Gómez, of Cochise County. She interviewed elderly Hispanic women and completed a series of three-page vignettes. Because she was interested in their personal lives, we occasionally are able to glimpse what life was like for them, which gives some insight into the restrictions that prevented them from writing. For example, in an interview with Doña Isabel Hernández, Gómez states that "Isabel Juárez (for that was the family name) never attended school in Bisbee and cannot understand or speak English at all." Doña Isabel and her sister were seamstresses. They supported their entire family from the work they did in a little room on the bottom floor of their home. In another interview with Martina Diaz, Martina says, "The respectable families were very proud and they imprisoned forever a girl who committed an indiscretion." And in an interview with Casimira Valenzuela (who was 82): "She is vague about dates and complete details, as her memory fails her and she can neither read nor write." Doña Casimira has knowledge of "home cures and remedies" and repays people's kindness to her by treating them. From an interview with Sra. Lola Romero: "Mrs. Romero knows no English at all, never having attended school in the U.S. Her younger sister was the only one of the family to attend school on the arrival of the family in Bisbee. She went to Central School, which was later torn down to make way for the larger brick building of today. There was no compulsion in the attendance of the children at school, so her sister, like most of the Mexican children going to school then, only went when she felt like it." And again in an interview with Doña Apolonia Mendoza, "Apolonia and an older sister attended school at Central for a short while, during which time she says they learned nothing at all, so their mother took them out of school so they could help her in earning the families living, which she did by taking in washing from families living on Chihuahua Hill."

The husbands of these women came to Bisbee mainly as miners, and many of the women had to earn a living doing laundry and serving as domestics or as clerks. There were few other opportunities for these women in those days. Bisbee was not a town without culture, however; there was a Mexican theater that regularly performed musical events, and there were many *bailes* (dances).

In *Women in Early Texas,* which chronicles the life of early pioneer women and includes biographies of early Spanish-speaking women who became civic leaders, it is clear that many of the women came from well-to-do families. "From an early age the children were carefully trained: in the meticulous practice of their Catholic faith; in love, respect, and implicit obedience to their parents; in the knowledge of, and strict adherence to family background and traditions; and in the elegant courtesy and social graces of the times." Girls were carefully sheltered, never leaving the home without a chaperone (*dueña*) or older companion. Quoting from the history of María Gertrudis Pérez Cordero Cassiano: "The Pérez girls were well educated, for women could own, inherit, administer, buy and sell property." María married the elderly Governor of Texas, who "so cherished his lovely eighteen-year-old bride that when he was absent, he authorized her to take his place and she conducted affairs of state in grand style and reviewed the troops as expertly as Queen Isabella."

The women who are known well enough to be mentioned in early histories of New Mexico, California, and Texas, generally came from wealthy families. However, even in the 1930s and 1940s few Chicanas were educated to be able to write, nor did they have the leisure to do so. If they had some education, they were likely to be the local schoolteachers, such as Fabiola Cabeza de Baca of New Mexico. Luis Leal and Pepe Barrón, in "Chicano Literature: An Overview" examine the stages in Chicano literature to determine at what point the literature written by writers of the Southwest has a reality and a "set of circumstances different from the Mexican" (in Baker, 12). No women writers are mentioned in their essay, and in many ways, these dates have no bearing on the women writing since 1848, because to be a female writer in those times was to be set apart to begin with. These early women authors often wrote with the sense of preserving the traditions that they saw vanishing. Perhaps when more diaries, memoirs, and other writings (which are still preserved) come forth, we will be better able to place these writers in their proper place. Nevertheless, it is also clear that musical events, theater, the oral traditions of *cuentos, corridos,* and poetry (along with the passing along of culture through recipes and remedies) all influenced women as well as men. In fact, some of the first "writing" was in the collection of cookbooks and household remedies in order to pass them along to female children or other women.

And what of women who may have been writing at this time, from the early twentieth century? Raymond Paredes, in his interesting and provocative article, "The Evolution of Chicano Literature," is one of the few critics who deals with early women writers in a serious way (in Baker, 33–79). However, he tends to criticize those writers from the early 1900s to 1940s for internalizing the class, sex, and racial stereotyping of the surrounding culture. He particularly criticizes writers from New Mexico for their excessive romanticism, their *hacienda* mentality, and their literary pretensions. He criticizes the women for their "gentility," because many of the ones who wrote came from an upper "more educated" class; and yet we know leisure time to be a necessity for writers of any gender, especially for women, tied as they are to nurturing familial obligations. Although many of Paredes' observations are accurate, it is rather amazing that women were writing at all.

About María Cristina Mena, writing in the early 1900s in English language magazines, Paredes says: "Mena was a talented story teller whose sensibility unfortunately tended toward sentimentalism and preciousness. She aimed to portray Mexican culture in a positive light but with great decorum: as a consequence, her stories seem *trivial* and condescending. . . . Occasionally she struck a blow at the pretensions of Mexico's ruling class, but to little effect. Mena's genteelness simply was incapable of warming the reader's blood" (Baker, 49–50). Paredes wishes Mena could have been "a braver, more perceptive writer," one who confronted social issues more forcefully (Baker, 50). He feels the same about writers in New Mexico, who portrayed the Spanish component of their heritage as the most important part of it. These writers, and there were a few women among them, seem to Paredes to describe "a culture seemingly locked in time and barricaded against outside forces" (Baker, 52). They saw the Spanish heritage of New Mexico through nostalgic eyes and essentially extolled the virtues of Spanish heritage over the Mexican or Indian heritage; a good illustration is the work of Nina Otero Warren. One product of her perspective is the society founded by Otero, aimed at pursuing Spanish customs and heritage. In her book, *Old Spain in Our Southwest,* everything of value is presented as an end product of Spanish (Castilian) culture. Nevertheless, such descriptions are valuable in preserving accounts of folk life and particularly the lives and duties of women that are not preserved elsewhere. One must recognize that they were among the first attempts at preservation of their lives against the overwhelming dominance of Anglo culture and language, and also against patriarchal norms.

Josephina Niggli is credited (by Paredes, among others) with the first genuine attempt to emphasize the authentic roots of Mexican Indian heritage in *Mexican Village,* 1945. Niggli is a neglected author who is beginning to be studied for her plays as well as her short stories. We must not forget, however, Fabiola Cabeza de Baca, who did write frontier stories and who documents the struggle of the *Nuevo Mexicanos* to keep their land and to preserve their heritage. Contemporary critics are studying these early writers for their strategies of resistance to cultural norms that threatened to erase their language and culture.

In early writing in Spanish (much of it published in Spanish-language newspapers), poetry was the craft most used by both men and women and generally it followed the dictates of classic and romantic styles. According to other findings, most poems were either dedicated to people, or were commemorative, religious, and patriotic texts. Mexican poetry and that of Hispanic tradition had arrived in almost every Spanish-speaking community with Spanish language newspapers in the United States, which printed the latest poetry from Spain and Latin America. Local writers consciously tried to follow these writers in themes, form, and content, and although many of these local writers were poor imitators, there was a great deal of authentic and original talent. Among them is Carmen Celia Beltrán, a poet who still lives in Arizona and who has written vigorously since the 1920s. Other women wrote occasional poems during the early part of this century, but there are none who have taken their careers as writers so seriously, perhaps, as Beltrán. Other women who were writing were María Guadalupe Valero, María Ibarra, May Stadden de Rojas, Catalina Iribe, Evangelina Cranz, and María Yoldi. Also in New Mexico, women such as María Esperanza López de Padilla were publishing poems in Spanish-language newspapers, and we include some examples of their work here.

Interestingly enough, many of the themes and topics covered by these women are frequently seen today in contemporary writing, even though the approach may be different. Therefore, the importance of family, the preservation of traditions, folkloric elements of healing, such as the activities of *brujas* and *curanderas,* are present in early writings as well as in contemporary ones. Common concerns and themes link the past with the present, weaving together the fabric of which women's lives are woven. These literary foremothers who told stories and sang songs, who passed on the details of their lives through the oral tradition, who wrote novels and poems and locked them away in boxes and drawers, are and have been the mainstay of our culture and of our creativity. Their daughters, granddaughters, and great granddaughters are just now writing their memory into history.

■ ■ ■

PART I: The Oral Tradition

Excerpts from "Una Vieja Y Sus Recuerdos."

Dictated by Doña Eulalia Pérez, 1877

This oral history is part of a series of oral histories of early pioneers in California collected under the directions of Hubert H. Bancroft. Eulalia Pérez spoke to Bancroft's assistant Thomas Savage, who gave us a description of her in 1877. "Whatever may be the real age of Madame Eulalia Pérez, she is certainly a very ancient person; there can be no doubt, from her personal appearance, that she is a centenarian." And later he comments, "Her memory is remarkly [sic] fresh on some things and much clouded on others, particularly on her age. She is at times flighty, but with patience, and by asking her questions only upon such matters as she could

be conversant with, I found no great difficulty in obtaining intelligible answers."
(This history was translated by Ruth Rodríguez in 1957.)

I, Eulalia Pérez, was born in the Presidio of Loreto in Lower California. My father's name was Diego Pérez, and he was employed in the Navy Department of said presidio; my mother's name was Antonia Rosalía Cota (Note: Michael White, her son-in-law, says Lucia Valenzuela). Both were pure Caucasians.

I do not remember the date of my birth, but I do know that I was 15 years old when I married Miguel Antonio Guillén, a soldier of the garrison at Loreto Presidio. During the time of my stay at Loreto I had three children— two boys, who died there in infancy, one girl, Petra, who was eleven years old when we moved to San Diego, and another boy, Isidoro, who came with us to this (Upper) California.

I lived eight years in San Diego with my husband, who continued his service in the garrison of the presidio, and I attended women in childbirth.

(There follows an account of her life, her husband's death, and comments on the mission priests for whom she begins to work in San Gabriel.)

When I came to San Gabriel the last time, there were only two women in this part of California who knew how to cook. One was María Luisa Cota, wife of Claudio López, superintendent of the mission; the other was María Ignacia Amador, wife of Francisco Javier Alvarado. She knew how to cook, sew, read and write, and take care of the sick. She was a good healer. She did needlework and took care of the church vestments. She taught a few children to read and write in her home but did not conduct a formal school.

On special holidays, such as the day of our patron saint, Easter, etc., the two women were called upon to prepare the feast and to make the meat dishes, sweets, etc. The priests wanted to help me out because I was a widow burdened with a family. They looked for some way to give me work without offending the other women. Fathers Sánchez and Zalvidea conferred and decided that they would have first one woman, then the other, and finally me, do the cooking, in order to determine who did it best, with the aim of putting the one who surpassed the others in charge of the Indian cooks so as to teach them how to cook. With that idea in mind, the gentlemen who were to decide on the merits of the three dinners were warned ahead of time. One of these gentlemen was Don Ignacio Tenorio, who they called the Royal Judge, and who came to live and die in the company of Father Sánchez. He was a very old man, and when he went out, wrapped up in a muffler, he walked very slowly with the aid of a cane. His walk consisted only of going from the Father's house to the church.

The other judges who also were to give their opinions were Don Ignacio Mancisidor, Merchant, Don Pedro Narváez, Navy official, Sergeant José Antonio Pico—who later became Lieutenant, brother of Governor Pio Pico, Don Domingo Romero, who was my assistant when I was housekeeper at the mission, Claudio López, superintendent at the mission, besides the Fathers. These gentlemen, whenever they were at the mission, were accustomed to eat with the Fathers.

On the days agreed upon for the three dinners, they showed up. No one told me anything regarding what it was all about, until one day Father Sánchez called me and said, "Look, Eulalia, tomorrow it's your turn to prepare dinner—because María Ignacia and Luisa have already done so. Let's see what kind of a dinner you'll give us tomorrow."

The next day I went to prepare the food. I made several kinds of soup, a variety of meat dishes, and whatever else happened to pop into my head that I knew how to prepare. The Indian cook, named Thomas, watched me attentively, as the Father had told him to do.

At dinner time those mentioned came. When the meal was concluded, Father Sánchez asked for their opinions about it, beginning with the oldest, Don Ignacio Tenorio. This gentleman pondered awhile, saying that for many years he hadn't eaten the way he'd eaten that day—that he doubted that they ate any better at the King's table. The others also praised the dinner highly.

Then the Father called Thomas and asked him which of the three women he liked best—which one of them knew the most about cooking. He answered that I did.

Because of all this, employment was provided for me at the mission.

(In 1821 she is appointed housekeeper of the mission.)

The duties of the housekeeper were many. In the first place, every day she doled out the rations for the mess hut. To do this she had to count the un-married women, bachelors, day-laborers, vaqueros—both those with saddles and those who rode bareback. Besides that she had to hand out daily rations to the heads of households. In short she was responsible for the distribution of supplies to the Indian population and to the Fathers' kitchen. She was in charge of the key to the clothing storehouse where materials were given out for dresses for the unmarried and married women, and children. Then she also had to take care of cutting and making clothes for the men.

They put under my charge everything having to do with clothing. I cut and fitted, and my five daughters sewed up the pieces. When they couldn't handle everything, the Father was told, and then women from the town of Los Angeles were employed and the Father paid them.

Besides this, I had to attend to the soap-house, which was very large, to the wine-presses, and to the olive-crushers that produced oil, which I worked in myself. Under my direction and responsibility, Domingo Romero took care of changing the liquid. Luis the Soap-maker had charge of the soap-house, but I directed everything.

I handled the giving out of leather, calf-skin, chamois, sheepskin, Morocco leather, fine scarlet cloth, nails, thread, silk, etc.—everything having to do with the making of saddles, shoes, and what was needed for the belt- and shoe-making shop.

Every week I delivered supplies for the troops and Spanish-speaking servants. These consisted of beans, corn, garbanzos, lentils, candles, soap, and lard. To carry out this distribution, they placed at my disposal an Indian servant named Lucio, who was trusted completely by the Fathers.

When it was necessary, some of my daughters did what I couldn't find the time to do. Generally, the one who was always at my side was my daughter María del Rosario.

After all my daughters were married—the last one was Rita, about 1832 or 1833—Father Sánchez undertook to persuade me to marry First Lieutenant Juan Marín, a Spaniard from Catalonia, a widower with family who had served in the artillery. I didn't want to get married, but the Father told me that Marín was a very good man—as, in fact, he turned out to be—besides, he had some money, although he never turned his cash-box over to me. I gave in to the Father's wishes because I didn't have the heart to deny him anything when he had been father and mother to me and to all my family.

I served as housekeeper of the mission for twelve or fourteen years, until about two years after the death of Father José Sánchez, which occurred in this same mission.

(She goes on to describe the life of the neophyte Indians at the mission and some other incidents of California history. She ends her narration with some songs.)

Eufemia's Sopapillas

As told by Catalina Gurulé and Patricia Gallegos

A story of the days when the forefathers of the Placitas people lived in the walled town of Las Huertas, a mile North of the present Placitas.

One day the men went to the mountains to hunt. They said they would be back before dark and told their women to lock the gates and keep all the children inside the walls. So that day the women worked in their houses and kept the children with them. Then a band of "wild Indians" came. They found the gates locked. They thought the people must be hiding somewhere so one of them climbed on top of the house that formed the corner of the wall, and another climbed up to look into the very small window. It was old Eufemia's house but the Indian could not see her because she was busy at the fireplace frying the last of her sopapillas. She had fried a lot of them because her men would be hungry when they returned from the hunt. There was no smoke from her chimney now for the fire was low. The Indian thought someone might be hiding down there, so down came his long stick with a spear head on the end of it. It went right into the *tinaja* of sopapillas. The poor old woman was frightened, but her mind worked fast. Because the spear head hit the bottom of the tinaja, the Indian would think he had speared somebody and would look for blood on it. She must do something to keep the Indians out there until the men came back. She put a sopapilla on the spear head and watched the stick go up the chimney. Then the stick came down again and she put another sopapilla on it. Again and again the stick came down until at last Eufemia had only one sopapilla left. And still the men had not come. It would take too long to make more sopapillas. What could she do? She moved back from the corner. She happened to look up. There was the Indian at the window eating one of her sopapillas. She must do something quick. She took up the tinaja and fast as she could move she stepped upon the adobe bench against the wall and threw the hot fat in the Indian's face. He cried out in pain. The other Indians thought he had been shot with an arrow. They ran away fast as they could go, leaving their companion screaming with the pain. Then the men came back. They put a rope around the Indian's feet and pulled him up over a tree and cut his throat—just as they would do an animal.

An Old Native Custom: La Curandera

Collected by the New Mexico Federal Writers' Project

In the days of long ago when there were no médicos in the now land of New Mexico, nor none trained scientifically to care for the sick and the suffering, self appointed healers called curanderos played important parts in the life of the native communities. Their curealls were of the lavish gifts of nature and free to all who collected them. From the traditions of their people those who collected them knew of their curative powers and how to administer them.

In the earliest days of las Placitas, a little house nestled close to Cerro Negro, the hill of black rock carved with Indian symbols, just to the north of the village. A house which became a kind of sanctuary for weary souls and a little temple of health for the sick. It was La Casa de La Curandera, Jesusita.

The name Jesusita and all of its forms have since been banned by the church. This Jesusita was a pious, honorable curandera devoted to the saints and her remedios. She had high faith in each of them.

She kept her house fresh and clean from the vigas which supported the ceiling of latas and the adobe mud roof, down to the hard earthen floor. Her walls were snow-white with yeso and the hand-hewn timbers of her wee windows and dwarf door were scrubbed to a saffron tint. Those who still have memories of La Curandera also tell of her house. Just inside her door stood a smooth, stout stick with grama grass bound tightly to one end of it by a piece of correa (leather string). That was her broom and first aid to household cleanliness in those old days.

La Curandera was a very small person, with slender, graceful hands with which she did half of her talking and much of her healing. She wore many petticoats, made of cloth she wove herself, and always she kept them fresh and clean. To one of them she fastened a little sack filled with the hair of every different form of life she could find. This would save her from the power of the witches as would the piece of cachana she wore about her person. A small piece it was with a hole pierced in it through which to run a string. This charm against witches was worn for many years upon the person of La Curandera and finally given to a grandchild to preserve her from the power of the witches. Jesusita feared the witches even more than she feared the devil; but then she was born in 1830.

Always there was a pleasant suggestion of a flower garden in the air in La Curandera's house. But, "Entren todos y miren alrededor ustedes." (Enter all and have a look around.)

Those vigas which supported the roof were festooned with drying herbs. Herbs which restored health, eased pain, and saved life. When these were dried they would be taken down and carefully put away for use. There was *yerbabuena* (mint), *guaco* (birthwort), *berraza* (water-parsnip): all superior remedies for *dolor de estomago* (hurt of stomach) as all stomach ailments were called in those days. But not all the *yerbas* good for this ailment were dried. There was *chan* (an Indian word) which was eaten when green, a pinch of salt added. There was *ramo de sabine* (twig of savin). Boil the leaves and make strong tea. Both these remedies were sure cures for cramps of the stomach. *Yerba de zorra* (fox weed) also made a desirable tea for stomach disturbances.

From the vigas hung much *poleo* (pennyroyal). It was the magic fever reducer. But an egg white, well beaten, added to the dry poleo and well mixed, a little salt sprinkled over it, was what really made the poleo effective. And it was effective, when spread as a poultice on a piece of cloth and covered with an equal sized piece of pin pricked paper. This poultice was bound to the forehead and soles of feet—paper side down—and it brought quick relief to victims of high fevers. So good a remedy was it that it is used to this day. A strong tea made from the reddish flower of the dried saffron (*yerba de azefrán*) was also an aid in reducing fever. It required some sort of sweetening for best results. Raisins made from the grape at home were used before the advent of "yellow sugar." *Azefrán* [sic] relieved colic.

La Curandera's house was sweetly scented by the drying *cilantro* (coriander). She would receive extra special gifts, perhaps a lamb or a kid for those precious aromatic seeds so coveted for flavoring soups, puddings, and *bizcochitos* (small biscuits).

La Curandera dried *mansanilla* in abundance (good old chamomile in English). That yerba was the baby medicine. It made excellent tea for the cure of colic, and it was considered a food substitute.

Cota (proper name should be *macha* and it is lamb's lettuce) when dried made a very popular drink good for almost any disposition towards general debility. It is popular to this day. Also it was cota that was dried in abundance in the old days and stored for using to light a fire when flint rocks furnished the sparks. Suspended from Jesusita's vigas was a plentiful supply of that yerba.

But not all of La Curandera's cure“alls were hung from the vigas to dry. Packed away in all those tinajas inside and upon the *tapanco* (the cupboard of the old days) were quantities of all the important roots and wonder-cures of her time. Prominent among the roots was *yerba del manza* which was indeed a life-saver, a killer of infections. The root was thoroughly boiled and bath water was made strong with it. The infected parts of the body were soaked in this water. Not once, but many times. No infection survived those repeated, sustained baths. To this day it is declared that the doctors of medicine, who came to the Territory of New Mexico in the early days, had no germ destroyer to compare with yerba del manza. Much of *yerba del lobo* (herb of the wolf) was stored in the tinajas. This root made a tea which was given to ease the first pains of childbirth.

Quiteria Outwits the Witch Nurse

As told by Rumaldita Gurulé

Rumaldita Gurulé, age 67, is the wife of José Librado Arón Gurulé and a descendant of one of the twenty-one families who received the Las Huertas Grant from the King of Spain, and who settled at La Madera, just over the Sandias from Placitas.

"Quiteria is the best nurse and she is young," the people said, and it made Doña Tomasa, the witch nurse, very jealous. So Quiteria was afraid of her and she tried to keep out of her way. The witch nurse might play an evil trick on her. Then one day somebody whispered to Quiteria that if she stood on Tomasa's shadow, Tomasa could not move, and then she would have power over Tomasa. At noon one day Doña Tomasa came to visit Quiteria. "Ah," thought Quiteria to herself, "I must keep her until her shadow grows a little." So she invited the witch nurse to eat dinner with her. The woman was hungry so she stayed and drank the good *atole* (a drink made of milk and the meal of the roasted and ground pueblo corn) and ate the tortillas. But she was in a hurry and soon she was leaving. Quiteria picked up her new *reboso* and followed Tomasa out the door. "See how fine my new reboso is. Touch it," and Quiteria came very close to the witch nurse and stood on her shadow. The witch nurse tried to move. She could not. So she acted very natural as if she did not wish to move. She talked of the people to Quiteria. She talked of the crops. She rolled many cigarettes and smoked them. Hour after hour passed. Then she knew Quiteria was keeping her there on purpose. She must get away. She cried out, "I am sick. Run quick. Get me some water!" Quiteria saw that she looked very pale, so she ran into the house for the water. When she returned, Doña Tomasa was gone.

Las Tres Gangozas (The Three Sisters)

As told by Guadalupe Gallegos

Once upon a time there lived a widow who had three daughters. Now these girls all had a defect of speech which caused them to speak with a sniffle and because of this none of them had ever been able to get a husband.

The three daughters were very beautiful, and it happened that one day a young gentleman caught sight of them. He was struck with their beauty and remarked to his two companions, "That old lady has the most beautiful daughters I have ever seen."

The young man and his two companions went to the old lady and asked for her daughters' hands in marriage. The old lady was very pleased and asked the young men to come to her house the following day to meet her daughters.

On this particular day the old lady found that she would be unable to be present when the young men called so before she left she told the daughters of what had happened and warned them not to speak in the young men's presence.

When the young men called the next day the girls heeded their mother's warning and spoke not a word. An hour passed and no one had spoken. Suddenly the coffee began to boil.

"The coffee is boiling," said the eldest sister forgetting her mother's warning.

"I'm going to tell mother that you talked," said the second sister.

"I'm the only one who didn't talk," said the third.

Upon hearing the defective speech of the sisters, the young men were very shocked and forgot how beautiful the girls were. They jumped up and left immediately, leaving their hats behind.

PART II: The Written Tradition

Asking for the Bride

Nina Otero-Warren

The Spaniard is dramatic in his love affairs. When a son of a *patrón* wished to become engaged, his father and uncles made a visit to the father of the girl to ask for the parent's consent to an engagement, following the old custom as expressed in the Spanish law of 1766, that no young people could marry without the consent of their parents. This law was to prevent marriages between people of different social positions. It was the intention of Spain to perpetuate the ruling class in the New Possessions. The father and uncles, on arriving at the home of the young girl, were received most formally. This was an occasion when the formal reception room was made ready in advance, for a visit of this nature was never a surprise, although convention required that it seem so.

After an exchange of courtesies, the father of the would-be groom presented a letter, which was received but not read. After a social visit, with wine and cookies served, the men departed, knowing only that a return visit would be made to deliver the answer before the month was over. The letter read:

"Most distinguished *Señor*:

"Most esteemed *Doña*:

"With our fitting regard and deserved affection, this informal note comes with the sole object of making your illustrious selves aware that our son, Felipe, is favorably disposed to your pleasing daughter, Consuelo. He wishes to place himself under your orders and to undergo the formality of the matrimonial ceremony in order better to serve you.

"We await, *señores,* your answer in the hope that you will pledge to us the most precious jewel of your house. This is our prayer. We abide by your final decision when it is your pleasure to answer us.

"We are, with highest respects,

At your orders,

Yours with all courtesy,"

Time passed. The young girl asked for in marriage during this interval did not see the youth to whom she was to be pledged by her parents. Word was sent to the young man's father as to the date of the return visit, so that he should not be absent on such an important occasion. All the members of the household felt the dramatic effect, whether the answer were to be favorable or otherwise. There was a speculation in the house of Felipe, among the younger members of the family. Eduardo, the small brother, ran into the room of his aunt, a widow who lived with them—"*Tía,*" the boy called. "Today Felipe will know whether Consuelo will be his wife or not. You know, Felipe looked sad. I think he knows he will be given the *calabaza*—the squash!"

"Do not be ridiculous," said his aunt. "Do you not know that the house of Aragón is the most distinguished in all this kingdom; that Felipe has cattle and sheep and horses and Indian slaves for his bride. No one could refuse such an offer!"

"But," continued Eduardo, "wouldn't it be funny for him to be given a squash? The yellow color would just suit Felipe and he is so jealous that he thinks if anyone visits in the hacienda of the Bacas he is in love with his *señorita.* I want him to get *calabazas;* he wouldn't be so everlastingly proud."

"His pride," said his aunt, "is of his family and his race."

"Look," said Eduardo, "here they come! See the big coach and oh! what lovely horses! I would rather have one of those horses than any girl."

The aunt had not heard this remark, as she was standing at a window looking at the guests.

The guests were received with great formality. Wine was served. No women ever took part in this special ceremony, though it was upon the mother's decision that the outcome depended. The visit was not a long one, for the answer, in the form of a beautifully written letter, was handed to Felipe's father.

After the guests had departed, the letter was eagerly read:

"Our Most Distinguished and
"Respected *Señor* and *Doña*:

"Greetings and happiness, and good returns in your business are our wishes.

"Most honored *Señor* and *Doña,* after greeting you we wish to notify you that we have made known to our young daughter, Consuelo, yours of date January 10, 1881, and have notified her that your son, Felipe, desires to be united with her by the bond of matrimony. She responded favorably to your request, and since we, because of the high respect in which we are pleased to hold you, have also agreed to your selection of our daughter, it is our duty as parents to make known to you our decision.

"Our doors will be open to you on the twenty-fifth of the present month at 2 o'clock in the afternoon, in order that you may be here to receive the pledge which you desire, and that you may arrange for the time when our children may pass on to be united by the means of the divine bond.

"With nothing more to say except to express the high respect in which we hold you,

                    "With sincerity, at your service,"

Preparations were immediately underway for the announcement of the engagement. This formal engagement is accompanied with as much ceremony frequently as the wedding itself.

The custom was for the groom-to-be to furnish the bride with a complete trousseau. Special marriage chests were carved and decorated. These were filled with fine linens, dainty underwear, house dresses, evening gowns, clothes for all occasions, of silks, satins, shoes of the latest pointed-toe styles. One chest contained the bridal outfit—a white satin gown trimmed with rose point-lace, a crown of way orange blossoms to be placed over the sheer veil, white satin slippers, lace gloves. On top of the clothes were two velvet boxes, one containing a string of pearls for the bride and the other the wedding ring.

Servants were sent to the home of the bride-to-be with wagon loads of provisions to prepare for the wedding which took place shortly after the announcement of the engagement.

On the day set, there was great excitement everywhere. The trousseau was brought at that time, and often the girl was so young that her thoughts were entirely on her new clothes. The two mothers fitted the dresses on the girl at this time, left the many gifts to be admired and made final arrangements for the wedding feast. The wedding feast took place in the home of the bride, but the bridegroom's family was completely in charge, and furnished everything for the occasion.

At the announcement of the engagement, there was usually a dance given and at this time the bride might wear one of the dresses from her trousseau. A wedding feast was truly a gay time, for with the grandees the celebration would last a week or longer, even though the bridal couple might have left for their own hacienda. The relatives particularly enjoyed it, for family relationships were cemented by the union.

The Field Crosses of the Farmers

Nina Otero-Warren

My fields were planted. Large rectangles of freshly tilled land lay brown in the sun. Wires were made tight to protect the crops from the cattle of the Indians who do not always confine their livestock to fences. I saw where the furrows were curved in the newly plowed ground, as horses had been guided to avoid old cedar and piñon stumps left after the clearing. On each of these stumps now stood a small cross.

The sun was setting as I approached the camp of my workmen. They had only just returned from the fields, for by them time is not reckoned by clocks, but by the length of the shadow.

I inquired of Anastacio, the foreman, his reason for "planting" crosses in my fields.

"That God may protect your crops, *Patrona*," he answered. "And that He may grant that your fields produce abundantly. You see, *señora*, in the olden days my grandfather used to tell us of the happenings here; and why some had success with their crops while others failed. Now, there is the story of the crosses. . . ."

"Tell it to me, Anastacio."

We sat by the small wood fire. The man had thrown a sheep's skin over old grass that I might be more comfortable.

"It was this way," he continued; "there lived in our community an old woman who was peculiar in her mind, and because of the strange things she said and her queer actions, she was called a witch. She lived alone in one small room. It was the duty of the community to see that she did not want either for food or for wood to keep her warm. Everyone took turns in leaving piñon logs and cedar sticks on her doorstep. The women saw to it that she had such food as she might need. As you know, *señora,* there is always a concern among us for the old and the unfit.

"One day, in the spring of the year, this old woman went about, as was her custom, 'whispering in the shadows.' There was great concern in her voice, so the people passing by stopped in to listen. The old witch told the men that there was a great storm coming. 'See the white clouds on the Sandia mountains,' she said. 'It is God's hand laying a cloth on His high altar to receive the pure snow. The heavens will freshen the earth. But it will then turn bleak, and the raindrops that fall on your fields will turn to hail which will beat down and make cold your young plants!'

"They all laughed at this witch. They said that she was simple-minded, for the skies were clear and the country flooded with sunshine.

"Days passed and the villagers watched their crops grow bigger and stronger. They had forgotten the first warning of the simple-minded old woman. They paid little heed to her mutterings and wanderings. How she insisted that everything would be lost to them unless they planted little crosses in their fields. 'Crosses are prayers to Our Master asking Him to watch over your corn and beans and squash plants. How will you have food for your families? How will I have food?' she wailed. 'Why, even Indians plant prayer-plumes in their fields!'

"Still other days passed and one night a cold wind came down from the mountains. The skies were overcast, the peaks of Truchas were white against the gray heavens. Some people wondered. Others said that it was time the spring rains came to feed the streams. But, *señora,* the clouds parted and the skies opened. The rain came down like many knives. The hail came, and beat all growing things to the earth. The following morning, the ground looked as though a blanket of ice had been laid over it. My grandfather said, 'It is a cold shroud for the young plants; the storm wished to hide its own damage.'

"The men went silently to their fields. Their crops were frozen and beaten down to the ground. In all this valley only one field had not shared in this ruin. An old couple had listened to the witch and had believed. They had nailed little wooden crosses to their fence posts and to the stumps of trees. Their fields were green. Their corn and bean plants were refreshed by the moisture and untouched by hail or frost. Silently and greatly humbled those men returned to their homes, their faith as real as their sorrow.

"Since that time, *patrona,* when we plant seed, and before the day's work is ended, we erect small crosses. And today, as the sun disappears behind the Jemez mountains bidding us rest, you will find in all your fields extending their arms in blessing over all your crops, not scarecrows—but The Field Crosses of the Farmers."

The Herb Woman

Fabiola Cabeza de Baca Gilbert

The next morning, as Doña Paula was preparing summer squash for drying, Señá Martina came by with a sack full of herbs. She had been out in the fields since dawn gathering medicinal herbs which she shared with her neighbors. Señá Martina was the *curandera,* the medicine woman of the village. Very often she went out to neighboring towns to heal persons from various maladies and her fame as a medicine woman stretched over many miles.

After greeting Doña Paula she sat down beside her and without being asked, she took over the task of slicing small squashes into circles in preparation for drying.

Doña Paula became curious to know if Señá Martina had discovered any new herbs.

"What did you bring me today?" she inquired.

"The usual remedies," she replied. "You need a new supply this year."

"Shall I spread them out to dry for you?" she asked as she reached for her sack.

Doña Paula went into the kitchen to get some string while Señá Martina spread out her herbs on the patio. She sorted the plants in neat piles ready for tying.

The medicine woman seemed so old and wrinkled to Doña Paula and she wondered how old she was. No one remembered when she was born. She had been a slave in the García family for two generations and that was all any one knew. She had not wanted her freedom, yet she had always been free. She had never married, but she had several sons and daughters. Doña Paula had heard many tales about Señá Martina. Some said the children belonged to the *patrón,* the master, under whom she had worked; others said they were his grandchildren. Doña Paula thought, "What right have I thinking of such things? They are children of God and they have been good sons and daughters. That is all that matters."

"Señá Martina, you will have to tell me the names of the plants and what their uses are. I can never remember from one year to another," said Doña Paula.

"You young people believe too much in doctors and you have no faith in plants," answered Señá Martina as she picked up a bunch of plants and tied them.

"When I was young, there were no doctors and we lived through many sicknesses.

"Children died from the evil eye because no one can compete with the devil, but they did not die from colic. Here is some *manzanilla,* camomile from my garden. A strong tea brewed from it cures the colic. It is always well to rub the stomach of the ailing child with camphorized fat and to keep him from eating solid food. A gruel made from wheat flour with a little sugar and anise seed helps to stop the diarrhea.

"Doña Paula, why don't you put down all the prescriptions that I give you each year? You who can write need not rely on your memory only, as I have for years. I cannot live forever and when I am gone you will have no one to ask."

"You are right," said Doña Paula. "I shall write them down." She had said the same thing for twenty years. But she kept on slicing squash.

Señá Martina sorting out herbs took a bunch of elder-berry flowers. "These," she said, "cannot fail to ease a fever and it is also a pleasant tea to drink. You should have a bush in your yard."

"Yes, of course," answered Doña Paula, "I have been telling José to bring a cutting from your garden."

"I brought you some dry rose petals, because with all your many tasks, I knew you would forget to gather some. Crushed rose petals mixed with powered alum are the best remedy for sore gums.

"I did not see any *azafrán,* saffron, in your garden this year and I know you will need it for seasoning. Do you remember when your children had the measles? You thought it was only a cold. When I gave them saffron tea, the measles broke out at once. The *curandera* knows a few things."

"Thank God for you, Señá Martina," said Doña Paula. "You have been an angel of mercy in our village for two generations and yet we do not appreciate you enough. We take you for granted."

Señá Martina did not seem to hear. She kept on sorting her herbs.

"This was a good year for *poleo,* pennyroyal, and I gathered bushels of it along the ditches. If the doctor tells you your children have tonsilitis don't let him cut the tonsils as everyone is doing; mix pulverized pennyroyal leaves with butter and rub the white spots in their throats. Take my word, they will not need a knife. It is even good for diphtheria."

"Diphtheria is contagious Señá Martina. It is better to let the doctor treat that."

"Be as you say—but I cured all my children without assistance from a doctor which I could not have afforded, anyway.

"When Juanito, my youngest, came down with it, I was all the doctor he had. Every night I rubbed him with camphorized whiskey to bring a good sweat and his throat soon healed with the pennyroyal and butter paste. Today he is as well as any one can be, although deaf, he is a healthy man.

"I dug out *canaigre* roots last evening which are so good for sore gums and loose teeth. They will tighten if you chew on the *canaigre* roots, and if I had practiced medicine on myself, I would have all my teeth instead only these two which you see. So would you, but you believe the dentist more than you do me."

Doña Paula wondered if Señá Martina were not right; but her daughters and Don Teodoro saw to it that she went to the dentist in town. She merely said, "We have to keep up with the times."

"Not with the times, Doña Paula, with your neighbors, or they will laugh at you. They have laughed at me, but I am too old to care so I laugh at them too.

"Last year Doña Refugio, who does not believe in my remedies, swallowed her pride and came to me with your future daughter-in-law. Her flux had stopped for over two months and the doctor could not bring it on. I did. Each night for nine days, I made her sit on a hot bath of strong *yerba de la víbora,* snake brush, in which I had dropped nine rounded stones. On the ninth day, there it was. It was only a cold in her insides."

"You know too much, Señá Martina. What are these roots here?"

"This is *inmortal,* spider milkweed. Grated and snuffed up into the nostrils cures nose catarrh and the grated powder dissolved in water is also good for nausea, stomach ache and for heart ailments.

"This is *contrahierba,* dorstenia contrayerba, which grated and dissolved in water can be used as an antidote for almost any poison and it is also good for the evil eye. When boiled until thick it serves as a tonic to build up the blood. This tonic is also the best known remedy to produce sweating.

"And this is *osha,* wild mountain parsnip. You know, you should never let your children go out to the fields without a piece in their pockets. Its odor keeps poisonous snakes away. Grated and put into diluted whiskey cures a cold quicker than all the doctors' medicines.

"I brought you some *cáscara de capulín,* choke cherry bark. I noticed you spinning some wool last year and I thought perhaps you would like to dye with it as we did for my masters. It produces a beautiful red and the *chamiza* here is for yellow. The *canaigre,* which you have already, is for brown. There are many others that can be used for dyeing, but I am more interested in the medicinal power of plants.

"Here is some *waco,* bee weed, which we Indians like to eat as greens, but it also makes a good tea for diarrhea and colic."

"How do you cook *waco* to take the bitterness out of it?" asked Doña Paula.

"That is simple. The secret is in using a metal kettle in which to cook it, but if you do not have a copper or iron vessel, drop a nail or a metal spoon into whatever container you use and the bitterness will be absorbed by the metal.

"For sores and ulcers, I brought you some *castilleja,* beard tongue. Stupes [poultices] made from it and applied soon heals them. I just found a few wild onion tops this year and I knew that you would need some; keep them well covered so that they will not lose their strength and use them as smelling salts for fainting spells.

"Did you gather *chimajá,* wild parsley, last spring? I had the rheumatism so bad after the cold winter that I did not go out in the hills."

"Yes, we brought some," answered Doña Paula, "I like it for flavoring fresh peas and also for dried pea soup. I have wanted to ask you, how do you prepare it for greens?"

Señá Martina thought for a while as its use for food was quickly disappearing and she had almost forgotten.

"Wash the tops carefully, place a layer of them in a pan, sprinkle with salt and dot with fat; place another layer and proceed as before. Cover with clean corn husks then sprinkle with water and place in the oven to cook. It takes a very short time to cook, not any longer than other greens which are cooked in steam on top of the stove."

"What is good for rheumatism?" asked Doña Paula. "Don Teodoro had such a spell of it last winter."

"There is nothing better than baths with snake brush. Boil it well and take a bath in it as hot as you can stand it. I would not be walking today if I had not done that for the last twenty years.

"It is getting late and you have supper to get, so I must be going," said Señá Martina.

"But there are still more herbs you have not told me about in that neat pile there."

"These are getting so scarce that I only brought you a few leaves; the men pull them up as weeds.

"Here is some *mariola,* rubber bush, which is so good for bringing down a fever. And this is *hediondilla,* creosote, to use for baths when there is high fever.

"Your girls will like some *poñil,* Apache plume, for washing their hair; it gives it luster and keeps it from falling out. I did not bring them *yerba de la negrita,* bristly mallow, this year, it is time they do it themselves. It will make their hair grow and there is nothing better for scalp irritations.

"I brought you some *mastranzo,* round leaved mint, from my garden, for poisonous insect bites; it kills aphids in plants too. This *estafiate,* wormwood, came from Doña Refugio's place; it cures severe headaches—just chew on it. Made into a tea, it has no equal for all stomach disorders.

"I hope to live another year, for when I am gone my remedies go with me and the doctors will get fat from your generosity.

"I did not gather *coto,* galium, and if the girls want some they can gather their own supply; the tea is good to drink and it cures stomach ulcers.

"I saw fields of *malvas,* common mallow, in your back yard. You can pick them yourself for I am getting too old and you might as well get used to doing it now. *Malva* stupes are a cure for all kinds of infections.

"And don't forget to have Don Teodoro bring some *amole,* yucca roots, when he goes after wood. The ladies in my day had beautiful hair but only because *amole* suds can make it so."

Señá Martina shook her apron, tied on her blue bandana and showed intentions of leaving as she said, "It is late and I must go, now. Next time that I come, I shall bring you some hand brooms. I have not had time to clean them and they are sure beauties this year."

"Have a cup of chocolate before you go," called Doña Paula from the kitchen.

The sack which Señá Martina had brought with herbs was resting by the kitchen door. It was full again. As she looked at it, she said, "You should not have done that, Doña Paula."

They were only idle words for she knew that her herbs would not let her go hungry. She boasted that the relief workers had never had to come to her house.

Cleofas M. Jaramillo

The memory of my grandfather and grandmother and many of my aunts is also the memory of old-time customs and ways of living. Aunt Dolores especially adhered strictly to the Spanish customs and was one of the outstanding examples of the dignified lady of the past.

She arrived one evening in her old fashioned cart, with her Indian maid sitting in the back on the old, low trunk. This was a marvel of antiquity, made of tanned hide, woven into squares and diamonds, the open spaces filled in with red flannel. Aunt Dolores had lost her husband, and left alone with her maid she sold her farm and home at Ocate and came to live with us.

On meeting the family, she gave each member the semblance of an embrace by stiffly placing the tip of her dainty, jeweled finger on the shoulder. She was at once accepted as one of the family.

Aunt Dolores' veneration for the old religious customs played a great part in her life. She would awaken the family early in the morning with her "Canto del Alba" (hymn at dawn).

Coro: Cantémos él álba	Let's sing the dawn,
Yá viene él día.	The light is coming;
Darémos gracias,	Let's give thanks,
Ave María!	Ave María!
Lós cínco Señores,	The five saints,
Dél cielo nós valgan;	In heaven help us.
Hó. Joaquín, humáno!	Ho, Joachim human!
Cuída nuestras álmas.	Take care of our souls.
Náce él álba, María	Born is the dawn, María,
Y él Ave tras élla;	And the Ave comes after her;
Desterrando lá nóche	Vanishing the night
Y nuestras penas.	And our troubles.

And this was her morning prayer, said after the hymn:

En este nuévo día,	On this new day,
Gracías té tributamos	Thanks we attribute Thee,
Hó, Díos omnipotente!	O, God Omnipotent,
Dueño dé todo ló criado.	Master of all created;
Vuestra divina cleméncia,	Thy divine clemency

Se há dignádo sacarnos	Has deigned to bring me
Dé la nóche obscura	Out of the obscure night,
á lá lúz dél sól claro.	Into the light of the clear sun.
Lleno está de tu gloría	Full of Thy glory
Todo el vasto teatro.	Is the vast theatre,
En el mundo cuanto existe,	That in the world exists.
Es óbra de tu mano.	It's the work of Thy hand.
Por vós nacen las flores,	By Thee the flowers bloom,
Reverdesen los campos,	The fields grow green,
Los árboles dan su fruta,	The trees bear their fruit,
El sól da sus rayos,	The sun gives out its rays,
El agua sus péces	The water its fish,
Los pájaros cantan	The birds sing Thy holy,
Tu nombre sánto, sánto.	holy name.
Dirigue Díos immenso	Direct, powerful God,
Y guia nuestros pásos.	And guide our footsteps,
Para qué enternamente,	So that eternally
Tú santa léy sigámos.	Thy law we may follow.

Aunt Dolores' salutations were always given in the name of God: "Buenos días les de Dios" and "buenas tardes les de Dios" were answered in the same manner: "God give you a good day." People although strangers, never passed each other without saluting this way.

In my grandfather's time the family gathered in the chapel for evening prayers; now the family knelt before Aunt Dolores' little altar. At the end of prayers the children and servants, one by one, knelt before the great aunt and my mother to receive their blessing and kiss their hand in sign of respect.

This blessing was always asked from parents and elders by the young before retiring and before starting on a journey.

Profound respect was always paid Aunt Dolores. Whenever she asked one of the servants or children to hand her her silver tobacco box and beaded *ojero*, they stood before her with folded arms, until she handed back the article to be put away. She often called out "Ave María" to a relative or friend she saw approaching. If the guest happened to be a man, he immediately removed his hat and stood with folded arms reciting the Ave María, to himself, and asked her to offer it.

This compact of the Ave María and the one of *valerse a la comadre* lasted through a lifetime, even when made in early youth. Those who compacted the "Ave María," locking their little finger with their friend's little finger, said:

"Cuantas hóras tiene el día,	All the hours the day has
Tiene el Ave María."	The Ave María has.

The ones who made the "comadre" compact repeated the following verses:

"Chiquitito de flóres no té derrames,	"Little flower basket, don't spill over,
Qué en esta vída y én la otra,	For in this life, and in the next,
Siempre serémos comádres."	We will always be *comadres*."
"Redondito, redondón,	"Round and rounded,
La que se vále a la comádre,	The ones that become *comadres*,
Se lé parte él corazón."	Their hearts split in two."

Prayer entered into every action or undertaking. Even in cooking, when starting to mix bread or any food, if you wanted it to come out specially good, the name of the Holy Trinity was invoked. A cross was marked on the bread dough before setting it away to rise.

When someone said or did something shocking, the one shocked pointed at him a cross formed by placing the thumb over the index finger, saying: "*póngote la cruz.*"

Among Aunt Dolores' heirlooms was her album bound in red plush, filled with quaint tin-type photographs of her relatives and friends, some of them wearing long curls and hoop skirts, their hands on their hips, every finger outspread to show the gold rings. Her most favored treasures were: her gold locket with a raised flower design in which was enclosed a ringlet curl of her mother's hair; a pair of gold *coquetas,* earrings with gold dangles like a fringe; a long gold *bejuco* caught together with a *centro,* ornamented with pearls set in black enamel, from which dangled a goldfish made of minute hinged scales that twisted as though it were alive; a necklace of round gold beads with a large bow-knot in the center, a long emerald pendant hanging from it; and the hand-hammered silver water pitcher and goblet which always stood on her table. Mela, her maid, kept this pitcher filled with fresh water, which she brought up from the spring at the foot of the hill. At the same time she used to bring up a *tinaja* full of water, carried on her head and never a drop spilled.

In the *trastero,* built in the wall and closed with hand-carved doors, was kept Aunt Dolores' set of fine china, little *posillos* (mugs), and her copper *jarra* imported from Mexico. These were brought out on special occasions, especially when serving the spicy, foamy Mexican chocolate to some distinguished guest, such as the bishops and other high dignitaries.

Ours was the home of priests, friends, and even mere acquaintances passing through to some other town. As old man Manuel once explained when he dropped in, in the midst of a big dinner for invited guests, leaving his muddy footprints on our varnished floor, "Jaramillo, I saw you had such a nice hay stack, I thought my horse would surely have a good feed here, not saying anything about myself."

Our city guests could not understand how anyone could drop in without an invitation, but this was almost an everyday occurrence. The cooks always had to be prepared for such emergencies.

Aunt Dolores especially went out of her way to entertain the religious guests. With great pride, she showed them her motto hanging over the door, "God Bless the Home," embroidered on *canavé* with delicately-shaded silk floss; her crucifix, *de Marfil,* a gift from *"Su Señoria el Obispo Lamy."*

When not entertaining guests, she busied herself knitting, embroidering, and supervising the making of her *mistela,* spiced wine, cosmetics, wax and tallow candles, and vegetable dyes. *Mistela* was made by adding sugar and spices to fine brandy and simmering the mixture for a whole day in an earthen pot, the top sealed tightly with a piece of dough. Green *chimaja* leaves boiled in a sugar syrup and strained were added to brandy for another kind of *mistela.*

Ground wild-rose leaves and romero were added to strained, melted beef marrow for homemade hair pomade.

Homemade hard soap was cooled, the top skimmed off into another pot and boiled with water until there was no lye left. The soap was cooled, cut up into shavings and put into a bag; the bag was put into a pail of water covered with corn husks and left to soak for three days, the water being changed every day. Then the bag was drained out of the water, the soap mixed with melon seeds, romero, wild rose leaves, and home-made bran starch; the whole mixture was ground into a paste and formed into little cakes, which were set out in the sun to dry. These *javonsillos* [sic] were used as face soap only and were kept as something very precious.

It was interesting to watch the making of tallow candles for use in the kitchen and of wax ones for the chapel altar. Long cotton strings were dipped into melted tallow or wax and hung on a string to cool. Starting at the other end, with the ones that were already cool, the candles were dipped again and again until they were of the desired thickness.

Mela sat on her bed, which was rolled on the floor against the wall by the window, spinning her *malacate* inside an Indian *escudilla,* twisting the fine wool carded from the finest sheepskins had been laid aside. The spun wool was then tied into skeins and boiled in the vegetable dyes of fadeless colors. Bunches of *brazil* sticks, *añil,* and a purple powder were imported from Mexico for this purpose. The *brazil* sticks cut up into shavings and boiled with the wool dyed it a rich brick red. The *añil* colored it indigo; yellow *chicoria* flowers, a pretty yellow, and the powder *azul presado,* a bluish purple. Yellow dyed wool dipped into blue *añil* turned it green. The wool from black and brown sheep were used in their natural color.

These fine wools were used to make hand-knitted hose and for embroidering *colchas,* bed covers. From coarser wool were woven blankets and long strips of black and white and brown plain *jergas* to cover floors.

When Grandmother Refugio came to visit the family, she always brought her work basket. Needlework was her pastime: she embroidered dainty scallops and eyelets on chemise yokes and attached the long loose part with shirring and dainty *panalito.* The servants trimmed theirs with pointed *piquitos.* Embroidery and shirring adorned her sons' shirt fronts; and fine drawnwork, the table napkins and cloths.

Chaquira, bead work, was Grandmother's speciality. With the finest needles and beads she worked hand bags, *ojeros,* little cases to hold the corn cigarette leaves, and tiny hearts used to join together the pink coral rosaries which she sent to *novios* for their engagements. These were used instead of rings.

These dames of old had their *desayuno* of *mistela* or chocolate with sweet cookies or fried *sopaipas* [sic] brought to their beds every morning. At four o'clock in the afternoon, after the *siesta,* they partook of the same drinks, varied with curlicued *biscochos, empanaditas,* or *puchas* and *marquezotes.* The recipe for puchas calls for twenty-four yolks.

The imported Mexican chocolate came already spiced and sweetened, but the most fastidious bought their own cocoa beans, pecan nuts, stick cinnamon, and maple sugar, and had them ground at home on a heated *metate* stone. The heat of the stone melted the nuts, formed the mixture into a paste. Out of it little round cakes were made, dried, and kept for future use.

The preparation of Spanish dishes requires much time and labor. However, with the aid of modern conveniences the work is now made much lighter than in olden times when the ingredients were ground by hand. But one is amply repaid for the labor by the appetizing flavor and attractive coloring of the dishes, for nothing quickens the appetite more than a stack of blue corn tortillas spread with pink onion and yellow cheese, red chile poured over this and a shredded, green lettuce garnish on top. . . .

Aunt Dolores was greatly missed when she passed away to the happy land she saw in her visions, while she fondled her rosary repeating her favorite "Ave María."

Mother brought out her black taffeta silk *mantona* to wear for the funeral. This silk cape was made with three lace flounces trimming the circular bottom, and the black lace veil fastened at the collar dropped over the head.

The *mantonas* were worn in mourning and at the church services during lent and Holy Week. On other occasions colorful, long silk *rebosos* were worn wrapped around the head or shoulders, tied in front with the two fringed ends thrown back over the shoulders. Elderly ladies wore the fine, black *stambre,* jersey shawls, wrapped over their heads, the long silk-fringed end thrown gracefully over the left shoulder. The length of the silk fringe denoted the wealth of the wearer. For dressy occasions the silk embroidered shawl was worn, and in the summer time, the long, scarf-like, lace *mantilla de castilla* or the triangular lace *pañueleta.* In the passing of these colorful wraps New Mexico has lost one of its attractive, typical customs.

* * * * *

Grandfather Lucero loved to see his grand-children around him, and to tell us about old times and his school days. Each pupil he said had to bring his own seat to school, and every morning an arm full of wood to heat the room.

Tobías, his teacher, strictly observed the old Spanish rules. He held no school on Saturdays, but his pupils went to the school house on that day at the usual hour.

Knocking at the door, each pupil called out: *"Jesús, José, Ave María."* The teacher asked from within, *"¿Quién toca la puerta de esta misión?"* (Who knocks at this mission's door?) The pupil answered, *"Yo buscando mi salvación, penitencia, penitencia."* (I, seeking my salvation.)

Here the teacher opened the door, and the pupil presented to him the *Pan del Sábado,* the Sabbath bread (bread, biscuits, or whatever he had to offer).

After all the pupils were assembled the teacher stood them in line, and the two pupils having the highest marks in their class were given a little stick. With this stick they went down the line hitting the hands that had not been washed and the heads that were uncombed.

An hour of religious instruction followed.

* * * * *

Grandfather's old-maid sister was quite amusing. She was very stately, tall and fair, with a delicate skin, for the sun or wind never touched it. She wore her long silver braids like a crown around her shapely head, which was always covered with a silk skullcap to protect it from the air. She ground roots and herbs, rubbing them on her temples and back of her head, to cure her continuous headaches, which she said were caused by *aire en la cabeza,* air in the head.

At night she pushed her bed into the farthest corner, away from doors and windows, placed two chairs on the side, and spread the bed cover over them, to screen off the air, which she said made whirls in the corners. When not occupied with her remedies or knitting, Aunt Cencionita made thin, long-necked, long-waisted, rag dolls for her nieces. When we begged her for thread to sew our doll dresses with, she would give us a long strip of muslin and show us how to pull out some strands and twist them into thread.

Tiodora, our nurse, went home to get married. After a few years of mother's good training, our maids usually won a marriage certificate and were soon selected as fine housekeepers.

Mela, Aunt Dolores' maid, was now promoted to the rank of nurse. She was not as patient as Tiodora. When the children refused to be quiet and go to sleep at night, she at once called to her aid the *Vieja Ganchos* or the *Orejas de Burro*. The Vieja Ganchos would appear crouching at the door with a long iron hook. Or the Orejas de Burro would stick in his long donkey ears, through a crack in the door. Immediately there was dead silence. But oh! those awful dreams during the night! I saw myself being carried out to the mountains hanging from the Vieja Ganchos' long hook, and would wake up stiff with fright, my heart thumping so hard that I could hear its beats.

I believe now that this fear of the *abuelos* and Lupe's ghost and witch stories, and the sore example put before us of bad children like the *mal hijo*, made our lives exceedingly timid. I was very young when the *mal hijo* passed through our village, but he impressed me for life. Mounted on a burro, he went from town to town preaching to the young showing them his clenched hand and the scar on his wrist where the knife turned and stuck when he raised it to strike his father. The earth had opened beneath him and swallowed him up to his waist. His mother ran for the priest, the priest came, and after many prayers and sprinkling with holy water the earth released him. Repentant of his sin, he promised to travel over the world, advising the young to respect and obey their parents.

Other strange characters passing through the village broke the quiet monotony. Turks and Arab gypsies, dressed in their picturesque garb, came peddling trinkets. They told the natives that they came from the Holy Land and that the rosaries and medals they were selling had been blessed in one of the Blessed Virgin's trays. This the poor people, in their simple faith, believed; took them in, fed them and bought their trinkets.

Flores Secas / Dried Flowers

Carmen Celia Beltrán

Mis ensueños fueron siempre
    deslumbrantes mariposas

que jamás quedaron presas
en el cáliz de una flor,
porque al roce de sus alas
los claveles y las rosas
marchitándose perdieron
su fragancia y su color.

En mi huerto sólo quedan
unas blancas tuberosas
que mis sueños incitaron
con sus galas y su olor;
las conservo, y así secas
esas flores luminosas
con sus pétalos perfuman
los recuerdos de un amor!

Fué un amor maravilloso!
Embriagándome de anhelo
escalé los arreboles
en la bóveda del cielo . . .
y después que el espejismo
de mi senda se alejó,
el recuerdo lo revive
descorriendo un tenue velo.

Fue como ave peregrina
que bajó en un raudo vuelo
a la fuente que a su paso
un remanso le brindó . . .

■

My fantasies were always
dazzling butterflies
that were never imprisoned
in the calyx of a flower,
because with the friction of their wings
the carnations and the roses
withered, losing
their fragrance and their color.

In my orchard there remained only
	some white tuberroses
which incited my dreams
	with their elegance and their smell;
I save them, and thus dried
	these luminous flowers
with their petals perfume
	the memories of a love!

It was a marvelous love!
	Drunk with eagerness
I scaled the red clouds
	in the arch of the sky . . .
and after the mirage
	distanced itself from my path,
the memory revives it
	drawing along a tenuous veil.

It was like a wandering bird
	that flew down in a rapid flight
to the spring which instantly
	tranquil water bestowed . . .

Quinceañera / Sweet Fifteen

Carmen Celia Beltrán

	¡Quinceañera dichosa! Por la senda florida
vas confiada y alegre hoy que puedes gozar
con la inmensa fortuna de vivir protegida
bajo un palio bendito en la paz de tu hogar.

	Que te siga brindando muchos goces la vida;
que tu límpido cielo no se llegue a nublar,
y la fe inquebrantable que en tu espíritu anida
sea el faro divino que te pueda orientar.

	Tus virtudes resaltan; la nobleza y decoro
que a tu gracia se adunan en fusión celestial
han de ser en tu vida el más grande tesoro.

Y si buscas la ruta del Palacio Real,
que Aladino te guíe con su lámpara de oro
y te dé Cenicienta su chapín de cristal!

■

Lucky sweet fifteen-year-old. Along the flowered path
you go full of confidence and happy that today you can enjoy
the immense fortune to be able to live protected
beneath the blessed roof in the peace of your home.

May life continue to give you many pleasures
may your clear sky never become clouded,
and may that unbreakable faith that dwells in your spirit
be the divine light that will guide you.

Your virtues stand out; the nobility and decorum
that in celestial fusion unite with your grace
will be the greatest treasure of your life.

And if you look for the road to the Royal Palace,
may Aladin guide you with his golden lamp
and may Cinderella give you her crystal slipper!

Drama en Mañanitas / Drama in the Early Mornings

María Esperanza López de Padilla

Despertaba yo muy de mañanita
cuando era todavía muy pequeñita,

Y salía con rumbo a las lomitas.
Me encantaba ir a ver las florecitas.
Todos los sacatitos y yerbitas
estaban cubiertos de rocío, en gotitas
que brillaban como de cristal cuentitas.
Y pensaba yo . . . mientras de puntitas
pisaba, para no despertar flores dormiditas,
. . . de donde vendrá esta humidad, estas aguitas
sobre toda la tierra en las mañanitas.

—Le preguntaré a mamá—sola me respondí
y en lo que yo ponderaba, de repente vi!
El Sol sonriente, con amor besó las lomitas,
el rocío desapareció, y vi las florecitas
destendiendo sus pétalos y ojitas
y claramente oí sus sonrientes rizitas,
ya despiertas y gustosas en el nuevo día.
Aunque tan pequeña, comprendí que se me había
concedido ver estas dramas tan hermosas
y de prisa corrí, con ojitos lagrimosos
A contárselo a mi muy amada mamacita,
la maravilla que vi en esta mañanita.

■

When I was yet so very, very young
I'd awaken very early in the morning

And I would walk toward the little hills.
It would enchant me to go see the little flowers
All the little grasses and little plants
were covered with droplets of dew
that glistened like little crystal beads.
And I thought, while on tiptoes I walked
So as not to awaken the tiny sleeping flowers.
All this moisture, these little waters,
Where does it come from, that it forms little pearls
To be found over all the earth in the morning?
"I will ask my mama," I answered myself,
and as I pondered, I suddenly saw
The smiling Sun, with love, kiss the little hills.
The dew disappeared, and I saw the tiny flowers
unfolding their little petals and leaves,
and clearly I heard their smiling laughter,
already awakened and delighted in the new day.

I, although so very young, understood I had been
allowed to *see* this beautiful drama
and quickly I ran, my eyes filled with tears
To relate to my very beloved little mother
the marvel I had seen on this morning.

María Esperanza

María Esperanza López de Padilla

"Esperanza se llamará nuestra niña,"
Dijo mi papá a mi padrino y madrina,
Amables señor y señora Ramírez . . . Ruperto y Benita.
"Pero, María, primero, por la Virgencita,"
Dijeron mi madrinita y mi madrecita,
Juntas, lo exclamaron como una sola voz,
Porque en sus corazones lo sentían las dos.
Mi padre y mi padrino con amor se miraron
Se dieron la mano y los cuatro se abrazaron
Y también ellos, como en una sola voz,
Porque en sus corazones lo sentían los dos,
Exclamaron, "Sí, natural es que se llame María,
Porque es costumbre nuestra, siempre y hasta el día,
Y para que Nuestra Señora sea su guía."

Mis padres eran del norte de Nuevo Méjico
Y mis padrinos eran del norte de Méjico
Pero las dos familias estaban recién venidas
A Pueblo, Colorado, hermoso estado en nuestro Suroeste
Y allí en los Steel Works se encontraron
Y con mi baptismo su amistad para siempre sellaron.

■

"Esperanza will be our girl-child's name"
Said my father to my godfather and godmother,
Gracious Señor and Señora Ruperto and Benita Ramírez.
"But first María, for honor to the Virgin,"
Said my godmother and my mother.
Together they exclaimed it as with one voice,
Because in their hearts, they felt the same sentiments.
My father and my godfather with love looked at each other
They clasped hands and the four of them embraced,
And they too, as with one voice
Because, in their hearts, felt the same sentiments,
Exclaimed, "Sí! Naturally her name shall be María,
Because it is our custom, always and to this day
And so that our Lady will be her life guide."

My father and my mother were from northern New Mexico
My godparents were from the north of old Mexico
But both families had recently arrived
at Pueblo, Colorado, lovely state in our Southwest,
And there at the Steel Works they had met
And with my baptism sealed their friendship.

Simplicidades / Simplicities

María Esperanza López de Padilla

Es siempre la simplicidad
lo que me trae felicidad.

Amapolas bailando en la briza
son rara hermosura.
Caritas radiantes en una sonrisa
me llenan de dulzura.

El aire travieso entre mis cabellos
me canta una canción.
Noches negras con millares de estrellas
veo con admiración.

Mañanas cristalinas,
las sierras escondidas
en espesas nublinas,
las ropas al sol tendidas,
miles de mirasoles en flor.
Mis bebés en el baño,
canciones de amor,
recuerdos de un año
son cosas muy sencillas,
pero alegran mis días.

El oro abundante de los trigales
es un tesoro.
El aroma de los pinos-reales
es cosa que adoro.
Un buen libro, una blanda silla

me gustan con sinceridad.
Cortinitas blancas en mi ventanilla
me llenan de felicidad.

■

It's always the simplicities
that bring me happiness.

Poppies dancing in the breeze
are things of rare beauty.
Little faces radiant in a smile
fill me with sweetness.

The playful wind through my hair
sings me a song.
Black nights with millions of stars
I gaze at with wonder.

Crystalline mornings,
the mountains hidden
in thick white clouds,
clothes hung out to the sun,
thousands of sunflowers in bloom.
My babies in their bath,
songs of love,
the memories of a year,
all these are very simple things
but they fill my days with happiness.

The abundant gold of fields of wheat
is a treasure.
The aroma of the pine trees
is something I love.
A good book, a soft chair
I sincerely do like.
White curtains on my kitchen window
fill me with happiness.

A Elena / To Elena

María Esperanza López de Padilla

Elena, eres para mí
La primera estrella de la tarde
Que con su luz plateada
Rompe el triste cielo.

Así tú,
Con la luz de tu mirada
Rompes
Mi obscura soledad

■

Elena, you are for me
The first star of evening
That with its silvery light
Breaks through the lonely sky.

Thus, you
With the light of your face
Break through
My dark solitude.

School

Esther Vernon Galindo

The Convent of the Holy Heart in Santa María la Rivera, in Mexico City, had four large buildings joined together by a series of passages, patios, and gardens, until it made a single unit. It faced the Santa María garden, where the boarders went every Sunday morning, excepting one weekend of each month when they were allowed to go home. All the buildings were surrounded by a high stone wall. Only through the second story windows did the girls ever get a glimpse of the street.

The first building housed the only room that had windows giving to the street. It was the reception room, immense, sparsely furnished containing little more than chairs placed in small groups, where parents who came on Sundays would sit with their children. There were small rugs on the wooden floor and a large statue of Christ. Beyond the reception room was the chapel, always beautifully decorated with fresh flowers. There the girls heard six o'clock mass every morning. Next was a small room which served as a dressing room for the school priest, and after that a corridor leading to the huge dining room with its raised platform in the center. Here one of the nuns read prayers in the morning and the lives of the saints at noon and night. Beyond the dining room were the kitchen and the pantries where the girls were never allowed. To the left were Mother Superior's office, the nuns' sewing room, their private chapel—a small exquisite room—and two or three mysterious rooms to which not even the boldest of the older girls had ever gained admittance.

A beautiful, well-cared-for garden surrounded by benches and corridors joined the first two buildings. There, unless it rained, the girls would gather with Sor Petra, the sewing sister, to mend on Saturday afternoons. In the second building were all the schoolrooms and the auditorium. Between the second and third building was the immense patio where the girls would play all sorts of games and where they went every day during their recess periods. In the third building half of the first floor served as the infirmary, or hospital, completely equipped with operating tables and everything needed for an emergency. On the second floor was a series of long dormitories with a nun at the head of the room and another one at the end to watch over the girls. This floor had a whole wing with bathrooms and showers where the girls bathed at five-thirty in the morning. The only manual work required of the boarders was making their own bed and polishing their shoes. Each bed was surrounded by a thick canvas curtain which allowed every bed to become a tiny room. The third floor housed all the girls who were too old to sleep with the younger ones. Among them were those who, for some reason, were still in the convent after they were seventeen. This floor was divided into small rooms with three beds in each for two girls and one nun. They had their own bathrooms. To the younger girls, this third floor was a very interesting floor indeed. The only other piece of furniture, either in the dormitories or in the bedrooms, was a plain bureau, or chest of drawers, where the girls' clean stockings, underwear, and sleeping garments were placed. The fourth and last building was never entered by any of the girls. It housed all the other nuns of the convent.

The rules of the convent were very strict indeed. Up at five-thirty, mass at six, breakfast at six-thirty, bed-making at seven. At eight everyone was in the schoolrooms. There was one recess at ten. Lunch was at twelve, and then a half hour of recreation. The afternoon classes began at one-thirty. Supper at six, from seven to eight study hall; then bedtime. All lights out by eight-thirty. On Friday afternoons, the out-of-town girls wrote letters home, letters which were given to the sisters unsealed. No letter went in or out without having been read by the nuns. On these Friday afternoons, the girls whose parents lived in town were allowed to read books handed out by the Sisters. On Saturday, the schedule was less exacting. The girls washed their hair, read, or played. On Sunday, after mass and breakfast, the girls were taken to the Plaza of Santa María to hear the music played by one of the city bands. They were allowed to talk all they wanted. Each small uniformed group was in the charge of a nun who watched it like a hawk. On Sunday afternoon, from three to five, parents were allowed to visit their daughters. Cousins could visit them only if accompanied by a brother or by a known member of the family. One Friday of each month the girls were allowed to go home after classes to stay until nine o'clock Sunday night. The greatest punishment for a girl was, of course, not to be allowed to go home and to be left alone at school.

Everyone had to wear uniforms, hated by the older girls: a pleated blue skirt, rather long, a white middy blouse, a passable dark red dress with pleated skirt, sailor collar, and white tie, brown shoes and brown stockings. But the horror of horrors were the hats! The older girls were punished time after time for not wearing them. The girls from the French convent—the Holy Heart's hated rivals—called the girls the "Tachuelas," the tacks, for they looked exactly like tacks. The dreaded hats were completely flat, with a wide, thick, stubborn brim. No one could do anything with those brims. No matter how much they were dampened and pressed to suit their wearers, they always took their original forms once they dried!

The total enrollment was large, but the nuns never allowed more than sixty to seventy boarders. The rest were either half boarders—girls who only ate the noon meal at school, or day pupils. All the servants in the convent were *hermanas legas,* religious women who at the time of their vows had not had the necessary money for their "dowry" but who were entitled to wear the habit and live the same life of penitence and renunciation as the nuns.

Sandra arrived in a state of rebellion. She hated the school, she didn't like the girls. She didn't think the Sisters were agreeable. At lunch the first day, when the serving Sister placed the meat plate in front of her, Sandra's indignation boiled over. She wasn't going to eat meat. She hated meat. And now that Mamacita wasn't here, she wouldn't eat it. She looked at her plate with disgust and pushed it away. The serving Sister came with the next course, and seeing Sandra's plate untouched she skipped her and began serving the rest of the girls.

"Eat your meat, Sandra," said the dining room Sister in a low voice at Sandra's elbow.

Sandra didn't answer. She pushed her plate further away. The sister tried again.

"Don't you like meat, Sandra?"

"No, Sister."

"Well, eat just a little of it."

"I won't. I don't like meat and you can't make me eat it!"

The Sister gave her a sharp look and without a word walked away. Nothing else was placed before Sandra. Not even dessert. When Sandra took her place at suppertime, she found her plate of meat exactly as she had left it. No bread, no butter, nothing else was in front of her. Let them! She wouldn't eat their horrible old meat. She would starve—that's what she would do. Daddy and Mamacita would be sorry they had sent her to this horrible school! But she was hungry. At breakfast next morning, her meat plate was still in front of her—nothing else. She was starving, and the hot chocolate smelled so good! Her mouth watered to see the rest of the girls having hot fresh bread, good thick chocolate, and golden eggs.

"Eat a little of your meat, Sandra," the Sister said softly.

Her mouth in a stubborn line, Sandra answered. "I am not hungry, Sister."

Without a word Sister walked away. Sandra drank water. She thought, "I am not going to eat their meat. I don't care if I starve! Serves Daddy and Mamacita right! I'll show them. When they come to see me they will see that I am sick and thin. They will be frightened and will take me away." She drank more water.

At noon, the eternal plate of meat was in her place. Not even a tiny piece of bread was placed before her. She was starving. By now the whole school knew of the clash of wills between Sister and Sandra, but no one said a word. All afternoon Sandra felt faint. Her ears rang and her knees were weak, but she wouldn't give in. At supper the plate of meat was exactly as she had left it. The meat was black and hard looking. She was tempted. She was so hungry! She made a gesture to take the plate, but she saw one of the girls looking at her. Instead she took the glass of water and drank it. That night she felt feverish. She could hardly sleep and when she did she dreamed of hot ears of boiled corn. She could even smell them. Next morning in chapel, she could hardly stand, could hardly keep still. When the long line of girls finally entered the dining room and sat down, she just didn't care. She reached for her meat plate, took her knife and fork, and cut a piece of the stiff, dried meat. As she was putting it in her mouth, Sister, at her elbow, said, "That meat looks a little dry, Sandra, let me get you something fresh."

Never had thick chocolate, hot fresh bread, and eggs tasted better!

Sandra learned her first lesson. She never knew how constantly the sisters had watched her wherever she was and how worried they had been about her. No one ever mentioned the incident to her.

Self and Identity

I was born a woman in a world that has conceived me for a role.
                                SYLVIA CHACÓN

*Today I speak their languages, both English and Spanish, but
I am neither, nor do I want to be . . . I am Chicana.*
                                DORINDA MORENO

yo soy[1]

                yo
        LORENZA CALVILLO-CRAIG

It can be argued, as it has for centuries, that art and literature have as their primary goal the exploration of human identity, and variations thereof. Identity of the artist, who grapples with visions of herself as reflected in images around her; identity of the writer, primarily with a poetic calling, who contemplates herself first as a finite entity and then as a human being in relation to her surroundings. For the minority artist and writer, immersed in a cultural context not easily ignored, self-definition is fraught with multiple views, with angles that reflect both universal and individual images of self. The complex problems and multitude of answers to "who am I?" "how do I see myself?" and "how am I seen by others?" are constantly explored by Chicana writers.

By virtue of their biculturalism, their bilingualism, and their identification, with an ethnic background that separates them from the dominant culture, Chicanas see their own being as inadequately represented by a single facet of reality. The life experiences of Chicanas mold a consistently repeated sense of "otherness," nurtured by feelings of alienation from both their Mexican and their American cultural modes; at times they despair in not finding an appropriate place as a safe haven, a cultural niche, or space of their own. So expresses Lorna Dee Cervantes:

---

1. I am \ I

I feel I am a captive
aboard the refugee ship.
The ship that will never dock.
El barco que nunca atraca.

Beyond coming to terms with the conflicts inherent in the search for personal definition, Chicana writers have also concerned themselves with class and race struggles ("My hopes exalted with the triumph of the *huelga* . . .") and the ways in which these struggles affect the self-image of an entire people. Most significant in this affirmation of individual and collective identity is the language use in dual code forms, which distinguishes Chicano literature as a general trait; code switching, a term generated by linguists, has become a literary variable necessary for the study of Chicano texts.

Chicanas define themselves in their writings as women of La Raza but also as very personal beings who are not primarily molded by color or culture or gender. They are woven by their own individual fiber:

don't call me for the Chicanos,
nor for my parents,
nor for women,
summon me for myself
     Marina Rivera

And they define themselves in manifestos, with a shout of self-knowledge: "I am, I am, yo soy, yo soy." Their identity is brown, both racially and culturally, but it also wishfully projects onto a glamour-magazine image that does not accept short legs, olive complexion, or Indian features. With an ironic twist, Chicanas are also superwomen, with split identities. They are daughters, granddaughters, sisters, cousins, friends; they are called *mija* (short for "mi hija," my daughter, either an affectionate or patronizing term). Chicanas take many forms, they are chameleonlike and respond to the needs dictated by their environment: "Soy chicana macana / o gringa marrana, / la tinta pinta / o la pintura tinta" (Margarita Cota-Cárdenas). A Spanish name betrays some Chicanas, for at times they are bereft of traditions ("My name hangs about me like a loose tooth" (Lorna Dee Cervantes). Yet Chicanas' names are all symbolic, full of future promises.

These names have edges and soft contours:

In English my name means hope. In Spanish it means too many letters. It means sadness, it means waiting. . . . At school they say my name funny as if the syllables were made out of tin and hurt the roof of your mouth. But in Spanish my name is made out of a softer something like silver.

     Sandra Cisneros

Chicana writers are painfully aware of the ancestral weight they carry on their shoulders, of the double-bind situation in which they must exist: that of being minority persons, members of a discriminated cultural group, and that of being women—a second-class majority. At the same time, they are also— and very much so—female: "Soy mujer / soy señorita / soy ruca loca / soy mujerona / soy Santa / soy madre / soy Ms" ("La loca de la raza cósmica," La Chrisx). They are women in childbirth, full-blooded females who, as artists, use a paradigm of poetic symbols to signify their earth and flesh identity: Chicanas are alone in their life-giving, in their life cycles, in their vital functions and their roles (Mora, Castillo, Bornstein, Cota-Cárdenas). They are blossom- ing nymphs or larvae in the process of metamorphosis; yet they are, at the same time, the non-entity, the non-female, the "other." Sometimes, a sense of un- reality overwhelms Chicana writers; they are intangible, like a wisp of smoke, they are invisible (Lizárraga). They are even an opaque darkness searching for itself.

The quest for identity and the pursuit of self-definition fill a spectrum of feelings and images: from political affirmation to transcendental opening, Chicanas can conform or rebel, can soar with eagles or descend to rage and despair. And they seek new images of themselves, new beliefs that will validate their femaleness and their humanity (Anzaldúa). Their whole being is under scrutiny, and yet their existence is not in question; they search, they continue to ask the question of metaphysical pursuit as well as the more mundane ones— albeit just as relevant—of social injustice (Angela de Hoyos). Their literary *personae* describe a multiplicity of roles, the prismlike quality of their facets: Chicanas are drop-outs, educated and Anglicized, dope-pushers or community organizers—and they are also the reflections on a window pane or on the black mirror or life; a tree, a pouring glass, a cat (Zamora, Rivera, Vigil-Piñón).

An integral part of a Chicana definition of self is made up of how writers see themselves as part of a family unit, at the center of responsibility but also— ironically—at the periphery of prestige and importance. *Essence* is defined *for* them; kinship lines and cultural roles give them a characteristic profile (Calvillo-Craig). They are nurturers, caretakers, learners. They are oppressed: they carry the names, the functions, the myths (Bornstein). Chicana identity is multiple, a reflection on circular mirrors: what others want from them, what their fathers mean, what their mothers mean, vis-à-vis what Chicanas want or know (Rivera, in the five parts of "Mestiza" in this volume). They are ugly or invisible daugh- ters (Cisneros, Lizárraga); they are torn between feelings for others and their own need of nurturing, love, and tenderness. On occasion, Chicanas do not like who they are or what others make them:

At some point I am afraid of the person that I am.
  Rejected—
  Dejected—
  Infected with the disease of lunacy.

Rina García Rocha

If Chicanas do not conform to the gender and sexual roles prescribed for them by their own culture and by society at large, they run the risk of not being real (Cunningham). And then Chicanas must give birth to themselves, in an epiphany of cultural and existential feeling; the butterfly and the tree grow forth. They alone are responsible for identity; they will bring themselves into the world, regardless of the bitter lessons of history. Chicanas emerge from their own roots, from their own blood (Alma Villanueva).

The texts contained in this chapter illustrate all points in the identity spectrum for Chicanas as writers and as women; but many more works by these artists are partially exemplary of their quest for self-definition and their unceasing search. We have included those that are particularly representative of both conceptual motifs and formal imagery, paying attention to variety as well as to generic diversity. Nevertheless, it can be seen in these selections that poetry constitutes a primary medium and a major literary mode for Chicana authors. We believe this reality to be even more relevant to an expression of self than perhaps to any other manifestation of Chicana visions; for it is through self-imagery that the artist and the woman delve deeper into the mysterious space of creativity.

■ ■ ■

So Not To Be Mottled

Bernice Zamora

You insult me
When you say I'm
Schizophrenic.
My divisions are
Infinite.

My Name
Sandra Cisneros

In English my name means hope. In Spanish it means too many letters. It means sadness, it means waiting. It is like the number nine. A muddy color. It is the Mexican records my father plays on Sunday mornings when he is shaving, songs like sobbing.

It was my great-grandmother's name and now it is mine. She was a horse woman too, born like me in the Chinese year of the horse—which is supposed to be bad luck if you're born female—but I think this is a Chinese lie because the Chinese, like the Mexicans, don't like their women strong.

My great-grandmother. I would've liked to have known her, a wild horse of a woman, so wild she wouldn't marry until my great-grandfather threw a sack over her head and carried her off. Just like that, as if she were a fancy chandelier. That's the way he did it.

And the story goes she never forgave him. She looked out the window all her life, the way so many women sit their sadness on an elbow. I wonder if she made the best with what she got or was she sorry because she couldn't be all the things she wanted to be. Esperanza. I have inherited her name, but I don't want to inherit her place by the window.

At school they say my name funny as if the syllables were made out of tin and hurt the roof of your mouth. But in Spanish my name is made out of a softer something like silver, not quite as thick as my sister's name Magdalena which is uglier than mine. Magdalena who at least can come home and become Nenny. But I am always Esperanza.

I would like to baptize myself under a new name, a name more like the real me, the one nobody sees. Esperanza as Lisandra or Maritza or Zeze the X. Yes. Something like Zeze the X will do.

Toma de nombre / Taking of Name
Miriam Bornstein

presiento
que el nombre que llevo a cuestas
peca por no definirme

no por falta de nombre
puesto que me sobra
sino
porque en una fórmula adquirida por costumbre
va una larga leyenda de virginidad y mitos
una preposición entregada en el cofrecito de las arras
y atada a mí
con el lazo de buena mujercita mexicana
cargo con el nombre de mujer casada
      soy
            fulana de tal
                    esposa de   fulano
                              madre de   zutano
y algunas veces presiento que solamente soy
      mujer de sola

■

I suspect
that the name which burdens me
sins for not defining me
not because of lack of name
since it is abundant
      but also
because in a formula acquired through habit
exists a ready-made legend of virginity and myths
a preposition contained in a "cofrecito de arras"[2]
      and tied to me
      with the rosary of the good little mexican woman
I carry my married name
      I am
            so and   so
                  wife of   so and so
                        mother of   so and so
and at times I feel that I am only
      a woman alone

---

2. A small chest containing twelve coins, which are blessed by the priest and given to the groom; then the groom hands the chest to the bride as a symbol of his promise to be a good provider. This custom is used in traditional Mexican wedding ceremonies.

By Your True Faces We Will Know You

Gloria Anzaldúa

I am visible—see this Indian face—yet I am invisible. I both blind them with my beak nose and am their blind spot. But I exist, we exist. They'd like to think I have melted in the pot. But I haven't, we haven't.

The dominant white culture is killing us slowly with its ignorance. By taking away our self-determination, it has made us weak and empty. As a people we have resisted and we have taken expedient positions, but we have never been allowed to develop unencumbered—we have never been allowed to be fully ourselves. The whites in power want us people of color to barricade ourselves behind our separate tribal walls so they can pick us off one at a time with their hidden weapons; so they can whitewash and distort history. Ignorance splits people, creates prejudices. A misinformed people is a subjugated people.

Before the Chicano and the undocumented worker and the Mexican from the other side can come together, before the Chicano can have unity with Native Americans and other groups, we need to know the history of their struggle and they need to know ours. Our mothers, our sisters and brothers, the guys who hang out on street corners, the children in the playgrounds, each of us must know our Indian lineage, our afro-*mestizaje,* our history of resistance.

To the immigrant *mexicano* and the recent arrivals we must teach our history. The 80 million *mexicanos* and the Latinos from Central and South America must know of our struggles. Each one of us must know basic facts about Nicaragua, Chile and the rest of Latin America. The Latinoist movement (Chicanos, Puerto Ricans, Cubans and other Spanish-speaking people working together to combat racial discrimination in the marketplace) is good, but it is not enough. Other than a common culture we will have nothing to hold us together. We need to meet on a broader communal ground.

The struggle is inner: Chicano, *indio,* American Indian, *mojado, mexicano,* immigrant Latino, Anglo in power, working class Anglo, Black, Asian—our psyches resemble the border-towns and are populated by the same people. The struggle has always been inner, and is played out in the outer terrains. Awareness of our situation must come before inner changes, which in turn come before changes in society. Nothing happens in the "real" world unless it first happens in the images in our heads.

El día de la chicana

Gloria Anzaldúa

I will not be shamed again
Nor will I shame myself.

I am possessed by a vision: that we Chicanas and Chicanos have taken back or uncovered our true faces, our dignity and self-respect. It's a validation vision.

Seeing the Chicana anew in light of her history, I seek an exoneration, a seeing through the fictions of white supremacy, a seeing of ourselves in our true guises and not as the false racial personality that has been given to us and that we have given to ourselves. I seek our woman's face, our true features, the positive and the negative seen clearly, free of the tainted biases of male dominance. I seek new images of identity, new beliefs about ourselves, our humanity and worth no longer in question.

Estamos viviendo en la noche de la Raza, un tiempo cuando el trabajo se hace a lo quieto, en el oscuro. El día cuando aceptamos tal y como somos y para en donde vamos y porqué—ese día será el día de la Raza. Yo tengo el compromiso de expresar mi visión, mi sensibilidad, mi percepción de la revalidación de la gente mexicana, su mérito, estimación, honra, aprecio y validez.

On December 2nd when my sun goes into my first house, I celebrate *el día de la Chicana y el Chicano*. On that day I clean my altars, light my *Coatlalopeuh* candle, burn sage and copal, take *el baño para espantar basura*, sweep my house. On that day I bare my soul, make myself vulnerable to friends and family by expressing my feelings. On that day I affirm who we are.

On that day I look inside our conflicts and our basic introverted racial temperament. I identify our needs, voice them. I acknowledge that the self and the race have been wounded. I recognize the need to take care of our personhood, of our racial self. On that day I gather the splintered and disowned parts of *la gente mexicana* and hold them in my arms. *Todas las partes de nosotros valen.*

On that day I say, "Yes, all you people wound us when you reject us. Rejection strips us of self-worth; our vulnerability exposes us to shame. It is our innate identity you find wanting. We are ashamed that we need your good opinion, that we need your acceptance. We can no longer camouflage our needs, can no longer let defenses and fences sprout around us. We can no longer withdraw. To rage and look upon you with contempt is to rage and be contemptuous of ourselves. We can no longer blame you, nor disown the white parts, the male parts, the pathological parts, the queer parts, the vulnerable parts. Here we are weaponless with open arms, with only our magic. Let's try it our way, the mestiza way, the Chicana way, the woman way.

On that day, I search for our essential dignity as a people, a people with a sense of purpose—to belong and contribute to something greater than our *pueblo*. On that day I seek to recover and reshape my spiritual identity. *¡Anímate! Raza, a celebrar el día de la Chicana.*

Soy hija de mis padres . . . / I am the daughter of my parents
Lorenza Calvillo-Craig

soy hija de mis padres
   nieta de mis abuelos
   hermana de mis hermanos
   prima de mis primos
   amiga de mis amigos

soy *lorenza*
   lencha
   lorraine
   wa
   panzas y
   mija
yo soy
soy
yo

∎

I am the daughter of my parents
   granddaughter of my grandparents
   sister of my brothers
   cousin of my cousins
   friend of my friends

I am *lorenza*
   lencha
   lorraine
   wa
   panzas and
   daughter

I am
I am
me

La Loca de la Raza Cósmica

la Chrisx

Dedico este trabajo a las mujeres Chicanas.
Está dedicado a las Locas / a las Reinas de la Raza Cósmica.

For as different as we all may seem,
When intracacies are compared,
We are all one,
        and the same.

Soy la Mujer Chicana, una maravilla
            Soy tan simple como la capirotada
and at the same time I am as complicated to understand as the Aztec
    Pyramids.
Soy la Reina de la Raza Cósmica (al estilo Califas) . . .

Soy mujer
soy señorita
soy ruca loca
soy mujerona
soy Santa
soy madre
soy Ms.
            Soy la India María
            soy la Adelita
Soy Radical
soy la Revolucionaria
soy la Chicana en los picket lines
soy la Chicana en los conferences
soy la Chicana en los teatros
            Soy la que hecha chingazos por su Raza
            soy el grito: "Chicano Power!"
            soy United Farmworker Buttons
            soy la Mexican flag

Soy la madre (El esclavo) de mi padre,
    de mi hermano, de mi esposo,
soy la comida en la mesa cuando llegan
    del jale
soy la que calienta los TV dinners
soy tamales at Christmas time
            Soy love-maker to my main man
            soy dreamer
            soy streetwalker
            soy la good woman
            soy la quien "mi carnal" hace rape
Soy shacking up
soy staying at home until I'm married
    or dead
soy dumping my old man, even though I'm
    pregnant with his child
soy getting married in Reno with the
    kids at home
soy getting married with 15 bridesmaids
    and champagne and cake
soy mother of 12, married at 14
soy staying together for the kids' sakes
soy la que se chinga pa' mantener a su
    familia
soy marianismo, living to love and support
    my husband and to nurture and teach
    my children
soy la battered wife
            Soy la drop-out
            soy the first in my family to graduate
            from high school
            soy la directora
            soy la poverty pimp
Soy "tank you" en vez de thank you
soy "chooz" en vez de shoes
soy refinada—educated in assimilated/
    anglocized/private institutions
            Soy la canería
            soy "silicon valley"
            soy los fields
            soy el unemployment

soy el welfare
soy la Avon lady
Soy la que va a visitar al Pinto
soy la que piensa que un pinto, es a bean
    Soy la political prisoner
    soy Saturday nights en el Drunk Tank
    soy Juvenile Hall
    soy week-ender at Elmwood
    soy la que mandan a Frontera, the
        California Women's Institute
    soy la que tiene Probation Officer
Soy the A.A.
soy the methadone clinic
soy being under psychiatric care
soy finding strength from within
    my Chicana Soul
soy someone who understands
    Soy dope-pusher
    soy straight
    soy preaching . . . and not listening to
        what I say
Soy el catechism
soy la Holy-roller
soy la que nunca se puede levantar for
    church on Sundays
soy wondering if there *is* a God
soy la Virgen de Guadalupe

Soy la low-rider
soy la cruzer en su Monte-Carlo
soy un ten-speed or walking
    Soy el Joseph Magnin's
    Soy la K-Mart
    Soy el Goodwill
    soy styling
    soy wearing tire sandals con sarape
Soy concerts cuando ando bien loca
soy el Disco, el Starlight, y el Palomar
soy el Hilton
soy the Texas Inn
soy the Knights of Columbus

Soy bragging about a good bato
soy echándole a él y a su mendiga madre
soy stepping out on my old man
soy being true
soy going out with my brother as chaperone
soy la que vive con double standards:
    My old man has a lover, but I'd
    be out on the streets if I had one
Soy la community organizer
soy not being able to get involved
    because my husband, or father,
    won't let me out at night
soy la madre que le hecha madres
    al principal
soy thinking my children's teachers
    are his second parents
        Soy alcohólica
        soy social drinker
        soy marijuana
        soy junky
        soy straight
        soy la natural high—Y que?
        soy glue sniffer
        soy white, red or yellow pills
        soy cristal
Soy el grito del Mariachi
soy salsa
soy Oldies but goodies
soy Freddie Fender
soy Little Joe
soy Vicente Fernández
soy la Vicky Carr
        Soy versos de la Santa Biblia
        Soy *True Confessions, Playgirl* or *Viva*
        soy Novelas de Amor
        soy Literatura Revolucionaria
        soy never reading at all
Soy spray painting on the wall
soy writing books
        Soy ojos negros y piel canela
        soy dying my hair a flaming red or yellow

Soy Mexicana
soy Mexican-American
soy American of Spanish Surname (A.S.S.)
soy Latina
soy Puerto Riqueña
soy Cocoanut
soy Chicana

Soy achieving a higher status en la causa
       de la mujer
          y del hombre Chicano

Con mucho cariño dedico esto a las Locas de la Raza Cósmica,
Y si no te puedes ver aquí hermana, solo te puedo decir
      "Dispensa"

Crisis de indentidad / Crisis of Identity or, "Ya no chingues . . ."[3]

Margarita Cota-Cárdenas

Soy chicana macana
o gringa marrana,
la tinta pinta
o la pintura tinta,
el puro retrato
o me huele el olfato,
una mera gabacha,
o cuata sin tacha
una pocha biscocha,
o una india mocha,
(me pongo lentes rosas o negros
para tomar perspectiva,
todo depende, la verdad es relativa)

---

3. The subtitle, "Ya no chingues . . ." is an idiomatic slang expression that can translate in various ways but here can be "Stop bugging me . . ." or more strongly "Stop fucking with me . . ."

la vista aguda
o ciega nariguda,
parece que sí
pero mira que no,
me entiendes, Mendes,
o no me explico, Federico,
están claras las cosas,
pues no es por las moscas . . .
Ya, ya cierra la boca
y si te parece poco,
te echo un jarro de mole
en el falso pinche atole.

■

Am I a false Chicana
or a gringa pig,
shady ink
or a shady painting,
the very picture of
or my breath smells fishy,
a mere gabacha[4]
or a cuata,[5] without equal,
a cookie pocha[6]
or a fractured india,[7]
(I put on rose- or dark-colored glasses
to take on perspective,
it all depends, the truth is relative)
I have sharp-eyed vision,
or I'm a sharp-nosed blind woman,
it seems that it's so
but really it's not,
or do you understand me, Mendes,[8]
or don't I make myself clear, Federico,
is everything clear now,

---

4. gringa
5. buddy, sister
6. an acculturated Chicana
7. "India mocha" in the original, referring to accusations that as a Chicana she "fractures" language and culture.
8. Mendes/Federico—expression equivalent to "so and so," "such and such"

well it's in spite of the moscas . . .[9]
Yea, shut your mouth now
and if that's not enough,
I'll throw a pot of mole[10]
in your stinking false atole.[11]

Oaxaca, 1974

Lorna Dee Cervantes

Mexico,
I look for
you all day in the streets of Oaxaca.
The children run to me laughing,
spinning me blind and silly.
They call to me in words of another language.
My brown body searches the streets
for the dye that will color my thoughts.

But Mexico gags,
¡Esputa!
on this bland pochaseed.

I didn't ask to be brought up tonta!
My name hangs about me like a loose tooth.
Old women know my secret,
"Es la culpa de los antepasados."
Blame it on the old ones.
They gave me a name
that fights me.

---

9. literally, "flies" that are buzzing around obscuring things

10. a spicy Mexican sauce

11. a bland white porridge, also from "darle en el atole," meaning to hit someone where it really hurts.

The Gift?

Sylvia S. Lizárraga

When was the first time I noticed I had the gift of making myself invisible? I know it was a gift because it didn't happen little by little and each time it became more perfect; I just became invisible all of a sudden, and really invisible. It was as if I erased myself, or was it that I was being erased? I don't know. The only thing I know was that I was still there, I knew that I was there, but nobody saw me. I remember the time my mother sent me to ask Don Tacho, the man who sold thread, buttons, ribbons and laces in the fil, if he would let her have some needles and a spool of thread on credit. My mother had gone to work early and she had asked me to do this errand because she needed the thread badly. I went to where Don Tacho had opened his box with all his pretty things and I waited my turn because there were many women buying. When it was my turn I told him my mother wanted those things and she would pay him next week. He knew my mother well and he knew me too because I always went with her when she bought from him. After I said that to him, Don Tacho just asked the person behind me what she wanted as if I wasn't even there. He just didn't see me. He didn't see me.

I'm sure he didn't see me because I stayed there the rest of the afternoon waiting for his customers to leave, but after everyone was gone he shut his box and left. And I was left standing there knowing that Don Tacho couldn't see me.

Another time I also felt sure I had suddenly become invisible was when my friend Teresa and I went to see this very important lady who was going to help us enter school. We were very happy when we knocked on the door. The lady opened it, said hello to Teresa, and we went into the living room. Her name was Mrs. Green and she was so educated and so nice. One could tell immediately that Mrs. Green knew a lot. She asked Teresa a lot of questions and I sat on the side waiting for her to talk to me, thinking about what I would answer. She talked for a long time, about an hour; she talked about the importance of education, and how she had struggled alone to get her education, and how no one had helped her. All alone she worked and worked till she found the way because no one taught her; and she repeated to us, Anyone can do what I did. Then she wrote Teresa's name on a list, she got up and went to the door. Teresa and I followed her. She said goodby, looking straight at Teresa as she had done for the whole hour, and she closed the door smiling. On our way home, Teresa and I made plans about when we would go to school; we were very happy, although inside I was thinking, How is it that

Mrs. Green didn't see me? The whole hour she talked with her eyes fixed on Teresa and I was there by her side, with my eyes fixed on her, but not even once did she realize I was there. I am sure she couldn't see me because not even once did she turn to where I was. And she was such a good person, she had talked about all the people she had advised on how to get an education. And I had been listening and watching although she couldn't see me.

Every time they can't see me I feel somewhat strange, as if I'm lacking something. Although I don't know what it could be, the only thing I know is that I'm missing something, because although I can see myself and I can see the people I'm with, they can't see me. At times I wonder, do they also feel something strange when they can't see me? Can they feel the *not* seeing me? or am I the only one who feels it because I know I'm there; because I am there, aren't I?

Chicana Studies

Rina García Rocha

If I wore my contact lenses,
all the marketable make-up &
Parisienne mode.
Would you say I was sensual if
I sprayed Chanel No. 5 in the
evening before you arrive?

If I gained five pounds or so
and suddenly my bust would
generously grow and show
Would you make love to me in
the day . . . at noon?
Under the magnified sun, when
you would obviously see my
yellow stained teeth, my zits,
my little crevices of wrinkles
on the sides of my eyes and lips.
Only shown when I smile,
if you look close.

Could you actually picture me?
A petite figure moving, embracing
your shoulders—uttering to you
exactly what you want to hear?

You, who go by fancy wrapped
packages! Can you understand
my mind?
The intricate weaving it embroiders.

Would you love me?
A woman who doesn't live by
Cosmopolitan standards?

Would you be able to detect me
Among the assembly line of Goddesses?

To Other Women Who Were Ugly Once

Inés Hernández

Do you remember how we used to panic
   when Cosmo, Vogue and Mademoiselle
      ladies would Glamour-us out of
         existence

                      so ultra bright
                      would be their smile
                      so lovely their
                      complexion

    their confianza based on
    someone else's fashion
    and their mascara'd mascaras
    hiding their cascaras[12] that hide

                      their ser[13]

I would always become

                      cold inside

---

12. shells
13. being

Que mataonda[14] to compete

to need
to dress right
speak right
laugh in just the
right places
dance in just
the right way

My resistance to this type of
existence

grows stronger
every day

Y al cabo ahora sé
que se vale[15]

preferir natural
luz to neon.

Women Are Not Roses

Ana Castillo

Women have no
beginning
only continual
flows.

Though rivers flow
women are not
rivers.

Women are not
roses
they are not oceans
or stars.

---

14. What a drag
15. Anyway, now I know that its better to prefer

i would like to tell
her this but
i think she
already knows.

Legal Alien

Pat Mora

Bi-lingual, Bi-cultural,
able to slip from "How's life?"
to *"Me'stan volviendo loca,"*[16]
able to sit in a paneled office
drafting memos in smooth English,
able to order in fluent Spanish
at a Mexican restaurant,
American but hyphenated,
viewed by Anglos as perhaps exotic,
perhaps inferior, definitely different,
viewed by Mexicans as alien,
(their eyes say, "You may speak
Spanish but you're not like me")
an American to Mexicans
a Mexican to Americans
a handy token
sliding back and forth
between the fringes of both worlds
by smiling
by masking the discomfort
of being pre-judged
Bi-laterally.

---

16. They are driving me crazy.

To live in the Borderlands means you

Gloria Anzaldúa

are neither hispana india negra española
   ni gabacha[17] eres mestiza, mulata, half-breed
   caught in the crossfire between camps
   while carrying all five races on your back
   not knowing which side to turn to, run from;

To live in the Borderlands means knowing
   that the india in you, betrayed for 500 years,
   is no longer speaking to you,
   that mexicanas call you rajetas,[18]
   that denying the Anglo inside you
   is as bad as having denied the Indian or Black;

Cuando vives en la frontera
   people walk through you, the wind steals your voice,
   you're a burra,[19] buey,[20] scapegoat
   forerunner of a new race,
   half and half—both woman and man, neither—
   a new gender;

To live in the Borderlands means to
   put chile in the borscht,
   eat whole wheat tortillas,
   speak Tex-Mex with a Brooklyn accent;
   be stopped by la migra at the border checkpoints;

Living in the Borderlands means you fight hard to
   resist the gold elixir beckoning from the bottle,
   the pull of the gun barrel,
   the rope crushing the hollow of your throat;

In the Borderlands
   you are the battleground
   where enemies are kin to each other;

---

17. a Chicano term for a white woman
18. literally, "split," that is, having betrayed your word
19. donkey
20. oxen

you are at home, a stranger,
the border disputes have been settled
the volley of shots have shattered the truce
you are wounded, lost in action
dead, fighting back;

To live in the Borderlands means
the mill with the razor white teeth wants to shred off
your olive-red skin, crush out the kernel, your heart
pound you pinch you roll you out
smelling like white bread but dead;

To survive the Borderlands
you must live sin fronteras,[21]
be a crossroads.

Mestiza

Marina Rivera

Poem in five parts

    i. what they want
they send word
just today just this hour
they will make me a poet
give thought to a book
invite me to read
but there is this matter
of more poems to be
constructed in shape of tortilla
lined like a serape,
threads bleeding
faces the color of coffee,
black eyes, a circle of ash
exactly placed on the proper day
in the center of each forehead.

they believe that downing me
in a swallow they have tasted every cup,

---

21. without borders

that if they chew me like a biscuit,
we are of the same dough.
mother, why don't they understand?

they would make me a ring
place it on one finger
that they might marry
all our nationality.
this people, this Mexican people
pieces of a plate
which in order to repair
they seek proud men of honor,
women of affection, of honey, of butter
giving sweetness to life.

they forget that we are people
they forget that the pieces
contemplated thus do not conform
one unto the other.
in whatever people:
the flower without seed
the scar which can't be seen
the salted heart
cage without bird
bird without song
song without lips—
tragedians, liars, drunkards
pieces which do not fit.

they would make me the button of a coat
so they could put it on
to demonstrate their love. us . . .
ay! what an immense body
yet they would clasp us like a lover
kissing all with one kiss
and we a bud opening,
a bud of one throat:
ya, ya, brother, I forgive you.

    ii. father
when a man could not go
he sent a dove.
my father could not go.

in those days even if
the mind were a waterfall
of light itself
they would tie you
by your tongue,
your feet without movement
because of your poverty.
to be eldest of ten poor children
is to shine for one cup of chocolate
with one piece of French bread.
having no meat, having no shoes
you ate your dreams, learned to walk
on your longings until they wore out.

my father could not go.
he sent a dove, he sent me,
groomed, tongue untied,
with fists of words.
one windy day he opened his hand.
she flew up leaving the brown earth
set to reach the rich white land.
dove of half-breed blood
dove of half-breed mind
which becomes smoke circling
over white earth, brown earth.
one side or another,
only death decides
when, the eyes wrinkling, going out,
she falls without choosing.

   iii. mother
dear mother, come forward
for it is you they are calling
you who watched your mother
die in the light of candles
in the house of adobe
the smell of death following
up the river, beyond the ranches
past the dusty road on which
you escaped your poverty.
known for your long lashes,
peddling eggs to buy cloth,

sewing on a pedal machine,
your sisters little lanterns
and you the butterfly of the dances.

today they come for my mother.
today they come for my father.
but they come late.
my parents did not arrive.

    iv. what I want
only I remain
a person of the middle
who battled in a brown-colored life,
battled in a life colored white,
and became strong,
strong enough to say:
don't call me for the Chicanos,
nor for my parents,
nor for women.
summon me for myself,
one woman
forgetting white people, brown people
remembering that the heart
is judged not by color
but by strength.
this Mexican plate cannot be fixed
because the pieces never took one form,
each man, each woman comprising a language
with dictionary loaned solely to listener
with ears pressed close to hear
movements of the individual soul.
we are rivers running slowly or fiercely,
deep or shallow, filthy or clean—
rivers which are born, cross, die and recross.

    v. what I know
if all the rest misunderstand
you will understand me, mother
you with a heart made of trodden earth
the movement of the sea in your
spiritual hands that don't smile anymore,
you whose only son waits in the

distant, fiery land of sudden death,
you mother who, when you raise the conch
to your ear, know that the sound
is not the music of the sea
but just song of one certain sea snail.

ever since

Veronica Cunningham

ever since
i kan
remember
i have been
slapped
with compliment
after compliment
and by these compliments
i have learned
many things
usually the people
meant
to share
a thought
or a feeling
of comfort
and usually
they failed

you're lucky,
you don't look Mexican.
you don't act
like a girl.
you can make something
of yourself.
you don't have
to tell anyone
you're a lesbian.

ever since
i kan
remember
i have shuddered
when someone
attempted
to crown me
with privileges
that
only demanded
of me
to deny
my (sex-
sexuality-
color-
class-
culture-) self
if i kant
live
this life
as i am
why live it
at all

I sing to myself

Alma Villanueva

There is something
I carry deep
within me
like an over-ripe
fruit, one whose use is past and
won't rot and merge
and gags me
now and then;
  it is the fruit
of bitterness and distrust.

oh yes, they planted the seed, but
I tended the soil . . .

I could weep and rage
against the man who never
stroked my child fine hair
who never felt the pride of
my femininity grow in his loins
   never desired me in a secret father's
      way
the man who
   dropped his seed in my mother's
   womb, then called it quits.
her pain haunted me for years,
the way she looked when she
talked about him, the
desire and need that rose to her eyes—
   it repulsed and attracted me.

I could weep and rage
against all those who
looked into my hungry eyes
and shifted theirs so quickly;
all those who didn't see
my love and need mirrored
naked in my eyes.
my thin, boyish body always
10 degrees colder than everyone
elses, shivering even in the heat;
never finding a breast to rest
and warm myself
   except once or twice
for awhile and then somehow
they'd slip or be dragged away—

I could weep and rage
against the man I loved;
who loved me at his leisure and
neglected my deepest needs, then
the final irony of his fear of
   (and final desertion)
my mounting self/love and strength

(how were you to know I
  would only love you
    more, if only you'd
  been equal
 to the taking)
there are times this fruit
galls me and yet
this fruit is strange; the
skin is so very beautiful but
the flesh is putrid and bitter

  —no, you don't fool me any longer—

I will swallow you whole and
accept and transform you
till you melt
in my mouth.
  (you/man only
    bit the apple:
      you must swallow
    death-
      I/woman give birth:
        and this time to
    myself)

Progenitor

Bernice Zamora

I am the padre
who drinks whiskey
until sun-up and
who makes love to
my virgin daughter
and her friends.

I am the madre
who stands dazed
before the coffin
of my young son

who shot himself in
his girlfriend's car.

I am the primo
who watched the child
play house with her friends,
then married her
at her own request.

I am the puta
who stands alone
on the grave of a
young man. I am
returning the lilies
he gave me.

I am all the children
and I am the abuelos
of dead children
whose resurrections
depend on
resurrections.

From "A Letter to Alicia"

Ana Castillo

finally we are ending the cesspool
of the 20's
i remember you
you don't fool me
with your designer jeans
designer makeup
sculptured nails
and glittering teeth
we shared the same jar of noxema
i covered for you at the ruins of monte albán
while you changed your tampon
before the eyes of gods and ghosts
and scorpions

you tolerated my cigarette smoke
binges drinking alone into oblivion
finally we are no longer young
women men deposit their confusion
in leaving us with their memories
of past loves and their dirty underwear
we no longer cry into our poems our work
my man done gone and left me and before
we get to the last verse the ass is knock
ing on the door again (maybe he left
something important behind? surely he
couldn't have grown up overnight . . . ?)
finally we've come to respect our own
privacy slipping into quiet moments with
a cup of tea or glass of mellow wine re
flect on the next project and life is
balanced even new york seems to make sense
chicago is not quite as resistant as once
i think i remember saying back at 21
can't wait for these next ten years to pass
anticipating a lot of pain like a decade
of pure heartburn and gas . . .

Whole

Ana Castillo

i love juana
because she is not me
which is why i can
say her name
outright
unlike poets who hold
their most precious secrets
to silence

we are lovers of
life and reflection she
believes i'm better at

the latter while she is
best at the first so we
report with great enthu
siasm so as not to leave
anything out

we are children to
gether playing the Grand
Madames off to the theatre
the posh at brunch
the avant garde at the cinema
we dress up we strip down
sometimes we take our daughter
then we are two and a half
or three or a triangle
and whole

Desert Women

Pat Mora

Desert women know
about survival.
Fierce heat and cold
have burned our skin.
Like cactus, we've learned
to pull in tender leaves,
to shoot spines
from soft aureoles, to hide
pain and loss by silence,
no branches wail or whisper
our sad songs. Our secrets
stay inside, only dried scars show
  if you get close
  if you dare push
  against our thorns.
But when we flower, we stun.
Like cactus, we've learned
to gulp and hoard.

THREE

Self and Others

You were proud of the woman blooming out of your
fourteen lonely years, but you cried
when you read the poem I wrote you.
        LORNA DEE CERVANTES

I remember you, Fred Montoya.
You were the first vato[1] to ever kiss me.
        BERNICE ZAMORA

If Chicanas as writers are primarily in search of their identities, as individuals and as a social beings, their self-concept is determined, to a great extent, in relation to others. This chapter could be said to deal with "relationships," as it shows the intimate links that are woven between the Mexican American female and family members, friends, and relations; it also illustrates, however, brief acquaintances with other individuals, in settings either of passion or violence. In literature, Chicanas' world perspectives are shaped and determined by their immediate female kin and the values they embody, and in addition male figures seem to take a secondary place. Seldom do the father and grandfather appear in a teaching or nurturing role ("Para Teresa" is an exception). Mostly they are seen setting up rules and imparting discipline in the home. In many instances, female households are shown in Chicana texts where role models—besides the more basic life functions—are performed by *abuelitas* (grandmothers) and mothers. In quite a few cases, the father figures appearing in poetry and prose are not only authoritatively repressive, they are frankly abusive. A common father image is that of a drunk returning home late at night, hitting, screaming, disturbing the peace: "we wake up / and it's him / banging and banging / and the doorknob rattling. . . ." (Cisneros). Sometimes fathers are presented through puzzling images—an ambivalent mixture of disdain and nostalgia. It

---

1. Guy, dude.

is only recently that writers have begun to have more exploration into the world of fathers (*The Toltec,* Ana Castillo). The few grandfathers that appear are distant figures, paternally kind but relatively unknown to the female adolescent or young woman (Vigil-Piñón, Quintana Pigno). Mothers are admired for patient ways, for survival skills, for homesteading virtues, and for crafts. They are seen as makers, doers, as women who did not have the opportunity to speak up, or even less to write, but who leave an indelible print on their children's lives: "you were the caravan master at the reins / driving your threaded needle artillery across the mosaic cloth / bridges / delivering yourself in separate testimonies" (Palomo Acosta). Aunts are also motherly and even enchanting; uncles are funny or sometimes cruel (Hernández, Mora, Rivera).

Chicanas as artists are mostly touched, however, when they write about the abuelita, everpresent in their narratives and poems. This aging female figure is revered, cherished, respected, treated with utmost love and care (Viramontes, Cervantes, Vigil-Piñón, Rivera). There is magic in that great mother figure, as if she were the kind fairy in olden tales, or the good witch who looks after children ("Abuelita Magic," Mora), or even the beautiful lady admired from afar, imagined in dreams ("El sueño de las flores," Cervantes). Abuelitas are traditional, carrying on their old Mexican customs and cooking (kitchen ingredients, tortilla-slapping sounds are part and parcel of grandmother texts). They pass on, and they are remembered through the rosy colored lenses of childhood memories. Unlike mothers, abuelitas almost never possess negative qualities; but the former can sometimes be pictured with traits that are similar to those of men ("mothers can be / jealous gods / Just like / husbands / Unforgiving and demanding," García Rocha).

Bonds with their own children are very strong in the world of Chicana writers. Daughters and sons are symbols of continuing life, of mysteries to ponder; they grow under their mother's gaze, and she worries about them, protects them, befriends them (Villanueva, Mora, Corpi, Cota-Cárdenas). The role of mother is part of the traditional outlook that constitutes a segment of their world vision; at the same time, they are also modern women, fighting against prejudice and sexism, facing society as best they can. Chicanas are armed with the wisdom of their foremothers, and they add to it the knowledge of their strong new selves, sometimes wavering but never going back in their struggles and their searches. This legacy they hope to pass on to their offspring: "I'll arm my daughter with a ring. / She'll slip it under her wedding mattress. / When he sleeps, she'll slit her finger, / smear the sheet" ("Plot," Mora).

Siblings are part of the family unit so dear to Chicanas, and they are treated with a special mixture of equality and humor, although sometimes a wistful tone creeps into the narrative line or the poetic discourse referred to brothers and sisters (Cisneros). They are not friends, they are bloodkin; and as such, there is a common mother lode of feeling between the writers and their siblings. Familial ties are strong and lasting, to be respected without question: "Papa makes us promise to lie / 3 kids we got remember it / but we got Arturo inside" ("Arturo Burro," Cisneros).

Though family life is peaceful and enriching when it revolves around female roles and kinships, it can be hard and cruel when domestic violence—usually in the form of a drunken father or stepfather—erupts. The older generation of women accepts this way of men toward their families, caused by routine and despair, exacerbated by alcohol. The younger Chicanas, however, as their literary world reveals, do not accept this harsh reality of abuse. In their relationships with lovers, Chicanas show themselves as traditionally loving and yielding ("Love Ritual," Mora) but also with a new kind of consciousness that does not let them bow to custom and social stereotyping ("Para un Revolucionario," Cervantes; "Do you take?" Zamora). A radical perspective will also appear in the work of poets who deal with nontraditional subjects (Cunningham and Cervantes on rape); this seems to be the counterside to romantic visions of womanhood, as dreams of flowers and illusions brought on by remembrances of abuelita's youth appeared to engender before. Images are mixed in their metaphors; pursuing a love fantasy seems to be equated with a past connected to the earth—brown, mother of brownness. So it is in Pat Mora's poems of love: the fickle lover is called back with ceremonies performed for the dead, flower and food and drink over the graves; a first night of physical loving is celebrated in a house surrounded by the desert, full of multicolored, flying birds. Nature is a compelling force, and for Chicanas—as for Chicanos—is seen as origin, as pristine mother of goodness:

> I have faith, Leticia
> our rural histories will prevail
> we can fight the elements of garbage
> and shall remain ourselves
>
> *Irene Blea*

And so shall Virginia and Teresa, as well as Leticia and all other friends present in Chicana literature, remain captured in the texts; they are the fictional witnesses of growing, of molding an adult personality and identity out of the old childhood ways. Hope is found in spite of differences; images of young women who shared school and *barrio* days are varied, empathetic, always wonderful companions of learning—"the brown thighs creeping out of our shorts, I read / you the poems of Lord Byron, Donne, / the Brownings." A common ethnic background, national roots shared in heritage, and customs prevail over social differences, over border divisions. For middle class Chicanas, the distinction between mistress and maid is guiltily observed: they are sisters in femaleness above all.

In childhood memories there were always female presences, soul or play mates, in touch with the inner person that was the writer at the time. But there were also the first male intrusions and encounters with reality and social mores adverse to women: "I said shame on me, and nobody / said a word to you" (Zamora). In other instances, male figures are not represented in the context of sex or friendship, but rather of family and fun, even though they are still recognized as a potential difficulty:

mi primo bien cool	my cousin real cool
me viene a sacar	comes to ask me
a bailar	to dance
gozando un rato	enjoying for a while
del simple gusto	the simple pleasures

"Remembering," Hernández

In their relationships, in defining themselves by connecting to others, Chicana writers build a world closely related to hearth and home but also adventurous, daring, nonconforming. Most of all, they see their own persons as independent entities, taught by their social context, but very much their own creation. Brought up on advice and admonitions, on tradition and custom, they nevertheless go on the wind and fly far from home. Away from their surrounding role models, they still make it in a hostile world; they are themselves—they are grown apart, with a space of their own—but they speak with a language learned from the tongues of their family women ("Crow," Cervantes).

In this chapter, we have included a varied sampling of new and established authors who show in their work how Chicanas are growing as artists, enriched with their past and their traditions but still "shadowed by no one." They continue to define for themselves a context of human depth, one toward which they feel deeply committed; their own "selves" are uniquely linked to others— by memory, by values, by rejection of inhumanity.

■ ■ ■

My Mother Pieced Quilts

Teresa Palomo Acosta

they were just meant as covers
in winters
as weapons
against pounding january winds

but it was just that every morning I awoke to these
october ripened canvases
passed my hand across their cloth faces
and began to wonder how you pieced
all these together
these strips of gentle communion cotton and flannel
nightgowns
wedding organdies
dime-store velvets

how you shaped patterns square and oblong and round
positioned
balanced
then cemented them
with your thread
a steel needle
a thimble

how the thread darted in and out
galloping along the frayed edges, tucking them in
as you did us at night
oh how you stretched and turned and rearranged
your michigan spring faded curtain pieces
my father's santa fe workshirt
the summer denims, the tweeds of fall

in the evening you sat at your canvas
—our cracked linoleum floor the drawing board
me lounging on your arm
and you staking out the plan:
whether to put the lilac purple of easter against the
red plaid of winter-going-into-spring
whether to mix a yellow with a blue and white and paint

the corpus christi noon when my father held your hand
whether to shape a five-point star from the
somber black silk you wore to grandmother's funeral

you were the river current
carrying the roaring notes
forming them into pictures of a little boy reclining
a swallow flying
you were the caravan master at the reins
driving your threaded needle artillery across the
mosaic cloth bridges
delivering yourself in separate testimonies

oh mother you plunged me sobbing and laughing
into our past
into the river crossing at five
into the spinach fields
into the plainview cotton rows
into tuberculosis wards
into braids and muslin dresses
sewn hard and taut to withstand the thrashings
of twenty-five years

stretched out they lay
armed / ready / shouting / celebrating

knotted with love
the quilts sing on

ser conforme

Evangelina Vigil-Piñón

my mother made me a beaded necklace
a beaded ring
and also a bracelet
gypsy colors
were the ones she used
indio colors but
fluorescent

and I think to myself
why is it that mothers always know
what kinds of things their daughters like
like when you were small and
she'd come home with two new dresses
one that you just loved
but expensive and
one that didn't strike
your fancy but was
cheaper

Haciendo Tamales

Cordelia Candelaria

Haciendo tamales mi mamá wouldn't compromise—
no mftr chili, no u.s.d.a. carne
nomas handgrown y home-raised, todo.
Oregano had to be wildly grown
in brown earth 'bajo la sombra.
Tamale wrappers had to be hojas
dried from last year's corn
nurtured by sweat—¿cómo no?
Trabajos de amor pa'enriquecer el saborcito.
To change or country
she wouldn't sacrifice her heritage.
Entonces, como su mamá antes y su abuelita
she made her tamales from memory
cada sabor nuevo
como el calor del Westinghouse where
she cooked them with gas under G.E. lights—
bien original to the max!

Beneath the Shadow of the Freeway

Lorna Dee Cervantes

1

Across the street—the freeway,
blind worm, wrapping the valley up
from Los Altos to Sal Si Puedes.
I watched it from my porch
unwinding. Every day at dusk
as Grandma watered geraniums
the shadow of the freeway lengthened.

2

We were a woman family:
Grandma, our innocent Queen;
Mama, the Swift Knight, Fearless Warrior.
Mama wanted to be Princess instead.
I know that. Even now she dreams of taffeta
and foot-high tiaras.

Myself: I could never decide.
So I turned to books, those staunch, upright men.
I became Scribe: Translator of Foreign Mail,
interpreting letters from the government, notices
of dissolved marriages and Welfare stipulations.
I paid the bills, did light man-work, fixed faucets,
insured everything
against all leaks.

3

Before rain I notice seagulls.
They walk in flocks,
cautious across lawns: splayed toes,
indecisive beaks. Grandma says
seagulls mean storm.
In California in the summer,
mockingbirds sing all night.
Grandma says they are singing for their nesting wives.
"They don't leave their families
borrachando."

She likes the ways of birds,
respects how they show themselves
for toast and a whistle.

She believes in myths and birds.
She trusts only what she builds
with her own hands.

4

She built her house,
cocky, disheveled carpentry,
after living twenty-five years
with a man who tried to kill her.

Grandma, from the hills of Santa Barbara,
I would open my eyes to see her stir mush
in the morning, her hair in loose braids,
tucked close around her head
with a yellow scarf.

Mama said, "It's her own fault,
getting screwed by a man for that long.
Sure as shit wasn't hard,"
soft she was soft

5

in the night I would hear it
glass bottles shattering the street
words cracked into shrill screams
inside my throat   a cold fear
as it entered the house in hard
unsteady steps   stopping at my door
my name   bathrobe   slippers
outside at 3 A.M. mist heavy
as a breath full of whiskey
stop it   go home   come inside
mama if he comes here again
I'll call the police

inside
a gray kitten   a touchstone
purring beneath the quilts
grandma stitched

from his suits
the patchwork singing
of mockingbirds

6

"You're too soft . . . always were.
You'll get nothing but shit.
Baby, don't count on nobody."

—a mother's wisdom.
Soft. I haven't changed,
maybe grown more silent, cynical
on the outside.

"O Mama, with what's inside of me
I could wash that all away. I could."
"But Mama, if you're good to them
they'll be good to you back."

Back. The freeway is across the street.
It's summer now. Every night I sleep with a gentle man
to the hymn of mockingbirds,

and in time, I plant geraniums.
I tie up my hair into loose braids,
and trust only what I have built
with my own hands.

mi mamá se sentaba / my mother would sit

Xelina

mi mamá se sentaba
   por horas
pegando su texas gold stamps
en libritos azul y amarillo
solamente así
lograba los sueños infantiles de sus siete hijos
my mother still believes in bargains

■

my mother would sit
   for hours
pasting her texas gold stamps
in little blue and gold books
the only way she had
of obtaining the child dreams of her seven children
my mother still believes in bargains

For the Color of My Mother

Cherríe Moraga

I am a white girl gone brown to the blood color of my mother
speaking for her through the unnamed part of the mouth
the wide-arched muzzle of brown women.

at two
my upper lip split open
clear to the tip of my nose
it spilled forth a cry that would not yield
that travelled down six floors of hospital
where doctors wound me into white bandages
only the screaming mouth exposed

the gash sewn back into a snarl
would last for years

I am a white girl gone brown to the blood color of my mother
speaking for her.

at five, *her* mouth
pressed into a seam
a fine blue child's line drawn across her face
her mouth, pressed into mouthing english
mouthing yes yes yes
mouthing stoop lift carry
(sweating wet sighs into the field
her red bandana comes loose from under the huge brimmed hat
moving across her upper lip)
at fourteen, her mouth

painted, the ends drawn up
the mole in the corner colored in darker larger mouthing yes
she praying no no no
lips pursed and moving

at forty-five, her mouth
bleeding into her stomach
the hole gaping growing redder
deepening with my father's pallor
finally stitched shut from hip to breastbone
 an inverted V
 Vera
 Elvira

I am a white girl gone brown to the blood color of my mother
speaking for her.

as it should be
dark women come to me
  sitting in circles
I pass through their hands
the head of my mother
painted in clay colors

touching each carved feature
  swollen eyes and mouth
they understand the explosion the splitting
open contained within the fixed expression
they cradle her silence
  nodding to me

Baby Doll

Rina García Rocha

Mothers can be
 jealous gods
Just like
 husbands
Unforgiving and demanding.

Saying
naughty girl,
naught ought
to have done that.
Naught, ought
to have said that.

I rake carefully
on their grounds—
gathering my fallen
words and actions
into a neat clump.

Neat & Bitter Clump.

And I . . .
am amazed still—
at me!
That I should
wait for those
candied coated loving
words of approval
from
     jealous gods.

The Album

Antonia Quintana Pigno

In the only photograph
the dark hair is combed
into a tight bun at
the nape of the neck.
The black dress with stiff collar
and long narrow sleeves
buttons at the front.
She does not smile.

Mama told us
when cars first appeared

Abuelita walked
in the fields
away from the roads.
One Sunday returning
from San Felipe mass,
she was run over
by a wino in a Model A.

And Abuelito, in a snapshot,
stands at his anvil,
tongs in one hand, in the other a hammer.
He wears a long leather apron,
goggles pushed high on his forehead,
his upper lip smudged with soot.

Grandpa never saw the
advent of the automobile.
The stroke came where he lay
beneath the red canopied wagon he was fixing
for the annual Albuquerque
                              Jubilee Parade.

Section 3 from *Mother, May I?*

Alma Villanueva

3.
my grandmother takes me to the first
day of school. everyone speaks
so fast. I can read and count
in spanish. I can say two poems
in spanish. you can't speak
spanish here. they don't like
it and the teacher is fat
and so white
and I don't like her. I run
home and my grandma says I can
stay. we
go to movies and chinatown and shopping.

she holds one side of the shopping bag, I
hold the other. we
pray and dunk *pan dulce* in coffee. we
make tortillas together. we
laugh and take the buses
everywhere. when we
go to the movies she cries and
she dances when she irons. I
comb her long hair and rub her
back with alcohol. one time
before we left the house, we
said our prayer and she was looking
for her hat and she was wearing
it and I
started to laugh and laugh and I
couldn't stop and she found
it on her head
and she spat–*grosera!*–and it
made me laugh harder and she gave
me the hand that meant a spanking
(and she never spanked me)
and she laughed too.
and when I flew she always
woke me gently—so the soul
  and the body will stay—and I
loved to fly
and dream. I was
always the strongest and the fastest. we
always said our dreams. she said
she knew when her four babies
were dying because they always
pointed up with their fingers
and they'd die in the night.
and I think she dressed me too warmly
and woke me gently
to trick death
to let me stay.

Mama Toña

Marina Rivera

I

The entry is one kiss of ours
for ten of yours, noisily.
You speak the words I comprehend
and the words they laugh at
when I speak them,
the words that flowed hardest,
like old butter, like lumps.
You sit and rock gently,
hands moving fast as rain.
You sit and hook the lines
that mesh into white squares,
joining the squares slowly,
parts of petals becoming
one translucent flower.
These are your words,
they bloom, they awe me
as the others do not.
You can make horses,
trees, even houses
as you make this brown house,
the one the rose vines cover,
rose against rust, wooden gate
scraping. You hold me
as though I count. You kiss me
noisily
and yet you do not know me.

II

Now you are patting dough.
The warm room. Plop, the
dough goes down round
as faces, flat as fear,
the money that ripples if I
spend it on that wood board.
The touch you use makes

everything come up smoothly,
even the dough. The white
feather-flour makes signets
on your hands. You pat everything.
You smooth it noisily.
The hands patting are words.
I am mute for they laugh at me.
We can talk and we do not speak.

III
You are the only one
the brothers' quarrels cease for.
You say all their names till you come
to the name that holds that fist back.
The blood of your sons is white,
is hot, flashes everytime I come.

IV
You have hands like my mother,
fleshy and warm. You are not like
some here. The pictures are
your words. They are like you,
delicate, small-boned, fanning light.
They blow in all the window frames,
masking dust, masking cracks.
they are your laughter,
When we kiss you, it is the signal
of leave-taking . . .

V
The day you die I come barreling
from Tucson, the road I do not
come up enough, to catch at your death.
But I am nothing to wait for.
I am only eyes, a wordless one.
I do not come in time.

VI
Death caused this rent in the middle.
It is not the flower, not the horse,
it is the house unraveling,
stitch by stitch.

The dough, the small tight map,
is spreading. Islands break off.

Death tips you out,
the one the rest depends on.

The Moths

Helena María Viramontes

I was fourteen years old when Abuelita requested my help. And it seemed only fair. Abuelita had pulled me through the rages of scarlet fever by placing, removing, and replacing potato slices on the temples of my forehead; she had seen me through several whippings, an arm broken by a dare jump off Tío Enrique's toolshed, puberty, and my first lie. Really, I told Amá, it was only fair.

Not that I was her favorite granddaughter or anything special. I wasn't even pretty or nice like my older sisters and I just couldn't do the girl things they could do. My hands were too big to handle the fineries of crocheting or embroidery and I always pricked my fingers or knotted my colored threads time and time again while my sisters laughed and called me bull hands with their cute waterlike voices. So I began keeping a piece of jagged brick in my sock to bash my sisters or anyone who called me bull hands. Once, while we all sat in the bedroom, I hit Teresa on the forehead, right above her eyebrow and she ran to Amá with her mouth open, her hand over her eye while blood seeped between her fingers. I was used to the whippings by then.

I wasn't respectful either. I even went so far as to doubt the power of Abuelita's slices, the slices she said absorbed my fever. "You're still alive, aren't you?" Abuelita snapped back, her pasty gray eye beaming at me and burning holes in my suspicions. Regretful that I had let secret questions drop out of my mouth, I couldn't look into her eyes. My hands began to fan out, grow like a liar's nose until they hung by my side like low weights. Abuelita made a balm out of dried moth wings and Vicks and rubbed my hands, shaped them back to size and it was the strangest feeling. Like bones melting. Like sun shining through the darkness of your eyelids. I didn't mind helping Abuelita after that, so Amá would always send me over to her.

In the early afternoon Amá would push her hair back, hand me my sweater and shoes, and tell me to go to Mama Luna's. This was to avoid another fight and another whipping, I knew. I would deliver one last direct shot on Marisela's arm and jump out of our house, the slam of the screen door burying her cries of anger, and I'd gladly go help Abuelita plant her wild lilies or jasmine or heliotrope or cilantro or hierbabuena in red Hills Brothers coffee cans. Abuelita would wait for me at the top step of her porch, holding a hammer and nail and empty coffee cans. And although we hardly spoke, hardly looked at each other as we worked over root transplants, I always felt her gray eye upon me. It made me feel, in a strange sort of way, safe and guarded and not alone. Like God was supposed to make you feel.

On Abuelita's porch, I would puncture holes at the bottom of the coffee cans with a nail and a precise hit of a hammer. Once completed, my job was to pack them with red clay mud from beneath her rose bushes, packing it softly, then making a perfect hole, four fingers round, to nest a sprouting avocado pit, or the spidery sweet potatoes that Abuelita rooted in mayonnaise jars with toothpicks and daily water, or prickly chayotes that produced vines that twisted and wound all over her porch pillars, crawling to the roof, up and over the roof, and down the other side of her house, making her small brick house look like it was cradled within the vines that grew pear-shaped squashes ready for the pick, ready to be steamed with onions and cheese and butter. The roots would burst out of the rusted coffee cans and search for a place to connect. I would then feed the seedlings with water.

But this was a different kind of help, Amá said, because Abuelita was dying. Looking into her gray eye, then into her brown one, the doctor said it was just a matter of days. And so it seemed only fair that these hands she had melted and formed found use in rubbing her caving body with alcohol and marijuana, rubbing her arms and legs, turning her face to the window so that she could watch the Bird of Paradise blooming or smell the scent of clove in the air. I toweled her face frequently and held her hand for hours. Her gray wiry hair hung over the mattress. Since I could remember, she'd kept her long hair in braids. Her mouth was vacant and when she slept, her eyelids never closed all the way. Up close, you could see her gray eye beaming out the window, staring hard as if to remember everything. I never kissed her. I left the window open when I went to the market.

Across the street from Jay's Market there was a chapel. I never knew its denomination, but I went in just the same to search for candles. I sat down on one of the pews because there were none. After I cleaned my fingernails, I looked up at the high ceiling. I had forgotten the vastness of these places, the coolness of the marble pillars, and the frozen statues with blank eyes. I was alone. I knew why I had never returned.

That was one of Apá's biggest complaints. He would pound his hands on the table, rocking the sugar dish or spilling a cup of coffee and scream that if I didn't go to mass every Sunday to save my goddamn sinning soul, then I had no reason to go out of the house, period. Punto final. He would grab my arm and dig his nails into me to make sure I understood the importance of cate- chism. Did he make himself clear? Then he strategically directed his anger at Amá for her lousy ways of bringing up daughters, being disrespectful and unbelieving, and my older sisters would pull me aside and tell me if I didn't get to mass right this minute, they were all going to kick the holy shit out of me. Why am I so selfish? Can't you see what it's doing to Amá, you idiot? So I would wash my feet and stuff them in my black Easter shoes that shone with Vaseline, grab a missal and veil, and wave good-bye to Amá.

I would walk slowly down Lorena to First to Evergreen, counting the cracks on the cement. On Evergreen I would turn left and walk to Abuelita's. I liked her porch because it was shielded by the vines of the chayotes so I could get a good look at the people and car traffic on Evergreen without them knowing. I would jump up the porch steps, knock on the screen door as I wiped my feet, and call Abuelita? mi Abuelita? As I opened the door and stuck my head in, I would catch the gagging scent of toasting chile on the placa. When I entered the sala, she would greet me from the kitchen wringing her hands in her apron. I'd sit at the corner of the table to keep from being in her way. The chiles made my eyes water. Am I crying? No Mama Luna, I'm sure not crying. I don't like going to mass, but my eyes watered anyway, the tears dropping on the tablecloth like candle wax. Abuelita lifted the burnt chiles from the fire and sprinkled water on them until the skins began to separate. Placing them in front of me, she turned to check the menudo. I peeled the skins off and put the flimsy, limp looking green and yellow chiles in the molcajete and began to crush and crush and twist and crush the heart out of the tomato, the clove of garlic, the stupid chiles that made me cry, crush them until they turned into liquid under my bull hand. With a wooden spoon, I scraped hard to destroy the guilt, and my tears were gone. I put the bowl of chile next to a vase filled with freshly cut roses. Abuelita touched my hand and pointed to the bowl of menudo that steamed in front of me. I spooned some chile into the menudo and rolled a corn tortilla thin with the palms of my hands. As I ate, a fine Sunday breeze entered the kitchen and a rose petal calmly feathered down to the table.

I left the chapel without blessing myself and walked to Jay's. Most of the time Jay didn't have much of anything. The tomatoes were always soft and the cans of Campbell soups had rusted spots on them. There was dust on the tops of cereal boxes. I picked up what I needed: rubbing alcohol, five cans of chicken broth, a big bottle of Pine Sol. At first Jay got mad because I thought

I had forgotten the money. But it was there all the time, in my back pocket.

When I returned from the market, I heard Amá crying in Abuelita's kitchen. She looked up at me with puffy eyes. I placed the bags of groceries on the table and began putting the cans of soup away. Amá sobbed quietly. I never kissed her. After a while, I patted her on the back for comfort. Finally: "¿Y mi Amá?" she asked in a whisper, then choked again and cried into her apron.

Abuelita fell off the bed twice yesterday, I said, knowing that I shouldn't have said it and wondering why I wanted to say it because it only made Amá cry harder. I guess I became angry and just so tired of the quarrels and beatings and unanswered prayers and my hands just there hanging helplessly by my side. Amá looked at me again, confused, angry, and her eyes were filled with sorrow. I went outside and sat on the porch swing and watched the people pass. I sat there until she left. I dozed off repeating the words to myself like rosary prayers; when do you stop giving when do you start giving when do you . . . and when my hands fell from my lap, I awoke to catch them. The sun was setting, an orange glow, and I knew Abuelita was hungry.

There comes a time when the sun is defiant. Just about the time when moods change, inevitable seasons of a day, transitions from one color to another, that hour or minute or second when the sun is finally defeated, finally sinks into the realization that it cannot with all its power to heal or burn, exist forever, there comes an illumination where the sun and earth meet, a final defiant burst of burning red orange fury reminding us that although endings are inevitable, they are necessary for rebirths, and when that time came, just when I switched on the light in the kitchen to open Abuelita's can of soup, it was probably then that she died.

The room smelled of Pine Sol and vomit and Abuelita had defecated the remains of her cancerous stomach. She had turned to the window and tried to speak, but her mouth remained open and speechless. I heard you Abuelita, I said, stroking her cheek, I heard you. I opened the windows of the house and let the soup simmer and overboil on the stove. I turned the stove off and poured the soup down the sink. From the cabinet I got a tin basin, filled it with lukewarm water and carried it carefully to the room. I went to the linen closet and took out some modest bleached white towels. With the sacredness of a priest preparing his vestments, I unfolded the towels one by one on my shoulders. I removed the sheets and blankets from her bed and peeled off her thick flannel nightgown. I towelled her puzzled face, stretching out the wrinkles, removing the coils of her neck, toweled her shoulders and breasts. Then I changed the water. I returned to towel the creases of her stretch-marked stomach, her sporadic vaginal hairs, and her sagging thighs. I removed the lint from between her toes and noticed a mapped birthmark on the fold of her buttock. The scars on her back which were as thin as the life lines on the palms of her hands made me realize how little I really knew of Abuelita. I covered her with a thin blanket and went into the bathroom. I washed my hands, and turned on the tub faucets and watched the water pour into the tub with vitality and steam. When it was full, I turned off the water and undressed. Then, I went to get Abuelita.

She was not as heavy as I thought and when I carried her in my arms, her body fell into a V and yet, my legs were tired, shakey, and I felt as if the distance between the bedroom and bathroom was miles and years away. Amá, where are you?

I stepped into the bathtub one leg first, then the other. I bent my knees slowly to descend into the water slowly so I wouldn't scald her skin. There, there, Abuelita, I said, cradling her, smoothing her as we descended, I heard you. Her hair fell back and spread across the water like eagle's wings. The water in the tub overflowed and poured onto the tile of the floor. Then the moths came. Small, gray ones that came from her soul and out through her mouth fluttering to light, circling the single dull light bulb of the bathroom. Dying is lonely and I wanted to go to where the moths were, stay with her and plant chayotes whose vines would crawl up her fingers and into the clouds; I wanted to rest my head on her chest with her stroking my hair, telling me about the moths that lay within the soul and slowly eat the spirit up; I wanted to return to the waters of the womb with her so that we would never be alone again. I wanted. I wanted my Amá. I removed a few strands of hair from Abuelita's face and held her small light head within the hollow of my neck. The bathroom was filled with moths, and for the first time in a long time I cried, rocking us, crying for her, for me, for Amá, the sobs emerging from the depths of anguish, the misery of feeling half born, sobbing until finally the sobs rippled into circles and circles of sadness and relief. There, there, I said to Abuelita, rocking us gently, there, there.

Mourning a Sister's Death

Irene Blea

when your sister dies
  do you say
    she was or is my sister
    he is or was my sister's child

erlinda, saying your name sounds rough
  like the life you lived:
  you led street gangs
    smoked
      and didn't go to school
      when others did

you've left children
  rough and lost like you
  scattered children
    like you were scattered—
      no one wants them, has time for them
      like they didn't want
          or have time for you

"what will happen to her children,
  what happened to erlinda,"
  mourners asked

she died an alcoholic
  displaced from rural birth
  and transplanted in an urban setting
  caught in a gringo world—
    once beautiful
      she died amongst the junkies
        pimps and whores
          of the asphalt city

To a Little Blond Girl of Heber, Califas

Margarita Cota-Cárdenas

that little sister of mine
was pretty, small tender
    but also very brave
    she wore cowboy boots
    a cowboy hat t-shirt and levis
she was always followed
    by little Wienie dogs

the Chapo the Chapa and the Chapitos
once she tried to take a molar from one
with a large pair of mechanics' pliers
and during Holy Mass
when communion was offered
to be precise
she said to Father Jean Vincent
—Cabrón. I am going to tell my papa
that you didn't want to give me the
white cookie.
Now
    well she's a mother   wife
       and she behaves herself.

Wimpy's Wake

Margarita Cota-Cárdenas

I
Imperial Valley, California.
UPA. MEXICAN NATIONALS SUFFOCATE IN BUTANE
TANK/TRUCK. ARREST MADE IN TRAGIC DEATHS OF ILLEGAL
ALIENS BEING TRANSPORTED BY U.S.–MEXICAN RING.
FARMWORKERS PAID FOR SMUGGLING ACROSS BORDER IN
SEALED TANK AND ON ARRIVAL IN U.S. ACCUSED CHARGED
SEVERAL COUNTS MURDER PENDING INVESTIGATION OF
NUMEROUS PRIOR CROSSINGS.

Salinas Valley, California.
API. TRAIN HITS TRUCK TRANSPORTING BRACEROS TO FIELDS.
MULTIPLE DEATHS TRAGIC END OF LONG ODYSSEY FOR MEXICAN
NATIONALS. ARRANGEMENTS FOR RETURN OF BODIES TO
MEXICO PENDING IDENTIFICATION. STATE AND FEDERAL
INVESTIGATION OF ACCIDENT IN PROGRESS.

San Joaquin Valley, California.
WU. MEXICAN AMERICAN RESIDENT OF FARM LABOR CAMP
DIES IN AUTO ACCIDENT. TRAGEDY BLAMED ON DEFECTIVE
BRAKES. VEHICLE HAD REQUIRED REPAIR FOR SOME TIME.
VICTIM LACKED MEANS FOR REPAIRS ACCORDING TO FELLOW
RESIDENTS OF LABOR CAMP.

II

My little brother, Plonquito, and I had a *velorio* for Wimpy outside the dining hall in the labor camp in which we lived in those days in Masterton, in the San Joaquin Valley in California.

The labor camp was made up of some green barracks with the gray building that was the kitchen and the dining hall in the center, not far from the entrance to the camp and the first row of barracks in which our family lived in two rooms. When the *carroza* arrived that afternoon at the camp, Plonquito and I ran to the bedroom window, bumping into cots and the blankets that served as walls and divided the room.

It had been a few days back that Wimpy had left to pick tomatoes with my dad and my uncles, but our friend never returned. "There was a wreck . . . ," Güero came to tell us, crying and twisting his straw hat in his hands. Wimpy and Güero were my mama's boarders, and they ate every day with us in the other room that served as living room, kitchen, and dining room, and Wimpy was always nice to my brother and me; he used to bring me funnybooks because they all knew that I liked to read and to imagine a lot; once he brought me a *Pepín* from Mexicali and he told me: "Remember the Mexican funnies?" And another day that he'd brought me some funnybooks, Patsy, my little sister who was only a few months old and who I was taking care of, fell on the cement floor, because I was reading my new funnies, and she got a big bump on the head by the time my mom and dad came home. They gave me a good spanking and they told everybody about it, and afterwards Wimpy and Güero used to make me real mad, making fun of me and calling me "Miss Funnybook," and sometimes I cried I was so embarrassed.

But Wimpy was always very nice to us, and that's why we ran to the window to watch him arrive that afternoon. He came in a long car, really big, black, and shiny, and we couldn't understand how he could sleep in that long box, which was also black, like our mama had told us.

When it got dark, cars began to arrive with families and friends that came to see Wimpy in the camp dining hall, because that's where they had put the long box that my mama had said Wimpy was sleeping in. And my parents went also to the *velorio,* but they didn't let us go, and I stayed behind but I was mad. Soon after, Güero arrived really scared, looking for my parents, because he said that Wimpy's brother, who was coming all the way from Ensenada, had smashed up in a car wreck. I wanted to give Wimpy the news, because he was my friend, and I just had to tell him, and so that's why I sneaked off anyway to the dining hall while the neighbor lady was busy with my little sisters.

"I've gotta go see Wimpy," I told Plonquito. I grabbed some funnybooks for company, and I crossed the road in the crickety dark and went toward where I could hear shouts and people talking once in a while . . . somewhere in the labor camp you could hear a radio with off-key mariachi music. When I got to a dining hall window, I could see some women inside; the men were already drinking outside of the hall, and they were talking and sometimes one of them would laugh nervously. The mariachi was singing ". . . si muero LEEjos de TIIIII. . . ." I began to think that a *velorio* was some kind of fiesta for Wimpy and my little heart was beating with anticipation, but first I had to talk with him, with my friend.

I couldn't see Wimpy's face and I went to another window that was right in front of the long box with its pretty lighted candles lined like a fence around it. There was my friend, and I was really surprised that now he had both eyes closed; I always thought that Wimpy slept with his good eye open just like that, and with one eye closed, but now, there was another Wimpy, all pale, and his curly hair combed real good, his face the color of the candles that surrounded him and pretending to be asleep.

I felt like my heart was going to pop out of my chest, like I was going to swallow my tongue, but I was about to call to my friend when Plonquito crept up, and I jumped with a start, frightened. "*Manita*, come home now because I'm scared . . . ," he said, but at that moment some *comadres* came out of the dining hall, crying and shouting, and a man came up to them to say "I'm really really sorry about Wimpy's dying," and he went back to the group of men with their bottles.

Plonquito and I stayed there a long time, thoughtful and trembling in the dark, holding hands tight and looking inside to where the candles and the little open door of the black box were. . . . I began to cry, feeling a heavy confusion, getting an anxious knot in my throat, because I hadn't been able to tell Wimpy that it was his brother that had died, that his brother would never get to come to the *velorio*, nor to anywhere else, and I just knew that someone must have made a mistake because he, Wimpy, was only supposed to be sleeping in his box and because there were only supposed to be dead people in the funnybooks, and then Plonquito and I left, running and crying, and my braids kept hitting me in the face and they felt really heavy and I threw my funnybooks far, very far away. . . .

Arturo Burro

Sandra Cisneros

Jacinto el pinto
María tortilla
Agustín es zonzo
tin tan tan

and we hide
yeah we hide
we got Arturo
inside inside
my brother
who spins his eyes

Mama says nothing
she never says nothing
Papa makes us promise to lie
3 kids we got remember it
but we got Arturo inside

He moves slow
like an elephant goes
and spits and spits
and never cries
and won't grow old
and won't grow old
my brother who spins his eyes

mente joven: nothin' like a pensive child. cold north wind flapping against his hair and tender face

Evangelina Vigil-Piñón

and you remember grandpa—
"Papá." le decían todos[2]
when he died
you were only age six
and you recall parientes
making you walk up to the corpse
and kiss its cold face and you
remember, too, how he used
to terrorize you into "un besito"
on his brown, leathersoft face
made rough by salt-and-pepper beard.
you so scared of him, whom you
hardly ever saw—
he'd prop you up and sit you on his lap
you frozen stiff with shyness and embarrassment
and he asking you things and you
not knowing how or what to answer
only that he was so desconocido
yet full of so much love
and so big and brown and strong
"salúdele a su abuelito," te decían[3]
and you recall how he would
always give you a bright shiny penny
pa comprar un chicle en el molino[4] next door
maybe you might get un premio![5]

---

2. Everyone called him
3. say hello to your grandfather, they would tell you
4. so you could buy gum in the store
5. prize

El sueño de las flores

Lorna Dee Cervantes

The things I remember most
I sift through again.

It's not lost because I have it
tucked away
somewhere behind memories
of the Paseo de las Flores,
la primavera when my grandmother danced,
lifting her skirts—to hear them tell it
she was a clear campana ringing
in their ears.
She was a Spanish dancer
who had an eye for the mandolineros.

Sometimes she is in my mirror:
la mexicana who emerges con flores,
con palabras perdidas,
con besos de los antepasados.[6]

Somewhere in a desert of memories
there is a dream in another language.
Some day I will awaken
and remember every line.

And I will whisper the Spanish
names of her lovers,
I will dance the lost steps of her dance.
I will find flores y flores,
find them and adorn her.

Otra vez,
I will find them in myself
again.

---

6. the Mexican who emerges with flowers, / with lost words / with kisses from our
ancestors.

On Meeting You in Dream and Remembering Our Dance

Denise Chávez

His little legs, dancing, dancing
the corrido
run-racing
against rice twisted floor
of some cousin's holy
union.

There is rhythm
in this dance
a sense of bandy-legged
pride, father,
an illplaced longing
for your sweetened flesh
and lost stories.

"They don't know, look at them,
they don't have the hop,
the salt of joy, you know the
desire of this dance,
father."

She, the bride, my cousin,
George's brother, her father,
George on the dollar, my
Grandmother, George, yes,
she looks that way,
browned.

This family
sectioned
creating wholes across desertlandscape
escape '
escape from
family, you can
not, they are a part of your dreams
you find yourself loving them
as you do that

state of wandering
through rooms you know
like your father's face,
his horseteeth,
not quite short enough,
but who can say:
"E.E.!"
or those goddamn Mexican
teeth look like hell, you bastard,
what's wrong with you,
anyway?

Chon

Marina Rivera

Running through the house, out the gate
you chased me, tortilla in hand, you a
long-legged wolf, me the moppet but fleet.
How would you have done it, Uncle?
How open my mouth of sharp, strong teeth
how stuff it down, since my nails were long
and my soles could have struck you in a fine spot.

We'd feast on ice cream but you'd wait longer,
knew how to sit, pretending to grey, to wizen
with the sun's setting that you might frighten
me with stories till the long, low dragging began.
The Indians going home, street dusty, pot-holed,
darkening, figures morose, hunchbacked
in the wagons. You saying how they'd come
for me soon, stuff me in their gunny sacks,
the roar of the wagons growing. I could not
see the mules' ribs but sensed them,
the wagons dragging, not rolling.
Later you would marry, have children,
come to axe our two pet ducks that you
might feast, careful to persuade in my absence,

cautious to gobble yours at home, the ducks
I loved to feed, hear, watch bathe
glistening at us in segments no one ate,
parts too unlike friends to bury.

Returning the tent, you hid the gash.
I can see you shivering,
determined to chop wood in the tent at night,
your strokes fiercer till you brought in
darkness through the wet smile in the canvas.
It was always your flaw:
That you would warm yourself through force.
And always the darkness falling on your head.
Immensely tired, going grey, the nose longer,
face thinner—I know I ought to forgive you.
The hatred of the small, brown child
is the hardest kind to change, Chon.

after the name-giving

Inés Hernández (T'oma'hto'hla'hkikt, Inés)

after the name-giving aunt tillie gave
me
  a beadwork purse
    deep purple
    background fuerte

color xochitl en el centro
sun kissed flower
though
the straps are
shuiyapa cured
you know
gringo so

auntie inez gave me
indian cured
buckskin
    for me
     to change
   them

To My Daughter

Alma Villanueva

to my daughter,
bringer of life

My daughter's flute sings high
and quivering;   such an improvement,
those first horrible, squeaky notes.
my daughter's body sings round
and womanly;   where's the skinny
girl with wounds on her knees?

here.   my daughter,
                 here.

I carry you so easily.
you barely span my fingertips
to elbow,   all stretched out:
my first born.
I preferred to keep you in,   like a
siamese twin. how, then, could we ever
be lonely?

such love recorded
in the red-mute brainy
placenta.

and I was too young
   (and ashamed)
to claim it,
ours.
  they left a stub of your

    cord hanging, a strange
     wounded, dried/blood
      thing—and when it
       fell off, I picked you up and
       ran the 4 blocks to
        St. Mary's crying because
        I knew your foot or
        your hand was
         next; and the nun laughed
         gently and asked
         'didn't they tell you?'
          I nodded, embarrassed-
          leaving, they'd told
           me 'to keep it clean' and
           I just assumed it
           would heal itself and
  stay.

a friend told me the myth
of the flute player; how he
carries seeds in his hump and brings
everything back to life-
 and I wonder how the most ancient
myths, told and retold before my
grandmother's mother's mother spoke
through her mother's blood, truly speaks
my questions-

 and I wonder how you grew
daughter/woman unthinkingly? they say
lack of love can stunt a child's growth:
perhaps there's a myth to explain
this one too.
perhaps those red/mute loves
stayed.
you are larger than
   (no twin, this one—
me.

Nuestros mundos / Our Worlds

Lucha Corpi / Translated by Catherine Rodríguez-Nieto

A Arturo

Sonrisas del mundo
envueltas en aire ráncido
Máquinas que nunca
se detienen a respirar.

Del otro lado de la mesa
ojos callados me miran
Manos pequeñas me ofrecen
un pedacito de pan.

Me conoces sin decirlo
Y a veces te sorprendo.

Aprendemos.

México tan lejano
pensamos los dos.

Reímos.

Creías que México estaba
más acá de Los Angeles.

No. Este es tu mundo
Aquí luchamos
Aquí vivimos.

Rumbo a la escuela . . .
No hay que comprar
en Safeway me recuerdas.

Y a veces me sorprenden
tus siete largos años.

■   *To Arturo*

Smiles of the world
wrapped in rancid air
Machines that never
stop for breath.

From across the table
quiet eyes watch me
Small hands offer me
a little piece of bread.

You know me without having to say it
and sometimes I surprise you.

We learn.

Mexico so far away
We both are thinking.

We laugh.

You thought Mexico was
closer than Los Angeles.

No. This is your world.
Here is where we struggle.
Here is where we live.

On the way to school . . .
—Mustn't shop at
Safeway you remind me.

And sometimes I am surprised
at your seven long years.

Plot

Pat Mora

I won't let him hit her. I won't
let him bruise her soft skin, her dark
brown eyes. I'll beg her to use the ring
snapped from a Coke can. That's my wedding
gift for my daughter.

My body betrayed me years ago, failed
to yield that drop of blood: proof
of virginity in this village of Mexican fools.

My groom shoved me off the white sheet
at dawn, spat insults. Had he planned to wave
the red stain at his drunken friends?
My in-laws' faces sneered *whore* and my neighbors
snickered at my beatings through the years.

I'll arm my daughter with a ring.
She'll slip it under her wedding mattress.
When he sleeps, she'll slit her finger,
smear the sheet. She must use the ring.
I don't want to split his throat.

The Toltec

Ana Castillo

c. 1955
My father was a Toltec.
Everyone knows he was *bad*.
Kicked the Irish-boys-from-Bridgeport's
ass. Once went down to South Chicago
to stick someone
got chased to the hood
running through the gangway
swish of blade in his back
the emblemmed jacket split in half.

Next morning, Mami
threw it away.

South Sangamon

Sandra Cisneros

We wake up
and it's him
banging and banging
and the doorknob rattling open up.
His drunk cussing,
her name all over the hallway
and my name mixed in.
He yelling from the other side open
and she yelling from this side no.
A long time of this
and we saying nothing
just hoping he'd get tired and go.
Then the whole door shakes
like his big foot meant to break it.
Then quiet
so we figured he'd gone.
That day he punched her belly
the whole neighborhood watching
that was Tuesday.
So this time we lock it.
And just when we got those kids quiet,
and me, I shut my eyes again,
she laughing,
her cigarette lit,
just then
the big rock comes in.

The Jewelry Collection of Marta la Güera

Mary Helen Ponce

Marta M., nicknamed *la güera,* was married to Don Roque, my father's
compadre, a man called Rocky by everyone but my father. She was slender, of

medium height with fair skin, dark eyes, a straight nose, and eyebrows that arched above her sad eyes. Her hair was worn in a stylish bob; her skin was like fresh buttermilk. From her tiny ears dangled gold earrings in the form of a cross.

A soft-spoken woman, Marta rarely raised her voice nor argued with her loud husband and equally loud kids. She rarely mixed with anyone outside her family, nor did she belong to the Altar Society. When I met her on the street, she smiled politely, then scurried off, her pale dress swishing below her slender knees.

I often visited with Marta's daughters Asunción and Adelina, both of whom went to a private Catholic school and stayed away from the rowdies that lived on Hoyt Street. Mostly I was friends with Adelina, or Lina, as I called her, who was my age, and equally chubby.

Marta and her family lived three blocks away, in a large house with a picture window and furniture bought in Los Angeles. A maroon horsehair sofa sat in the living room; next to it a glass coffeetable. On one wall stood a china cabinet with glass doors which held Rocky's whiskey glasses and assorted candy dishes. To the side were what were called "occasional chairs" covered in a floral print of maroon and green. In the dining room was a mahogany table with eight velvet-covered chairs, two at the head and foot; the others faced each other. Atop the polished table sat crocheted doilies edged in purple, starched stiff, which from afar resembled large fans. In the center of each doily sat a fruit or flower arrangement.

The roomy house had several bedrooms. Asunción's was next to the bathroom; Lina's was toward the back. I thought Lina's bedroom the prettiest of the two, although both had twin beds and a dresser set. Lina's room had pink dotted swiss curtains at each window; the curtain ties were of pink grosgrain ribbon, similar to those used on my curls. Next to Lina's bed was a small table on which sat a ceramic lamp with an etching of a man and woman dressed in silks and lace. The two reminded me of George and Martha Washington's pictures found in textbooks, except for the powdered wigs.

Atop Lina's bed was a pretty taffeta bedspread. Fluffy pillows of various shapes: hearts, squares, and rounds nestled against each other. Each pillow was of pink satin covered in a white crocheted design, made by her grandmother. I thought Lina's family was terribly rich! Not only did they have a fine house, but each girl had her own bed. At home three of my sisters shared a bed!

Marta and Rocky were considered very social. This surprised me being that Marta appeared to be without friends. They gave parties throughout the year: *bautismos,* birthdays, and Christmas parties. Once they gave a party to which my parents were invited. I went too, not because I was invited but because Lina, spoiled rotten, and at eleven already bigger than her mother, threw a fit and insisted I be invited or she would throw a super fit.

"Ay Dios mío, how can you talk that way to your mother?"

"Like this see. *Con la boca*."

"Is this how I raised you? To be so . . ."

"If she don't come I'll break yer dish."

During the party, while Lina served enchiladas saturated with yellow cheese, potato salad, grape punch, and lots of rice and beans, I walked around the house, looking at everything. I ran my hand over the smooth velvet cushions in the living room, fingered the glass ashtrays on the coffeetable, then went into the bathroom and locked the door.

I tiptoed on maroon tile to inspect the white tub and enclosed shower that in the dim light shone like masses of chrome. I fingered the fancy faucets, nearly burning my hands with the hot water that gushed from the one marked H, then flushed the toilet by pulling the handle on the tank. It made a quiet noise compared to the loud gurgling noise made by ours at home. Our toilet, installed by my father when he remodeled our bathroom, had a tank suspended over the commode with a handle and chain that released what I called "Niagara Falls." Often while sitting atop the seat I kept my head sideways just in case the tank fell on me.

That night, while the adults talked, Lina and I snuck into her parent's bedroom.

"Close the door."

"Okay."

"Lock it, I said!"

"I did, see?"

Lina first opened her mother's closet to show me an assortment of dresses, jackets, and coats, including something called a "Wallaby," a fake brown fur that was then quite popular. Lina let me try on the coat while she struggled into a red "box" coat called a Chesterfield, then we both stood in front of the mirror. I looked like a fat bear, Lina like a red refrigerator. Undaunted, we next inspected her mother's size 5 1/2 shoes, none of which fit but looked pretty on our hands. Many had shiny buckles or buttons made of leather. A pair of black-and-white shoes called spectator pumps lay on the closet floor. These were identical to those belonging to my sister Nora, except she wore 6–7. To the side were slippers called "mules" in movie magazines, with pom-poms near the toes.

Exhausted from putting things back in their places, we then took a short break to allow Lina to sneak into the kitchen for goodies. She returned with a glass dish crammed with cookies, pie, cakes, and *empanaditas*. While we gobbled the treats, Lina pulled out a drawer from the maple dresser next to the wall. Inside, on a velvet pad, lay her mother's jewelry: pins, earrings, a rhinestone necklace, a string of matching pearls said to have come from Japan, and assorted trinkets that against the soft velvet, glowed as though alive.

Lina explained that every time her parents had a fight Rocky (as she called her father) lost his temper and hit la güera. The next day he vowed not to do it again. A contrite Rocky climbed into his shiny Buick, then drove to San Fernando to the best store in town where he had a standing account, to buy his wife a small trinket or two.

The jewelry was offered to Marta in exchange for the forgiveness she always gave. The ruby earrings, Lina explained, as she picked her nose, were bought when Rocky punched Marta in the ribs, cracking two at a time. The silver bracelet was given her after Rocky, furious at Marta for smiling at the butcher, twisted Marta's wrist until it cracked. The diamond earrings, tiny droplets of clear shiny crystals, Lina told, wiping her mouth full of jelly, were presented to Marta when, in a rage, Rocky pushed her against the kitchen counter and fractured her collarbone.

Lina was not the least bit ashamed to talk about her parents nor was she afraid of being overheard. *No tenía vergüenza!* Often, while waiting for her to come out to play I heard her screaming at her terrified mother. From far away she sounded just like Rocky.

"You better buy me that dress, or else . . ."

"But mija, it's not your size!"

"Buy it anyway or . . ."

"Ay sí, mijita. Just don't get mad!"

That night we sat cross-legged on the fluffy pink bedspread edged in lace that covered *la güera's* bed like frosting on a cake. I munched on a cookie as piece by piece Lina sifted through her mother's jewelry and recounted their history.

"The opal ring is from Mexico," Lina said, brushing cake crumbs on the pink bedspread. "Rocky went there on business with his friends. When he came home he had something called VD—and the ring, and gave them both to my amá. She gots real sick, but nobody knew what it was. The doctor wanted to examine Rocky, but he said no." Rocky, it seems, called Marta a whore, saying she got the disease from screwing around while he was away. He swore to divorce her until Padre Juanito, sent for by Lina's saintly grandmother, talked him out of it.

"These are from Japan. See how they shine?" Lina held a string of matching pearls to the light, then slowly hung them on me. They were so heavy! I could barely keep my head up. I looked at myself in the mirror then gently removed the necklace and handed it to Lina who continued the story. "One day Rocky came home drunk. He was angry cause his workers had not shown up on time. He caught my mama in the kitchen, then chased her to the bedroom and smacked her until she passed out. The doctor said my apá broke her nose, but Rocky called him a God-Damned liar and told my grandma my mama fell on the maple dresser. Rocky felt real bad. He was scared too cause he thought the doctor might report him. After he paid the doctor—cash—he bought the pearls. The next day we got dressed up and went to visit mama at the hospital. She had a private room, so I got to sit on her bed. Right before we got there Rocky stopped to buy flowers, you know, at the place on the corner. They cost ten dollars. Rocky felt bad. He bought me and Asunción small bouquets too. I dried mine later, but Asunción threw hers in the garbage. She hates Rocky."

"Do you?"

"Neh. Besides, she asked for it."

"Huh?"

"Cause she tried to talk back."

"What about the pearls?"

"What about them?" Lina said, stifling a yawn. She got off the bed, then put the pearls back in their velvet bed. I followed her out the room and to the kitchen where we gorged on chocolate cake.

Marta, she later told me, did not immediately comprehend the pearl's perfection, nor beauty. Her swollen nose and eyes ringed with purpose were covered with gauze. But in time she wore them. They were added to the collection of pins and earrings lying in the drawer.

Soon after, Rocky gifted his wife with a new jewelry box with velvet-lined drawers, one large enough to hold the growing jewelry collection of Marta la güera.

Do You Take?

Bernice Zamora

so you wish to marry me,
wash for me, clean for me,
type my papers, tie my shoes,
iron my clothes, and cook for me.
So it would please you to be
this woman's wife.

No, querido.
I would not ask
that of another
human being.

Para un Revolucionario

Lorna Dee Cervantes

You speak of art
and your soul is like snow,
a soft powder raining from your
mouth,
covering my breasts and hair.
You speak of your love of mountains,
freedom,
and your love for a sun
whose warmth is like una liberación
pouring down upon brown bodies.
Your books are of the souls of men,
carnales with a spirit
that no army, pig or ciudad
could ever conquer.
You speak of a new way,
a new life.

When you speak like this
I could listen forever.

Pero your voice is lost to me, carnal,
in the wail of tus hijos,
in the clatter of dishes
and the pucker of beans upon the stove.
Your conversations come to me
de la sala where you sit,
spreading your dream to brothers,
where you spread that dream like damp clover
for them to trod upon,
when I stand here reaching

para ti con manos bronces that spring from mi espíritu[7]
(for I too am Raza).

Pero, it seems I can only touch you
with my body.
You lie with me
and my body es la hamaca
that spans the void between us.

Hermano Raza,
I am afraid that you will lie with me
and awaken too late
to find that you have fallen
and my hands will be left groping
for you and your dream
in the midst of la revolución.

A Woman Was Raped

Veronica Cunningham

a woman
was raped
by her father
yesterday
and she was only
thirteen
and
i never laugh
at rape jokes
another woman
was raped
on her first date
and
i kant laugh
at rape
i just kant laugh

---

7. for you with bronzed hands that spring from my spirit

at rape
another
was raped
by a man
of a different
color
political
perhaps,
fucked
for sure
another woman
by her husband
but that's
with the law
of property
and another
and another
and another
they have been
violated
by more
than a penis
they've suffered
by the law
with policemen
in the courts
in society
inside themselves
  with guilt
  or shame
because
people believe
the victim
  should be
  blamed
and i'll be raped
with every
woman
yet
i kant laugh
i kant forget

For Virginia Chávez

Lorna Dee Cervantes

It was never in the planning,
in the life we thought
we'd live together, two fast
women living cheek to cheek,
still tasting the dog's
breath of boys in our testy
new awakening.
We were never the way they had it planned.
Their wordless tongues we stole
and tasted the power
that comes of that.
We were never what they wanted
but we were bold. We could take
something of life and not
give it back. We could utter
the rules, mark the lines
and cross them ourselves—we two
women using our fists, we thought,
our wits, our tunnels. They were such
dumb hunks of warm fish
swimming inside us,
but this was love,
we knew, love, and that was all
we were ever offered.

You were always alone
so another lonely life
wouldn't matter.
In the still house
your mother left you,
when the men were gone
and the television droned
into test patterns, with our cups
of your mother's whiskey
balanced between the brown thighs
creeping out of our shorts, I read
you the poems of Lord Byron, Donne,

the Brownings: all about love,
explaining the words
before realizing that you knew
all that the kicks in your belly
had to teach you. You were proud
of the woman blooming out of your
fourteen lonely years, but you cried
when you read that poem I wrote you,
something about our "waning moons"
and the child in me
I let die that summer.

In the years that separate,
in the tongues that divide
and conquer, in the love
that was a language
in itself, you never spoke,
never regret. Even
that last morning
I saw you with blood
in your eyes, blood
on your mouth, the blood
pushing out of you
in purple blossoms.

He did this.
When I woke, the kids
were gone. They told me
I'd never get them back.

With our arms holding
each other's waists, we walked
the waking streets
back to your empty flat,
ignoring the horns and catcalls
behind us, ignoring what
the years had brought between us:
my diploma and the bare bulb
that always lit your bookless room.

Crow

Lorna Dee Cervantes

She started and shot from the pine,
then brilliantly settled in the west field
and sunned herself purple.

I saw myself: twig and rasp, dry
in breath and ammonia smelling.
Women taught me to clean

and then build my own house.
Before men came they whispered,
Know good polished oak.

Learn hammer and Phillips.
Learn socket and rivet. I ran
over rocks and gravel they placed

by hand, leaving burly arguments
to fester the bedrooms. With my best jeans,
a twenty and a shepherd pup, I ran

flushed and shadowed by no one
alone   I settled   stiff in mouth
with the words women gave me.

FOUR

Spaces

spaces are the things you know exist
the talents that go unrecognized
                    IRENE BLEA

No one told me
So how was I to know
that in the paradise
of crisp white cities
snakes still walk
upright?
        ANGELA DE HOYOS

The response to environment by Chicana writers encompasses both interior and exterior landscapes. Landscape can be defined as a perceptual response to the land: its natural features, in terms of mountains, rivers, and deserts, as well as its human features—houses, towns, and cities. One's psychological space as well as one's physical location in landscape are interconnected. Spaces are "perceived" according to one's own cultural shaping; a sense of place or alienation from place can be an aspect of landscape. Landscape is also inevitably tinged with smells, foods, colors, emotional connectedness, psychological closeness or distancing, nostalgia, and individual history. The idea of landscape is, therefore, a complex one that often is shaped by individual history, culture, and emotions. How Chicana writers respond to their interior and exterior environment and to natural and human spaces are the subjects of the explorations in this chapter.

The early Hispanic women writers included in this study, generally writing in English in the early twentieth century, were already feeling a sense of loss of culture, and history, as well as economic losses. The New Mexican writers, particularly Fabiola Cabeza de Baca, Nina Otero-Warren, and Cleofas Jaramillo, were acutely aware of the passing of Hispanic economic and social power, and were concerned about preserving in writing what they considered to be "their" stories, "their" heritage. Consequently, they recorded in an autobiographical manner folktales, family tales, and their own experiences and history. They also felt it important to record recipes in cookbooks that extolled the native ingredients and preparation of Mexican, Spanish, and New Mexican foods. The harvest from the land was, therefore, important to the cultural landscapes of these women.

The overriding perception in terms of response to natural landscape on the part of these early writers is that the Southwest of their youth was a fertile, pastoral garden of Eden, blessed by cool crystal waters and verdant springs—the desert landscape, while barren at times, was, when it rained, also a "field" of cactus, gamma grass, and yucca. Pastoral, romantic elements in this psychological landscape included the sense of community well-being as a varied set of people, Native Americans, and Hispanics lived on the land in harmony (at least according to these writers). The Edenic, idyllic living is destroyed by the coming of Anglo settlers, the disintegration of the Hispanic economic and social systems, and change; traditional ways are no longer possible. The sense of dismay at the loss of Spanish land grants and the disintegration of the culture are reflected in the natural landscape, which, destroyed by drought and antiquated land use practices, is imaged as a sand-filled house and barren environment.

In the words of Cabeza de Baca, all that remains of the Hispanic presence in many areas are Spanish place names—place names that new arrivals, speaking no Spanish, are unable to understand, place names that have lost their significance. Thus, for these New Mexican writers, the geographical landscape parallels the cultural, social landscape.

The loss of a rural, agricultural way of life and disconnection from land and place in the twentieth century are followed by a migration on the part of many families to the towns and cities. The New Mexican experience is paralleled in Texas, California, Arizona, and Colorado. Often, the Spanish-speaking families lived together in Spanish-speaking neighborhoods—at times also settled by newly arrived immigrants from Mexico. The continual waves of new immigration reinforce "Mexicanness" in terms of food, language, and culture, while at the same time placing economic and social strains on the already established residents in these areas. Many of the neighborhoods deteriorated over the years and became urban, Spanish-speaking ghettos. The word *barrio,* which simply means neighborhood, is translated is some areas as "slum."

The change from rural to urban often signals a change from exterior spaces to interior spaces. Where before writers may have commented on mountains, rivers, and even towns from an exterior perspective, we begin to see the transformation to interiors of rooms and houses—spaces that then become traditional "female" spaces. The move to the city also institutes more compartmentalization of women's lives. These interior spaces are often enclosing and narrowing. Kitchens, which epitomize women's work in terms of food preparation and production, also delineate symbolically the nurturing aspect of many women.

In much Chicana literature, kitchens are closely associated with grandmothers and with cultural values related to the Spanish language and family traditions. Food is generally commented on in terms of Mexican staples—*tortillas, frijoles,* and *tamales*—not in terms of more Americanized food. And while the kitchen can enclose and enslave, generally speaking it is a nourishing and nurturing safe haven where the writers can return for emotional and psychological sustenance in terms of female support via their *abuelitas,* mothers, and sisters.

The houses of these urban settings are also seen in terms of the ambivalent images of kitchens and food. On the one hand, as in Sandra Cisneros' *The House on Mango St.,* it may be a poor dwelling and not the home her family wants, a house to be ashamed of vis-à-vis the outside world; nevertheless, it may also be a structure that protects and nurtures the female, one in which growth takes place.

Venturing forth from home into the school situation, the first truly "public" space the child experiences is often traumatic for both female and male children, as recorded in the literature. Those Chicanas writing often experienced now questionable education practices of language and culture denial. They were often punished both physically as well as psychologically for speaking Spanish in school. Many who came from rural or immigrant families may have suffered the trauma experienced in encountering cultural as well as language difference for the first time. Their encounters with these traumas is clearly recorded in their memories and in their writing. The school then is often portrayed as a negative space, a space of shyness and culture shock, of racial intolerance where one eats tortillas or rice sandwiches and everyone laughs at you, a place populated by generally uncomprehending teachers, nuns, and principals.

Often in this literature other public spaces fare equally badly. Any confrontation with the "outside" dominant culture produces conflict of cultural values and a varying degree of interactions with authorities. These writers, often the only bilingual speakers in their families, become translators. Their "translations" make them the mediators between two cultures, between the public sphere of school and work, and their families. Thus Lorna Dee Cervantes becomes the "translator" for foreign mail, that is, bills, government notices, and so forth, and Alma Villanueva becomes the "translator" between her aging grandmother and hospital authorities.

In addition, such public spaces as hospitals and doctors' offices are seen as other negative spaces. Social systems and institutions designed to help and provide services for those in need are also shown in a bad light, although perhaps realistically, in this literature.

For the adult, the city is thus seen as a jungle where women are on a frontier fighting for survival against overwhelming forces of poverty, drugs, and death. The city, shining land of opportunity, signals only struggle and often destruction for them, their families, and their culture. The barrio, as opposed to the city, however, once again represents a dual image. There is poverty in the barrio; there is sickness; there is desperation; yet there is also a sense of connectedness to family, neighbors, and community. The barrio may cause fear in the hearts of outsiders; yet, as Cisneros states in "Those Who Don't," "we aren't afraid. We know the guy with the crooked eye is Davey the Baby's brother, and the tall one next to him in the straw brim that's Rosa's Eddie V. and the big one that looks like a dumb grown man, he's Fat Boy, through he's not fat anymore nor a boy" (Cisneros, *House,* 29).

Another public place that symbolizes the emancipation of Chicanas—their freedom from traditional home and societal—values is the *cantina* (bar, tavern). Much Chicana literature is written about what critic María Herrera-Sobek calls "cantina" culture. That is, Chicanas symbolically enter public places formerly reserved for, or inhabited only by, men. Herrera-Sobek sees this as the "seizing" of public space by women.

When Chicana writers turn once again to outdoor spaces, it is the freeway that symbolizes both destruction and progress. Generally, freeways have been built through the slum areas, and often in southwestern and western cities this has been the Spanish-speaking barrio. As Patricia Preciado Martin says, "The Freeway has cut the river from the people. The Freeway blocks the sunshine. The drone of the traffic buzzes like a giant unsleeping bee, a new music in the barrio" ("The Journey"). Yet the freeway, such an integral part of modern life, also symbolizes freedom, the ability to travel, to return to one's roots, or to travel to find new ones.

The psychological space of living between two or more cultures, languages, and histories is part of the mestiza consciousness that pervades all of the works in this chapter. It is also a part of the consciousness that permeates other works in this anthology. Crossing borders, bridging borders, or simply recognizing the limits of the borders are an integral aspect of Chicana writing and of Chicana literature. Thus the texts in this chapter illustrate the plurality of spaces that Chicanas inhabit, from the specifically female environment to the public arenas of their social and cultural interactions.

■ ■ ■

La Casa / The House

María Herrera-Sobek

Te veo parada
desolada
con los rayos del sol
salpicados
en tu cabellera
de tejas negras.
Oscura
sola
quedas como la cueva
de un hermitaño
al cual se le ha
apagado su fuego.
Tus entrañas
sólo emiten
silencio.
El fuego
que ensanchaba
tus paredes
que bailaba
en las ventanas
y abría tus puertas
se ha alejado.

Ahora
taciturna
sólo sueñas
pensativa
escuchas
los pasos lentos
de las nubes
que a tus espaldas
murmuran
compadecidas
de tu enorme
vacío.

■

I see you standing
desolate
with the sun's rays
spattered
on your hair
of black roof-tiles.
Dark
alone
you remain like the cave
of a hermit
whose
fire has died down.
Your bowels
send out only
silence.
The fire
that widened
your walls
that danced
on the windows
and opened your doors
has gone away.

Now
taciturn
you dream alone
pensive
you listen to
the slow steps
of the clouds
that murmur
at your shoulders
compassionate
of your enormous
emptiness.

kitchen talk

Evangelina Vigil-Piñón

speaking of the many
tragedies that come in
life most times unexpectedly
I uttered with resolution,
"nunca sabe uno lo que le va
traer la vida de un momento
al otro."[1]

sintiendo en un instante
todo lo que ha sentido en su vida
responde mi abuela
"no, pues no,"[2]
thought perfectly balanced
with routine rinsing of coffee cups and spoons
"¡qué barbaridad!
pues si supiera uno,
¡pues qué bárbaro!"[3]

New Year's Eve

Rina García Rocha

Did you seem to forget in the old
days back in '61–'62?
When all the aunts, grandma and you—
Be in the kitchen making tamales?
Some teaching their teenage daughters
to spread masa evenly over corn
husks.

---

1. "No one ever knows what life has in store for one, from one moment to the next."
2. Feeling in an instant everything she has felt in her lifetime my grandmother responds, "No, certainly not."
3. "How absurd! / if one only knew. / How incredible!"

It was New Year's Eve
and everyone under one roof.
The men drinking, talking music and
politics, sitting in the living
room smoking cigarettes.
The Christmas tree still standing
looking six feet tall.
Up,
    Up on top a Santa Claus with a
flashing red light for a nose.

Tamales won't be done until
ten o'clock or eleven o'clock

The women would say.

While we, the children ran from
one room to another screaming,
not it! not it!

Pedro Infante's voice pierced above
our heads from the cheap phonograph.
Dancing began on the dining room
floor.
Mommies swished their bell shape
dresses,
Fathers with those baggy trousers.

It was polka time, that New Year's Eve
in our five room apartment . . .
remember?

Section 5 from *Mother, May I?*

Alma Villanueva

5
the nun asked to look at
my hands. I thought she thought
they were beautiful, so I

put them out
and she hit them with
a ruler. it hurt it hurt
and she told me to
put them out
again and I wouldn't and she
tried to grab my hands so
I grabbed the ruler and hit
her and ran
home and my grandma let me
stay when she saw
my hands. there was
a beautiful young nun who
spoke spanish and english and she
sat in the dark on the other
side of the cage. the metal was black
and cold and beautiful. it had flowers
and I loved to put my face on it, it
felt so good and cold.
and when she came and sat and spoke
her voice was very warm. she
said she came from mexico. I
bet she didn't let them shave
her head. this boy who was
very bad sat behind me
and he put his fingers in my *nalgas*
when we prayed at him, he'd
smell them and smile. he
whispered one time in the yard
—they all have bald heads—

Spaces like the Barrio

Irene Blea

"they left spaces in my mind"
    that's what it's like
        living in the barrio

spaces are left in the mind
   knowing something else exists
      but you're addicted to the city
         family and friends

it's safe there in the barrio
   you can handle it
      no one expects anything
         all you have to do is stay alive
            and keep out of trouble

spaces are the things you know exist
   the talents that go unrecognized
      because the fear of failing
         while grasping opportunity
            that exists elsewhere
               is much too overwhelming

The Truth in My Eyes

Rina García Rocha

Taking a walk down 26th street
passing "La Luz del Norte,"
the strip joint,
Veracruz Barber Shop,
Doña Lupita's Supermercado,
and the currency exchange with the sign
  "Se Habla Español"
Ah, Latino Barrio
Is this the ghetto?
Passing Mexico Lindo Photo's
a window display of staring faces
nicely printed up
specializing in weddings and passport pictures

I see a shop full of dreams

Then there are still the slick catty women
with streaked Frankensteinish hair,

with black crescent eyeliner
Didn't realize time went on to the 70s
People, People all from the same nation
Living, hassling, packed
Two boys down the block been shooting rats with
their B-B guns behind a capitalist back door restaurant
Wild game available and plenty

Came up close to a dead body of one of the rats

Came up close enough to see how the shiny little bodies of
the flies nested
filth—
Disgust,
as I smash the maggots on the cobble stone alley . . .

The Journey

Patricia Preciado Martin

Dedicated to my sister, Elena,
and my husband, Jim:

In the warm and sun-filled days
I remember in the haze
The happy sounds of children laughing,
The rustle of the cottonwoods.
Now all is old and cold and dark
Underneath Presidio Park.

The bell rings, the bus slows, and finally stops. I get off at the corner of
Fifth and Congress. One North Fifth Avenue. The MARTIN LUTHER KING JR.
APARTMENTS. LOW COST HOUSING FOR THE ELDERLY. Gray concrete walls
five stories high. Honorable Mayor James M. Corbett, Jr. Honorable Coun-
cilmen Richard Kennedy, Kirk Storch, Conrad Joyner, Rudy Castro, and John
Steiger. *Anno Domini* 1969.

I go through the double-wide glass doors of the apartment building.
(ENTER HERE ONLY.) Electronically operated. The high-ceilinged waiting
room is painted bright yellow (to make it seem cheerful). The room is bare
except for a few weatherbeaten chairs and scarred coffee tables cluttered with
tattered magazines. GOOD HOUSEKEEPING—"Decorate A Bedroom With

Sheets." U.S. NEWS AND WORLD REPORT—"The Effect of Arab Oil Prices on Wall Street." COSMOPOLITAN—"How To Tell If Your Husband Is Faithful." The black-and-white TV drones on, addressing no one in particular. The elevator clanks along noisily. (UP: DOWN: PRESS BUTTON ONLY ONCE.) A few viejitos are coming and going with purpose. Some are waiting for the mail. Some are waiting for visitors. Some are just waiting.

And Tía is there, as always. Every Saturday. Summer or winter, spring or fall, for the last two years. Except when the weather is too cold or too wet. It can never be too hot. Her small delicate figure is nearly lost in the big overstuffed chair (Donated by the Cochran Family; In Memory of Our Son, Lawrence, Jr.; Cochran Realty and Investments). Tía is waiting for me. Quietly, primly, regally, her hands folded in her lap. She is wearing a shawl and a small knit hat. A flowered print dress and black stockings and shoes.

"Ah, mihijita, ya llegaste." I take her arm, and she rises to her feet, not without difficulty. On one arm she carries a straw bag, and on the other a worn black umbrella (just in case). We walk slowly out the wide glass doors (EXIT HERE ONLY) into the late morning sunshine.

"Qué bueno que llegaste temprano. Tengo mucho que hacer, y la tienda está lejos. It is good that you arrived early. I have a lot to do, and the store is far away."

We begin our walk; our journey. Every Saturday she insists on taking the same route. Across town. Down Congress Street. Past the Regal Cigar Store (MAGAZINES, CIGARS, NOVELTIES). Past the Discount Clothing City (GANGAS HOY! 60 DAYS TO PAY! SE HABLA ESPAÑOL). Past the empty store windows with the dusty, limbless mannequins. We walk slowly, without talking. We turn on South Sixth Avenue and go south, past the numerous bars and liquor stores. A hippie plays a guitar for quarters in front of the O.K. Bar. We walk past Armory Park. Winter visitors are playing shuffleboard in the sunshine and winos are sleeping in the grass. On Ochoa Street we turn west again and walk toward the gleaming white towers of the Cathedral. San Agustín. The Dove of the Desert. The pigeons flutter over our heads when the noon bells chime. Sr. Enríquez, the old bell chimer, died long ago. He climbed the rickety stairs to the bell tower three times a day for more years than anyone could remember. One day he climbed up and played the Noon Angelus and never climbed down again. They found him with the bell rope still in his hands. Now the Angelus is a recorded announcement.

Tía laboriously climbs the concrete steps to the vestibule of the Cathedral. I open the heavy carved doors for her and she makes her way into the cool darkness. The perfume of the incense from the early morning funeral Mass still lingers in the air.

(Sra. Juanita Mendoza. Born in Tucson of a Pioneer Family, Grandfather

Eight Children. Twelve Grandchildren. Seven Great-Grandchildren.)

Down, down, the long corridor Tía walks until she reaches the side chapel of the Virgen de Guadalupe. La Madre de Nosotros. La Reina de Las Américas. She lights a small vigil candle and prays for the souls of husbands and brothers and sons. The ones who have died or lost their souls in Los Angeles. Father Carrillo walks by, intent on something. Cuentas and almas. Bills and souls. El Padre. Son of Barrio Anita. The pride of the people. "Y cómo estás, Doña Luz?" He grasps her hand warmly.

We walk out once more into the brightness. Past an elegant old home that is now a funeral parlor. Down South Meyer and west on Cushing Street. Past a sign that says Barrio Histórico. THIS AREA HAS BEEN OFFICIALLY DESIGNATED AS AN HISTORICAL LANDMARK AND IS OFFICIALLY REGISTERED WITH THE NATIONAL REGISTER OF HISTORICAL PLACES. In Bronze. Most of the houses in the Barrio Histórico are owned by Mr. Kelly Rollings, a local automobile dealer and millionaire and amateur anthropologist. He owns the old Robles House. It is now the Cushing Street Bar. "EAT, DRINK AND BE MERRY IN AN AUTHENTIC RESTORED OLD ADOBE."

"That's where the Robles' lived," Tía tells me, in Spanish. "They had a piano. The Señora played beautifully. Everyone would come to listen. People would leave flowers on her doorstep." She continued. "On Sundays we would all walk down for the Paseo in the Plaza of the Cathedral. Sometimes we would walk down to the river. (It had water then! Can you believe that the Santa Cruz had water?!) In the summers we would picnic under the cool shade of the cottonwood trees. Everywhere there was music."

We continue south on Convent Street. Mr. Ortega is sitting on his porch. He pays his rent now to Coldwell and Banker, based in New York. "Buenas Tardes, Doña Luz." "Buenas Tardes, Don Felipe." We walk on slowly. Tía continues. "His father and his grandfather had tierras by the river. Everywhere it was green. They grew flowers and vegetables. And oh! The flowers! The perfume was everywhere in the summer breezes. His father, Don Raimundo, sold vegetables from a cart. All of us children would run after the cart. He gave us free sugar cane. Now the river is dry. The milpas are gone and the people are gone. (The river had water then! Can you believe that the Santa Cruz had water?!)

The Freeway had cut the river from the people. The Freeway blocks the sunshine. The drone of the traffic buzzes like a giant unsleeping bee. A new music in the barrio.

On down South Convent. Past the old Padilla House. THIS HOUSE IS A REGISTERED HISTORICAL LANDMARK. In brass. It is being renovated. The sign has gone up. LOS ARCOS. ANTIQUES, PRIMITIVES, AND COLLECTIBLES.

At last we arrive at our destination. Romero's Convent Street Market. Tía opens the screen door. RAINBOW BREAD IS GOOD. Rafael Romero. Patriarch of the Barrio. Mr. Rollings has offered him a good price. Mr. Romero has no price, but he has no sons either. "Buenas Tardes, Doña Luz." "Buenas Tardes, Don Rafael." Tía fills her bag. The ancient cash register rings and whirs metallically. Queso blanco. Salsa de tomate. Campbell's Chicken Noodle Soup. White bread. Tortillas de maíz. Tortillas de harina. Cheerios. Pan Mexicano. Coffee. Saladitos for me. "Gracias Doña Luz. Hasta luego."

Then around the corner. Down South Main. I follow unquestioning. I know that the journey is not over. There is always one more destination. Toward the Tucson Community Center Complex. The Pride of Tucson. MUSIC HALL. LITTLE THEATRE, CONVENTION HALL. CONCERT ARENA. URBAN RE-NEWAL. Honorable Mayor James M. Corbett, Jr. Honorable Councilmen William Ruck, Ramon Castillo, Richard Kennedy, Robert Royal, and Conrad Joyner, *Anno Domini,* 1971. Concrete walls, and steps, and fountains. Fountains, fountains, everywhere. (The river had water then! Can you believe that the Santa Cruz had water?!)

The pace of Tía quickens now. I follow her, carrying the straw bag laden with groceries. We walk past the Concert Hall to the vast parking lot of the Community Center Complex. A billboard reads: CONCERT TONIGHT. ALICE COOPER. SOLD OUT. We stop in the middle of the parking lot. The winter sun is warm. The heat rises from the black asphalt. The roar of the Freeway is even more distinct. It is the end of the journey. I know what Tía will say.

"Aquí estaba mi casita. It was my father's house. And his father's house before that. They built it with their own hands with adobes made from the mud of the river. All their children were born here. I was born here. It was a good house, a strong house. When it rained, the adobes smelled like the good clean earth."

She pauses. She sees shadows I cannot see. She hears melodies I cannot hear. "See, here! I had a fig tree growing. In the summer I gave figs to the neighbors and the birds. And there—I hung a clay olla with water to sip from on the hot summer days. We always had a breeze from the river. I had a bougainvillea; it was so beautiful! Brilliant red. And I had roses and a little garden. Right here where I am standing my comadres and I would sit and visit in the evenings. We would watch the children run and play in the streets. There was no traffic then. And there was laughter everywhere."

"Ah, well," she sighs. "Ya es tarde. It is time to go." I turn to follow her and then turn to look once more to the place where her casita once stood. I look across the parking lot. I look down. "Tía, Tía," I call. "Ven!" She turns and comes toward me. "Look!" I say excitedly. "There is a flower that has pushed its way through the asphalt! It is blooming!"

"Ah, mihijita," she says at last. Her eyes are shining. "You have found out the secret of our journeys."

"What secret, Tía?"

"Que las flores siempre ganan. The flowers always win."

We turn away from the sun that is beginning to drop in the West. I take her arm again. There is music everywhere.

Refrain

ABUELITA, ABUELITA,
ABUELITA, NO LLORES.
TE TRAIGO, TE TRAIGO, TE TRAIGO
UNA RAMITA DE FLORES.[4]

was fun running 'round descalza

Evangelina Vigil-Piñón

barefoot is how I always used to be
running barefoot
like on that hot summer
in the San Juan Projects
they spray-painted all the buildings
pastel pink, blue, green, pale yellow, gray
and in cauldrons tar bubbling, steaming
(time to repair the roofs)
its white smoke filling summer air with aromas of nostalgia
for the future
and you, barefoot,
tender feet jumping with precision
careful not to land on nest of burrs or stickers
careful not to tread too long on sidewalks
converted by the scorching sun into comales
"¡se puede freír hasta un huevo en esas banquetas!"
exclamaba la gente

---

4. Grandmother, grandmother / Grandmother, don't cry. / I bring you, I bring you, I bring you / a little bunch of flowers.

ese verano tan caliente[5]
no sooner than had the building wall/canvasses been painted clean
did barrio kids take to carving new inspirations
and chuco hieroglyphics
and new figures drawings of naked women
and their parts
and messages for all
"la Diana es puta"
"el Lalo es joto"
y que "la Chelo se deja"[6]
decorated by hearts and crosses
and war communications
among rivaling gangs
El Circle
La India
pretty soon kids took to just plain peeling plastic pastel paint
to unveil historical murals
of immediate past well-remembered:
más monas encueradas[7]
and "Lupe loves Tony"
"always and forever"
"Con Safos"
y "Sin Safos"
y que "El Chuy es relaje"
and other innocent desmadres de la juventud[8]
secret fear in every child
que su nombre apareciera allí
y la música de los radios
animando[9]

> "Do you wanna dance under the moonlight?
> Kiss me baby, all through the night
> Oh, baby, do you wanna dance?"

---

5. "you can fry an egg on those sidewalks!" / the people would say / that hot summer
6. "Diana is a whore" / "Lalo is a queer" / "Chelo is easy"
7. more naked-women drawings
8. youthful peccadillos
9. that their name would appear there / and the radio music / blaring

was fun running 'round descalza
playing hopscotch
correr sin pisar las líneas—
te vas con el diablo[10]

was fun running 'round descalza
shiny brown legs leaping with precision
to avoid nido de cadillos[11] crowned with tiny blossoms pink
to tread but ever so lightly on scorching cement
to cut across street glistening with freshly laid tar
its steam creating a horizon of mirages
rubber thongs sticking, smelting
to land on cool dark clover carpet green
in your child's joyful mind
"Got to get to la tiendita, buy us
some popsicles and Momma's Tuesday Light!"

was fun running 'round descalza

Caminitos[12]

Carmen Tafolla

The pathways of my thoughts are cobbled with
  mesquite blocks
    and narrow-winding,
  long and aged like the streets of
    san fernando de bexar
      y la villa real de san antonio.

pensive
  y callados
cada uno con su chiste[13]
  idiosyncracy
    crazy turns

---

10. go with the devil
11. birds' nest
12. little roads
13. and silent / each one with their joke

that are because they are,
   centuries magic
      and worn smooth,
         still intricate.
cada uno hecho así,[14]
   y with a careful
      capricho touch,
         así.

They curl slowly into ripples,
   earthy and cool like the Río Medina
            under the trees
silently singing, standing still,
   and flowing, becoming,
      became
         and always as always,
            still fertile, laughing, loving,
               alivianada
            Río Medina,
               under the trees,
                  celebrating life.

They end up in the monte, chaparral,
   llenos de burrs, spurs
      pero libres[15]
Running through the hills freefoot
   con aire azul,[16]
blue breaths peacefully taken
   between each lope
      remembering venado,
         remembering conejos,[17]
            remembering
               where
                  we came from.

---

14. each one made like that
15. full of . . . but free
16. with blue air
17. deer . . . rabbits

Roads

Barbara Brinson Curiel

I. HIGHWAY 12, LODI TO DIXON, LUNES

I migrate into my history
these cool mornings
I return weekly
to the first graders,
expecting to yank them
from these fields
with ditto sheets and chalk.

Mis abuelos
pensaron haberse ya lavado
todo este polvo
de sus pies y manos
con el agua tubérculo
de San Francisco

Pero regresan en mí.[18]
Tomatoes rise to greet us:
dusty red moons.
They border our camp
on three sides.

II. JUNCTION, HIGHWAY 12, DIXON

Morning glories are pressed
into maestra's hand.

All day
tiny fingers

braid songs
into my hair,

reach
for an open palm,

for gold rings
around the valley sun.

---

18. My grandparents / thought they had already washed off / all of this dust / from their feet and hands / with the tubercular water / of San Francisco / But they return in me.

They search for tides
in irrigation canals.

III. WINTER, LODI
I dream of you, all of you,
huddled against brothers and sisters
in icy beds.

I dream of your empty cupboards
in Texas,
Jalisco,
Michoacán.

I dream of
young birds,
their mouths stretched open,
of armless grape trees
standing in fog.

Here, in the Sacramento Valley,
corn husks
lie slivered on frozen fields;
this year's tomatoes
have fallen from your hands
into other people's jars.

Like seeds,
you are left out to dry
over Winter.

Only God has arms
enough to warm you.

The Valley of the Sun

Gina Valdés

Father Agustín was determined to celebrate Christmas Day with the
farmworkers of the valley. He had prepared a special sermon and several
Christmas songs he had collected as a boy in Mexico. As he neared the Valley
of the Sun he saw the dark clouds clustered above him, shading everything.

The green hadn't dried, it was only hidden like the sun. The animals huddled in the corrals protecting themselves against the storm. He recalled the last confrontation with Father Doherty, the rector of The Holy Trinity.

"If you don't want me to come, why don't you learn Spanish so you can serve all the people of the valley."

"They're the ones that should learn English."

"The shepherd always learns to call his flock."

"They're not my flock."

"All of the Catholics in town are, and they all deserve to be treated well."

"They don't support the church as they should, like the other people of this town."

"They don't have as much money as the other people."

"They earn the same."

"How can you talk so much nonsense? You're an incredible man. Besides having so many prejudices, you try to cover them up with stupid lies."

"Watch your words; you're speaking to your superior."

"My superior is in heaven; only He tells me what to do. He and my people. And anyway, I only speak the truth."

"When 'your people' give more money to the church, I'll treat them better."

"They give what they can. They don't have more money. You want to take the food from their mouths?"

"Or the beer. They've got money for that—for beer and for parties."

"Since you don't have zest for life, you don't want anyone else to have it."

"That's enough of your insults! I know what I'm doing. And if you continue to harass me, I will call the bishop and tell him of your rudeness."

"I will also speak to the bishop."

"He won't listen to you."

Father Agustín clenched his teeth and his anger leaped out of his eyes to strike Father Doherty. He saw the rector turning pale. He knew that what he was saying was true, since he had tried to contact the bishop on several occasions without any luck. He knew that he had to look for other resources. "Do as you please, but I will continue to come. The people of the valley need me; you don't take care of them, so I will. And as long as they ask me to come, I'll keep on coming."

Candles glittering in the dark, scent of burning wax, of tinkling incense, glistening eyes of saints, echoes of litany, red wounds of the sacrificed Christ, impassioned devotion, penance, reverence. With these images stamped on him, Agustín the altar boy left Todosantos, Michoacán, with his parents and five brothers, seeking, like many, a house with water, light, and indoor plumbing, three meals a day. In California they worked from farm to farm, finding in each what they had tried to escape. He didn't lose his love of hymn and candle, and always after work he walked to the nearest church. It had been ten years since he had been ordained and had worked as a priest in many town churches in California. As soon as he became close to the people, he was transferred.

Night was approaching, darkening the valley further. As usual Father Agustín arrived at the church half an hour before mass. The doors were open and there were already people inside. He stepped out of his car and entered Father Doherty's office. The spacious, well-ordered room was lit by a single weak lamp that in the dark room looked like a piece of sun trapped between black clouds. He found Father Doherty as usual, sitting at his desk examining papers with his shaky pale hands. The two men looked at each other like animals of different species. The rector caught the priest's gleaming black eyes and hair, fast panther movements. Father Agustín noted Father Doherty's old snake head, small eyes, dry narrow mouth.

"I'm here as I told you last Saturday, to give Christmas Day mass."

"You can't give mass."

"What?"

"You didn't call me."

"Last Saturday I told you I was coming."

"But you didn't confirm it. I've told you many times that it's necessary to do so."

"The people are waiting for me; I have no time to argue."

"Neither do I. Go tell them that there won't be any mass, to go home."

"Don't you know how hard it is for them to come to church? Many of them live in the hills, out of town, and today they have come in the rain, some on foot, only to hear mass."

"I already gave mass this morning."

"In English. The bosses already had mass. Now it's the workers' turn."

"You're not saying mass. That's an order. And if you don't follow my orders, you'll have trouble."

"Don't try to scare me with your threats. I know the politics of the church as well as you do. It doesn't scare me."

"Well, if you know so well, you know what you're in for." Father Agustín began to put on his frock, and Father Doherty continued talking.

"Why are you changing? You're not saying mass."

"Whether you like it or not, I'm saying mass. Because I promised to do so, and because like all good Christians, they deserve it."

"When they support the church like good Christians, then they'll deserve mass."

"You can't put a price on people."

"The church doesn't run by itself."

"It doesn't lack anything.

"Because I know how to handle money. Not like these people who . . ."

Father Agustín left Father Doherty talking to himself and walked into the church that was by now filling. Father Doherty followed him to the altar, repeating to him in a weak voice that reached Father Agustín's ears like a hiss. "Don't prepare anything, you're not giving mass."

"I came to give mass and that's what I'm going to do."

"Don't speak so loud."

"That's the way I speak, so I can be heard."

"They're not good Christians, they don't deserve mass."

"You want to take away Saint Joseph from them, you want to take away Mary, what do you want to leave them, the donkey?"

"Leave this church! You're not saying mass!"

Standing in the middle of the altar, Father Agustín turned to face the farmworkers who filled the church and said to them, "He says no, but I say yes." When he turned toward the altar again, Father Doherty was no longer there. Suddenly, everything darkened as if the black clouds had entered the church. "He turned off the lights. That's going too far." He noticed that several people were shivering. "He's turned on the air conditioning. That's the limit!" He saw some of the parishioners hiding in their coats and moving closer to each other. He walked down the altar steps and said, "Sometimes the devil enters even into the church. Wait for me a minute. I'll be back."

Soon after Father Agustín stepped out of the church the lights went on. When he reentered the church the lights went off and the air began to cool again. He took a lit candle from the altar and began to light the other candles. Several people stood up and helped him light all the candles in the church. When the priest noticed that many had buttoned their coats and settled in their seats, he began mass.

Everyone prayed and sang with the same enthusiasm as Father Agustín, accompanied by the tapping of the rain. When he stood in the pulpit and saw the golden hue of the church, he felt the candles not only gave light, but warmth. He stepped down to stand closer to the people. Saving the sermon that he had prepared, he spoke what he felt at the moment, as fervently as he prayed and sang. "Let's blow life into faith and hope."

Everyone stood up to sing one last Christmas song of celebration. Father Agustín kept on singing in his strong voice as he walked towards the door. From there he gave his farewell to everyone present, shaking their hands firmly, wishing them a Merry Christmas, and promising that he would return the following Saturday.

When he stepped out into the street, Father Agustín saw that the black night had swallowed a few clouds, and that the moon was beginning to taste the night.

Fecundating

Bernice Zamora

A carved and jutting mountain
waits for us in Southern Colorado.
There are chokecherries to be picked,
piñons to be roasted, and
alfalfa fields to harvest
before the snows come.

The mountain heaves for us.

El retorno

Gloria Anzaldúa

All movements are accomplished in six stages,
and the seventh brings return.
—I CHING

Tanto tiempo sin verte casa mía
mi cuna, mi hondo nido de la huerta.
—"SOLEDAD"[19]

I stand at the river, watch the curving, twisting serpent, a serpent nailed to the fence where the mouth of the Río Grande empties into the Gulf.

I have come back. *Tanto dolor me costó el alejamiento.* I shade my eyes and look up. The bone beak of a hawk slowly circling over me, checking me out as potential carrion. In its wake a little bird flickering its wings, swimming sporadically like a fish. In the distance the expressway and the slough of traffic like

---

19. So much time without seeing you my house / my cradle / my deep nest of the orchard. (A song sung by the group *Haciendo Punto en Otro Son*.)

an irritated sow. The sudden pull in my gut, *la tierra, los aguaceros.* My land, *el viento soplando la arena, el lagartijo debajo de un nopalito. Me acuerdo como era antes. Una región desértica de vasta llanuras, costeras de baja altura, de escasa lluvia, de chaparrales formados por mesquites y huizaches.* If I look real hard I can almost see the Spanish fathers who were called "the cavalry of Christ" enter this valley riding their burros, see the clash of cultures commence.

Tierra natal. This is home, the small towns in the Valley, *los pueblitos* with chicken pens and goats picketed to mesquite shrubs. *En las colonias* on the other side of the tracks, junk cars line the front yards of hot pink and lavender-trimmed houses—Chicano architecture we call it, self-consciously. I have missed the TV shows where hosts speak in half and half, and where awards are given in the category of Tex-Mex music. I have missed the Mexican cemeteries blooming with artificial flowers, the fields of aloe vera and red pepper, rows of sugar cane, of corn hanging on the stalks, the cloud of *polvareda* in the dirt roads behind a speeding pickup truck, *el sabor de tamales de rez y venado.* I have missed *la yegua colorada* gnawing the wooden gate of her stall, the smell of horse flesh from Carito's corrals. *He hecho menos las noches calientes sin aire, noches de linternas y lechuzas* making holes in the night.

I still feel the old despair when I look at the unpainted, dilapidated, scrap lumber houses consisting mostly of corrugated aluminum. Some of the poorest people in the U.S. live in the Lower Rio Grande Valley, an arid and semi-arid land of irrigated farming, intense sunlight and heat, citrus groves next to chaparral and cactus. I walk through the elementary school I attended so long ago, that remained segregated until recently. I remember how the white teachers used to punish us for being Mexican.

How I love this tragic valley of South Texas, as Richardo Sánchez calls it; this borderland between the Nueces and the Rio Grande. This land has survived possession and ill-use by five countries: Spain, Mexico, the Republic of Texas, the U.S., the Confederacy, and the U.S. again. It has survived Anglo Mexican blood feuds, lynchings, burnings, rapes, pillage.

Today I see the Valley still struggling to survive. Whether it does or not, it will never be as I remember it. The borderlands depression that was set off by the 1982 peso devaluation in Mexico resulted in the closure of hundreds of Valley businesses. Many people lost their homes, cars, land. Prior to 1982 U.S. store owners thrived on retail sales to Mexicans who came across the border for groceries and clothes and appliances. While goods on the U.S. side have become 10, 100, 1000 times more expensive for Mexican buyers, goods on the Mexican side have become 10, 100, 1000 times cheaper for Americans. Because the Valley is heavily dependent on agriculture and Mexican retail trade, it has the highest unemployment rates along the entire border region; it is the Valley that has been hardest hit.

"It's been a bad year for corn," my brother, Nune, says. As he talks, I remember my father scanning the sky for a rain that would end the drought, looking up into the sky, day after day, while the corn withered on its stalk. My father has been dead for 29 years, having worked himself to death. The life span of a Mexican farm laborer is 56—he lived to be 38. It shocks me that I am older than he. I, too, search the sky for rain. Like the ancients, I worship the rain god and the maize goddess, but unlike my father I have recovered their names. Now for rain (irrigation) one offers not a sacrifice of blood, but of money.

"Farming is in a bad way," my brother says. "Two to three thousand small and big farmers went bankrupt in this country last year. Six years ago the price of corn was $8.00 per hundred pounds," he goes on. "This year it is $3.90 per hundred pounds." And I think to myself, after taking inflation into account, not planting anything puts you ahead.

I walk out to the back yard, stare at *los rosales de mamá*. She wants me to help her prune the rose bushes, dig out the carpet grass that is choking them. *Mamagrande Ramona también tenía rosales.* Here every Mexican grows flowers. If they don't have a piece of dirt, they use car tires, jars, cans, shoe boxes. Roses are the Mexican's favorite flower. I think, how symbolic—thorns and all.

Yes, the Chicano and Chicana have always taken care of growing things and the land. Again I see the four of us kids getting off the school bus, changing into our work clothes, walking into the field with Papí and Mamí, all six of us bending to the ground. Below our feet, under the earth lie the watermelon seeds. We cover them with paper plates, putting *terremotes* on top of the plates to keep them from being blown away by the wind. The paper plates keep the freeze away. Next day or the next we remove the plates, bare the tiny green shoots to the elements. They survive and grow, give fruit hundreds of times the size of the seed. We water them and hoe them. We harvest them. The vines, dry, rot, are plowed under. Growth, death, decay, birth. The soil prepared again and again, impregnated, worked on. A constant changing of forms, *renacimientos de la tierra madre*.

> This land was Mexican once
>   was Indian always
>   and is.
>   And will be again.

Drought: San Joaquin Valley, Winter

Barbara Brinson Curiel

This winter, canaries
curled up on the bottom of
their cages to die.

Needles on Christmas trees
are brittle as thin glass.

In root cellars,
vegetables turn to slime.
Past winters were filled
with the scent of tangerines.

We look for halos around the moon.
Umbrellas dream in the backs of closets,
their seams rotting.

Crowded in my bed,
death curls around my head
and around my feet for warmth
We dream of rivers and howling dogs.

Fields are dry ridges of a fingernail.
My throat is dry.
Insistent feathers curl into a noose around my heart.

Sailboats knife the brown Mokelumne: white shark fins.
Only tumbleweeds along the highway grow fat.

La Gran Ciudad

Angela De Hoyos

for Mireya Robles

I
No one told me
So how was I to know
that in the paradise

of crisp white cities
snakes still walk
        upright?

Una mujer de tantas
sola
    divorciada
    separada
    largada[20]
    —what does it matter?—
llegué a la gran ciudad
con mi niño en los brazos
por sembrar su camino trigueño
con las blancas flores
    de la esperanza[21]

(. . . but how quickly they wilted
beneath the scorching breath of evil.)

    2
El barrio, indefenso:
the pit of the poor.
Mi raza: el ay por todas partes.

When I couldn't pay the rent
the landlord came to see me.
Y la pregunta, que ofende:
    Ain't you Meskin?
    How come you speak
    such good English?
Y yo le contesto:
    Because I'm Spanglo, that's why.
. . . Pero se cobró
el muy pinche
        a su modo.[22]

---

20. one woman among many / alone / divorced / separated / deserted

21. I arrived in the big city / with my child in my arms / to plant its dark road / with the white flowers of hope

22. but the jerk / charged anyway / in his own way.

3

And every day the price of hope goes up.
Every day in the bleak pit
the sun casts a thinner shadow
(algún día nos olvidará por completo.)

    Hijito, nos comemos hoy
    esta fiesta de pan
    o lo dejamos para mañana?[23]

4

So where is the paradise?
In the land of the mighty
where is the shining
    —THE EQUAL—opportunity?
Can I skin with my bare teeth
the hungry hounds of night?

. . . lárgeunse con su cuento
a otra parte![24]
    I know better.

The Border

Gina Valdés

    The Border
a wall of barbed lies,
a chain of sighs, a heart
pounding, an old wound.

Aladdin hawks his magic
lamps, Ali Baba rounds up
his thieves, Lone Ranger
joins Texas Rangers,
Dark Vader trains Storm

---

23. (some day it will forget us completely.) / Son, shall we eat today / this fiesta of
bread / or shall we leave it for tomorrow?
24. take your fairy tales / to some other place

Troopers, El Santo wrestles
Batman, La Llorona howls.

Chaplin and Cantinflas
waddle up a hill, roll down,
Siqueiros paints the sky
blood red, Dali pastes
a purple moon, lights
the smile of the Cheshire
cat.

Hide and seek, kick the can,
Cowboys and Indians,
chess, dominoes, tin marin,
la lotería, a world loaded
on each back.

Trails of broken glass
glittering like stars.

A bolted door without walls,
a broken window where
a vulture sits and waits.

A cross of stones
extending to the four
points, each stone a prayer,
each prayer a murmuring stone.

A dry river, fish gasping
for air, air of whirling moons,
bed of rock, pillows of fluttering
bats, dreams of phosphorescent
doves in flight.

Flying horses, flying bullets,
flying rocks, violent eyes
smelling heat, capturing sighs.

The border is a wall
of barbed lies, a sigh
of chains, a pounding heart,
a fresh wound on an old cut.

tía juana u glisten

Xelina

tía juana u glisten by night
sequined by dangling city lights
by day u are shrouded with misery
groping for a bite to eat
  oh tía juana
esos perros scrounging tus calles
y el mosquero swarming la basura tirada
  oh tía juana que nos cure el shaman
ah, tía juana disculpe pero hoy tiene demasiados
  enfermos americanos
    venga mañana
mañana volveremos a subir el cerro
a pie por los baches
arrastrando tus piernas dolorosas
hinchadas con venas moradas
mañana tenemos cita en la casa de cartón
tal vez esos güeros con sus carruchas elegantes
  no vendran tan temprano
      tía juana

■

tía juana u glisten by night
sequined by dangling city lights
by day u are shrouded with misery
groping for a bite to eat
  oh tía juana
those dogs scrounging your streets
and the flies swarming in the thrown trash
  oh tía juana hopefully the Shaman will cure us
ah, tía juana, I'm sorry but you have too many
  sick americans
  come back tomorrow
tomorrow we will climb the hill again
on foot through the batches
dragging your painful legs
swollen with purple veins

tomorrow we have an appointment with the house of
  cardboard
maybe those anglos with their elegant cars
  won't come so early
    tía juana

tavern taboo

Evangelina Vigil-Piñón

I hate to be pssst at
I hate to be pssst at
me cae pero sura

I hate to walk by a man and be pssst at
I hate to sit at a table at some mistake joint
and be pssst at

ya ni los viejos en el Esquire
no different than other viejos no doubt
pero se mantienen
es todo

FIVE

Myths and Archetypes

I came to be known as Malinche
and Malinche came to mean traitor.
CARMEN TAFOLLA

Who wore her black shawl, black
gloves the day she walked, chin high,
never watching her feet, on the black
beams and boards, still smoking,
that had been Upton's Five-and-Dime.
PAT MORA

We all need a mythology to live by. Culture uses stories, myths, heroes and heroines to create role models. Stories transmit moral values, tell us ideally how we should live, help us distinguish correct behavior from incorrect, and identify those traits considered desirable by a group or society.

Because cultural values and norms circumscribe women's lives so strongly, it is particularly interesting to see what myths, historical and cultural heroines, and social role models writers choose to write about. Although myths may be in some part culturally set for both men and women, often the heroines chosen by female writers may be different from those chosen by male writers, they may show different aspects or attributes from those of male writers, or may coincide with values held by male writers. Many of the myths and archetypes singular to Chicana literature are presented in this chapter.

The Catholic religion with its emphasis on the personal intervention of the Virgin Mary and its cult of Marianismo (that is, to emulate the Virgin, one should emulate her characteristics of faith, self-abnegation, motherhood, and purity), of course, heavily influenced many Hispanic women who look to the intervention of the Virgin in their daily lives. In Mexico, the Virgin of Guadalupe, the first *mestiza* madonna, with her miraculous appearance to Juan Diego, was an important symbol. The introduction of the Virgin in an area known to be the sacred worshiping place of an important Nahuatl goddess, Tonantzín, facilitated the native Mexican's acceptance of this "Indian" deity. Moreover, the Virgin of Guadalupe represents the merging of European and Indian cultures since she is, in some senses, a transformation or "rebirth" of the native goddesses; Tonantzín is, interestingly enough, an aspect of the female deity Coatlicue.

Coatlicue was the strangest goddess of pre-Spanish America. . . . The metaphysical conceptions of death and resurrection that came together in her as the "filtheater" belong to the oldest ideas of mankind. . . . temple was erected for her as Tonantzín (our mother), on the site of which there stands today the church of the "Virgen de Guadalupe," the patron-saint of the Mexican Indians (Anton, 58).

It is interesting to compare the main characteristics of the Nahuatl deity to those of the Christian deity to see where they differ and where they coincide. Coatlicue was characterized as:

> goddess of love and of sin, she created life/devoured life, she was the symbol of ambivalence of all human life, personification of awesome natural forces, monster who devoured the sun at night/brought it to life in the morning, ageless, beginning and end, threatening/beneficent, represents birth *and* death. Coatlicue, therefore, represents all aspects of a dual nature and is a cyclical figure. (Anton, 59)

The characteristics of any of the Christian Virgins, whatever their names or titles might be, would include the following: purity, as in freedom from all sin, role as mother of Christ and of all Christians, dignity as Queen of Heaven and Earth, Helper of the sick, Mother of good counsel, Comforter of the afflicted, Queen of Peace. Moreover, it is *through* her, not *to* her, that humans pray since "love and honor paid to Mary are always an expression of thanksgiving and adoration to her son" (Johnson, 247). The Virgin of Guadalupe, then, is a unilateral figure, representation of those values considered positive by European cultures.

What becomes clear upon examining these characteristics is that those traits of the Nahuatl deity not acceptable to the Church were dropped: they were considered inappropriate to the virtuous symbolism of a Catholic virgin, mother of God. Because the Catholic Church was a system heavily promoting the all-knowing, all-encompassing power of God the Father, it was necessary to negate the powerful characteristics of Tonantzín (Coatlicue) in her attributes of judging, creating, and destroying. She was independent, wrathful, competent; her power to create and destroy was autonomous, as was that of most of the Nahuatl deities; it was a power not emanating solely from a central male figure.

The Virgin of Guadalupe was not the only virgin venerated by Mexican Americans in the United States (another one was La Conquistadora, an image that accompanied the Spaniards to the New World, also an important figure), but she was the most central one. Those role models that were most like her were, of course, also central to the literature. Dutiful mothers, wives and daughters, teachers, nurses, and helpful figures of all kinds abound in the writings of both males and females.

The Virgin of Guadalupe represents certain values considered positive: unselfish giving, intercessor between earth and spirit, and ideal qualities of motherhood, characteristics important to people everywhere. However, she is also sometimes seen by many Chicana writers, ironically, as a symbol of failure. In the personal relationship Chicano culture has with its saints, the Virgin is seen often as not active enough, and though she may be the patron saint of contemporary popular culture—as seen in lowrider manifestations—she is also clearly seen as the image of the unattainable. She has failed to intercede for her people in the United States; she advocates acceptance and endurance, not action. In an interesting juxtaposition, she is often connected with the Statue of Liberty, also a symbol of failure, for this statue promises justice and equality for all, a promise certainly unfulfilled in many writers' opinions. Thus, as cultural heroines, particularly in the early days of the Chicano Renaissance, we see in a prominent place not the Virgin of Guadalupe but rather the figures of heroines of the Mexican Revolution. These figures are *guerrillera* figures: *soldaderas* who followed their men into war and at times fought beside them—as in the particular case of one heroine popular in legend and corridos, La Adelita. Although no "revision" or complex exploration of these figures in Chicana literature has emerged, it is clear that an identification exists between revolutionary fighters for justice, land, and food, and contemporary writers. Thus, although the essential goodness of the Virgin of Guadalupe is acknowledged, she cannot emerge as a cultural heroine for these authors without some transformations (see "Little Miracles, Kept Promises").

Perhaps the directly opposite female to the Virgin Mary is the Eve/Lilith figure. In Mexican as well as Chicano culture, she is the Malinche/La Llorona figure. La Malinche/Malintzín/Doña Marina is the Aztec woman who was sold into slavery by her family. When she was fourteen, she was given again, among twenty women, to Hernán Cortés when he arrived in Mexico. Because she had the ability to speak both Nahuatl and Maya, and because Cortés had in his retinue a Spaniard, Jerónimo de Aguilar, who had been shipwrecked on the Yucatan coast and who spoke Spanish and Maya, she was from the beginning placed in a central role as translator. From there she became Cortés' mistress. Her name became synonymous with that of the conqueror and by the twentieth century in Mexico, the word *Malinche* or *malinchista* was identified with a person who betrays his or her country. The historical Malinche went on to have a child by Cortés, and when he was ordered to bring his wife to the new world, Malinche was married off to one of his soldiers, Don Juan Jaramillo. She died in relative obscurity at the age of twenty-four.

The image of La Llorona, the weeping woman, brought together both Indian and Spanish folklore and legend. In both cultures there were prevalent images of women who either had their children murdered and could not rest thereafter, whose spirits continued to roam, appearing to those who rode or walked deserted roads, particularly crossroads. In some tales La Llorona murdered her own children, and her cries could be heard during the night. La Llorona was connected both to Spanish medieval notions of *ánimas en pena,* spirits in purgatory expiating their sins, and to the Medea myth. She was also closely identified to Aztec cultural heroines: the Mocihuaquetzque ("valiant women"), who died in childbirth. They were the only Aztec females to achieve afterlife in the place of the heroes, and they were venerated by warriors who believed that carrying the third finger of the women's left hands into battle would protect them. It was also believed they had supernatural powers, and *brujos,* witchdoctors, would try to obtain their hair or their left arms. After their deaths, their families had to guard their graves so their bodies would not be mutilated. However, when these women had achieved afterlife, they were known as *cihuapipiltin,* night ghosts, who lay in wait at crossroads, wished epilepsy on children, and incited men to lewdness. In addition, they were vaguely connected to attributes of Coatlicue who also, at times, roamed the crossroads.

The mysterious forces combined in La Llorona, life-giving and death-taking (and also, it should be remembered, forces attributed to Tonantzín) made her a scapegoat in the Hispanic United States: she was thought to be the cause of children's drowning, since she was associated with rivers and ditches as well as crossroads. Today in New Mexico, for example, La Llorona is the symbol on signs warning children to stay away from ditches.

The images and mythology about La Llorona and La Malinche coalesce in folklore until in many areas in the Southwest they are one and the same woman. In general, the image is a negative one, tied up in a vague way, with sexuality and the death of children: the negative mother image. For La Malinche, sexuality is connected to her liaison with Cortés and subsequent betrayal of her people. In the case of La Llorona, she often appears to young men who are roaming about at night and who believe she is a young girl or beautiful young woman and, as they approach her (with sexual intent in mind), she appears to them as a hag or as death personified. The union of the two figures is clearly seen, for example, in Rudolfo Anaya's *The Legend of La Llorona,* where the historical figure of La Malinche evolves into that of the mythical crying woman.

Chicana writers' responses to La Malinche/La Llorona are varied and complex. One thing is certain, nevertheless: in their writing these two figures are almost never confused—the identities of the two women remain clear and defined. For Chicana writers, their relationship to La Malinche is one which has undergone constant examination and reevaluation since the Chicano Renaissance. The number of essays written by Chicanas on La Malinche is quite astonishing, both for their variety and their approaches. The points of identification for these writers seem to arise from the following:

1. La Malinche was the Indian woman taken by the conqueror and raped, so to speak, by her historical and cultural circumstances. She was, therefore, "conquered" by the Spanish male and a victim of both her family and her historical circumstances. Chicana writers find it difficult to place the symbolic blame of history on a woman who was a victim and not an instigator.

2. La Malinche also stands for the conquest of the Indian race by European whites who not only hold power but also consider themselves superior intellectually, socially, and culturally. The Indian roots of Chicano culture were for a long time denied, as Mexican-Americans attempted to assimilate into the dominant culture. The resuscitation of La Malinche as part of the process of acknowledged *mestizaje* brings her also into the forefront as the symbolic mother of a new race. Recognition of La Malinche as a complex figure with both positive and negative aspects would imply, therefore, integration of these Indian roots.

3. La Malinche and language: the meaning of translation. Part of Malinche's historical importance has been her ability to translate for Cortés, thus giving him knowledge and power over the Indian tribes. History tells us that La Malinche chose to aid Cortés, saving his life on more than one occasion. Chicana writers identify with the act of interpretation as they shift consciously from one language to another, from one culture to another. In the power structure they always have to take into consideration their relation to the dominant culture. Thus the writers' identification with the act of translation or interpretation, and of culture shifting, is closely aligned with the figure of La Malinche.

4. La Malinche as survivor. Many Chicana writers think of La Malinche as a woman who had and made choices rather than as the woman so often portrayed as the passive victim of rape and conquest. Because she possessed the power of language and political intuition and knowledge, they see her as a woman who deliberately cast her lot as a survivor—a woman who, with a clairvoyant sense, cast her lot with the Spaniards in order to ensure survival of her race and a woman who lives on in every Chicana today. It was often because of Malinche's diplomacy and intelligence that a more total annihilation of the Indian tribes of Mexico did not occur. And it is in her capacity as intercessor and helper that La Malinche takes on the attributes of the Virgin of Guadalupe.

The figure of La Llorona is quite different for Chicana writers. In popular folklore she approximates all those ancient Nahuatl deities who had life-giving and life-destroying abilities. One of these was Tonantzín, near whose shrine the Virgin of Guadalupe appeared, but many other Nahuatl female deities were also recognized for that creative and destructive ability; among these is the terrible goddess Coatlicue. La Llorona is also symbolic of Chicano culture, whose children are lost because of their assimilation into the dominant culture, or because of violence and prejudice. Associated with water, drownings, and the mysterious forces of night, La Llorona comes to represent the unpredictability of nature. For Chicana writers, La Llorona represents mourning for their lost culture, their lost selves. The search for self, in terms of Nahuatl myths, has also included the redemption and reassumption of the total power held by the Nahuatl female deities—the negative as well as the positive, control over one's own destiny, the active side rather than the passive side identified with the Virgin of Guadalupe. Thus Sandra Cisneros, in "Woman Hollering Creek," can play on the folklore surrounding La Llorona and turn her into an active heroine (Cisneros, *Woman Hollering Creek*, 43–56).

Another historical and cultural heroine is Sor Juana Inés de la Cruz. Sor Juana, a seventeenth-century nun, epitomizes both empirical as well as intuitive knowledge. She was a woman astute enough to know that if she accepted traditional norms, married, and had a family she would have no time for reflection and intellectual pursuits. On occasion she defied authority, as when told it was unseemly for a woman and a nun to pursue intellectual study; this is clearly seen in her *Letter.* Sor Juana argued that to stop her studying would be to defy God, who must have given her intelligence for some reason. When ordered to put away her books, she complied, only to pursue her study of physics and empirical knowledge by writing on natural laws evident in cooking and household chores; she thus elevated the everyday work of women into the realm of science. The stark reality of her final years of silence, when, while obeying the order to end her studies, she gave away her library and attended to her sister nuns during an epidemic, culminated in her death at an early age. All the qualities of Sor Juana—her fierce love of knowledge, the brilliance of her writing, the power of her language, her independent spirit and agony, and her final silence—intrigue and inspire the writers of today. She was not a quiet, long-suffering woman, but an intellect who made her own choices, living out her life as an independent entity.

It is interesting to note that one of the most prominent of contemporary feminist heroes is the *curandera/partera*/healer. As a hero she incorporates a complex series of characteristics seen as important values for the Chicana writer today. She also evidences values seen as negative by the dominant Spanish Catholic culture but incorporated by Indian cultures as part of the life cycle. She is a figure, like that of La Llorona, who emerges from the history and traditions of two cultures: the Indian herb women—folk doctors who taught the Spanish arrivals their knowledge, and the folk healer that the Arab culture had brought to Spain and whose healing traditions the Spaniards continued upon their arrival in the New World. The curandera is close to nature, possessing both intuitive as well as cognitive skills. She is a powerful figure and is seen throughout Chicano writing, even in the early authors. Tales of Cabeza de Baca and Otero-Warren bear witness to this. The fact that the curandera has emerged as a powerful figure in the writing of both males and females demonstrates not only her enduring qualities as myth and symbol but also the close identification of the culture to this figure. Chicana writers feel a particularly intimate connection. Part of her strength lies in the curandera's relationship to earth and nature—she understands the cycles of development and destruction, thus harking both to the past and to the future. She incorporates intuition and rationality, she studies power and harnesses it, she understands humans as well as animals, she listens, and she takes an active role in her environment. However, and perhaps this is the secret of her attractiveness, she also has the capacity to fight evil with destruction. She can and *does* seek vengeance and revenge. She is careful, however, to retaliate only against the evildoer and not in general—so evil is always dealt with in the particular.

Thus, like the Virgin, the curandera has the capacity for intervention between earth and spirit, but her world is a much more equal one, where accepting patriarchal rule is not the norm. She has the capacity to heal—but like the Nahuatl deities, she also has the capacity for death and destruction. Another ability of this curandera/bruja is an alchemistic one: her ability to effect transformations. From raw materials she makes precious jewels. This is also the unique talent of the writer, and it is clear that the identification of Chicana authors with the curandera, and their belief that writing is a form of both exorcising and controlling evil, and of healing, forms the nexus between them and this powerful image. The curandera figure has thus, in a powerful way, redeemed the Nahuatl dualities and fully incorporated the Indian myth to the Catholic one.

This chapter offers a sample of how Chicana writers view their cultural myths and archetypes, incorporate them into their texts, and transform them in poetic and creative substance.

■ ■ ■

Aztec Princess

Pat Mora

Her mother would say, "Look in
the home for happiness. Why do you stare out
often with such longing?" One day,

almost in desperation, her mother said,
"Here. See here. We buried your umbilical
cord here, in the house, a sign that you,
our girl-child, would nest inside."

That night the young woman quietly dug
for some trace of the shriveled woman-to-woman
skin, but all she found was earth, rich earth,
which she carefully scooped into an earthen jar
and carried outside to the moonlight
whispering, "Breathe."

Marina

Lucha Corpi / Translated by Catherine Rodríguez-Nieto

I. MARINA MOTHER

They made her of the softest clay
and dried her under the rays of the tropical sun.
With the blood of a tender lamb
her name was written by the elders
on the bark of that tree
as old as they.

Steeped in tradition, mystic
and mute she was sold—
from hand to hand, night to night,
denied and desecrated, waiting for the dawn
and for the owl's song
that would never come;
her womb sacked of its fruit,
her soul thinned to a handful of dust.

You no longer loved her, the elders denied her,
and the child who cried out to her "mamá!"
grew up and called her "whore."

II. MARINA VIRGIN

Of her own accord, before the altar
of the crucified god she knelt.
Because she loved you, she only saw
the bleeding man, and loved in him
her secret and mourning memory of you.

She washed away her sins
with holy water, covered her body
with a long, thick cloth
so no one would know
her brown skin had been damned.

Once, you stopped to wonder
where her soul was hidden,
not knowing she had planted it
in the entrails of that earth
her hands had cultivated—
the moist, black earth of your life.

III. THE DEVIL'S DAUGHTER

When she died, lightning struck in the north,
and on the new stone altar the incense burned
all night long. Her mystic pulsing
silenced, the ancient idol
shattered, her name
devoured by the wind in one deep growl
(her name so like the salt depths of the sea)—
little remained. Only a half-germinated seed.

IV. SHE (MARINA DISTANT)

She. A flower perhaps, a pool of fresh water . . .
a tropical night,
or a sorrowful child, enclosed
in a prison of the softest clay;
mourning shadow of an ancestral memory,
crossing the bridge at daybreak,
her hands full of earth and sun.

La Malinche

Carmen Tafolla

Yo soy la Malinche.

My people called me Malintzín Tenepal
the Spaniards called me Doña Marina

I came to be known as Malinche
    and Malinche came to mean traitor.

they called me—*chingada*

                                  Chingada.
(Ha—¡Chingada! ¡Screwed!)

    Of noble ancestry, for whatever that means,
I was sold into slavery by MY ROYAL FAMILY—so
that my brother could get my inheritance.

. . . And then the omens began—a god, a new civilization, the downfall of our empire.
    And *you* came.
    My dear Hernán Cortés, to share your "civi-
lization"—to play a god, . . . and I began to *dream* . . .
                          I *saw*
                          and I *acted*.

I saw our world
    And I saw yours
        And I saw—

                another.

And *yes*—I helped you—against Emperor Moctezuma
Xocoyotzín himself.
I became Interpreter, Advisor, and lover.
    They could not imagine me dealing on a level
        with you—so they said I was raped, used,
                chingada
                  ¡Chingada!

But I saw our world
        and your world
            and another.

No one else could *see*.
        Beyond one world, none existed.
And you yourself cried the night
the city burned
        and burned at your orders.
The most beautiful city on earth
                        in flames.
You cried broken tears the night you saw
                        your destruction.

My homeland ached within me
        (but I saw *another*).

Another world—
        a world yet to be born.
And our child was born . . .
        and I was immortalized *Chingada*!

Years later, you took away my child (my sweet
mestizo new world child)
            to raise him in your world
            You *still* didn't see.
                You *still* didn't see.
And history would call *me*
                            Chingada.

But Chingada I was not.
        Not tricked, not screwed, not traitor.
For I was not traitor to myself—
        I saw a dream
            and I *reached* it.
                Another world. . . . .
                            la raza.
                            la raaaaa-zaaaaa . . .

La Malinche a Cortez y Vice Versa /
La Malinche to Cortez and Vice Versa

Angela de Hoyos

(o sea, "El Amor No Perdona, Ni Siquiera Por Amor") /
(or, "Love Does Not Forgive, Not Even for Love")

ELLA Dame tu nombre, mi amo y señor,
      para que me adorne.
      Cómo quisiera
      grabarlo aquí, junto con el mío en la arena.
      Es que soy tuya, y quiero que lo sepa
      todo el mundo.

EL   Todo el mundo
      ya lo sabe
      mi querida Marina. No necesitas
      adornos superfluos.
      Yo te quiero y eso basta.

> *Y entre paréntesis El se dijo:*

> *Además, hrrrmmmppp!!! es indigno*
> *que un hombre blanco*
> *de mi noble estatura*
> *se enlace*
> *con una sencilla esclava, hrrmmpp! Es cierto*
> *que es una hembra a todo dar, pero no.*
> *Esta chatita patarrajá ya se está haciendo*
> *demasiadas ilusiones, hrrrmmmppp!!!*

ELLA Sí, amo y señor mío, tienes razón.
      Ya lo sé que me quieres
      y perdona mi necedad. Es que nosotras
      las mujeres siempre soñamos con imposibles.

> *Y entre paréntesis* ELLA *se dijo:*

> *Huh! y para eso te di*
> *mi sangre y mi pueblo!*
> *Sí, ya lo veo, gringo desabrido,*
> *tanto así me quieres*

que me casarás
con tu subordinado Don Juan,
sin más ni más
como si fuera yo
un kilo de carne
—pos ni que fueras mi padre
pa' venderme a tu antojo
güero infeliz. . . !!!

Etcétera, etcétera.

■

SHE   Give me your name, my master and lord,
so that it can beautify me. How I wish
to engrave it right here, next to mine in the sand.
I'm yours and I want the whole world
to know it.

HE   The whole world
knows it already
my dear Marina. You don't need
superfluous adornments.
I love you and that's enough.

     And between parenthesis He told himself:

        Besides, hrrmp!!! it's unbecoming
for a white man
of my noble stature
to marry
a simple slave, hrrmpp! It's true
that she's a lovely woman, but no.
That short carpetbagger is already creating
too many illusions, hrrmmmppp!!

SHE   Yes, my lord and master, you're right.
I know that you love me
and forgive my stupidity. It's that
we women always dream of the impossible.

     And between parenthesis SHE *said to herself:*

        Huh! and for this I gave you
my blood and my people!
Yes, I see it now, insipid gringo

you like me so much
that you want to marry me
to your subordinate Don Juan,
without my say so
as if I were
a pound of flesh
—well it's not like you were my father
to sell me at your whim
ungrateful white man . . . !!!

Etcetera. Etcetera.

Somos la Tierra[1]

Beverly Sánchez-Padilla

"la india de raza cautiva"[2]
with legs open, only to be penetrated,
    open, center pink with the calling grace
    open, wetness with smearing lush
    open, calling to be one with you
    open, 7 UP and chenin blanc in the belly button
    open, to be sucked into the ocean that is our fugue.
"la india de raza cautiva"
with arms that hold to please, to give and to give.
    and the tearless cry, i cannot hear,
    and the silent yell, that pierces my ears,
    with an end that never ceases, soy la tuya.
"la india de raza cautiva"
you have never been forgiven
for your stoic acceptance,
for your humble welcome,
for your spiritual passivity.

    (Ese Cortez never knew that this was only one life of many, and its
funny how the gringo thinks he can think better than us, even when TIME
is what we have on our side.)

---

1. We are the earth
2. The Indian woman of the captive race

porque, sí señor soy la india[3]
Y el ritmo, from the hearts with our men we make more hearts.
Never will we be captive.

Malinche's Discourse

Margarita Cota-Cárdenas

Are you Malinche a malinche? Who are you (who am I malinche)? seller
or buyer? sold or bought and at what price? What is it to be what so many
shout say sold-out malinchi who is who are / are we what? at what price
without having been there naming putting labels tags what who have bought
sold malinchismo what other
-ismos invented shouted with hate reacting striking like vipers like snakes
THEIR EYES like snakes what who what
"I am going to tell you some stories, my children, some very short stories,
interspersed sometimes they may appear they may be perhaps confused but it's
that one must go on with this thread this thread of
FEW WORDS ARE NECESSARY TO HE/SHE THAT UNDERSTANDS WELL (ha ha
you only have to push the buttons right right and it's easy ha ha ha pull pull
the right strings and you'll see how he/she dances how they dance like a mari-
onette like a puppet)
"They came in symbolic numbers: they were twelve, the *conquistadores* ahem
the missionaries I mean, the spiritual missionaries and we had a lot of crises of
of identity of of beliefs of of -isms because they were our lords whom we had
awaited for so long they had come to rescue us from a bloody pyramidal
funereal heritage and we wanted to believe in SOMETHING and some of us
helped them I believed them because it was the best thing right? it was the
best thing right?
AND YOU BOUGHT IT LIKE I SAY AND YOU BOUGHT IT LIKE I SAY OH YOU'RE
A REAL
"Don't let them do it to you, damn you Carlos, you have to ask ARGO GUENO
SOMETHING REAL JUICY why don't you look at me, Miss Len, why. . . ?
OH WERE YOU THERE WHEN THEY CRUCIFIED MY . . . Were you there?
"Using the latest terminology and it's so useful nowadays, I'm going to tell
you about my formative years: at the age of five, more or less, I left off being

---

3. because yes sir, I am that Indian / and the rhythm

the favorite eldest daughter of my tribe, when some very immediate relatives sold me, to some more distant buddies, who bought me . . . at what price? I don't know, I only remember that I went kicking that I wanted my mama that why had my papa abandoned me yes yes I went yelling loud too why why and they said tie her up she's too forward too flighty she think's she's a princess thinks she's her father's daughter thinks she's hot stuff that's it doesn't know her place a real threat to the tribe take her away haul her off she's a menace to our cause that's it only learned to say crazy things to say accuse with HER EYES and they didn't want then troublemakers in their country.

YES YOU BOUGHT IT LIKE I SAY OH YOU BOUGHT IT

"The country, well I suppose Mexico, Aztlán . . . ? Well, it could have been a little more to the north or a little more to the south, it makes no difference now, what I was telling you was my version that's it, my version as . . . as a woman, that's right, and they can establish the famous dialectic with the other versions that you already know very well . . . Oh don't act as if you don't understand, don't put me on now. . . .

AND TO HE/SHE WHO DOESN'T UNDERSTAND WELL A LOT OF WORDS WITH DRAWINGS CAUSE YOU BOUGHT IT LIKE

"We had waited for him a long time, that's what I remembered when I saw him, *pero* the first thing I felt was an attraction like well like a woman and he a man. . . . That's what I first felt . . . there were others more blond than HE and others that were dark-haired and even others like us (on the outside anyway, right?) but why don't they want to understand that I did it all because of love and not because of any hate nor any ambition. . . . A traitress . . . ? Because of our language, that I helped them that I sold my people . . . ? You know what, you know a lot about -isms and -acies but I advise you, my children, to look for the answer inside and to look further than the labels implanted and thrown out in reaction hate violence. . . . What's wrong is that we're very smart, very bright, and we learn certain things very well that frankly keep on being the same pyramidal funereal hierarchal structure . . .

CAUSE YOU BOUGHT IT LIKE I SAY WELL THERE WAS ANOTHER WAY

Another Way To Be

Another Way Rosario Another

"And what I Malinche malinche am telling you, is: SHOW ME. Because from what I've seen, not in every case that's true, is that we go on being, in name of every cause, *chingones y chingadas* . . . those who fuck you and those who are fucked . . . for a change of subject . . .

BREAK THE TIES TO YOUR MYTHS

". . . or for a change . . . the *chinga*-doer and el/la *chinga*-dee . . . HAVEN'T YOU SEEN IT YET? (and still you go on)

MAKE SHREDS OF THE CORDONS TO YOUR

(and the dirty linen, malinchee, and your dirty linen is coming coming
looking for you look)
BRRIIINGGG . . . BRRIINNGG . . .
". . . Halo, yes, it's me, Malin . . . Len, Lencha . . . Oh, how's everybody,
Loreto, it's been a while since you . . . Oh, really, you're right, it was just day
before yesterday, yesterday . . . yeah, the funeral was yesterday but I couldn't
. . . Yes, that must be it, a crisis of . . . my nerves . . . (that's all that was
missing now, don't you think ha ha Maleench' Mah-leehncheeh) . . . what?
. . . I'm sorry, what were you saying, Loreto? No, no I haven't written
anything new (it's all old all right ha and still you) but I keep thinking about
it, turning it over and over as if that way I can see things better . . . I know, I
know, I'm somewhat discombobulated . . . I've even started to imagine that
someone is following me that something is going to happen to me, well it's
like I told you the other night . . . And you, what's new? Treacherous? . . . Oh
the *chota* is treacherous . . . at least those two cops, right . . . You don't say. . . .
But . . . But that can't be, because Puppet never . . . No, it's just that because
of my nerves, Memo hasn't been able to tell me everything . . . the other day
he was going to tell me something . . . well, the truth about how it really
happened, about the death . . . Assassins . . . Well, what are you . . . what can
be done? God, Loreto, but I've tried to write more and I've just got too much,
too many pressures and I'm getting confused and my jotquequis are hurting
. . . what? You know, the truth, the real, real low-down is that . . .
WHEN YOU WERE YOU WERE ALL A CHILD CHILDREN YOU WERE YOU
ALL WERE VERY BRAVE AND NOW AND NOW THAT THERE'S NO TIME LEFT
NOW
". . . and as I was saying to you yesterday, my daughters, *lo Cortés no quita lo
valiente* . . .
TO ONE WHO UNDERSTANDS WELL YOU ONLY NEED A FEW BUT AFTER
CENTURIES OF POOLS OF WELL THEN MAYBE
". . . Let's talk turkey, class . . . Well, that means that we ought to discuss
today's topic openly and in-good-faith-ly, that's how I prefer it. Well then,
Ester, what do you think of Miguelito's comment . . . Yes, what he said about
the bad effect of feminism on the movement . . . What do you think, Ester
. . . ? Is feminism bad or good . . . etc. . . . ? Oh, you don't want to say . . . ?
You're . . . afraid . . . ? What are you saying, Miguelito . . . ?
". . . that the chicano/mexican/latin family has to maintain itself intact, that
traditions are more important for the good, for the future, Profesora. I think,
that's just what my dad and my grandparents were saying last night, that all
this stuff about women's liberation is just bourgeois women's junk, those
women that have idle time to write and to draw and to . . . discombobulate
themselves . . . like my dad said last night . . . I'm sorry, but the movement

needs its women . . . well to struggle for the *causa* . . . Ester, why are you
crying . . . What's wrong with you . . . ?
WHY ARE YOU CRYING QUE TE PASA
(ha ha, like I've told you, don't stick your nose in it, don't stick your nose in
because it's CHINGOS AND CHINGOS OF BLOOD and still you)
You leave class humming "Some day my prince will come . . . " and you laugh
and you laugh Cinder-Malinsheesh (What did I say . . . ?)
WHO'S TO BLAME WHO WELL YOU BOUGHT IT LIKE THAT WAY CAUSE THEY
SOLD IT LIKE I SAY WHO'S TO BLAME CENTURIES AND CENTURIES WILL IT
HAPPEN TO THEM WILL IT HAPPEN
You keep being afraid of you don't know what of SOMEONE who wants you to
shut up for you not to ask questions not to challenge not to NOOOOOOOOOOOO
and the insomnia with Puppet and other signs of the barrio about which you
had never thought before or much and that now that there's no time left . . .
(and this rage started to enter you suppurating and you begin to write poetry
at all hours and you strike out at everything now) One long poem, you entitle
"A tombstone for Puppet," with a pachuco's cross drawn by lines around the
poem, like like like . . .

        the cross that the little dude has on his left
        hand, goes from his thumb to his index finger
        what is that Puppet you say and the batito
        looks at you HIS EYES don't you know what it is,
        Miss Len? don't you know? you tell him
        that your cousin Boni in the Eastside of where
        was it now it was so long ago in El Centro
        that's it your cousin Boni had a small cross
        and his camaradas also he said
        and they were always together and they loved
        life and they weren't afraid of anyone NOBODY NAIDE
". . . Between two cultures, that's how the pachucos found themselves in Los
Angeles, Tucson, in El Paso . . . Between two systems, in a conflictive state
which resulted in . . . THEMSELVES . . . because they were themselves only,
because they wanted to be something not from over there nor from over here
because anyhow both sides saw them the same way THEY THEMSELVES in
their own eyes there was IN THEIR EYES
                Another Way to Be
                   Another Way to Not-Be the Others
                     But rather THEMSELVES
(oh sure, sure, and what was it that happened to them CAN'T YOU GET IT YET?
DIDN'T YOU SEE IT IN THE NEWS?)

"Doña Marina, do you really think that people can change, that there can really be something better . . . history, well it doesn't assure me much that . . ."
"Yes, yes, my daughter, except the part about death . . . Well, if you've died already, then it's only in people's memory in their fantasies in the goodbad versions that . . . That's the only thing, if you're dead already . . ."
". . . Well how can you know if you're dead . . . ? (hahahahaha keep it up little donkey) Isn't it too late by the time you realize that you've . . . Answer me that one, Profe Malinchi . . ."
DID YOU BUY LIKE I SAY OH DID YOU
". . . hee, hee, it's easy, it's easy to know, my daughters my sons it's easy: If you can still open your eyes, then, well you haven't blin blin blinked them for the last time, if you still can open your eyes, then . . . Well then I tell you that you can still kick . . . some . . .
WELL MY COMADRE LA LLORONA IS CALLING ME I STILL HAVE TO TEACH HER TO NOT PUT UP WITH SHIT TO OPEN HER EYES BECAUSE THERE'S SOMETHING REALLY GOOD

Malinche Past:
Selection from *Paletitas de guayaba*
Erlinda Gonzales-Berry

The train stops on the edge of a headland that projects itself toward the center of the waters of an enormous lake. She looks out the little window and in the distance she sees a city that appears to be suspended over the very heart of the lake. She dresses quickly, grabs her suitcases and abandons her compartment. In the hallway she runs into Lencho who blocks her way so she can't get by. She turns quickly to flee in the opposite direction but his aggressive arms have already enveloped her waist; pressing his lips close to her ear he pleads with her to stay on the train while the other passengers get off. His breath is a hot flame that engulfs her in a hypnotic trance. His hands move agilely under her red sweater and his erect organ traces her hips like a blind man's cane seeking the doorway of an unknown building. She feels thick waves of juices descend and instinctively she begins to undulate in a slow and deliberate rhythm, her wide hips against the stiff organ that demands an opening. Suddenly, she remembers that the train has stopped and she thinks surely they must be in Mexico D.F. She slips away from Lencho's arms like bland gelatin and with her erect breasts pointing out the way, she runs toward the door of the train.

The morning light hurts her sleepy eyes and she barely avoids slipping on the stairs. When at last she recovers her normal vision she begins to discern the movement of a beautiful and intricate human kaleidoscope which glides in an improvised dance on the wide clean streets. Hundreds of young men, barefoot and in loincloths that barely cover their private parts, slide alongside the station like olympic skaters, offering to rent canoes and transportation to the new arrivals. Young girls in white *huipiles* and black braids tied with rainbow ribbons offer mangoes, pineapples, sweet potatoes, cooked corn, and other things to the weary traveler. She walks slowly opening a path through the multitude as it mills around to a collective beat. The smells of the street, the merchandise, and the bodies pressed together assault her nose and make her feel like vomiting. Suddenly, two dwarfs appear before her, both in white loincloths and green and pink waistbands. They tell her that their mistress has sent them to find her and indicate she should board the canopied canoe adorned with green feathers and silver embroidery. Stupefied by the carnival that slithers before her eyes, which feel as if they had lived in the most abject sensory deprivation until the moment of leaving the train, she obeys without saying a word. She has no idea where the jovial dwarfs are taking her, but at the same time she feels an obscure impulse to follow them. They travel for several hours in the canoe along a wide causeway that unites the headland with the distant city, whose towers and masonry buildings light up impressively beneath the tropical sun. Upon arriving on firm ground the canoe passes into one of the many canals that cross the city like liquid sidewalks and on whose banks appear houses of red tezontli and whitewashed adobes of one or two stories, each one with a lush garden on the roof. Each oar stroke brings them closer to the white pyramids that spring up like mirages against the enormous backdrop of transparent blue. Amazed, she looks from one side to the other thinking that what she sees "is a dream" because "she's seeing things she had never imagined, or seen, nor even dreamed." That it isn't a dream is proved by her delicate sense of smell which receives the aroma of thick layers of putrefied blood that adorn the steps of the sacred temples. As if this weren't sufficiently disconcerting to the new arrival, along her field of vision appears an enormous abacus whose hundred beads consist of grotesque skulls heaped on bamboo stakes like sinister gargoyles on silent and capricious guard. For the second time that morning she feels the impulse to empty all the contents of her stomach through her mouth. As swiftly as this physical reaction appears, it subsides and her attention turns to the scene that slowly and marvelously unfolds as the canoe passes through a carved arch in the wall of a building which afterwards she will discover is one of the castles of the Great Lord of Tenochtitlan. The canoe docks at an enormous garden that rests tranquilly inside the four walls of the magnificent castle.

A woman whose noble aspect reveals itself in her dress and in her presence awaits her. How beautiful you are. She speaks with enthusiasm. I've been very conscious that my behavior would produce a beautiful and strong race of people. Seeing you pleases me and recompenses the insults and the thrashing that history will bestow on me.[1]

Taking her by the arm the two begin to walk through the garden. The woman delivers a long speech in a voice, now serene, which contrasts sharply with the content.

Mari, you have had the good fortune to arrive before the imminent destruction of this beautiful city. From what you have seen today, the temples, markets, palaces, this garden, only fragments will remain as testimonies.

These strangers our gods have sent us are a destructive plague. Although they are few in comparison to the number of our people, their triumph is inevitable. Even if our great lord were able to act decisively and if we could stop this greedy wave of fire-spitting men, others would come and others and finally troops of them to yank the last flower of our race, sending every last one of us to rest in the shadows of Mictlan. The end of the world as we know it is inevitable; however it is possible and necessary to save what we can. Ours is a beautiful race, strong and fertile. Nevertheless there are among us some who would destroy it with internecine battles; we are trapped and fixed within a circle of time because of our constant strife the cause of which is hunger for damn power and the desire to maintain this level of luxury. If the dirt-eating feathered ones of the provinces didn't produce with the pure sweat of their labor food and goods, if they didn't extract the resources of our mother earth, it wouldn't be possible for the distinguished eagles and jaguars to live like this;

---

1. Marina was at this time in the morning of life. She is said to have possessed uncommon personal attractions and her open, expressive features indicated her generous temper. She always remained faithful to the countrymen of her adoption; and her knowledge and customs of the Mexicans, and often of the designs, enabled her to extricate the Spaniards, more than once, from the most embarrassing and perilous situations. She had her errors, as we have seen. But they should be rather charged to the defects of early education, and to the evil influence of him to whom in the darkness of her spirit she looked with simple confidence for the light to guide her. All agree that she was full of excellent qualities, and the important services that she rendered the Spaniards have made her memory deservedly dear to them; while the name of Malinche—the name by which she is still known in Mexico— was pronounced with kindness by the conquered races, with whose misfortunes she showed an invariable sympathy.

and to ensure this order they must divide and conquer, they must impose constant war. And now those false gods take advantage of our disunity to defeat us. Our chiefs, Mari, it gives me great pain to say so, are weak either in mind or in body. Some want to fight to save the moment. Those are the weak in mind because they don't understand that that provokes the anger and the greed of these barbarians. Prince Cuauhtemoc, for example, will resist until they burn his feet, and the future creators of myth will render him homage and they will erect monuments to him, but what historians won't admit is that if Falling Eagle triumphs it will only be a triumph of the moment because in the end, the King from overseas will send us his last servant to destroy our race.

It seems to me that the realm of this King Don Fernando is in critical condition. His people find themselves in a state of profound depression. Knowing they live on a dead-end street overwhelms them. They are trapped in worn-out models, and their old myths are losing their cosmic meaning. They search for an exit from that quagmire that surrounds them everywhere, and this, our world, will be their salvation. They come armed with profound doubts and this will force them to destroy our world . . . with swords, with crosses, with phallus. And Moctezuma, my poor little lord of the crooked cane, the priests have him by the balls with their magic and superstitions. He has the most noble soul that will ever walk this earth, but he's weak and his fear of the gods will make him collaborate with them, Mari, but listen well. I want you to understand my actions so that one day when you are wounded by the words "Hijo de la Chingada" you will understand what motivates me. Look, the women in this society, as in yours, are mere objects; they are chattel; they are the property of their fathers first and then of their husbands. The only honor that is given to them in this culture is to be sacrificed, if they are virgins. Great honor! Look, the priest, the princes, the merchants, the artisans, the warriors all are men. We women are primarily the mirrors that reflect the male image so that he will recognize who he is; then we're their playmates in bed, and finally receptacles and incubators of their grains of corn. We are relegated to the world of shadows and silence, but this silence engenders the word that flounders about in its own bile and finally becomes resentment, outrage, and also song. And to this word is added another and another, and in the end they form a long and strong chain that surrounds us and strangles us. We can succumb, die asphyxiated by words that never found their voice, or we can conjure, with all the portents of heaven and hell, that voice and hurl it out onto the world of men. Before it, they will show their real tendencies—solitude, reticence hidden behind masks and sexual organs that discharge like bows and arrows, harquebuses, and guns. Can you imagine Mari if we unite every single chain of words of every single woman in the world what power that would generate? And we could use that power to create a society where everyone would be naked without shame or lies or weaknesses to hide; a world where work, the fruit of that work, and our mother earth would be divided evenly, a society where everyone, men and women, would take care to nourish and to educate our daughters and our sons so they could learn to work with grace, with honesty, with creativity, and with human compassion. We women are strong, Mari; our strength comes from the silence imposed upon us by social and legal hands that have gagged our mouths.

Look, I find myself at the crossroads of a treacherous road. A history of infamy and degradation follows me. Not once, but twice, I have been sold like common merchandise, once by my mother and again, like a slab of meat, by my lord, who in turn expected to receive the good graces of Cortés. Ah, Cortés. At last we talk about my lover of the crooked legs, about that beast of the white gods, that astute bearer of the sword, master of games and of manipulation, persistent seeker of glory and fame. From the start I recognized in his eyes that spark that impels humans to commit the most desperate acts on the road to success. Everywhere he looked he saw our caciques vacillate before him; he wasn't a god, yes he was a god, maybe he was a god. I decided to put an end to their vacillations. I slept with him and I have discovered that he makes love like any mortal, recklessly and full of complexes because of the limitations of his instrument. And also I have discovered his lust for power. I have decided to align myself with him to absorb that power certain to be his, and thus alter the destiny of my people who find themselves on the road to annihilation. I will use the force of my voice and offer it to Cortés, converting myself into his tongue and his procuress. Yes, the necessary link between his world and ours. My object is to help him achieve his imperious plans through the word and though compromise. I see this as the only way to save our race because this is what most obsesses me in this critical moment. Because of me many have died, in Cholula, thousands of brave warriors—and many more will die before this is finished. But in the end, if my collaboration with this bewitching devil is necessary to assure that we don't all die, I am ready to sell myself. What difference does it make if I repeat what has already been? But in this case my sale is the result of my exercising my own will, which doesn't allow me to accept passively the total destruction of my people. My act of betrayal, as history will call it, promises to inject the seed of our flower in the new order that invariably will gather with the four winds. Without my act of collaboration our race will disappear and will give to this empire a pure race of false gods, weak and anemic before the greatness, the majesty, and the caprice of our natural habitat. However, because of my actions a new mestizo race will be born in whose veins will flow the strength of my blood, of my will, and my feminine word. You, Mari, are the future fruit of my womb, the flower of my betrayal.

[I have decided to narrate this dream in the third person because it seems to me that in dreams we always see ourselves from the outside. Although we are actors within that same dream, a sort of doubling exists that allows us at the same time to perceive visually the action as omniscient observers. Well, omniscient only in the sense that part of us feels distanced from the actions. The other part continues emotionally connected to the action. That is precisely what is happening as I am constructing this text. Part of me feels distanced and objective, the other part is emotionally involved in the events narrated by Mari.]

Malinchista, A Myth Revised

Alicia Gaspar de Alba

(It is a traditional Mexican belief that La Malinche—Aztec interpreter and mistress of Cortés—betrayed her own people in exchange for a new life. It is said that La Malinche bore a son by Cortés, the first mestizo of Aztec and Spanish blood, whom she later sacrificed when Cortés threatened to take the boy to Spain. Some say that the spirit of La Malinche is La Llorona.)

1
The high priest of the pyramids feared La Malinche's
power of language—how she could form strange syllables
in her mouth and Speak to the gods without offering
the red fruit of her heart. He had visions of a white
man who would change her ways with an obsidian knife.

2
La Malinche hated the way Cortés rubbed his cactus-
beard over her face and belly. The way his tongue
pressed against her teeth. She was used to smooth
brown lovers who dipped beneath her, who crouched
on the ground and rocked her in the musky space
between their chests and thighs.

3
When the child was born, his eyes opened Aztec black,
his skin shone café-con-leche. His mother wet his
fine curls with her saliva to make them straight.

His father cursed the native seed in that first
mixed son.

4

They slept under the black silk of a Tenocha sky,
the hammock molded around the two bodies: a woman's
buttocks heavy after childbirth, an infant weighted
by the shadows in his skull. A coyote lurking near
the river could smell their blood.

5

The woman shrieking along the littered bank of the
Río Grande is not sorry. She is looking for revenge.
Centuries she has been blamed for the murder of her
child, the loss of her people, as if Tenochtitlan
would not have fallen without her sin. History
does not sing of the conquistador who prayed
to a white god as he pulled two ripe hearts
out of the land.

Como Duele[4]

Adaljiza Sosa-Riddell

Ese, vato,[5] I saw you today
en Los y Sacra
en Santa Barbara, Sanfra
and everywhere else.
You walked, Chicano chulo,
eagle on your jacket,
y "carnales y carnalas,"[6]
y "Que Viva la Raza."

But where were you when
I was looking for myself?
As if I didn't know.

---

4. How it hurts. This poem has consistently and erroneously been attributed to
Lorenza Calvillo-Craig because of a pagination error in *El Grito* 7:1 (September, 1973).

5. Hey, buddy

6. brothers and sisters

Where the MAN and
all his pendejadas[7]
sent you,

> To Dartmouth, Los Angeles City College,
> Barber's School, La Pinta,
> Korea, and Vietnam; too many of you
> returned wrapped como enchiladas
> in red, white, and blue.

A Chicano at Dartmouth?
I was at Berkeley, where,
there were too few of us
and even less of you.
I'm not even sure
that I really looked for you.

I heard from many rucos[8]
that you
would never make it.
You would hold me back;
From What?
From what we are today?
"Y QUE VIVA"
Pinche, como duele ser Malinche.[9]

My name was changed, por la ley.[10]
Probrecitos, they believed in me,
That I was white enough
to stay forever,
that I would never find you again.

I found you, Chicano,
but only for a moment,
Never para siempre.[11]
Temilotzin died the morning after,
Malinche.
It's too late.

---

7. stupidity
8. old people
9. How it hurts to be Malinche
10. by the law
11. for ever

The world does not wait
for indecision,
neither do Chicanos.

And mis pobres padres[12]
taught me
not to hurt
others too much.
Malinche, pinche,
forever with me;
      I was born out of you,
      I walk beside you,
      bear my children with you,
      for sure, I'll die
      alone with you.
Perhaps I died before,
when I said good-bye
al barrio y al Cruiser.
He went to road camp,
por grifo y peleonero.[13]
While I was saved—
for what?

Pinche, como duele ser Malinche.
Pero sabes, ese,
what keeps me from shattering
into a million fragments?
It's that sometimes,
you are el hijo de la Malinche, too.

Go 'Way from My Window, La Llorona (1)

Cordelia Candelaria

Get lost, lady! ¡Andale!
Far away and forever! ¡Vete! but not

---

12. my poor parents
13. for drugs and fighting

Like sinks of dirty water swallowed by the drain
To rise again in cesspools, not like
A fat black roach swept away
Returns with crowds at midnight. But vanish,
Weeping Bitch, out of my life
Como el sudor de mi sobaco.[14]
You've hounded me beyond belief, scaring
My childhood away from me, spooking
My sleep to reels and reels of horror shows
Until the time
Of my passage afuera de la casa[15]
And the reality of your unreality
Turned me into the taste of moldy brine
At the bottom of a jar, into Goneril
seeing her father as you make me see mine.
And my mother.
Married forever in sickness and in sickness
Till death parts them in sickness
And in loudness
at midnight, in beatings and blood
And weeping children and everyone big
Drunk and endings of kisses happily forever
Sickness, befitting the passionate prelude.
Go!
Follow your babies llorando
Into the rolling water del río
Let them stare you clear-eyed into Hell.

La Llorona

Cordelia Candelaria

At Sixteen

i'm forever blowing bubbles
blowing bubbles in the air

---

14. Like the sweat from my armpit
15. away from home

they fly so high
nearly reach the sky
they fade and
      and when she realized she did not have it
         she fell apart inside
      no, no, she cried
         frantic
      yes, yes, of course it's here
      she crooked a smile to fettle up
         her scrambled heart
      ever alert it might turn up
      turn up someplace, she looked
      and looked and didn't tell
         ¡ay, qué sorpresa![16]
      and when she realized
      she *could* not have it
         gritó a todas madres
         a scream so sharp, so piercing
      its volume popped each fragile sphere
         adrift in air
      and left her looking
      looking, long before the weeping

Portrait by the River

La luz es todo: light is crucial
Its tawny hues the weight of dusk
Sifted by random shards of a retreating sun.
The current curves silent
As thick brushstrokes of a watercolor drying darkest blue.
The splash of ripples as she bends to rinse tired feet
Paint her flesh an instant shine
Bright as tears, or hope.

Persistent footsteps round every shore
De Tehuantepec a Chapala
De Campeche a Culiacan
De rio a rio, de calor al frio
Lavando   llorando   andando[17]

---

16. oh, what surprise!
17. From river to river, / from heat to cold / washing crying walking

The reticence of her slow movements
Remembers the tons of sleepless time pressed upon
Her weary flesh from shore to shore—
Bony hands pressing feeling into each toe,
Fingertips dampening back stray wisps of hair, gray on black.
Slow motion inscribes, too, a final image:
Each haunted glance
She sinks into the camera of river's reflection
Returns her babies' outstretched hands to her,
Shivering cold and wet:
                    La hambre eterna.[18]

La Llorona

Naomi Quiñonez

When La Llorona comes to me
vulnerability turns compassion
the haunting melody of her song
wanders as wounded and random
as her legend through the rivers
and alleyways of my existence.
La Llorona—madre perdida
who searches eternally
the phantom murderess
who has killed her children,
the rejected mother
of desgraciados.
All-giving and all-loving
the all-forgiving part of my being
that is negated.
La madre bendita
La mujer fuerte
La puta madre
La soldadera
La india amorosa

---

18. eternal hunger

La mujer dolorosa:[19]
But who can understand
that a woman sentences to death
the child she brings
into the world.
La Llorona, the feminine
haunts us if we fear her
comforts us if we understand.
La madre who grieves
at bringing children into a world
that may destroy them
and will kill them.
La Llorona, contradiction
of life and death,
who sacrificed her children
to haunt the weak
and comfort the living.
La mujer sagrada[20]
the defiled woman.
She makes her peace
with those who respect vulnerability
and draw from her strength.

Witches' Blood

Alma Villanueva

Power of my blood, your secret
wrapped in ancient tongues
spoken by men who claimed themselves
gods and priests and oracles—they
made elaborate rituals
secret chants and extolled the cycles,
calling woman unclean.

---

19. the blessed mother / the strong woman / the whore mother / the *soldadera* girl / the
loving Indian [woman] / the suffering woman
20. the sacred woman

men have killed
made war
for blood to flow, as naturally
as a woman's
once a month—
men have roamed the earth to find
the patience of pregnancy
the joy of birth—
the renewal of blood.
  (the awful, bloody secret! o woman
      you dare birth
        yourself)

call me witch
call me hag
call me sorceress
call me mad
call me woman
  do not call me goddess.
I do not want the position.

I prefer to gaze in wonder, once
a month at my
witches' blood.

The Three Sisters

Sandra Cisneros

They came with the wind that blows in August, thin as a spider web and barely noticed. Three who did not seem to be related to anything but the moon: one with laughter like tin and one with eyes of a cat and one with hands like porcelain. The aunts, the three sisters, *las comadres,* they said.

The baby died. Lucy and Rachel's sister. One night a dog cried and the next day a yellow bird flew in through an open window. Before the week was over the baby's fever was worse. Then Jesus came and took the baby with him far away. That's what their mother said.

Then the visitors came . . . in and out of the little house. It was hard to keep the floors clean. Anybody who had ever wondered what color the walls were came and came to look at that little thumb of a human in a box like candy.

I had never seen the dead before, not for real, not in somebody's living room for people to kiss and bless themselves and light a candle for. Not in a house. It seemed strange.

They must've known, the sisters. They had the power and could sense what was what. They said come here and gave me a stick of gum. They smelled like kleenex or the inside of a satin handbag, and then I didn't feel afraid.

What's your name, the cat-eyed one asked.

Esperanza, I said.

Esperanza, the old blue-veined one repeated in a high thin voice. Esperanza . . . a good good name.

My knees hurt, the one with the funny laugh complained.

Tomorrow it will rain.

Yes, tomorrow, they said.

How do you know? I asked.

We know.

Look at her hands, cat-eyed said.

And they turned them over and over as if they were looking for something special.

She's special

Yes, she'll go very far.

Yes, yes, hmmm.

Make a wish.

A wish?

Yes, make a wish. What do you want?

Anything? I said.

Well, why not?

I closed my eyes.

Did you wish already?

Yes, I said.

Well, that's all there is to it. It'll come true.

How do you know? I asked.

We know, we know.

Esperanza. The one with marble hands called me aside. Esperanza. She held my face with her blue-veined hands and looked and looked at me. A long silence. When you leave you must remember always to come back, she said.

What?

When you leave you must remember to come back for the others. A circle, understand? You will always be Esperanza. You will always be Mango

Street. You can't erase what you know: You can't forget who you are.

Then I didn't know what to say. It was as if she could read my mind, as if she knew what I had wished for, and I felt ashamed for having made such a selfish wish.

You must remember to come back. For the ones who cannot leave as easily as you. You will remember? She asked as if she was telling me. Yes, yes, I said a little confused.

Good, she said rubbing my hands. Good. That's all. You can go.

I got up to join Lucy and Rachel who were already outside waiting by the door, wondering what I was doing talking to three old ladies who smelled like cinnamon. I didn't understand everything they had told me. I turned around. They smiled and waved in their smoky way.

Then I didn't see them. Not once or twice or ever again.

Hands

Pat Mora

The woman walked quickly down the dusty streets of Juarez. Every few seconds she would glance behind her, checking to see that Miguel was not following. It was a foolish fear. Her husband knew that every morning she rose early and left their three small rooms wearing her black *mantilla,* going to the dark church.

She put her cool palms to her cheeks. Feverish.

"What is happening to me?"

She walked faster. She could remember when she had seemed calm, slow, like the river. The women around her would cry often, fight. But not Cuca. The women came to her with their problems, stories of husbands who threw plates, sons who staggered home drunk. And she dispensed wisdom like Solomon. She had prayed often then for humility, had knelt before the heart of flickering candles at church. Yet the secret pride remained.

Now she smiled sadly at the woman she had been. Now it was she seeking help from another woman, if the witch was a woman.

Bruja, the townspeople called her. She lived alone in a small house a half mile from the last city street. The priests warned that her magic was black, evil, smelling of the devil. But when, day after day, Cuca had dug her nails into her palms until her hands ached all night; when night after night Miguel entered her bed smelling of another woman, Cuca decided that she would reach for any help.

For she loved Miguel.

At first, years ago, when she saw him at dances or after church, she had convinced herself that her love was pure. Wasn't she a good Catholic girl seeking a man to reform, seeking a union more spiritual than physical? Before she went to sleep then she would think of how his lips would feel on hers— soft, gentle, undemanding.

She walked faster. She walked faster thinking of the first time he touched her. He had smiled slowly at her quick response, at her soft moans when he kissed her deeply, when he touched her breasts lightly with the palms of his hands.

Through the years the song of Miguel's touch remained. To her neighbors she was an attractive, religious woman. But at night or on Sunday afternoons, she and Miguel wrapped their legs around each other and rocked to their secret music.

But the music had begun to fade. Two months ago Cuca had cried after their lovemaking.

"What?" asked Miguel.

"You don't stroke my body anymore. I bore you." Cuca did not like to discuss sex. The words had caused her pain.

Miguel patted her head, got dressed, left for a few hours. They never spoke of the change again, but the lovemaking became shorter, less often.

Cuca had reached the edge of Juarez. She began down the dirt road to Bruja's house. She had seen this woman at the market. She dressed in black— black blouse, long black skirt, black shawl wrapped around her head. The gossips said Bruja's gray hair reached to her waist and that when she danced alone in the desert, the moonlight did not dare touch the gray strands that spun round and round.

Cuca's palms were damp as she carefully walked up the two steps leading to the small porch. Jars of herbs covered most of the rotting planks. A pungent smell almost frightened Cuca away.

But his hands.

She wanted Miguel's hands back on her body. She wanted to feel his desire warm, under his skin.

She knocked. Bruja opened the door.

Her eyes were pale blue. They stung Cuca much as the herb smell had stung her nostrils.

Bruja walked to the table in the center of the room. Cuca followed her, darting quick glances at the chipped furniture, the old black stove, the small bedroom adjoining the larger room.

Bruja sat and motioned for Cuca to sit opposite her. Cuca wanted to run.

"I am thirty-eight," she thought. "And I want to run to my mother. But my mother is dead, and the Virgin ignores my prayers."

"What do you want," asked Bruja. Her voice was flat. She began to shred dried herbs into a mayonnaise jar.

"I am embarrassed to be here," said Cuca. "I am embarrassed to have such a weak body."

"You look healthy," said Bruja.

"But I *need,*" said Cuca slowly. "I need my husband back."

"He has gone to Texas?" asked Bruja watching Cuca's face with her pale eyes.

"No. No, he is in Juarez. He is in my bed. But I know that when he touches me in his sleep, it is her he wants. He opens his hands wide, reaching for her large breasts."

"You have seen this woman?" asked Bruja still showing no interest or emotion.

Cuca dug her nails into her palms. "Yes," she whispered. "I followed him to her room. I've stood across the street and watched her. I've seen her stand before her mirror admiring her body, remembering his hands pressing on her skin as they once pressed on mine."

Cuca bit her finger. She hated for others to see her weakness. Only Miguel had seen her lose control. "Yes," he would say urgently. "Let go. Let go. I'll bring you back."

Bruja looked out the window for a long time.

"I hear you shrink things," said Cuca.

Bruja looked at her.

"I hear you shrunk a man's private parts."

"Is that what you want me to do to your husband?" asked Bruja with a trace of a smile.

"I want you to shrink her breasts. I want you to make her flat like a boy. I want him to feel bones beneath her skin and to long for my warm softness. And I'll be there waiting. I will take him back. And we will rock wildly in the dark."

Bruja said nothing.

The sound of their breathing filled the room.

Finally Bruja went into the bedroom. She returned with a small jar of brownish power.

"I can make her breasts disappear," said Bruja. "I can't promise that your man will return."

"I know my Miguel. He will return."

"Ten American dollars," said Bruja.

Cuca was surprised at the amount, although she didn't show it. She had saved carefully this last month. She had known she must either pay to have Masses said or see Bruja. And one didn't ask the Lord to remove a woman's breasts.

"You must sprinkle this powder outside her door every day for a month. Each day the breasts will grow smaller. At the end of the month your husband will feel bones."

Bruja then reached into a large basket. She removed needle, thread, stuffing, and a small, crude cloth figure. Her fingers worked quickly. Soon she handed Cuca the cloth doll.

"Each morning after your husband leaves for work, snip a bit of the breasts from this figure. Guide the magic, but slowly, slowly."

Cuca paid Bruja. She stuffed the powder and doll into her purse and left quickly. She half-ran all the way back to her neighborhood.

The next morning she could hardly wait for Miguel to leave.

"You seem nervous," he said.

As soon as she was sure he'd left the block, she went into the bathroom with a pair of scissors and the cloth figures. She pulled hard at the cloth nipples and snipped a small piece from each. She flushed the cloth away and hid the doll under her slips and gowns.

She then hurried to the woman's small room. She walked by the door, sprinkled the powder carefully, and walked on.

That day she was supremely happy. She smiled at her neighbors and spent hours in her kitchen cooking *chiles rellenos,* and *flan.*

That evening while Miguel was gone she knelt by the bed and said the rosary. Seldom had she felt as devout.

The ritual of snipping, flushing, sprinkling, continued day after day. At the end of the week Cuca was frantic to know if her money had been well spent. She stood, partly hidden, across from the girl's room and waited.

In time the young woman stood before her mirror wearing only a thin lilac gown. She looked in the mirror for a long time, then turned to the side. She cupped her hands to her breasts then slowly looked at her palms.

Cuca smiled. She wanted to throw back her head and laugh. She wanted to dance on the girl's bed. Instead she walked home quickly.

Snip. Flush. Sprinkle.

"You can only go once a week," she said to herself. She bought a low-cut blouse and began wearing it in the evenings, after supper. She would catch Miguel staring at her, and she would smile softly.

She began to sleep facing him again. And she waited for the music to return.

At the end of the second week, she again hid across from the girl's window. Cuca bit her finger as she waited.

In time the girl stood before the mirror, again wearing only a thin gown. The sight of the girl's small breasts caused Cuca to bite so hard she tasted blood.

She walked to the market and bought a bag of milk candy for the neighborhood children. "It is a sweet life, little ones," she said as she returned their smiles of surprise. "Sweet, sweet."

She washed the gown Miguel had always liked most on her. She remembered how she would say, "Poor green gown, you are never left on me long enough to be appreciated."

And Miguel would whisper, "I want to appreciate you."

That night Cuca started yawning early. "You look tired, Miguel. Don't go out."

Miguel frowned. "Business," he said. He returned late, but Cuca was still awake. Waiting. She pulled the bodice of the gown to reveal more of her warm flesh.

Miguel lay staring at the ceiling, Cuca edged closer to him. She licked her lips, slowly.

"Miguel," she finally said softly.

"Yes, Cuca, yes," he said with a sigh, and he rolled her over and began to rub her back slowly, very slowly until he fell asleep.

Cuca began to dig her nails into her palms again. In the morning she wanted to throw Miguel out of the house so that she could pull out the doll. The breasts were almost gone now. A month had almost passed.

Cuca returned to her hiding place behind a large, old tree on the girl's street. This time Cuca did not have to wait at all. The young girl was standing before the mirror wearing a skirt and no blouse. She was naked from the waist up. The girl was running her hands over her hard, flat chest, moving her hands up and down, pressing into the bones. Smiling.

And Cuca remembers that at night now, Miguel would roll her over in his sleep, and rub her back. He would almost hurt her as he stroked the smooth lines slowly, and then more and more quickly, and his breathing would grow heavy.

1910

Pat Mora

In Mexico they bowed
  their heads when she passed.
   Timid villagers stepped aside
    for the Judge's mother, Doña Luz,
who wore her black shawl, black
  gloves whenever she left her home—
    at the church, the *mercado,* and the *plaza*
      in the cool evenings when she strolled
        barely touching her son's wrist
          with her fingertips,
who wore her black shawl, black
  gloves in the carriage that took her
    and her family to Juarez, border town, away
      from Villa laughing at their terror when
        he rode through the village shouting,
          spitting dust,
who wore her black shawl, black
  gloves when she crossed the Rio Grande to
    El Paso, her back straight, chin high,
      never watching her feet,
who wore her black shawl, black
  gloves into Upton's Five-and-Dime,
    who walked out, back straight, lips quivering,
    and slowly removed her shawl and gloves,
      placed them on the sidewalk with the other
        shawls and shopping bags
          "You Mexicans can't hide
          things from me," Upton would say.
          "Thieves. All thieves.
          Let me see those hands."
who wore her black shawl, black
  gloves the day she walked, chin high,
    never watching her feet, on the black
      beams and boards, still smoking,
        that had been Upton's Five-and-Dime.

Josefina's Chickens

Gina Valdés

It was during The Depression, and Josefina Portillo's prices had gone up along with everyone else's. But in spite of her exorbitant fees, Josefina la curandera's patients were numerous and growing. Her fame as a healer extended to both sides of the U.S.–Mexico border and reached its peak in the California barrio where she resided.

Josefina was a bosomy woman in her late fifties, and she wore her long white hair in two braids pinned on top of her head. She had a high laugh and when she laughed her bosom moved up and down. When she was not attending to her patients, she was working on an herb garden that filled her back yard. The rest of the time she spent caring for her 20 chickens. In the last few weeks, not only Josefina's cures, but also her chickens had become the main topic of conversation in the barrio.

"I can't go on like this, comadre," said one woman to another at the neighborhood mercado. "I haven't been able to sleep well all week; something must be done about Josefina's chickens."

"I haven't been able to sleep a complete night either, we should do something, somebody should tell her to keep her chickens quiet."

"I can't understand it comadre, all other chickens I know of sleep at night, something must be wrong with Josefina's chickens."

Several other women joined the conversation.

"Ay!" said Romelia. "Those chickens are driving me and my husband crazy; he wants to speak to her."

"That's a good idea," agreed the women.

"I told my husband not to."

"But why? Somebody should speak to her."

"Let someone else do it, I'm too indebted to her. She cured my boy of dysentery."

"How about you Cuca? She has never cured you or your family of any ills."

"Not me. Never know when I might need her. Besides, I wouldn't want to anger a curandera."

Not only the neighbors had grown restless with Josefina's chickens, but her sister Consuelo, who lived with her, was no longer willing to be kept awake at night by 20 noisy chickens. She stood in front of Josefina who was tending a mint plant. They were not far from the chicken coop where the 20 chickens lay, apparently asleep. "Look at them," shouted Consuelo in her high voice. "They sleep all day and cackle all night. If you don't get rid of those chickens, we'll soon have chicken mole."

"My chickens don't cackle all night, you're exaggerating as usual. They're fine little creatures, fine chickens."

"They'll make good mole," said Consuelo shuffling away.

"You stay away from my chickens!"

The truth was that Josefina herself had been worrying about the chickens. She went into her bedroom, locked the door, took out a small notebook and pencil from a locked drawer, sat on a wicker chair with the notebook and pencil on her lap and closed her eyes. A few minutes later she opened her eyes and began to write in the notebook. The first word she wrote was "bewitched." She thought of this for a moment. "Who could have done it?" "Consuelo," she wrote in her notebook. Consuelo hated her chickens more than anybody else. She hated them since the first day that Josefina had brought them home, even before they had begun to cackle at night. She crossed out Consuelo's name. "She has the motives, but she doesn't have the power," thought Josefina. "No. Consuelo couldn't bewitch a flea." A list of relatives and neighbors ran through her mind, but she dismissed them all. No one had the power. "A prowling animal," wrote Josefina. She crossed it out. "A dog can't jump the high fence around the house, and there are no coyotes in the city except those that chase women, not chickens." The image of a lean cat drooling in front of the chicken coop filled her mind. "Maybe a very hungry cat. Maybe." She closed her notebook, placed it back in the drawer, locked it, walked out of the room, and locked the door as usual. She always kept her bedroom locked whether she was in it or out of it. Consuelo stood nearby watching her and shaking her head.

"Spying on me again? Why don't you find something useful to do."

"I could slaughter your chickens."

"You stay away from them. I'm warning you."

Josefina put on the wide straw hat that she always wore when she went out in the sun. She stood in front of the chicken coop and observed the chickens. They all lay on the floor immobile, their eyes glazed. She glanced over the fence next to the chicken coop. On the other side of the fence lived her younger brother Severino, his wife Carlota, and their seven children. She thought of the children. "Little devils, everyone of them." She looked at the chickens, and then at the fence. "Maybe it's one of Severino's brats." But Josefina had doubts. Her brother's children never went near her house—they were afraid to do so. Whenever one of them ventured near the women's house they invariably caught them in one of their arguments and sneaked away for fear of being caught in the fight.

Severino worked hard at various jobs in order to support his family. But with seven children, and in such hard times, it had become an impossible task. So Severino reached a desperate solution.

A large storage room in back of Severino's house served as the Portillo Distillery. He could brew a fine drink—flavorful and potent: 100 percent proof. He put on a white starched apron and began his work with the seriousness of a chemist. He began early in the morning and worked for long hours brewing and bottling the strong liquor. As soon as he finished he called a neighbor who was an old friend of his, and together they began the tasting ritual. They began with a small spoon, then they used a larger spoon, then a glass, and finally they graduated to the sealed bottles. Eventually, the two men passed out and when they came to, they started all over again. During the intervals that the two men were passed out, Carlota went into the room and took the bottles. She worked quickly, sometimes with the help of a daughter or son, taking as many bottles as she could.

Carlota was strongly opposed to her husband's bootlegging, but not for moral reasons since it was The Depression and they had many children to feed. And it was not for fear that Severino might be caught, since that meant that he would be jailed and that was the only way she could hope to keep him at a distance. Her main objection was that he never made any money at it.

Carlota passed the bottles over the fence to the eager hands of Josefina. Josefina was always cheerful at brewing times, she had good use for the bottles. While her younger brother drank the profits, she became a wealthy woman. Josefina sold her brother's brew as an expensive cure-all. Carlota often wondered whether her patients used the brew as medicine or if they went along with Josefina's game and bought the bottles as medicine but used it as the liquor that it was, but during those times Josefina's fame as a curandera soared.

What neither Carlota nor Josefina knew was that the liquor bottles weren't the only thing passing over the fence. When brewing was completed, Severino took the powerful sediments and threw them over the fence and into the chicken coop. The chickens went straight to it becoming hopelessly drunk.

When The Depression was over, everyone in the country rejoiced. But few were as ecstatic as Carlota, Consuelo, and Josefina's neighbors—they no longer had to contend with drunk chickens; now they could all return to their usual problems.

Adelita

Ana Montes

Adelita,
Gentle with the dead,
Fierce in battle,
Loving in faith,
And side by side you bled.

Your heart
                    broken
by the sights of bodies
strewn in the fields of war.
Yet, you remained.

Adelita,
Today you are called
                 Chicana.

Woman of women
Amor de la Revolución
Sangre de la tierra
Flor entre de los muertos.[21]

Chicana,
You still struggle.

Adelita,
You fought long and hard
A gun in your hand;
A gleam in your eyes
and faith in your heart.

Your mind and body were ravaged,
Your people suffered,
Your families lost.
Yet you remained,
You withstood the battles of hate,
And left a trail of hope.

Note: This poem is printed as it was originally published, although it is part of a longer work.

21. Love of the revolution / blood of the earth / a flower among the dead

You saw what other revolucionarios saw,
You killed when necessary,
You fell like them all.

Guerrillera Soy / I Am A Warrior Woman

Inés Hernández

Con cada gota de mi sangre
con todo mi mente y mi ser
con cada suspiro
pensamiento
lágrima y anhelo

con cada coraje que paso
y en cada demuestra de amor

En cualquier momento
que me 'ncuentras

Guerrillera soy

■

With each drop of my blood
With all my mind and my being
With each sigh
thought
tear and longing

With each rage that I feel
and in each demonstration of love

At whatever moment
that you find me

I am a warrior woman

Sor Juana

Estela Portillo Trambley

ACT I: Synopsis

Convent of St. Jerome, Mexico City, 1693. Sor Juana is warring with herself and her capacity for passion. She has become ill from self-flagellation and self-denial. She atones for her sin of pride and passion by serving the poor. Flashbacks into Sor Juana's life reveal some of her background. She dreams about her childhood with her two slaves, Andrés and Juana. She dreams about her relationship with Bernardo, a young nobleman who is betrothed to Laura. Juana will not be able to marry well because she is illegitimate. Unable to study at the university because she is a woman, she nevertheless shows her brilliance at court. She becomes a nun feeling knowledge will be the path to her salvation. Her relationship to Father Antonio, her confessor, is explored.

ACT II: Scene 1

The next evening. Rosary bell is heard. Juana, sitting crosslegged in bed, wearing a sackcloth wrapper, is playing a flute very softly, awkwardly, stopping every so often to touch it. She stops to listen to church bell, then covers face with hands. A tray of untouched food sits on one of the boxes. Sor Feliciana enters, crosses to tray, inspects it. Juana puts flute under pillow.

SOR FELICIANA   You didn't touch your food.

SOR JUANA   I drank my tea. Stopped the shivering . . .

SOR FELICIANA   (*Crosses to bed, touches Sor Juana's forehead.*) You're still feverish. Did you sleep?

SOR JUANA   I don't want to sleep—I don't want to dream.

SOR FELICIANA   (*Sits on bed next to Sor Juana.*) I wanted to spend the day with you. We went out for wood and had such problems!

SOR JUANA   There's no more coal?

SOR FELICIANA   Supply wagons cannot get into the city. They're ambushed by the people up on the mountain. No fruits or meat . . .

SOR JUANA   They're starving, those people up on the mountain. They need the food more than we do. It's all so different, so terrifying. (*Crosses to window.*) Look, out there, the *locutorio*,[22] silent, dark. Over a year now. Is the whole world like that now?

---

22. parlor where nuns received visitors; literally "talking room."

SOR FELICIANA   They're all dark now, all the locutorios of Mexico. Don't you remember? The Commissary of the Inquisition decided on that long before the burning of the city. I hear they are dark all over Spain, too.

SOR JUANA   Sinful. Isn't that what the locutorios are supposed to be? And my plays? And all the festivals for the saints? I believe it now. My whole life was sinful . . .

SOR FELICIANA   That's not the truth, Sor Juana. The locutorio of St. Jerome, thanks to you, was the spiritual center for the devout. Great people, great minds, gathered out there. They all found a path to your door. You have always been faithful to the precepts of St. Jerome, to knowledge.

SOR JUANA   Faithful to knowledge, but not to my vows . . .

SOR FELICIANA   You're never going to get well with all that guilt inside of you. You never did anything wrong. You, of all people, the most gentle, the most wise.

SOR JUANA   I miss the garden so. Where there were flowers, there are turnips now. But we cannot eat flowers, can we . . .

SOR FELICIANA   After rosary services I'm coming back with hot soup, and you're going to eat it. I'm going to make you. Food, rest will get you well . . .

SOR JUANA   You think so? I wonder where he is right now . . .

SOR FELICIANA   Who?

SOR JUANA   My confessor, my tormentor . . .

SOR FELICIANA   The last I heard, Father Antonio was leading a wagon train with food and medicine for the starving of Zacatecas. No harvest there.

SOR JUANA   Always with the poor, the sick, the hungry. But he knows how to gain Heaven, on earth as well. I didn't understand before, but now I wish I had spent my life the way he has. But he's so old. He shouldn't travel long distances any more. If only I could see him, talk to him one more time . . .

SOR FELICIANA   Oh, dear Aunt, you will see him. Sor Catarina has sent for him.

SOR JUANA   But he was forbidden to ever see me again.

SOR FELICIANA   That won't stop him if he knows you have been ill.

SOR JUANA   Oh, dear God, thank you for the hope! Days will be good again just waiting for him! (*Rosary bell rings again.*)

SOR FELICIANA   (*Kisses Sor Juana, crosses to door.*) I must go now, but I'll be back after services. (*Exits.*)

SOR JUANA   (*Crosses to window.*) I miss the flowers so!

(*Light fades on cell, comes up on flashback area. A table down right; a chair with a flower basket full of bouquets next to it. Sor Juana enters with a handful of* cut ribbons; Sor Feliciana follows. St. Jerome has been the home of Sor Juana for seventeen years. She wears a tunic of white wool, blue-edged, double-sleeved. Outside sleeve is bell-shaped, giving a certain elegance to the habit. Over the tunic is a long black scapulary (two small slips of cloth almost the length of the tunic underneath). The scapulary is six inches shorter than the tunic. On the front piece of the scapulary is an image over the chest area. Emblem of the Annunciation, the Virgin Mary standing to the right of a recliner where a book lies open. The left hand of the Virgin lies on the book. Opposite the Virgin, on the other side of the recliner, is the imprint of the Archangel Gabriel with folded white wings. On her head, Sor Juana wears a white toque and over that a long black veil. On her waist is a wide leather belt with a brass buckle. On her feet, plain black closed shoes and cotton stockings. Around her neck and falling parallel to the scapulary is a black rosary (fifteen mysteries). The large gold cross of the rosary is adjusted high on the left sleeve of her tunic. The habit of the Order of St. Jerome. Sor Juana and Sor Feliciana put a ribbon around each of the bouquets. A children's choir begins to sing as they go about their labor.)

Aquella zagala
Del mirar sereno
Hechizo del soto
Y envidia del cielo

La que el mayoral
De la cumbre excelso
Hirió con sus ojos
Hirió con sus ojos . . .

(Harmony without lyrics is heard.)

SOR FELICIANA   The legend of the nymph. How beautiful, your words, your music.

SOR JUANA   My farewell gift for Lisi. The nymph that disappears in light. Oh, why must the people we love leave us . . .

La ninfa del valle
Donde nací
Vuela, bailando
La escala de luz

En alto peñasco
Donde tiembla el sol
Canta la ninfa
Canta, canta
Con voz celestial.

SOR FELICIANA   There. All done. After they sing, each child will offer a bouquet to the Count and the Countess.

SOR JUANA   Overwhelmed by flowers. My last festivity for them. They love this garden so, dear Count, dearest Lisi.

SOR FELICIANA   Dr. Pavón is due any minute now.

SOR JUANA   Oh dear, I forgot all about the interview. I suppose I must find the time since I said I would, but I do have so many preparations yet for the festivities tomorrow.

SOR FELICIANA   Would you like to see him here in the garden?

SOR JUANA   Yes, send him out here.

(*Sor Feliciana exits. Sor Juana notices her slave.*)

SOR JUANA   There you are. Go tell Timoteo I would like the chairs set up this afternoon. A canopy over the Count and Countess' chair.

SLAVE JUANA   Mistress . . .

SOR JUANA   Let's see. I've taken care of the pastries, the chocolate came in from Chiapas. The Count's favorite wine must be chilled. And more flowers—of course, I must see to the flowers. (*Notices her slave.*) Go, girl, do as I say.

SLAVE JUANA   You said I could go and see Andrés.

SOR JUANA   What?

SLAVE JUANA   You forgot about Andrés. . . .

SOR JUANA   Oh, I'm sorry. It did slip my mind. How is he? You saw him yesterday?

SLAVE JUANA   He beat bad. He and Camila hide. I go take them food.

SOR JUANA   You must be careful not to implicate yourself.

SLAVE JUANA   He my brother.

SOR JUANA   What he did is considered a most serious crime. He has run away from Don Martín many times before, but this time he turned on his master. That is a serious crime. Have you heard? Is Don Martín dead?

SLAVE JUANA   Don Martín evil man. Good if he die.

SOR JUANA   May God forgive Andrés.

SLAVE JUANA   And you?

SOR JUANA   Juana!

SLAVE JUANA   I beg you buy Andrés away from Don Martín!

SOR JUANA   You know I spoke to him about it, again and again. A stubborn man—a slave is a slave to him.

SLAVE JUANA   The Count, the Countess, your friends—they could make him. They are important people. They could force Don Martín.

SOR JUANA   You don't know what you're talking about. It's a delicate subject. There are certain unspoken rules about a master and his slaves. I cannot take sides.

SLAVE JUANA   You forgot Andrés was like your brother long ago.

SOR JUANA   I have not forgotten. But that was long ago. It's a different world.

SLAVE JUANA   You not love Andrés. You not care. Andrés and Camila go to mountain where people hide. Soon they will fight!

SOR JUANA   Fight? That is only fearful talk. It will not come to that.

SLAVE JUANA   You do not see because your nose in book all the time.

SOR JUANA   Enough. If only all men were equal. Perhaps some day this will be, through the help of God, knowledge.

SLAVE JUANA   Your head stuffed with words, Sister. Pretty, silly words, Sister.

SOR JUANA   How dare you!

SLAVE JUANA   You say I is like your sister.

SOR JUANA   You are also my slave.

SLAVE JUANA   Then why you say we is equal?

SOR JUANA   Go to Andrés. Help him as best you can. Tell him I will pray for him.

SLAVE JUANA   Many starve on mountain.

SOR JUANA   I will pray for them too.

SLAVE JUANA   That will not fill their bellies.

SOR JUANA   Prayer moves mountains . . .

SLAVE JUANA   Don't move mountains. Just give more food.

SOR JUANA   I said enough! Now go.

SLAVE JUANA   (*Turns to go, then stops.*) Andrés and Camila will not come back this time. They will not be caught. They have wagon and gun.

SOR JUANA   May God keep them safe. (*Watches Slave Juana go, puts hand to forehead as if head hurts.*) Why must the world change so? I remember slaves singing at the plow. But I was a child then. I cannot bridge the years anymore. Oh my, I must see to those flowers. (*Sor Feliciana enters with Dr. Ignacio Pavón, a Peruvian poet who has come from Lima to interview Sor Juana.*)

SOR FELICIANA   Sor Juana, this is Dr. Ignacio Pavón. He has come all the way from Lima, Peru, just to interview you.

DR. PAVON   Sor Juana Inés de la Cruz, a great honor. (*Kisses her hand.*)

SOR JUANA   Dr. Pavón.

SOR FELICIANA   You'll forgive me. I have duties to attend to.

DR. PAVON   Thank you for leading me to this garden and to this great lady.

SOR FELICIANA   Goodbye, Dr. Pavón. (*Exits*)

SOR JUANA   You have caught me in the midst of preparations—a farewell party for the Count of Paredes and his wife, Lisi.

DR. PAVON   I am intruding . . .

SOR JUANA   On, no, please! This is the perfect time. I need someone to cheer me up. A poet, you are!

DR. PAVON   A humble one in the light of your great fame. Beautiful place,
     St. Jerome.
SOR JUANA   My home for seventeen years.
DR. PAVON   Fruitful years.
SOR JUANA   They have not been idle. May I offer you some refreshment?
DR. PAVON   Not at the moment, thank you. I have come across an ocean to
     set eyes on the Tenth Muse.
SOR JUANA   So, I am pursued into pagan temples! My church is Christ's
     church.
DR. PAVON   In your writings, you have given that Christian humanity to the
     pagans. You cannot deny you love the Greeks.
SOR JUANA   The Greeks are the open door to our humanity. Tell me of your
     work, your country.
DR. PAVON   What does a poet do? I'm a man coiled in his own passions,
     unwinding, discovering, and sometimes, and mind you only sometimes,
     attempting to re-create with words some kind of energy lost in my
     people. A sad attempt to remold our poor misguided civilization.
SOR JUANA   Unwinding passions—how beautifully you put it. We are crea-
     tures of passion, are we not? Writers! What a lot we are!
DR. PAVON   All I've read by you, of you, is full of passion.
SOR JUANA   My greatest passion has been to learn and learn and learn. My
     way to God.
DR. PAVON   There is, of course, your strong faith.
SOR JUANA   I shall share a secret with you.
DR. PAVON   A secret?
SOR JUANA   You journalists are always looking for something new. For a long
     time now, I have come to believe that my love for knowledge is much
     more than a passion. It's madness.
DR. PAVON   Madness? I don't understand . . .
SOR JUANA   Some time ago, a holy and candid abbess who was my superior
     forbade me to study. I was ordered not to read a single book. She believed
     that knowledge was a form of inquisition. I did as I was told. I did not
     study. I did not even take a book into my hands. A very difficult thing for
     me to do.
DR. PAVON   She had no right . . .
SOR JUANA   Oh yes, she did! She was a most holy abbess. She was true to
     her vows. She lived by faith alone. Her path to God was different from
     my own. Well, when I could no longer read, I found myself overwhelmed
     by a curiosity. I studied the things that God created, all around me—little
     things. One morning walking through the doorway to my bedroom, I

observed that though the lines of the two sides of the hall were parallel and its ceiling was level, the eye pretended that its lines leaned toward each other and that its ceiling was lower in the distant part. I inferred that visual lines run straight, but not parallel, forming a pyramid figure. I told myself that was the reason the ancients doubted that the earth was spherical. But then I told myself it could be a trick of the eyesight. Thoughts came like this one, one after another, day after day. It was like a fever consuming me. More than a passion.

DR. PAVON   But such journeys of the mind are exciting.

SOR JUANA   My mind would not rest. I remember watching the little girls we teach here at St. Jerome playing with a top one day. I noticed the easy movement of the spherical form and how long the impulse lasted once it was independent of its cause. I ran to the kitchen and took a handful of flour. I sifted it on a table, then took the top and spun it on the table. I spun it thus to see if the circles made by its movements were perfectly circular or not. I discovered that only some spiral lines lost their circularity as soon as they transmitted their impulse. Then to my mind came the thought that in the study of music, harmony is circular. A spiral! Such thoughts invaded my mind, invade my mind still these days, though I now spend long hours reading, experimenting. God wants me to understand my universe. Did you know I had been accused of heresy for doing what I do? The Bishop of Puebla does not approve of me. They would like me to study more of the sacred theology. Little do they know that both can be reconciled . . .

DR. PAVON   You have found a way . . .

SOR JUANA   Of course! Without Rhetoric, how could I understand the figures, the tropes, the locution of the Holy Scripture? Or, without Physics, how could I understand the many natural problems of the nature of sacrificial animals? Without Arithmetic, could I understand the computations of days, months, hours, weeks as mysteries, as were those of Daniel? How without Geometry could I measure the Holy Chest of the Testament and even the Holy City of Jerusalem, whose mysteries thus measured form a cube? All those dimensions! And the marvelous distribution of all its parts! Without Architecture, how could I understand the Great Temple of Solomon? God Himself was the Architect who gave the disposition and plan. The Wise King was only the foreman who executed it. They accuse me of loving knowledge more than God.

(*Light fades out on flashback area, comes up on cell area. Sor Juana is still by the window, looking out. She suddenly turns, crosses to bed, takes out flute from under the pillow. Plays a few notes softly, then touches it tenderly.*)

SOR JUANA You gave this to me, Andrés. Your one possession. You and Juana said goodbye forever. Yes, it was forever! We were children, free. (*She plays a few more notes, then hugs flute, crosses to window again.*) Oh, God, are You out there in the hovels where children cry of hunger? Are You out there in the ashes that were the marketplace, where the hanging tree sways with the wind? Are You here, with me and my pain? No! I want to remember happy times. The garden full of people and laughter . . . the last party we ever had in the garden. The very last one. Even then the sounds of a wounded world, heavy with pain, hung in the air.

(*Light fades on cell area, comes up on flashback area. There are three chairs, very ornate under a canopy. The center chair is raised slightly above the others. A single ordinary chair is outside the canopy. Sor Juana is seated on the raised chair. The Count de Paredes sits to her right. Lisi, his wife, sits to her left. Dr. Pavón sits on the single chair outside the canopy.*)

LISI I shall remember this day. The children were lovely, all our friends so kind! I hate to say goodbye to Mexico.

COUNT I too shall miss Mexico, though I confess the Mexico outside these walls is not to my liking. The Indian, the zambo, has forgotten the good we have brought to this new world. We civilized a primitive people. Now they turn against us.

DR. PAVON I equate civilization with violence, M'Lord. The white man has been less than a humanizing force.

COUNT Did you hear about Don Rafael Martín? Attacked by one of his slaves. Found unconscious in the granary.

SOR JUANA Will he die?

COUNT He'll recover, but two slaves are gone, his wagon, his horse, and stores from his warehouse. Who is safe these days!

SOR JUANA Humane masters, perhaps. Don Martín treats his slaves like animals.

COUNT Do you condone the crime?

SOR JUANA I don't condone crime, but all circumstances must be understood before the word "crime" is given to a single desperate act.

COUNT Those runaway slaves have a good head start into mountain country. Don Martín's soldiers gave up the chase. I suppose you're glad the two slaves escaped. I'm afraid the mountains have their own merciless bondage. They may starve, freeze to death, become the prey of wild animals.

SOR JUANA May God protect them and keep them safe.

COUNT Would you say the same prayer for Don Martín?

SOR JUANA There is no need. He is surrounded by comfort and care.

LISI   M'Lord, let's enjoy our last visit to St. Jerome. Oh, the memories I take
with me—music, laughter, brilliant conversation. Sor Juana drawing,
quoting her poetry, or passionate over a new scientific finding. Sor Juana,
the center of our lives . . . I shall miss you so, dear friend.

COUNT   We should not be at odds, Sor Juana. I know you love us well. Ah,
the peace of this place. Such flowers!

SOR JUANA   I shall miss you both. Six years. I've known you and loved you
both for six years. And you have done so much good, M'Lord.

COUNT   I hope that during my reign I made the right decisions. I tried to. I
pride myself in being a man in touch with the times. But dreams erode.
The world is full of wolf packs and each great nation in time falls victim.

SOR JUANA   Ah, Dr. Pavón. There is much to say about His Excellency. He
has been a compassionate ruler, just and right as if he were born to be
nothing less.

DR. PAVON   I have heard the like said of him. But you are right, dear Count,
the wolf packs are growing. When I arrived in Vera Cruz, a French pirate
ship had gone into Acapulco and carried off forty women.

COUNT   The Gulf is infested. Another problem for the new viceroy.

DR. PAVON   Ah yes! Count Monclova is a favorite of the Peruvian court. Has
an arm made of silver. Lost it in a naval battle. For many years he was the
companion of Her Excellency, the Vicereine of Peru. He carries a gold
casket aboard his ship. It's said to be full of gold and diamonds and a
bone belonging to St. Rose of Lima. It is his protection against pirates.
He will rule with a silver arm . . . preferable to ruling with an iron hand,
eh? (*Laughs.*)

LISI   Alas, he has no wife. No one to lead him to this wonderful place. I
daresay he will come to meet you, Sor Juana, and will attend one of your
gatherings in the locutorio.

SOR JUANA   I fear it will not be so. There is the weight of too much
criticism—of me, of St. Jerome, of locutorios in general. It can only
get worse.

LISI   You have our protection even from across the sea.

SOR JUANA   I know it and I thank you.

LISI   Whatever happens, your work will be published. I'm taking all you have
ever written to a publisher in Madrid.

SOR JUANA   They are the only children I have conceived. Imperfect but they
are yours . . .

LISI   They shall belong to the world . . .

(*Light fades on flashback area, come up on cell. Sor Juana sits on bed and
begins to play flute. Stage slowly darkens.*)

ACT II: Scene 2

(The next afternoon. Sor Juana and Sor Feliciana are standing over the boxes.)

SOR JUANA   I want all articles and letters in this small box. Books in the large one.

SOR FELICIANA   Are you up to doing this?

SOR JUANA   Of course I am. Look at me. You fed me last night. I ate every-thing this morning. My fever's gone—and Father Antonio might come today. It's Wednesday, isn't it? He always came for tea on Wednesdays when he was in the city, remember?

SOR FELICIANA   Don't set your hopes too high.

SOR JUANA   It's a beautiful day, isn't it? Anyway, let's put all these things away. Once everything is put away I shall feel that I have turned another page in my life, and the page is clean, waiting for new experiences. We shall bury these things deep in the dungeon of this convent.

SOR FELICIANA   There's no dungeon.

SOR JUANA   Very well. We shall store them somewhere dark where spiders can build their webs. I do not want my past.

SOR FELICIANA   I see your guilt did not disappear with the fever.

SOR JUANA   He will never recognize this place. I don't even have a table to serve tea! I must have a table.

SOR FELICIANA   We'll find one if he comes.

SOR JUANA   Of course he's going to come. Let's start with this box.
(She kneels on floor and starts taking books and papers from a box to sort them. Comes across a copy of her love sonnets. She turns the pages.)

SOR FELICIANA   What's that?

SOR JUANA   Poems . . .

SOR FELICIANA   May I? *(Sor Juana hands book to her.)* Your sonnets! How beautiful.

SOR JUANA   Not now . . .

SOR FELICIANA   Wait! *(She begins to read.)* "Love begins, a faint restlessness, a burning wakeful anxiety, growing in slopes, transections, feeding on tears, entreaty . . ."

SOR JUANA   Ancient, ancient feelings.

SOR FELICIANA   Your feelings?

SOR JUANA   All mine. The pain of youth.

SOR FELICIANA   *(Continues reading.)* "Love, shadow of my scornful good, bewitched image, fair illusion for which I'd gladly die, sweet confection, for which I live in torment . . ."

SOR JUANA   They sound so awkward—such rash feelings.

SOR FELICIANA   Someone hurt you very much.

SOR JUANA   We suffer so when we are young. The howls of my pain.

SOR FELICIANA   Is that why you took the veil?

SOR JUANA   Who knows one's reasons for doing those things that change one's life? What comes to mind is a childhood memory. There was a mulatto on my grandfather's farm, a misshapen man, an idiot, they used to say. Even as a child I could read the hurting loneliness in his eyes by the way he walked and held his head. Poor creature! One morning when the dark was dissolving, I followed him out into the desert, wondering what he did out there so early in the morning. He ran to the middle of a sand hill. The wind moaned and the dust curled under his feet. He held up his arms as if pleading with the morning sky, then fell to his knees. Suddenly he raised his head and howled. Just howled—a long, sad, empty sound that ran into the stillness of the sun. That was his loneliness, his pain. He freed himself of the heavy cutting burden, to face the day.

SOR FELICIANA   How sad. What happened to him?

SOR JUANA   He disappeared. I always imagined he had walked off into the desert and found a place where he was like everyone else. Those words are just the way I howl.

SOR FELICIANA   Your sensitive, beautiful words?

SOR JUANA   Why not? The writing of those sonnets washed me clean. The anger, doubt, bitterness, all washed away.

SOR FELICIANA   Who was he?

SOR JUANA   A young nobleman, foolish and unwise, no different from myself.

SOR FELICIANA   It must have been so painful . . .

SOR JUANA   The grave agony that begins with desire, then that sudden rushing melancholy, evaporating contradictions. Those are the contradictions.

SOR FELICIANA   (Reading through the pages.) You speak of deception, again and again. (Reads.) "Triumph, my love, you who kills me with disdain. And he who loves me, I myself, kill, for he loves in vain. I do not know if love is hate, or hate is love, for both are fires that prick the skin and move the heart and sweeten all the air."

SOR JUANA   He will come today. I know he will . . .

SOR FELICIANA   It's not a certainty.

SOR JUANA   I am not at my best . . . my wool tunic, the blue-edged one— the embroidered scapulary, the one from Spain. . . . Look at me—so disheveled.

SOR FELICIANA   All you have is what you're wearing.

SOR JUANA   How stupid of me! I forgot. Is there some tea left in the kitchen? Just a little. (Looks around room.) He will be shocked, the way I look, the room—so empty, bare.

SOR FELICIANA   You sold everything. Do you regret it? All your beautiful things, your books, your instruments.

SOR JUANA   No! There's no regret. My empty cell will please Father Antonio. It vexed him so, my having all those luxuries. May God forgive me! Is it three o'clock? He always came at three . . . so punctual!

SOR FELICIANA   It's closer to five.

SOR JUANA   Five . . . No! Sister Catarina sent for him. It's been two weeks now.

SOR FELICIANA   We have not received word as to his whereabouts. The fact that it's Wednesday doesn't mean . . .

SOR JUANA   I wanted him to come today. I need him to help me creep out of this darkness. Never mind the books. We'll see to them later. I'll watch for him at the window.

SOR FELICIANA   Do you want me to watch with you?

SOR JUANA   No. Go about your business. Thank you. I'd rather sit here by myself.

SOR FELICIANA   I'll check on the tea—just in case . . .

SOR JUANA   Yes, yes—do that.

SOR FELICIANA   (*Crosses to exit, turns.*) I'll stop by after supper.

(*Sor Juana, staring out into the garden, doesn't answer. Sor Feliciana leaves.*)

SOR JUANA   I have cast off pride, possessions, so my flight to Heaven will not be cumbersome. Oh, Father, you were right! Knowledge more easily breeds arrogance than it does humility. Oh, Father Antonio, I know myself now! I've opened the door to the prison I created. It's not a blind creature you will see before you. . . . No more . . .

(*Light fades on cell, comes up on flashback area. There is a statue of the Virgin Mary backing a font of holy water. To the left is a confessional. Sor Juana comes out of the confessional, crosses herself, goes to font, dips fingers in holy water, crosses herself again. Father Antonio comes out of the confessional. Sor Juana turns, hands reaching out to welcome her confessor.*)

SOR JUANA   My prayers of penitence can wait!

FATHER ANTONIO   You are forgiven, my child.

SOR JUANA   Trees are blooming, and the last time I saw you I was worried about the frostbite on your nose. (*Touches his face after looking at it intently.*) There are tired lines around your mouth. You are too old for long trips over mountains! Where were you?

FATHER   Manzana. I found a miracle there. (*Takes out folded printed sheet from pocket, hands it to Sor Juana.*) See . . .

SOR JUANA   (*Unfolding sheet.*) My mysteries! I wrote them a long time ago. Where did you find them? Manzana—an Indian village, isn't it?

FATHER   Isolated, and now its people are dying of the plague like flies. I exhausted all my energies, not fighting for peoples' lives, but preparing them for Heaven. The last rites become swollen ritual words in my mouth. So many! One night, they forced me to rest and gave me a fish for supper. I sat down at a table, too weary to protest and unwrapped my fish. There it was—your mysteries.

SOR JUANA   Someone wrapped a fish with it?

FATHER   There it was, your name, your words, at a time like that! I forgot my hunger and fatigue. I read your prayer by a wavering flame in the cold room—your fourth mystery to the Virgin Mary. It made me new. I read it again and again and held it in my hand while I slept. A miracle.

SOR JUANA   These were distributed in the *catedral,* thousands of them, two years ago. This one fell into your hands . . . and all those months I longed for you so, imagined you falling off a horse, or getting sick. There was no more waiting at the gate for you, and somehow days became blurred and empty.

FATHER   When there is time to breathe or rest, you are in my thoughts, too.

SOR JUANA   But my prayers have been answered. I hear you were recalled by the bishop. I heard the Tribunal had reprimanded you for neglecting your duties as an officer of the Inquisition. You have been ordered to remain in Mexico City and I'm glad, glad, glad!

FATHER   I doubt that you are glad about my misfortune.

SOR JUANA   It isn't that to me! Someone younger, with more energies, can take your place with those people.

FATHER   How little you understand. North of Coahuila—immolation— anger against the God we gave them. Their most insane pagan god is better to them than the God given to them by the Conquistadores.

SOR JUANA   They have lost the Way . . .

FATHER   I'm not so sure. I have been one of them for too long not to understand their anger and their fear.

SOR JUANA   All that I care about is that you're safe and that you're here and that I shall see you often.

FATHER   How blind you are, my daughter. The palace, the convent, that is not the world—nor those books that consume your life.

SOR JUANA   I know that these are rebellious times.

FATHER   How well you mouth the words of your masters.

SOR JUANA   My masters!

FATHER   For almost two decades you have spent your life writing, singing the praises of the masters. Villancicos for a long parade of viceroys, vicereines—*loas* and sonnets about the Spanish great. Your praises have been bountiful for those who have conquered your people, exploited them.

SOR JUANA They are my friends. They are the only world I know . . .

FATHER Have you forgotten your beginnings? You are *mejicana!*

SOR JUANA I will not take sides! I dream, I hope for, I work for the brotherhood of all men . . .

FATHER What substance is there in the words you write, the ideas you express, when in this very city you hear the sad songs of the zambo slaves living in the hovels behind the rich man's house? The cry of women whose children are in pain because of hunger? Look upon the earth to find your Heaven, child. It is not in pretty words.

SOR JUANA Why do I wait for you with such eagerness? There is no peace between us.

FATHER Have you made peace with yourself?

SOR JUANA I do not know what you mean. I just confessed my sins to you. You have absolved me . . .

FATHER Oh, the triviality of your sins! You're not even aware of your sins!

SOR JUANA You don't love me! You take such pleasure in trying to destroy what I believe . . .

FATHER What you believe! It's what you are that's important. Look to your own people.

SOR JUANA What would you have me be?

FATHER In Fresnillo, where I was born, there is a dry, brittle shrub that clings ferociously to life. Its roots dig into the sand the hostile sun violates. The tempestuous wind twists the shrub, strips it, wounds it, until it structures itself against its own nature, pulling away, pushing away, just to stay alive, just to survive. Its thorns, empty of the milk of hope, prick your finger. The shrub shrivels up against the violence around. That is the Mexican today—the Indian—the zambo slave. My spirit is like that shrub, my soul, my passions. I am a Mexican, so I fight! I beg money off the rich, I hide the fugitive, I scramble around for food and medicine, because their hunger, their pain, their enslavement, their deaths wound me, consume me . . .

SOR JUANA I feel with you, but you must understand—I fight the same struggle. My voice carries all over, my words of love, compassion, brotherhood, peace . . .

FATHER I'm speaking of human beings—not words!

SOR JUANA You refuse to understand!

FATHER And you refuse to see!

(*Light fades on flashback area, comes up on cell area. Sor Juana is still by window.*)

SOR JUANA   He's not coming. He may never come. (*She crosses to a box on the floor and rummages through it desperately until she finds a packet of letters. She looks through them until she finds the one she is looking for. It is a letter written to her by one Sor Filotea de la Cruz. She stares at it, then crumbles it in her hand.*) They deceived me with this! Conspiracy! The Holy Company against one lone woman. Cowards! (*She begins to sob.*) They took him away from me . . . they took him away from me . . .

(*Light fades on cell area, comes up on flashback area. May 1691. The Bishopric in the diocese of Bishop Don Miguel Fernando de Santa Cruz, in Puebla. Bishop is sitting behind desk, looking at three documents. A published postulate written by a renowned Jesuit, Father Antonio Vieira, an intellectual giant, entitled The Greater Good of Jesus. The second document is a letter written by Sor Juana as an answer to the third document, supposedly a letter written by one Filotea de la Cruz, Convent of the Holy Trinity. Father Juan Ignacio, the Bishop's secretary, enters.*)

BISHOP   We have a problem.

JUAN IGNACIO   You speak of Sor Juana Inés de la Cruz.

BISHOP   Precisely. Hostile forces within the Church and outside the Church are shifting and changing to create dissension. As the Bishop of Puebla, it is my duty to maintain some kind of balance.

JUAN IGNACIO   I understand, Your Holiness.

BISHOP   Don Francisco Aguiar y Seijas has changed the face of Mexico.

JUAN IGNACIO   Our esteemed Archbishop has seen to it that all comedies in print be burned and has successfully replaced his most holy book among the faithful, Consolations for the Poor.

BISHOP   You can imagine what he thinks of Sor Juana's pagan plays! Mexico shall be well rid of impure customs, sinfulness. Sor Juana may find herself in the Index one of these days. When our Archbishop first came to Mexico six years ago, he found a country beset by vices, devoid of virtues. The time has come for great piety among the faithful. Festivities in the Church have been abolished, convent locutorios are now closed. You would think Sor Juana would see the light, but her pen has not stopped. And her latest—her criticism of Vieira—that is too much for the Holy Company to endure. A hornet's nest . . .

JUAN IGNACIO   Of course! Her Athenagoric letter. It has caused a sensation. She claims it was not meant to be published.

BISHOP   I had it published. I also called it, appropriately, the Athenagoric Letter. Rather well titled, wouldn't you say?

JUAN IGNACIO   A clever insinuation on your part. She does love the Greeks. It's there, in all she writes. She is an Athena.

BISHOP   I assumed that if I had it published, she would be proved a fool!

She is a fool! How dare she criticize the postulate of the most brilliant of Jesuits!

JUAN IGNACIO   There is no greater Catholic Predicator than Father Antonio Vieira. '

BISHOP   The audacity of that woman! A man of the world! One who has mingled with great minds! To find himself opposed by this upstart—a nun with a parochial mind! He must be highly amused.

JUAN IGNACIO   A great part of the public is siding with Sor Juana.

BISHOP   I simply cannot believe—refuse to believe—that the ravings of a simple-minded maid should be preferred over the subtle discernment of the Holy Scripture in Vieira's argument. But then, Vieira's views are beyond common intelligence.

JUAN IGNACIO   A great man.

BISHOP   A man of action too! A long service as adviser to the king of Portugal, and later, standing before his Christian pulpit in Brazil, he gave voice to the abuses of the rich. He fears not! The powerful Brazilians used their influence at the Vatican to have him censored. But he went to Rome himself and pleaded a brilliant case before the Pope. Even the Pope gave in . . . Vieira went back to Brazil with a papal order in his pocket exempting him from the jurisdiction of the Grand Inquisitor. Vieira's postulate questions the old dogmas. So, no one agrees with him. They dare not! And many just simply cannot grasp the brilliance of his concepts. Then came Sor Juana with a rehash of old stale beliefs—the kind that people cling to. That woman is a parrot. Oh, she praises with rhetorical passion. She loves, she discusses, she reasons, she exalts . . . then, there's that curious humility in her words—so female. How dare she! A mere—mere . . .

JUAN IGNACIO   Woman. Your plan didn't work, then. When both arguments were published side by side, she was not discredited.

BISHOP   The public applauds her! This cannot be forgiven. That *gongorina*[23] feeds the reading public the fare they prefer. I should have foreseen it. Vieira's postulate on the "greater good of Jesus" makes people uncomfortable. The greater good, he forwards, is God's deliberate absence from Mankind. That is a shocking idea to the ordinary layman or the ordinary churchman. Why didn't I foresee . . .

JUAN IGNACIO   Everywhere one goes, everything one hears—well, a battle on church doctrine is well on the way.

BISHOP   She must be forced to put down her pen.

---

23. Term used in the seventeenth century to refer—critically—to an educated woman writer.

JUAN IGNACIO   I doubt that it is possible . . .

BISHOP   My dear Father, you give up too easily. I have found a way. I sent for Father Antonio Núñez de Miranda. She loves him well—too well, I'm afraid.

JUAN IGNACIO   I doubt that Father Antonio can persuade her.

BISHOP   His absence from her life might persuade her! I hear she is eager for his visits. She relies and depends on him. Off and on, they have been companions for almost a lifetime. He will come to see me this very day. In fact, I expect him now. (*Pause.*) Before he arrives, I would like to take you into my confidence regarding a delicate matter.

JUAN IGNACIO   How can I be of service . . .

BISHOP   Remember the letter I dictated to you a month or so ago? (*Goes to table, picks up letter from Sor Filotea and hands it to Juan Ignacio.*)

JUAN IGNACIO   I remember it well. At the time I thought it strange that you did not sign your own name to it but used the name Sor Filotea, Convent of the Holy Trinity, Puebla de los Angeles. I know you had your reasons.

BISHOP   Very good reasons.

JUAN IGNACIO   It was a kind letter—praising Sor Juana's considerable talents, stating great affection for her.

BISHOP   I thought that if Sor Juana read the letter as from a fellow sister, a woman, she would heed the soft current of advice I offered. In the letter I urged she give up her worldly writings and return to her vows.

JUAN IGNACIO   Did she answer you?

BISHOP   Oh, yes. She sent the letter to the Convent of the Holy Trinity addressed to Sor Filotea. It was turned over to me.

JUAN IGNACIO   How did she reply?

BISHOP   See for yourself.

(*Crosses to table, picks up the answer to Sor Filotea written by Sor Juana, hands it to Juan Ignacio. As Juan Ignacio reads the letter, Bishop paces floor around his secretary.*)

BISHOP   It's no use. She refused my advice. Look, pages and pages explaining her obsession—yes, I said obsession! Things of the mind control her. Oh, she is humble and apologetic. See? All a trick, I assure you. A letter of merit, I agree, but one that reveals the stubbornness of her nature. So this scheme failed. (*Pause.*) I shall ask a favor of you. Do not mention this letter to anyone. It could prove an embarrassment . . .

(*There is a knock at the door. Juan Ignacio opens it to Father Antonio. Juan Ignacio leaves as Father Antonio enters.*)

BISHOP   Ah! Father Antonio—it has been a long time.

FATHER ANTONIO   Your Holiness.

BISHOP   I hope you have had a taste of our hospitality here in Puebla.

FATHER   Yes. Thank you.

BISHOP   Come, sit down. I have brought you here all the way from the capital for good reason.

FATHER   Your message said the "utmost urgency."

BISHOP   It is—and you are the only solution.

FATHER   I—am a solution?

BISHOP   The problem is Sor Juana Inés de la Cruz.

FATHER   That furor over her criticism of Vieira? It has gotten out of hand. Her criticism was not meant for publication. It was her own private exercise.

BISHOP   She has said that of all her writing, yet it seems to get published in Madrid. Her words exercise a modesty that she does not truly have.

FATHER   I know her—and I do know her very well—to be a modest person. She has never considered what she calls her "scribblings" worthy of print.

BISHOP   You, who know her so well, believe her?

FATHER   It is not a matter of belief. Sometimes our own words belie us. What motivates her to write, to some extent, is an audience. It's a worn ritual in her life. She claims she is pressed by others to write. But her writing is her own search for God.

BISHOP   Absurd! When has this woman been true to her vows? That is the way to God!

FATHER   Hers is not an ordinary case. The world makes demands of her, the court . . . she has a genius, a talent.

BISHOP   Indeed! If this is foremost in her life, why even pretend piety? She serves not God, but the world! What happened to her vow of poverty? Where is her humility?

FATHER   The locutorio of St. Jerome has never made it possible. She has been a light, drawing to her the writers and intellectuals of her time. You cannot blame her for the circumstance of her fame. The church was very pleased by this not so long ago.

BISHOP   You, my dear Father Antonio, know that times have changed. The locutorio of St. Jerome is now closed as are all locutorios all over Mexico. Our Archbishop considers the frivolities that locutorios are famous for a mark of shame in church history.

FATHER   I doubt that history will see it thus.

BISHOP   You are a member of the Inquisition Council. You know very well the severe austerity that cloaks the Church these days. Sor Juana's horizons differ greatly from those of our Archbishop. Now—this thing with Vieira.

FATHER   It was not of her own doing. She was urged to write it.

BISHOP   Who does she blame?

FATHER   She blames no one in particular. According to her—many people. Sor Juana does not run from any labor that gives her the exercise of reason. She admires Vieira greatly. She stands in awe of his intellect.

BISHOP   I know! I know! Nevertheless, what did she do? You must admit her postulate cannot compare with Vieira's. She says nothing that has not been said before.

FATHER   I will not judge either argument. Each has its merits.

BISHOP   There is the matter of her worldly possessions. Her cell is a luxury in itself—expensive gifts, fine furniture, thousands of books! The gardens of St. Jerome are a showplace.

FATHER   How am I a solution to all this?

BISHOP   She is very well aware of the Church's displeasure. She is aware of her enemies, yet even after the Vieira episode, she wrote a silva for the Viceroy, Count Galve. And those new villancicos in honor of St. Catherine . . . She's very, very clever.

FATHER   You still have not answered my question.

BISHOP   In time. First, I must make you see why you are the last resort. You have read her villancicos on St. Catherine?

FATHER   They are pure music and her most intimate convictions.

BISHOP   They are a weapon against her censors!

FATHER   I can't believe that you . . .

BISHOP   Wait! Hear me out first. Sor Juana has many persecutors, so she claims. Did not St. Catherine suffer the great persecutions of Maximino? Sor Juana is accused of confusing the scholars of our day. Was it not the same with St. Catherine? St. Catherine, as Sor Juana puts it, was a martyr to Wisdom. Do you not agree that Sor Juana believes herself to be the same? St. Catherine was condemned to a horrible death, placed on a wheel of knives, then beheaded. But her wisdom triumphed even over her death. The angels carried her up to Moses' mountain to be buried. So our Sor Juana stands before us, the martyr, the triumphant one. Do you think she would like her own Mt. Sinai?

FATHER   It's not fair! Your whole argument is a distortion . . .

BISHOP   Very well! You do not see it my way, but on one thing you have to agree: Everything she writes has the stamp of arrogance!

FATHER   I cannot help you if you think that way.

BISHOP   This is an order from the Inquisition Tribunal, Father Antonio. I'm afraid it's not a matter of choice.

FATHER   What order?

BISHOP   You are forbidden to see her again.

   (*Lights fade on flashback area, come up on cell area. Sor Juana puts down the letter, crosses to window again, looks out into the night.*)

SOR JUANA They took you away from me. I did not believe that you would do as they ordered. Ah, but you, the true Jesuit, must obey. Why did they torture me by taking you away? That last time you warned me that my words were my own prison. Words, I told you, are all I have. Words caress me, fulfill me, warm me . . . not any more, not any more, not any more! I must not write, you said. I cannot help it, I said, I succumb, my fingers nervous, careless, to please others—imperfect scribblings. I'm only a woman incapable of changing worlds. You warned me about what was happening outside the walls of this convent: missions abandoned in the province of Coahuila . . . Indian uprising . . . multitudes hiding and starving in the mountains. I didn't want to hear about the world falling apart! I had my compass, books, pen, harp. I had conceived a world of my own in my mind. The mind knows passions, feelings, beauty, order, I said. I listen only to the reasoning dimensions of scientific laws, human poetry, philosophy, the words of God . . . a city had to burn, a brother had to die, and you left me—before I could understand. My journey is at an end, my purpose chills, but I wait. Oh, I wait for you, Father, and a tenderness grows inside of me—the resurgent language of the heart. I dare not open this window to breathe in the spring, for I would die of longing—for God? For you? It's grown so dark, I must have some light in here. (*Goes to box where candle stands, lights it.*) Your single flame is like my heart, impervious, waiting, like stars lost in the immense darkness of the sky. (*Crosses window, opens it; sounds of night birds are heard, she looks at sky.*) How silent you are! How sweet is the night! Oh, but I remember the bells! The bells that pierced the sanctuary of my world.

(*Light fades on cell, comes up on flashback area. The church bells of the whole city are ringing. On the walk leading from the garden to the chapel of the convent, Sor Juana waits for Sor Feliciana to catch up. From a great distance the muffled sounds of shouting and screaming and the sounds of gunfire are heard. The red glow of a burning city inflames the skies. The Viceroy's palace, the marketplace in the Plaza Mayor, municipal buildings are on fire.*)

SOR FELICIANA Where have you been?

SOR JUANA I was down by the gate. The sacristan from San Angel came with the latest news.

SOR FELICIANA Has the fire been contained?

SOR JUANA Yes, but the marketplace was burned to the ground, and the Viceroy's palace suffered from the fire too.

SOR FELICIANA Thousands came down from the mountains, from the starving pueblos. They headed for the palace, ragged Indians, women, children . . . they came down only to beg for food.

SOR JUANA   Is it true all the houses closed their windows so as not to hear them?

SOR FELICIANA   Even at the palace. The crowd screamed for the Viceroy, then someone picked up a stone and threw it at a window when no one answered. Soon, everyone was throwing stones. Some of the starving made their way to the warehouses behind the palace, broke down the doors and took the grain. Then someone threw a torch.

SOR JUANA   And the Viceroy? His family?

SOR FELICIANA   They fled to the monastery of San Francisco, where they were given refuge.

SOR JUANA   The sacristan told me the Archbishop headed a procession out of the *catedral* to appeal to the crowds, calling among the faithful. They threw stones at the Archbishop, so he went back to the *catedral*.

SOR FELICIANA   The palace guard and the soldiers from the garrison opened fire on the people.

SOR JUANA   Fired among women and children? Those starving people have no weapons!

SOR FELICIANA   All the faithful in the city are being called to prayer.

SOR JUANA   Volumes and volumes and volumes of prayers.

SOR FELICIANA   Come, we must hurry.

SOR JUANA   The sky is red with anguish.

SOR FELICIANA   Come, we must not be late.

(*Slave Juana runs in greatly frightened, face stained with tears, falls to knees before Sor Juana.*)

SLAVE JUANA   Sister . . .

SOR JUANA   What's wrong?

SLAVE JUANA   Andrés . . .

SOR JUANA   What about Andrés?

SLAVE JUANA   He is here, in the garden, hurt.

SOR JUANA   Blessed Mother! (*Motions for Slave Juana to lead her to him.*)

SOR FELICIANA   Sor Juana . . .

SOR JUANA   Go on, go to prayer. I'll take care of this.

SOR FELICIANA   But, Sister . . .

SOR JUANA   Go on, I said.

(*Sor Juana follows Slave Juana to garden; Sor Feliciana goes toward chapel. Andrés lies prone on the ground. Sor Juana kneels beside him, strokes his face.*)

SOR JUANA   Andrés, can you hear me?

ANDRES   Yes . . .

SOR JUANA   Where is your wound? Were you shot?

ANDRES   Yes . . . my leg.

SLAVE JUANA   He tired, Sister. Soldiers chase him. He got away. We got to
   hide him. (*Sor Juana looks at wound, rips worn leg of cotton pants.*)
SOR JUANA   He's bleeding still. We need something to staunch the wound.
SLAVE JUANA   My poor brother! My poor brother!
SOR JUANA   Go get some clean cloth and some wine from the cupboard.
   (*Slave Juana is still crying.*) Did you hear me?
SLAVE JUANA   I get them—I get them. Will my brother die?
SOR JUANA   Of course not. Stop crying and hurry. (*Slave Juana exits.*) Juana
   says soldiers were chasing you. Did they see you come here?
ANDRES   I run fast—is dark . . .
SOR JUANA   Why were they chasing you?
ANDRES   I kill soldier . . .
SOR JUANA   Why?
ANDRES   He shot Camila—she with child. He shot her in the stomach.
SOR JUANA   Oh, my God, no! (*She kisses Andrés' face and holds him close.*) I'm
   so sorry. They went straight to Heaven, Andrés, straight to Heaven. Oh
   my brother, your pain is my pain.
ANDRES   I killed him with his own gun.
SOR JUANA   May God forgive you.
ANDRES   You not know Camila . . .
SOR JUANA   I'm sorry. But she must have been beautiful. I wish . . .
ANDRES   What you wish?
SOR JUANA   Why didn't I go to you, to your family? I feel so badly about
   not . . .
ANDRES   No time to cry now. That was long ago. I remember like dream.
   You are the little girl?
SOR JUANA   Yes, my brother. I have your flute. I still play the song you
   taught me. . . . Forgive me, Andrés!
ANDRES   Don't cry, coya, the sky is smiling.
   (*Sor Juana holds him close, crying. Slave Juana returns with cloth and wine.
   Sor Juana puts bottle to Andrés' lips. He drinks. She tears piece of white cloth into
   shreds, uses one to staunch blood, then binds the wound. She uses another piece to
   cleanse his face very tenderly.*)
ANDRES   (*Tries to raise himself.*) I hide . . .
SLAVE JUANA   You hide him here, Sister.
SOR JUANA   Yes, yes . . . but where? I know! The main altar in the chapel.
   There's room there. After the service this evening we'll take you there.
   Now, you must stay in my room. Can you walk?
ANDRES   Yes. (*He holds on to Slave Juana and Sor Juana.*)
SOR JUANA   This way . . .

(There is pounding at the convent gate. The sound of a soldier's voice: "Open this gate, in the name of the Viceroy!" *Someone else calls out,* "Break it down. He's in there. Break it down!" *Sound of hacking on wood as the two women lead Andrés away.*

Lights fade on flashback area. Slowly a red haze comes up on cell. The sound of a flute is heard. Sor Juana, sitting on the center of cot, crosslegged, is playing the flute. She stops.)

SOR JUANA   I am without illusion now—distrusting even stars. *(Leaves bed and goes to window.)* And dreams? Persuasions of the blood. *(She plays flute as she crosses down center.)* But dreams have freed me as faith has not. That dream, that first dream, where I was one with God. I still remember the terror of my smallness. A sleeping world—my spirit leaving the vegetative state of my body. I flew to the pyramidal shadow of the earth until it came to touch the lunar sky. Ah . . . through me poured a great silence. All things were purified. I became a whirlwind. Yes! a whirlwind penetrating the immensity of Heaven. My eyes saw thousands and thousands of things, variations that confused my understanding. And I hungered so to understand! Secrets beyond me . . . I felt the breath of God. I knew my smallness then. Suddenly, the terror! I felt Him, my God! *(She begins to play the flute again.)* Remember, Andrés? My brother . . . you taught me that song when I was but a child. They dragged you away from here and put a rope around your neck. Your eyes were dark with fear. I saw you dangling from the hanging tree. My eyes cannot erase it. My mind cannot erase it. A sovereign fact, this death of yours which was . . . a death of me. Oh, the raw concreteness of the world! The mind is not enough, is it? Oh, I have wept loudly in the dark and felt a copious guilt. . . . And that dark, mysterious flow where no words exist—I found it, didn't I? Faith . . .

ACT III: Synopsis.

Again 1693. Juana's cell. Father Antonio visits Sor Juana. He finds her cell is empty—she has given her possessions to the poor. In 1695 Father Antonio dies. Sor Juana has discovered that she could not find God through knowledge, that He is in all the life around her. She has learned humility and acceptance of faith. Sor Juana dies in 1695, two months after the death of her beloved confessor.

444 Years After

Carmen Tafolla

To Guadalupe

If I gathered roses for you . . .
Like Juan Diego stumbling through the cactus,
wearing only calzones and faith
with his tilmantli,
  —I would smother them into
    my jeans jacket
    because I never had a tilmantli.

If I gathered roses for you . . .
(After all, it's still the doce de diciembre,)
but there are no hills on my block,
And the Bishop is *used* to miracles—
He's a Chicano.
  —would my jeans jacket sprout
    an embroidered vision
    of the same old Lupe
    with stars in her cloak
    but standing on a pick-up
    truck with melons?

If I gathered roses for you . . .
The prettiest and sweetest ones I could steal!
But all of them with a little note that says
"Me junté una dozena,
pero nomás te traigo seis,
porque la otra media dozena
se las di a mi querido,
con una canción y un poema,
y todo mi amor."[24]
  —Would you understand?

    I think so,
    because despite what the Aztecs think
    You're a Chicana too.

---

24. I gathered a dozen / but I only bring you six, because the other half dozen / I gave to my loved one / with a song and a poem / and all my love.

So 444 years from now,
I'll *still* gather roses for you.

(And for him.)

Little Miracles, Kept Promises

Sandra Cisneros

Exvoto Donated as Promised
On the 20th of December of 1988 we suffered a terrible disaster on the road to Corpus Christi. The bus we were riding skidded and overturned near Robstown and a lady and her little girl were killed. Thanks to La Virgen de Guadalupe we are alive, all of us miraculously unharmed, and with no visible scars, except we are afraid to ride buses. We dedicate this retablo to La Virgencita with our affection and gratitude and our everlasting faith.

> Familia Arteaga
> Alice, Texas
> G.R. (Gracias Recibido / Thanks Given)

Blessed Santo Niño de Atocha,
Thank you for helping us when Chapa's truck got stolen. We didn't know how we was going to make it. He needs it to get to work, and this job, well, he's been on probation since we got him to quit drinking. Raquel and the kids are hardly ever afraid of him anymore, and we are proud parents. We don't know how we can repay you for everything you have done for our family. We will light a candle to you every Sunday and never forget you.

> Sidronio Tijerina
> Brenda A. Camacho de Tijerina
> San Angelo, Texas

Dear San Martín de Porres,
Please send us clothes, furniture, shoes, dishes. We need anything that don't eat. Since the fire we have to start all over again and Lalo's disability check ain't much and don't go far. Zulema would like to finish school but I

says she can just forget about it now. She's our oldest and her place is at home helping us out I told her. Please make her see some sense. She's all we got.

Thanking you,
Adelfa Vásquez
Escobas, Texas

Dear San Antonio de Padua,

Can you please help me find a man who isn't a pain in the nalgas. There aren't any in Texas, I swear. Especially not in San Antonio.

Can you do something about all the educated Chicanos who have to go to California to find a job. I guess what my sister Irma says is true: "If you didn't get a husband when you were in college, you don't get one."

I would appreciate it very much if you sent me a man who speaks Spanish, who at least can pronounce his name the way it's supposed to be pronounced. Someone please who never calls himself "Hispanic" unless he's applying for a grant from Washington, D.C.

Can you send me a man man. I mean someone who's not ashamed to be seen cooking or cleaning or looking after himself. In other words, a man who acts like an adult. Not one who's never lived alone, never bought his own underwear, never ironed his own shirts, never even heated his own tortillas. In other words, don't send me someone like my brothers who my mother ruined with too much chichi, or I'll throw him back.

I'll turn your statue upside down until you send him to me. I've put up with too much too long, and now I'm just too intelligent, too powerful, too beautiful, too sure of who I am finally to deserve anything less.

Ms. Barbara Ybáñez
San Antonio, TX

Dear Niño Fidencio,

I would like for you to help me get a job with good pay, benefits, and retirement plan. I promise you if you help me I will make a pilgrimage to your tomb in Espinazo and bring you flowers. Many thanks.

César Escandón
Pharr, Tejas

DEAR DON PEDRITO JARAMILLO HEALER OF LOS OLMOS

MY NAME IS ENRIQUETA ANTONIA SANDOVAL I LIVE IN SAN MARCOS TX I AM SICK THEY OPERATED ME FROM A KIDNEY AND A TUMOR OF CANCER BUT THANKS TO GOD I AM ALIVE BUT I HAVE TO GET TREATMENTS FOR A YEAR THE KIMO I AM 2 1/2 YEARS OLD BUT MY GRANDMA BROUGHT ME THAT YOU AND OUR LORD WHO IS IN THE

HEAVENS WILL CURE ME WITH THIS LETTER THAT I AM DEPOSITING
HERE ITS MY GRANDMA WHO IS WRITING THIS I HOPE EVERYBODY WHO
SEES THIS LETTER WILL TAKE A MINUTE TO ASK FOR MY HEALTH

ENRIQUETA ANTONIA SANDOVAL
2 AND A HALF YEARS OLD

I LEOCADIA DIMAS VDA. DE CORDERO OF SAN MARCOS TX HAVE
COME TO PAY THIS REQUEST TO DON PEDRITO THAT MY GRANDDAUGH-
TER WILL COME OUT FINE FROM HER OPERATION THANKS TO GOD AND
THOSE WHO HELPED SUCH GOOD DOCTORS THAT DID THEIR JOB WELL
THE REST IS IN GODS HANDS THAT HE DO HIS WILL MANY THANKS WITH
ALL MY HEART.

YOUR VERY RESPECTFUL SERVANT
LEOCADIA

Oh Mighty Poderosos, Blessed Powerful Ones,
    You who are crowned in heaven and who are so close to our Divine
Savior, I implore your intercession before the Almighty on my behalf. I ask
for peace of spirit and prosperity, and that the demons in my path that are the
cause of all my woes be removed so that they no longer torment me. Look
favorably on this petition and bless me, that I may continue to glorify your
deeds with all my heart—santísimo Niño Fidencio, gran General Pancho
Villa, bendito Don Pedrito Jaramillo, virtuoso John F. Kennedy, and blessed
Pope John Paul. Amen.

Gertrudis Parra
Uvalde, Tejas

Father Almighty,
    Teach me to love my husband again. Forgive me.

s.
Corpus Christi

Seven African Powers that surround our Savior—Obatala, Yemaya, Ochún,
Orunla, Ogun, Elegua, and Shango—why don't you behave and be good to
me? Oh Seven African Powers, come on, don't be bad. Let my Illinois lottery
ticket win, and if it does, don't let my cousin Cirilio in Chicago cheat me out
of my winnings, since I'm the one who pays for the ticket and all he does is
buy it for me each week—if he does even that. He's my cousin, but like the
Bible says, better to say nothing than to say nothing nice.
    Protect me from the evil eye of the envious and don't let my enemies do
me harm, because I've never done a thing wrong to anyone first. Save this
good Christian who the wicked have taken advantage of.

Seven Powers, reward my devotion with good luck. Look after me, why don't you? And don't forget me because I never forget you.

Moises Ildefonso Mata
San Antonio, Texas

Virgencita de Guadalupe,

I promise to walk to your shrine on my knees the very first day I get back, I swear, if you will only get the Tortillería la Casa de la Masa to pay me the $253.72 they owe me for two weeks' work. I put in 67 1/2 hours that first week and 79 hours the second, and I don't have anything to show for it yet. I calculated with the taxes deducted, I have $253.72 coming to me. That's all I'm asking for. The $253.72 I have coming to me.

I have asked the proprietors Blanquita and Rudy Mondragón, and they keep telling me next week, next week, next week. And it's almost the middle of the third week already and I don't know how I'm going to do it to pay this week's rent, since I'm already behind, and the other guys have loaned me as much as they're able, and I don't know what I'm going to do, I don't know what I'm going to do.

My wife and the kids and my in-laws all depend on what I send home. We are humble people, Virgencita. You know I'm not full of vices. That's how I am. It's been hard for me to live here so far away without seeing my wife, you know. And sometimes one gets tempted, but no, and no, and no. I'm not like that. Please Virgencita, all I'm asking for is my $253.72. There is no one else I can turn to here in this country, and well, if you can't help me, well, I just don't know.

Arnulfo Contreras
San Antonio, Tejas

Saint Sebastian who was persecuted with arrows and then survived, thank you for answering my prayers! All them arrows that had persecuted me—my brother-in-law Ernie and my sister Alba and their kids—el Junior, la Gloria, and el Skyler—all gone. And now my home sweet home is mine again, and my Dianita bien lovey-dovey, and my kids got something to say to me besides who hit who.

Here is the little gold milagrito I promised you, a little house, see? And it ain't that cheap gold-plate shit either. So now that I paid you back, we're even, right? Cause I don't like for no one to say Victor Lozano don't pay his debts. I pays cash on the line, bro. And Victor Lozano's word like his deeds is solid gold.

Victor A. Lozano
Houston, TX

Dear San Lázaro,

My mother's comadre Demetria said if I prayed to you that like maybe you could help me because you were raised from the dead and did a lot of miracles and maybe if I lit a candle every night for seven days and prayed, you might maybe could help me with my face breaking out with so many pimples. Thank you.

Rubén Ledesma
Hebbronville, Texas

Santísima Señora de San Juan de los Lagos,

We came to see you twice when they brought you to San Antonio, my mother and my sister Yolanda and two of my aunts, Tía Enedina and my Tía Perla, and we drove all the way from Beeville just to visit you and make our requests.

I don't know what my Tía Enedina asked for, she's always so secretive, but probably it had to do with her son Beto who doesn't do anything but hang around the house and get into trouble. And my Tía Perla no doubt complained about her ladies' problems—her ovaries that itch, her tangled fallopians, her uterus that makes her seasick with all its flipping and flopping. And Mami who said she only came along for the ride, lit three candles so you would bless us all and sweep jealousy and bitterness from our hearts because that's what she says every day and every night. And my sister Yoli asked that you help her lose weight because *I don't want to wind up like Tía Perla, embroidering altar cloths and dressing saints.*

But that was a year ago, Virgencita, and since then my cousin Beto was fined for killing the neighbor's rooster with a flying Big Red bottle, and my Tía Perla is convinced her uterus has fallen because when she walks something inside her rattles like a maraca, and my mother and my aunts are arguing and yelling at each other same as always. And my stupid sister Yoli is still sending away for even stupider products like the Grasa Fantástica, guaranteed to burn away fat—*It really works, Tere, just rub some on while you're watching TV*—only she's fatter than ever and just as sad.

What I realize is that we all made the trip to San Antonio to ask something of you, Virgencita, we all needed you to listen to us. And of all of us, my mama and sister Yoli, and my aunts Enedina and Perla, of all of us, you granted me my petition and sent, just like I asked, a guy who would love only me because I was tired of looking at girls younger than me walking along the street or riding in cars or standing in front of the school with a guy's arm hooked around their neck.

So what is it I'm asking for? Please, Virgencita. Lift this heavy cross from my shoulders and leave me like I was before, wind on my neck, my arms swinging free, and no one telling me how I ought to be.

Teresa Galindo
Beeville, Texas

Miraculous Black Christ of Esquipulas,
Please make our grandson to be nice to us and stay away from drugs. Save him to find a job and move away from us. Thank you.

Grandma y Grandfather
Harlingen

M3r1c5l45s Bl1ck Chr3st 4f 2sq53p5lls,
3 1sk y45, L4rd, w3th 1ll my h21rt pl21s2 w1tch 4v2r M1nny B2nlv3d2s wh4 3s 4v2rs21s. 3 l4v2 h3m 1nd 3 d4n't kn4w wh1t t4 d4 1b45t 1ll th3s l4v2 s1dn2ss 1nd sh1m2 th1t f3lls m2.

B2njlm3n T.
D2l R34 TX

Milagroso Cristo Negro de Esquipulas,
Te ofrezco este retrato de mis niños. Wáchelos, Dios Santo, y si le quitas el trago a mi hijo te prometo prender velitas. Ayúdanos con nuestras cuentas, Señor, y que el cheque del income tax nos llegue pronto para pagar los biles. Danos una buena vida y que les ayudes a mis hijos a cambiar sus modos. Tú que eres tan bondadoso escucha estas peticiones que te pido con todo mi corazón y con toda la fe de mi alma. Ten piedad, Padre mío. Mi nombre es Adela O.

Elizondo
Cotulla TX

Milagroso Cristo Negro,
Thank you por el milagro de haber graduado de high school. Aquí le regalo mi retrato de graduation.

Fito Moroles
Rockport, Texas

Cristo Negro,
Venimos desde muy lejos. Infinitas gracias, Señor. Gracias por habernos escuchado.

Familia Armendáriz G.
Matamoros, Tamps. México

Jesus Christ,
    Please keep Deborah Abrego and Ralph S. Urrea together forever.

                                        Love,
                                        Deborah Abrego
                                        Sabinal, Texas

Blessed Virgen de los Remedios,
    Señora Dolores Alcalá de Corchado finds herself gravely ill from a com-
plication that resulted after a delicate operation she underwent Thursday last,
and from which she was recovering satisfactorily until suffering a hemmorhage
Tuesday morning. Please intercede on her behalf. We leave her in the hands of
God, that His will be done, now that we have witnessed her suffering and
don't know whether she should die or continue this life. Her husband of
forty-eight years offers this request with all his heart.

                                        Señor Gustavo Corchado B.
                                        Laredo, Tejas

Madrecita de Dios,
    Thank you. Our child is born healthy!

                                        Rene y Janie Garza
                                        Hondo, TX

Saint Jude, patron saint of lost causes,
    Help me pass my English 320, British Restoration Literature class and
everything to turn out ok.

                                        Eliberto González
                                        Dallas

Virgencita . . .
    I've cut off my hair just like I promised I would and pinned my braid here
by your statue. Above a Toys "Я" Us name tag that says IZAURA. Alongside
several hospital bracelets. Next to a business card for Sergio's Casa de la
Belleza Beauty College. Domingo Reyna's driver's license. Notes printed on
the flaps of envelopes. Silk roses, plastic roses, paper roses, roses crocheted
out of fluorescent orange yarn. Photo button of a baby in a *charro* hat.
Caramel-skinned woman in a white graduation cap and gown. Mean dude in
bandanna and tattoos. Oval black-and-white passport portrait of the sad uncle
who never married. A mama in a sleeveless dress watering the porch plants.
Sweet boy with new mustache and new soldier uniform. Teenager with a little
bit of herself sitting on her lap. Blurred husband and wife leaning one into
the other as if joined at the hip. Black-and-white photo of the cousins *la* Josie

and *la* Mary Helen, circa 1942. Polaroid of Sylvia Rios, First Holy Communion, age nine years.

So many *milagritos* safety-pinned here, so many little miracles dangling from red thread—a gold Sacred Heart, a tiny copper arm, a kneeling man in silver, a bottle, a brass truck, a foot, a house, a hand, a baby, a cat, a breast, a tooth, a belly button, an evil eye. So many petitions, so many promises made and kept. And there is nothing I can give you except this braid of hair the color of coffee in a glass.

Chayo, what have you done! All that beautiful hair.

Chayito, how could you ruin in one second what your mother took years to create?

You might as well've plucked out your eyes like Saint Lucy. All that hair!

My mother cried, did I tell you? All that beautiful hair . . .

I've cut off my hair. Which I've never cut since the day I was born. The donkey tail in a birthday game. Something shed like a snakeskin.

My head as light as if I'd raised it from water. My heart buoyant again, as if before I'd worn *el* Sagrado Corazón in my open chest. I could've lit this entire church with my grief.

I'm a bell without a clapper. A woman with one foot in this world and one foot in that. A woman straddling both. This thing between my legs, this unmentionable.

I'm a snake swallowing its tail. I'm my history and my future. All my ancestors' ancestors inside my own belly. All my futures and all my pasts.

I've had to steel and hoard and hone myself. I've had to push the furniture against the door and not let you in.

What are you doing sitting in there in the dark?

I'm, thinking.

Thinking of what?

Just . . . thinking.

You're nuts. Chayo, ven a saludar. All the relatives are here. You come out of there and be sociable.

Do boys think, and girls daydream? Do only girls have to come out and greet the relatives and smile and be nice and *quedar bien*?

It's not good to spend so much time alone.

What she do in there all by herself? It don't look right.

Chayito, when you getting married? Look at your cousin Leticia. She's younger than you.

How many kids you want when you grow up?

When I become a mommy . . .

You'll change. You'll see. Wait till you meet Mr. Right.

Chayo, tell everybody what it is you're studying again.

Look at our Chayito. She likes making her little pictures. She's gonna be a painter.

A painter! Tell her I got five rooms that need painting.

When you become a mother . . .

Thank you for making all those months I held my breath not a child in my belly, but a thyroid problem in my throat.

I can't be a mother. Not now. Maybe never. Not for me to choose, like I didn't choose being female. Like I didn't choose being artist—it isn't something you choose. It's something you are, only I can't explain it.

I don't want to be a mother.

I wouldn't mind being a father. At least a father could still be artist, could love some*thing* instead of some*one,* and no one would call that selfish.

I leave my braid here and thank you for believing what I do is important. Though no one else in my family, no other woman, neither friend nor relative, no one I know, not even the heroine in the *telenovelas,* no woman wants to live alone.

I do.

Virgencita de Guadalupe. For a long time I wouldn't let you in my house. I couldn't see you without seeing my ma each time my father came home drunk and yelling, blaming everything that ever went wrong in his life on her.

I couldn't look at your folded hands without seeing my *abuela* mumbling, "My son, my son, my son. . . ." Couldn't look at you without blaming you for all the pain my mother and her mother and all our mothers' mothers have put up with in the name of God. Couldn't let you in my house.

I wanted you bare-breasted, snakes in your hands. I wanted you leaping and somersaulting the backs of bulls. I wanted you swallowing raw hearts and rattling volcanic ash. I wasn't going to be my mother or my grandma. All that self-sacrifice, all that silent suffering. Hell no. Not here. Not me.

Don't think it was easy going without you. Don't think I didn't get my share of it from everyone. Heretic. Atheist. *Malinchista. Hocicona.* But I wouldn't shut my yap. My mouth always getting me in trouble. Is that *what they teach you at the university? Miss High-and-Mighty. Miss Thinks-She's-Too-Good-for Us.* Acting like a *bolilla,* a white girl. Malinche. Don't think it didn't hurt being called a traitor. Trying to explain to my ma, to my abuela, why I didn't want to be like them.

I don't know how it all fell in place. How I finally understood who you are. No longer Mary the mild, but our mother Tonantzín. Your church at

Tepeyac built on the site of her temple. Sacred ground no matter whose goddess claims it.

That you could have the power to rally a people when a country was born, and again during civil war, and during a farmworkers' strike in California made me think maybe there is power in my mother's patience, strength in my grandmother's endurance. Because those who suffer have a special power, don't they? The power of understanding someone else's pain. And understanding is the beginning of healing.

When I learned your real name is Coatlaxopeuh, She Who Has Dominion over Serpents, when I recognized you as Tonantzín, and learned your names are Teteoinnan, Toci, Xochiquetzal, Tlazolteotl, Coatlicue, Chalchiuhtlicue, Coyolxauhqui, Huixtochihuatl, Chicomecoatl, Cihuacoatl, when I could see you as Nuestra Señora de la Soledad, Nuestra Señora de Remedios, Nuestra Señora del Perpetuo Socorro, Nuestra Señora de San Juan de los Lagos, Our Lady of Lourdes, Our Lady of Mount Carmel, Our Lady of the Rosary, Our Lady of Sorrows, I wasn't ashamed, then, to be my mother's daughter, my grandmother's granddaughter, my ancestors' child.

When I could see you in all your facets, all at once the Buddha, the Tao, the true Messiah, Yahweh, Allah, the Heart of the Sky, the Heart of the Earth, the Lord of the Near and Far, the Spirit, the Light, the Universe, I could love you, and finally, learn to love me.

Mighty Guadalupana Coatlaxopeuh Tonantzín,
What "little miracle" could I pin here? Braid of hair in its place and know that I thank you.

                                        Rosario (Chayo) De Leon
                                        Austin, Tejas

Gullible

Margarita Cota-Cárdenas

how patiently
              how lonely
                                        you weave your
tapestries
         Penelope
he's over there Circeing himself
              taking his sweet time

you're working so prettily
a symbol now of patience
                    slowly slowly slowly
for so many years   a lovely example
                    weaving   unweaving
                              frustrated years
                                   or
he satisfied you through egotistical telepathy

                                   or
                         you had a lover

Cuento de Hadas / Fairy Tale

Angela de Hoyos

She was a bonafide storybook princess.
Romantic. Impractical. A delicate
princess of innocence, born to blush
in the midst of a cynical
go-go, buy-bye world.
                    (O yes, María,
who knows why, but anachronisms do happen.)

And so she dreamed and dreamed. She dreamt of
Prince Charming and the happily-ever-after.
Fantasizing halcyon utopias
     she convinced herself
     that all of God's creatures
     (for her sake)
          were ideally endowed
          with the best of platonic aspirations,
gently lulled
               in the poetry of perfection.

Until one night (the story relates)
     she discovered her consort-prince
          in the form of a macho-man
               stepping out on the sly.

Desperate she hit the panic button, shouting
    HELP! O MY GOD . . . DO SOMETHING! . . .
        But God just sat on His throne in the sky
        and never so much as blinked an eye

. . . and the story is vague
as to what happened then, but
she never never never again
blindly believed
        in deities, or
             in men.

Mi Reflejo

Lydia Camarillo

Who goes there?
    It is I,
Don't you recognize me?
    You made me your prostitute,
    Me hiciste tu esclava,
    Conquistaste y colonizaste mi gente.[25]
    You alienated me from my people.
    Me hiciste la "Vendida."[26]
¿Ya no te ACUERDAS de mí?
    Qué Poca Memoria Tienes,[27]
    I have come to pay your dues,
    I have come to FREE my people.
        I AM MALINCHE.

Who goes there?
    It is I,
Don't you remember me?
    Your chauvinism impedes my inner growth,
    quemaste mis libros,[28]

---

25. You made me your slave / you conquered and colonized my people
26. You made me a traitor
27. Don't you remember me? / What a short memory you have
28. you burned my books

you smashed all women's hopes,
you destroyed my life.
¿Ya no te ACUERDAS de mí?
I am the scientist:
the gifted;
the one with all wisdom,
Yo soy la mujer hermosa.
He venido con Malinche,[29]
I have come to make you pay.
I have come to LIBERATE my people;
the oppressed.
Yo soy
SOR JUANA INES DE LA CRUZ.

Who goes there?
It is I,
Don't you recognize me?
I've stood behind your shadows,
siglo tras siglo.
He sido prisionera de tus males,
He llorado por mis hijos,[30]
I have slept on blood-stained sheets,
while my womb longs to give birth.
¿Ya no te ACUERDAS de mí?
Yo soy el fruto de mi gente,
llena de amor,
y capaz de matar.[31]
I am "creation,"
Vida con Vida,
Y Arte.
I have come with Malinche and Sor Juana.
He venido a hacerte pagar.[32]
I have come to be part of the INSURRECTION of my people,
the oppressed.
I AM FRIEDA KAHLO.

---

29. I am the beautiful woman / I have come with Malinche
30. century after century / I have been a prisoner of your evil / I have cried for my children
31. I am the fruit of my people / full of love / with the capacity to kill
32. I have come to make you pay

Who goes there?
    It is I,
Don't you know me?
    I am the mother of the people.
    I am the symbol of fertility,
    pride,
    strength,
    beauty,
    and wisdom.
    I am the "SPIRITUAL TRUTH" of my people.
    He venido a traer "luz"[33]
    I have come with Malinche, Sor Juana, and Frieda.
    I have come to guide them to the EMANICIPATION
    de mis HIJOS.
Yo soy TONANTZIN,
    la Virgen Morena,
        I AM LA VIRGEN DE GUADALUPE.

Who goes there?
    It is I,
Don't you remember me?
    Soy la fuerza de mi gente.[34]
    I am the invincible.
    Soy la Revolucionaria.
¿Ya no te ACUERDAS de mí?
    Perhaps you have forgotten,
    the outright plunder you have caused.
He venido a Recordarte:
    QUE mis Hijos se mueren de Hambre,[35]
    while you sit in a French restaurant
    De lujo.[36]
Have you forgotten,
    how many of my people have died unjustly?
    Se te ha Olvidado cuántos pintos hay.[37]

---

33. I have come to bring light
34. I am the strength of my people
35. I have come to remind you / that my children are dying of hunger
36. luxury
37. You have forgotten how many prisoners there are

QUE POCA MEMORIA TIENES,
    YOU,
      have exploited and oppressed my people.
But I have come to tell you!
    "BASTA!"[38]

Si somos espejos de Cada una,[39]
    Soy Malinche,
      Soy La Virgen de Guadalupe,
        Soy Sor Juana Inés de la Cruz,
          Soy Frida Kahlo,
          Soy Mujer.

I am the reflection of the oppressed.
    I am half the struggle . . .
        Y mi compañero la otra.[40]

I have come to knock at your door,
    A Decirte,
    "NO MAS!"[41]

WE ARE THE REVOLUTION!

---

38. Enough!
39. If we are the mirrors of each other
40. And my companion the other
41. To tell you, No longer.

Writers on Language and Writing

it is my nature
as woman and poet
to give birth

ALMA VILLANUEVA

I like to tell stories. I tell them inside my head.
SANDRA CISNEROS

I cup the algae in my free hand
and smear it on my face for inspiration
MARGARITA COTA-CÁRDENAS

It has been said that one of the most characteristic traits of contemporary literature is that it speaks about itself; that is, the poetic or narrative *personae* of the authors address the subject of writing in their writings. This they do as a way of exploring not only the meaning of language written on the page, but also the significance of the literary act itself. In this sense, Chicana literature is indeed a child of the present. Text after text, whether poem, short story, essay, or novel, comes back to the expression of a creative consciousness that acknowledges its creation, its doings with a pencil, a pen, a typewriter, or a computer.

Musings about becoming, or being, a writer are common enough in literary works ("A House of My Own," Cisneros). Longing for the ability to *say,* to paint the world as seen though the eyes of the creator, to play with words and their mysterious power, is also a recurring motif in many texts; so is the search for inspiration, the waiting for that spark that will ignite or trigger a verbal explosion (Vigil-Piñón, Cervantes). And so it is in the Chicanas' literary world: writing is a need that knows no restraints, no boundaries. These women acknowledge, sometimes with resignation, the demanding tasks self-imposed on a writer:

words we picked up, wiped off
cleaned up, prepared and served
as canapés to the lordly lords
that they might digest . . .

Bernice Zamora

Writing, especially for a poet, is a lonely profession, one which exacts an almost religious fervor from its practitioners ("Maybe a Nun After All," Mora). It is thankless, and yet it is fulfilling; it is a duty "fraught with fettered chores" ("Restless Serpents," Zamora). It is a trade compared to that of a sorceress; bewitching, yet apparently foolish, frivolous to the uninitiated: "I spill my whole life on you / and don't even know who you are" ("Como embrujada," Vigil). How do Chicanas define their writing inclination, their activity? It is "just telling the stories of life," or feeling deeper than others want to do; it is reviewing every day, when "little pieces of oneself" fall to the ground. Or it could be anything to be considered with words: the most mundane and even vulgar happening could be subject matter for art. Or perhaps it is, as one poet affirms "to see the contours of the / world and make / a myth to share" (Villanueva). Whether sacred or profane, the activity that ensues from inclination and necessity is always like a little bit of magic that happens to one: a magician's trick (Mora). At the same time, it is part of the writers' routine and compulsion; poets walk around their streets, their well-known towns or neighborhoods, searching for raw materials, seeking "inspiration"—and getting it from the ordinary, the familiar, the trivial (Silva, Cervantes). Chicanas' muses can be evoked by Juliet or Minerva (Gonzales-Flores, Cisneros); they are ancestral spirits or sometimes very modern women. Chicanas' literary works come from their bloodstream, or from their womb; they are "criaturas sedientas" (thirsty infants); they are seeds; they are night visitors. Often, the act of producing a poem is equated to giving birth, to the climax of sexual pleasure; it is catharsis, a bodily need.

Writing is, then, a mixture of light and shadow; of the magic and the mundane. And it can be linked with day-to-day life at home, at work, in the streets of the *barrio*; for some poets, words come between loads of laundry, between the leaves of lettuce they are washing at the sink. This is not exclusive to the world of Chicanas; this "poetry as a household activity" comes with being female. Sometimes the writers are surprised at the imaginary beings that populate their world, at the feelings that seem to overwhelm them, like capricious madness, like birds, like clouds, and waves ("Poema," Hernández). On other occasions, they try to dismiss the importance of writing by becoming literal: poems are nothing but "words on paper / that yellows or blows away" (Castillo). But blown away they are, in a metaphor of wind and amazement at what *the word* is: an insight into meaning, into possessing reality, into *knowing*.

For in writing, the domain of words, the poet finds a refuge from reality while describing it. No matter how much Chicanas have written about mothers and *abuelitas*, about ethnic prejudice, about belonging to a hybrid culture, no matter how insistent the voice that recognizes their rights and their desire to *be*, Chicanas also imagine a mythical, wonderful universe where nature and humans live in harmony, where peace is tangible, where there are no "politics of oppression," where skin color will cease to be an issue. And poetry becomes a dream of dancing on rooftops; writing is the poet's country, her homeland. Instead of a babel of confusion to be found in languages, the tongues that speak out of texts are order itself; they make sense of chaos. Writing is a "tower of words" that does not hinder meaning, but sustains it (Cervantes).

For the storytellers among Chicanas, writing is recording the memories of childhood; it is putting down in graphic signs what ordinary life events signify. It is a way of keeping track of what growing up "different" meant; it is the art of cultural preservation by means of capturing the flow of time and people in their lives. While poetry for Chicanas is more lyric and introspective, by the very nature of the beast, narrative is more associated with the stuff of life itself as it unfolds in a subculture. It is the happenings of childhood, adolescence, and young adulthood, preserved in their full flavor by means of a time frame and a definite space: working class neighborhoods, mostly Hispanic, in San Diego, in Chicago, in Imperial Valley. And then writing becomes the art of painting, with fine brush strokes, what a visit to the lonely *barrio* chapel might be ("The Moths," Viramontes), or what it would mean to rebel against the family's rigid customs ("The Paris Gown," Estela Portillo Trambley), or what life could become if one had the talent to get a degree in higher education, as in *The House on Mango Street*. In the latter book, Minerva wrote poems and Alicia went to college; and Esperanza, the protagonist, dreamed—in Woolfian fashion—of a "house of my own," with room for books and stories, "nobody's garbage to pick up after." "Only a house quiet as snow, a space for myself to go, clean as paper before the poem" (Cisneros). In that sense, Chicana storytellers are the keepers of the flame of female culture within their ethnic group; they are *raconteuses* who speak for all those others, mostly women, who had no syllables to paint with: "I come from a long line of eloquent illiterates" (Cervantes).

This is one of the reasons why language itself is so important to Chicana writers, as well as to their male counterparts. Deprived of meaning in a society that does not understand their mother tongue, Mexican immigrants must learn those "thick words" if they want to help their children in school, or later if they want to help themselves make sense of their surroundings. Spanish is seen as a language of family culture, but it is, unfortunately, lost to children of Chicanas (Quintana Pigno). The images of ancestral tongues are so powerful that they become poetic subject matter ("Our Tongue Was Nahuatl," Castillo); they are not only the tool for conquering reality and meaning, but also the nostalgic symbol of a glorious past that is now preserved only in the mythical concept of Aztlán.

Poetry is also seen, at least, as an absorbing obsession and as a tyrannical mistress. It interferes with life's duties, with chores and with family affections. Writing must occur; but it should give way to life itself. Inspiration, however, can keep a writer awake; and it is described as an obnoxious presence, as a nagging friend or guest, who will have to be barred from the inner premises of the soul if it should persist in its calling (Cota-Cárdenas, "Lírica fanática" and "Desveladas inútiles").

This chapter underlines the importance of language and language arts for Chicana writers. Given the primary importance of mastering the tools of their craft, they have a particular blessing and a special difficulty: that of being bilingual or even multilingual. As such, Chicanas write in two or more codes, or when writing in only one they are ever mindful of the ambiguity of speech and its multiple facets. When English-monolingual, they bemoan their shortcomings, which amount to being bereft of their heritage ("Oaxaca, 1974," Cervantes). But mostly this collection of writings by Chicanas shows the introspective mood in which authors consider their art, what it means to them to live by words, to create with linguistic symbols. It shows Chicanas as poets, as writers of short stories: it shows them as artists in search of meaning.

■ ■ ■

A Poet's Job

Alma Villanueva

A poet's job
is to see
the contours of the
world and make
a myth to share
for others to see
    to make a reality;
a point from where the
world spins-
and if stubborn and persistent enough,
  the point from where the
    universe whorls:
right here.

It Is My Nature

Alma Villanueva

It is my nature
as woman and poet
to give birth
over and over
always to birth
a daughter, a son, a poem;
     to nurture the seed / the young
     to start again and again
     to see in the old, the new-
                  the whole
     again and again

all I ask
     (is it too much?)
is to be born
new:
     always to be born
          slick and wet and blood / red new
until the still and
timeless core
of me
decides the
smell and heat
of birth is
repugnant

Creations

Irene Blea

sometimes lost in the amazement
     of something to relate to
          we must create

i create poems and poetry
to hold my dreams
tell of my despair

drink from the cups i created
one such amazing day

Cuentista: Story-teller

Pat Mora

She carries a green river in her arms.
Alive, it rises, sloshes, boundless play
of rolling light. She tempts with a silver
splash, says, "*Una vez* this desert sparkled:
fish. Cold waves rolled over these bare mountains."
Ripples, fins stream in our skin, muted song.
Even our stiff bones sway. She says, "The land
dried. Crawl into caves. Still water echoes."

At night, wet chants stream through her hair like fish
through water fronds. In sunlight, they vanish
like the moon. She carries a green river,
heavy, unpredictable, but it hums.
In any desert, she can bow her head
and sip—from her own arms.

Clever Twist

Pat Mora

The best revenge is
pouring the tears
into a tall, black hat
waving a sharp No. 2 pencil
slowly over the blue echoes

then   gently, gently
pulling out
a bloomin' poem.

Restless Serpents

Bernice Zamora

The duty of a cobra's master
is fraught with fettered chores.
Spite strikes the
humbling stroke of
neglect—coiling,
recoiling, pricking
the master's veins
of lapse, draining
a bounded resurrection
to numb the drumming
pain. Lyrics,
lyrics alone soothe
restless serpents.

From all corners
precision humming
and rhythmic sounds
fill the mindful
master who laps
about the droppings
of disregard. Lyrics,
lyrics alone soothe
restless serpents, strokes
more devastating than
devastation arrived.

Como la semilla / Like the Seed

Lucha Corpi / Translated by Catherine Rodríguez-Nieto

Como la semilla en espera
de la benevolente lluvia
el verso sediento calla.
Su quietud se desparrama
en los adentros y me asusta
su sequedad mustia y blanca.

■

Like the seed that waits
for gentle rain
my thirsting poem is silent.
Its quietude scatters
inside me and I am frightened
by its withered whiteness.

Protocolo de verduras / The Protocol of Vegetables

Lucha Corpi / Translated by Catherine Rodríguez-Nieto

El mundo exige
diplomacia estricta:
Me dicen que aun
entre las legumbres
existe el protocolo;
y ya dentro de la casa
no hay tiempo
ni para la melancolía
soledad desvestida,
porque debo atender
los asuntos
del día de plancha
y escribir versos

cuando puedo
entre el ir y venir
de la tempestad
en el lavadero.

Así, no me reproches
si te recuerdo
en el agua sucia
en el verde de las hojas
cuando riego las plantas,
entre repollo y pimienta
a la hora de la cena;
si te leo entrelíneas
de la *Civilización*
y sus descontentos.

■

The world demands
impeccable diplomacy.
Protocol exists,
or so they say,
even among vegetables;
and in my house
there's no time any more
even for melancholy,
that is loneliness laid bare,
because I must tend
to the affairs
of ironing day,
and write poems
when I can
between the shifting winds
of the tempest
in the laundry.

So don't reproach me
if I recall you
in wash water,
or among the leaves
of thirsty houseplants,
or between cabbage and pepper

at dinnertime;
if I read you between the lines
of *Civilization*
and Its Discontents.

Para el consumidor / For the Consumer

Miriam Bornstein

considero que fui parte del circo
aplaudí a lo romano ante jugadores cristianos
me divertí con gladiadores futbolistas
y la virgen de la macarena
me amarré como todos a un comercial
que por sólo un minuto
interrumpía mi programación
pero un día
al asesinar la mañana
con el sofocante rumor de las calles
los zumbidos de caras indiferentes
a cada paso me topé conmigo misma
ellos son yo
son yo misma
y desde entonces
me dieron ganas de ser bruja
y jugar a la vida con poemas

■

I believed I was part of the circus
I applauded the Roman against the
Christian players
I was entertained by football gladiators
and the Virgin of The Macarena
I attached myself like everyone else
to a commercial
that for only a minute
interrupted my programs
but one day

upon the death of the morning
with the suffocating rumor of the streets
the noises of indifferent faces
with each step I bumped into myself
They are me
I am myself
I felt like being a witch
like playing at life with poems

Maybe a Nun After All

Pat Mora

Motels are my convents.
I come alone
give workshops, readings.

I lock my door twice,
smell solitude, taste quiet
away from fast music, telephones,
children tugging, "Mom, Mom."

I remove my dust-
y clothes, slip on
a loose white gown.
Before I sleep, I say
My poems, old, new
say lines over and over
wrestling with demon words.

I wake early
mumbling phrases,
litanies
holding a pencil
rather than beads.

I shower, wrap my hair
in a white towel.
My face is pale, my body
hollow.

Visions of Mexico While at a Writing Symposium in Port Townsend Washington

Lorna Dee Cervantes

"This world understands nothing
but words and you have come into it
with almost none."
ANTONIO PORCHIA

México

When I'm that far south, the old words
molt off my skin, the feathers
of all my nervousness.
My own words somersault naturally as my name,
joyous among all those meadows: Michoacán,
Vera Cruz, Tenochtitlán, Oaxaca . . .
Pueblos green on the low hills
where men slap handballs below acres of maíze.
I watch and understand.
My frail body has never packed mud
or gathered the full weight of the harvest.
Alone with the women in the adobe, I watch men,
their taut faces holding in all their youth.
This far south we are governed by the law
of the next whole meal. We work
and watch seabirds elbow their wings
in migratory ways, those mispronouncing gulls
coming south
to refuge or gameland.

I don't want to pretend I know more
and can speak all the names. I can't.
My sense of this land can only ripple through my veins
like the chant of an epic corrido.
I come from a long line of eloquent illiterates
whose history reveals what words don't say.
Our anger is our way of speaking,
the gesture is an utterance more pure than word.
We are not animals
but our senses are keen and our reflexes,
accurate punctuation.

All the knifings in a single night, low-voiced
scufflings, sirens, gunnings . . .
We hear them
and the poet within us bays.

Washington

I don't belong this far north.
The uncomfortable birds gawk at me.
They hem and haw from their borders in the sky.
I heard them say: Mexico is a stumbling comedy.
A loose-legged Cantinflas woman
acting with Pancho Villa drunkenness.
Last night at the tavern
this was all confirmed
in a painting of a woman: her glowing
silk skin, a halo
extending from her golden coiffure
while around her dark-skinned men with Jap slant eyes
were drooling in a caricature of machismo.
Below it, at the bar, two Chicanas
hung at their beers. They had painted black
birds that dipped beneath their eyelids.
They were still as foam while the men
fiddled with their asses, absently;
the bubbles of their teased hair snapped
open in the forced wind of the beating fan.

there are songs in my head I could sing you
songs that could drone away
all the Mariachi bands you thought you ever heard
songs that could tell you what I know
or have learned from my people
but for that   I need words
simple black nymphs between white sheets of paper
obedient words   obligatory words   words I steal
in the dark when no one can hear me

as pain sends seabirds south from the cold
I come north
to gather my feathers
for quills

Poem For The Young White Man Who Asked Me How I, An Intelligent, Well-Read Person Could Believe In The War Between Races

Lorna Dee Cervantes

In my land there are no distinctions.
The barbed wire politics of oppression
have been torn down long ago. The only reminder
of past battles, lost or won, is a slight
rutting in the fertile fields

In my land
people write poems about love,
full of nothing but contented childlike syllables.
Everyone reads Russian short stories and weeps.
There are no boundaries.
There is no hunger, no
complicated famine or greed.

I am not a revolutionary.
I don't even like political poems.
Do you think I can believe in a war between races?
I can deny it. I can forget about it
when I'm safe,
living on my own continent of harmony
and home, but I am not
there.

I believe in revolution
because everywhere the crosses are burning,
sharp-shooting goose-steppers round every corner,
there are snipers in the schools . . .
(I know you don't believe this.
You think this is nothing
but faddish exaggeration. But they
are not shooting at you).

I'm marked by the color of my skin.
The bullets are discrete and designed to kill slowly.

They are aiming at my children.
These are facts.
Let me show you my wounds: my stumbling mind, my
"excuse me" tongue, and this
nagging preoccupation
with the feeling of not being good enough.

These bullets bury deeper than logic.
Racism is not intellectual.
I can not reason these scars away.

Outside my door
there is a real enemy
who hates me.

I am a poet
who yearns to dance on rooftops,
to whisper delicate lines about joy
and the blessings of human understanding.
I try. I go to my land, my tower of words and
bolt the door, but the typewriter doesn't fade out
the sounds of blasting and muffled outrage.
My own days bring me slaps on the face.
Every day I am deluged with reminders
that this is not
    my land
    and this is my land.

I do not believe in the war between races
    but in this country
    there is war.

Declaration on a Day of Little Inspiration

Lorna Dee Cervantes

I pound these streets for poems.
Los viejitos, los vatos, los perros
y los perdidos,
the giant piss-stream of freeway

which covers my barrio,
sops my Atlantis;

none of these will own up
and give me the taste
of ripe literature.

I write the same poem everytime
about beans and tortillas sin salsa,
about "¿Quién soy yo?"
Flushing this anger is easy

pero el otro
is harder to unfold.

It stays shut like a wet piece of paper.
It's a word I don't remember;
an automatic genuflection
that I can't explain.

And it haunts me like an old corrido,
this love that has no words,
this love for my Raza
which is a poem.

Literary Wetback

Alicia Gaspar de Alba

When Bostonians hear me speak Spanish and ask me what country I'm from, I say I come from the border between Tejas and Méjico. Nobody asks me what side of the border I'm talking about, and I don't tell them, mainly because, to me, the border is the border, and it would not make any sense to divide it into sides. It is the place that it is, the country that it is, because of the influence and the inbreeding of the Mexican and the North American cultures. As proud and grateful as I am about having grown up in La Frontera, I do recognize its problems, cultural schizophrenia being the one that most concerns me in my writing. By way of exemplifying what I mean by cultural schizophrenia, I would like to share with you some of the highlights of my formative years.

I was born into a strict, Mexican-Catholic family that treasured, above everything else, all of its ties to el Méjico real: customs, values, religion, and language. That this strict Mexican-Catholic family had its residence in the United States was a question of economic circumstance rather than personal preference.

At home I was literally forbidden to speak English, and any of my aunts or uncles could rap me on the head if they heard me disobeying the rule. At school I could only speak Spanish in my Spanish class, otherwise I would be fined a quarter for each transgression. At the same time we ate Mexican food in the school cafeteria. Most of the women who worked in the kitchen were from across the river, and cheap labor is especially appealing to convent schools.

As you can see, cultural schizophrenia set in early. At home I was pura Mejicana. At school I was an American citizen. Neither place validated the idea of the Mexican-American. Actually, I grew up believing that Mexican-Americans, or Pochos, as my family preferred to call them, were stupid. Not only could they not even speak their own language correctly (meaning Spanish), but their dark coloring denounced them as ignorant. Apart from being strict, Mexican, and Catholic, my family was also under the delusion that, since our ancestors were made in Madrid, our fair coloring made us better than common Mexicans. If we maintained the purity of la lengua Castellana, and didn't associate with Prietos or Pochos, our superiority over that low breed of people would always be clear.

To safeguard me lest I become infected by that kind of people, my grandparents enrolled me in a private Catholic girls' school—a luxury which they were certain Pocho families could not afford or even aspire to. To make sure that my Spanish remained "pure," my grandmother had me do two hours of Spanish lessons at home every evening. "Forgetting my Spanish"—meaning not just the language, but the accent as well—was the equivalent of losing my virginity.

But I had no intention of forsaking either my mother tongue or my cherry; both were integral to my survival in the family. English, on the other hand, the forbidden tree of knowledge that I could diagram with my eyes closed, was a reward that my family could never give me, and, therefore, a rebellion. My brother and I used to sneak conversations in English, even swear words, behind my Grandma's back. I would write hour after hour in my journal/portable confessional, playing with the forbidden words and sentences as if they were a hieroglyphics that only I could read. I wrote and performed my first play in the fourth grade, and in the eighth grade I had my first essay published. Neither of those pieces had anything to do with cultural schizophrenia (although the play *was* about racial discrimination), but they had everything to do with my becoming a writer.

I don't know when I decided that I was a Chicana writer, or if I decided at all. It must have happened during my junior year in college, when I was enrolled in a Chicano Literature class which, of course, I kept a secret from my family. Until I took this class, I had seen myself adamantly as Mexican. Chicanos, in my illuminated opinion, had no language, no country, and certainly no culture. They all wore zoot suits and lived in the tenements of the Second Ward; their graffiti did to buildings what their dialect did to the Spanish language. I was no goddamn Chicana!

How was I to know that zoot suits comprised a culture of their own? That graffiti was symbolic expression, a language of the barrio, as intricate and full of meaning as poetry itself? Who would have told me that Chicanos practiced the same rituals, listened to the same music, believed the same superstitions, ate the same food, even told the same jokes as my purebred Mexican family? Needless to say, my cultural schizophrenia transcended the realm of my unconscious and became a conscious demon, grinning over my shoulder at every turn.

But it wasn't until the Chicano Literature class exposed me to poems and stories about La Llorona, the mythic Weeping Woman of my own childhood fears who more than once had peeked into the windows of my darkest nightmares, that I really started to locate myself within La Raza. Chicanos did have a heritage after all, and I was living it! At home I was Mexican and spoke only Spanish, and yet we celebrated Thanksgiving and the Fourth of July. At school, my language was English and we pledged allegiance to the American flag, and yet we prayed to the Virgen de Guadalupe. Naturally, imperceptibly, this bilingual/bicultural identity became the controlling image of my life, and nowhere did it manifest itself more than in my poetry.

Domingo Means Scrubbing

our knees for Church.
'Amá splicing our trenzas tight
with ribbons, stretching
our eyes into slits. Grandpa
wearing his teeth.

Domingo means one of our tíos
passing out quarters
for the man with the basket
and me putting mine under
my tongue like the host.

Then menudo and Nina's
raisin tamales for dessert.
Our tías exchange Pepito
jokes in the kitchen
while we sneak a beer
into the bathroom,
believing the taste
will make our chi-chis grow.

Domingo means playing
a la familia with all our cousins,
me being the Dad cause I'm
the oldest and the only one
who'll kiss the Mom
under the willow tree.

After dark,
our grandmothers pisteando
tequila on the porch, scaring us
every little while: *La Llorona
knows what you kids are doing!*
'Amá coming out of the house
to drag the girls inside
pa' lavar los dishes.

Domingo means scrubbing.

Chicanos are lucky because our heritage straddles two countries and feeds
off two traditions, as the "Domingo" poem illustrates, but Chicano culture
feeds tradition as well, with change, with individual history, with contemporary vision. In a paper I wrote about the place of Chicana literature in the
wide, white world, I explained the Chicana writer's role as "historian, jour-
nalist, sociologist, teacher," and, let me add, activist, like this:

> The Chicana writer, like the curandera (medicine woman) or the bruja
> (witch) is the keeper of the culture, keeper of the memories, the rituals,
> the stories, the superstitions, the language, the imagery of her Mexican
> heritage. She is also the one who changes the culture, the one who breeds
> a new language and a new lifestyle, new values, new images and rhythms,
> new dreams and conflicts into that heritage, making of all of this brou-
> haha and cultural schizophrenia a new legacy for those who have still
> to squeeze into legitimacy as human beings and American citizens . . .

So you see, I have always been a Chicana, and I have always wanted to be a poet. The bridge between my identity and my writing has become a symbolic border that I cross at will, without a green card, without la migra or el coyote.

Now, there is another bridge to cross, one I have migrated far away from home to find: the invisible bridge between the marginal and the mainstream literary worlds. Like any frontera, this one requires the "right" credentials or the right coyote to get me across. Without either one, all I am is a literary wetback, but that too has its own magic. I would like to close with my National Anthem.

La Frontera

La frontera lies
wide open, sleeping beauty.
Her waist bends like the river
bank around a flagpole.
Her scent tangles in the arms
of the mesquite. Her legs
sink in the mud
of two countries, both
sides leaking sangre
y sueños.

        I come here
mystified by the sleek Río Grande
and its ripples and the moonlit curves
of tumbleweeds, the silent lloronas,
the children they lose.
In that body of dreams,
the Mexicans swim for years,
their fine skins too tight to breathe.
Yo también me he acostado con ella,[1]
crossed that cold bed, wading
toward a hunched coyote.

---

1. I too have slept with her

Refugee Ship

Lorna Dee Cervantes

Like wet cornstarch, I slide
past my grandmother's eyes. Bible
at her side, she removes her glasses.
The pudding thickens.

Mama raised me without language.
I'm orphaned from my Spanish name.
The words are foreign, stumbling
on my tongue. I see in the mirror
my reflection: bronzed skin, black hair.

I feel I am a captive
aboard the refugee ship.
The ship that will never dock.
El barco que nunca atraca.

Linguistic Terrorism

Gloria Anzaldúa

Deslenguadas. Somos los del español deficiente.[2] We are your linguistic
nightmare, your linguistic aberration, your linguistic *mestisaje*, the subject
of your *burla*. Because we speak with tongues of fire we are culturally crucified. Racially, culturally and linguistically *somos huérfanos*—we speak an
orphan tongue.

Chicanas who grew up speaking Chicano Spanish have internalized the
belief that we speak poor Spanish. It is illegitimate, a bastard language. And
because we internalize how our language has been used against us by the
dominant culture, we use our language differences against each other.

Chicana feminists often skirt around each other with suspicion and hesi-
tation. For the longest time I couldn't figure it out. Then it dawned on me. To
be close to another Chicana is like looking into the mirror. We are afraid of

---

2. Tongueless. We are those with deficient Spanish.

what we'll see there. *Pena.* Shame. Low estimation of self. In childhood we are told that our language is wrong. Repeated attacks on our native tongue diminish our sense of self. The attacks continue throughout our lives.

Chicanas feel uncomfortable talking in Spanish to Latinas, afraid of their censure. Their language was not outlawed in their countries. They had a whole lifetime of being immersed in their native tongue; generations, centuries in which Spanish was a first language, taught in school, heard on radio and TV, and read in the newspaper.

If a person, Chicana or Latina, has a low estimation of my native tongue, she also has a low estimation of me. Often with *mexicanas y latinas* we'll speak English as a neutral language. Even among Chicanas we tend to speak English at parties or conferences. Yet, at the same time, we're afraid the other will think we're *agringadas* because we don't speak Chicano Spanish. We oppress each other trying to out-Chicano each other, vying to be the "real" Chicanas, to speak like Chicanos. There is no one Chicano language just as there is no one Chicano experience. A monolingual Chicana whose first language is English or Spanish is just as much a Chicana as one who speaks several variants of Spanish. A Chicana from Michigan or Chicago or Detroit is just as much a Chicana as one from the Southwest. Chicano Spanish is as diverse linguistically as it is regionally.

By the end of this century, Spanish speakers will comprise the biggest minority group in the U.S., a country where students in high schools and colleges are encouraged to take French classes because French is considered more "cultured." But for a language to remain alive it must be used. By the end of this century English, and not Spanish, will be the mother tongue of most Chicanos and Latinos.

So, if you want to really hurt me, talk badly about my language. Ethnic identity is twin skin to linguistic identity—I am my language. Until I can take pride in my language, I cannot take pride in myself. Until I can accept as legitimate Chicano Texas Spanish, Tex-Mex and all the other languages I speak, I cannot accept the legitimacy of myself. Until I am free to write bilingually and to switch codes without having always to translate, while I still have to speak English or Spanish when I would rather speak Spanglish, and as long as I have to accommodate the English speakers rather than having them accommodate me, my tongue will be illegitimate.

I will no longer be made to feel ashamed of existing. I will have my voice: Indian, Spanish, white. I will have my serpent's tongue—my woman's voice, my sexual voice, my poet's voice. I will overcome the tradition of silence.

My fingers
move sly against your palm
like women everywhere, we speak in code . . .
Melanie Kaye/Kantrowitz[3]

Julieta's Muses

Judy Gonzales-Flores

Julieta, de color café, full-chested, with flowing hair, awaits the dawn.
She lies like a sleepy ocelot in her lumpy, make-shift bed. In meditative half-
slumber, images arise to her vision. Dancing Indian princess, flowers swirling,
Julieta's deepest fantasies tease her awareness. She longs to compose a few
lines—"Chicana, Chicana, have you ever written a line? Is your reality the
same as mine?" She muses to herself, thinking about her fantasies, her lovers,
whatever she can conjure. Others may conjure up their lovers' favorite dishes,
but Julieta conjures up their most languid fantasies. Still half-sleeping, she
moans softly, confused about the day to follow. Shall she leaflet the campus,
spreading the joy of the mujeres' first literary magazine, or shall she help the
vatos organize the workers' march? She knows what she wants, but is it what
she should do? An impish, brown face, como su sobrino, pingo que es,[4]
smiles in her mind's eye. Her muse, chavalito mocoso,[5] tells her to spread joy.
"To hell with should do's" availing of her muse for impish strength, "I'll go
with my girlfriend, and we shall create our magazine. We will write of swirling images, human love, liberation, God, rosas que brotan, almas hondas y
satisfechas,[6] our muses, sensual impish, shall guide our awareness. Of consciousness we shall create!"

Oh hell, Julieta berates herself, her poetry, remembering her sadness, her
despondency with the vatos, who tease the women for their silly endeavors.
The lines of sensual poetry drift into semiconscious—"Julieta, heart fond of
love, of passion, brown eyes like diamonds, radiate life and the need for joy."
She remembers her lover, his vibrating touch and soft words of encouragement. How long has she been without him, yet she can remember his steady,

---

3. "Sign," in *We Speak in Code: Poems and Other Writings*. Pittsburgh: Motherroot
Publications, Inc., 1980), 85.

4. like her cousin, weird as he is,

5. snotty little kid

6. roses that blossom, deep and satisfied souls

true assurance that her seeking is right and true? Why can the others not be as he is? Why the taunting? She can write and will, of liberation, of human life bursting to the copete of the goblet! Then Julieta becomes a river, flowing water of past, present, of future, for there has never been a yesterday, every day is today. The river bears her name and flows onward, giving life, as holy water of bygone rituals.

They Are Laying Plans for Me — Those Curanderas

Teresa Palomo Acosta

For Carmen Tafolla

those curanderas know
they can heal me

so they have come to lead me,
those curanderas,
back to myself

at some point in their plot
they wanted to put in a part
a scene
where they
lay their hands upon my head
give me their sacred bundle of magic
to banish my wounds and fears

in their story line
this has been their ancient role

but
they have digressed with me
(to say among themselves) that
I have forgotten
the strength
of their medicine

so instead must send me
another healer: Chicana Poeta
to bring me home in another way

to make my journey with her words
about la raza's lives
to build the bridge
from their spirits to mine
to bring me from the shadows
to see myself entire
and become
in time
my own curandera

Poema Inédito / Unpublished Poem

María Herrera-Sobek

Se me escapó
el sonido del poema
que tocó a la puerta.

Dormida,
sin aliento
lo dejé ir
y se alejó
para siempre
perdido
entre los pliegues
del olvido.

■

The sound of the poem
knocking at the door
escaped me.

Asleep
without breath
I let it go
and it went away
forever
lost
among the folds
of memory.

Mi Poesía / My Poetry

María Herrera-Sobek

Mi poesía
me persigue
entre botes de hojalata,
entre chiles y tomates,
manzanas y duraznos,
escobas y basura
que otro día
eran mi única canción.

My poetry
follows me
between tin cans
between chiles and tomatoes
apples and peaches
brooms and garbage
that on another day
were my only song.

Mi poesía
surge entre chillidos
de niños
y esposos lastimados
por la explosión
de pluma
que sangra
y deja
gusanos destripados
en las páginas.

My poetry
bursts out between cries
of children
and husbands hurt
by the explosion
of a pen
that bleeds
and leaves
gutted worms
on the pages.

Mi poesía
me asalta
entre ríos de caricias
que recibo
de impacientes amantes
en desesperada competencia
con mi pluma.

My poetry
assaults me
among the rivers of embraces
I receive
from impatient lovers
in desperate competition
with my pen.

Dedicated to American Atomics II

Margarita Cota-Cárdenas

Writing poems
sitting in the deep end

of an empty Tucson swimming pool,
I cup the algae in my free hand
and smear it on my face for inspiration,
feeling life connecting glowing kinship
in this desert Atlantis.

Lírica fanática / Fanatic Lyric

Margarita Cota-Cárdenas

te hablo en serio
     poesía
   si en paz no me dejas
     no
       se lavarán platos
       ni caritas consentidas
     no
       se harán camas
       ni tareas
       ni comidas
me estás desbaratando   demasiado pláticas
   tú déspota
              déjame un par de días
 o ya   no
      no te dejaré entrar
        mi único huesped
       a mi roperito

■

I speak to you seriously
     poetry
   if you don't leave me alone
     the dishes won't get washed
     nor spoiled little faces
     work won't get done
     nor meals cooked
You're undoing me
   you despot

leave me for a few days
or I won't
let you enter
my only guest
in my little closet

Desveladas inútiles / Useless Sleeplessness

Margarita Cota-Cárdenas

Poesía,
déjame dormir;
pronto me llaman
unas manitas morenas
y me absorben
mis ciclos
acabándose
en narración

■

Poetry
let me sleep
soon   little dark hands
will call me
and my cycles
will absorb me
finishing themselves
in narration

The Confession

Naomi Quiñonez

I must confess
I have been off the planet earth

for 3 days and 3 nights
posing as myself
in a rather shabby disguise
imposter to those
who never knew me
in the first place.

I have been caught
writing poetry
instead of monthly reports,
disciplined for daydreaming
at budget meetings.

And more recently
I faded from view
only to become a silhouette
playing piano in a dark room
serenading oblivious
breakdancers, and equally
oblivious breaking lovers.

People winced in concern
when I astrally projected
from a Parkview business meeting
into the L.A. cityscape
where I was last seen
cavorting with a fellow Eulipian
over fishburgers & fries
by candlelight
exchanging here and nows
and toasting
gin & platonics at Yee Mee Loo's.

I was lost at rush hour
for two of those three days
and nirvana was a freeway offramp
at 6th and Olympic
where I found shelter
at a 7-11, the urban temple of
immediate gratification.

And I must confess—with urgency
that there is a method

to my madness, as I have made madness
my lover, for those long lost nights
of repeated anti-climaxes.

The method is a destination
with no map
an awkward silence
a deliberate and premeditated rage
posing as confusion.
The method is an unworldly love
for certain earthlinks
that can never grow roots.

I've been off now
for 3 days & 3 nights,
have given up
all my worldly possessions:
    Sights for sore eyes (scratched glasses)
    Financial insecurity (unbalanced checkbooks)
    Senseless direction (Santa Ana Freeways at 8 a.m.)
    Illusionary lovers (fill in the blank please)
All at the risk of being taken seriously
and given nothing in return.

But the party is over
Stuporvision ebbs
and I'm back
to 9 to 5 certainties
and the questionable security
of my name, rank and serial number.

I must confess
you were right
to look at me sideways
(never look a madwoman in the eye)
accuse me of having vacated the premises
without so much as giving a 30 day notice
or a clue to my whereabouts.

But you were fettered and fastened
to your obligations
and I have none, save my own madness
and an unwavering tendency towards
confessions—after the fact.

como embrujada[7]

Evangelina Vigil-Piñón

how strange
to have this compelling urge
to write to ghost readers.

I spill my whole life on you
and don't even know who you are.

I don't understand it.
I've always been taught
to be very careful who you trust.

Qué confianza, verdad?[8]

Paradox

Ana Castillo

You ask me
if it is possible to emanate
joy
eased from the matrix
in my poem's end
the merciless castration.

What are the poems
but words on paper
that yellows or blows away?

i cannot write of the unspoken
poem created in shadows
as dusk turns a flat into a place
for ghosts and one, so white
next to my obscure origin as when

---

7. as if bewitched
8. What confidence, right?

virgins' hearts were torn pulsating
in fear of immortality.

Your paintings will not tell
of the perfection of aftermath
and future history losing substance.

Never will a monocled critic
spy my cynical laugh in geometric oils
a synchronized sigh, a whisper
meant only for one ear to appraise
when you've gone: "I have work—
it cannot wait." i freeze time
until you return.

Mango Says Goodbye Sometimes

Sandra Cisneros

I like to tell stories. I tell them inside my head. I tell them after the mail-
man says here's your mail. Here's your mail he said.

I make a story for my life, for each step my brown shoe takes. I say, "And
so she trudged up the wooden stairs, her sad brown shoes taking her to the
house she never liked."

I like to tell stories. I am going to tell you a story about a girl who didn't
want to belong.

We didn't always live on Mango Street. Before that we lived on Loomis
on the third floor, and before that we lived on Keeler. Before Keeler it was
Paulina, but what I remember most is Mango Street, sad red house, the house
I belong but do not belong to.

I put it down on paper and then the ghost does not ache so much. I write
it down and Mango says goodbye sometimes. She does not hold me with
both arms. She sets me free.

One day I will pack my bags of books and paper. One day I will say goodbye to Mango. I am too strong for her to keep me here forever. One day I will
go away.

Friends and neighbors will say, What happened to that Esperanza? Where
did she go with all those books and paper? Why did she march so far away?

They will not know I have gone away to come back. For the ones I left
behind. For the ones who cannot out.

SEVEN

Growing-up

Mother, Father
there's no passing the cup
I'm going to be a troublemaker
when I grow up.
                DEMETRIA MARTÍNEZ

I thought then
I would like to be a nun with
long white veil floating in the wind
mounted on horseback
like the actress María Felix
            MARGARITA COTA-CÁRDENAS

Recovery of the past through memories of childhood; coming into knowledge of the person they are now by examining the growing-up period; identification of social and cultural forces that shaped and influenced their lives: these
are some of the forces that lie behind the series of "growing up" poems and
stories or *"bildungs"* tales written by Chicana writers. The adventures of the
hero/heroine that shape their destinies and bring self-knowledge and self-realization are part of the genre of self-development brought about by schooling
or other forces in society; this is the *Bildungsroman,* or it could also be called
Entwicklungsroman, the novel of development (Pratt, 13). These moments of
self-realization and growing up arc not only seen in the short story and the
longer narrative, but can also be found in the poetry which is included here.

The growing-up stories and poems written by Chicanas are part of the
chain of searching that forms a general theme in Chicano literature: the quest
goes on for moments of insight into what has made Chicanos and Chicanas
what they are today. For writers such as Rolando Hinojosa, Tomás Rivera, and
Rudolfo Anaya, their well-known works (*Klail City, . . . Y no se lo tragó a tierra,*
Bless Me, Ultima) are tales of young boys growing into manhood or self-knowledge through the acceptance of the symbols, happenings, and circumstances of
the past, and the subsequent integration and unification of these as their destiny. For them it is the winning of the kingdom of consciousness, heritage, and
self. On the other hand, the bildungstales, or stories of development written
by women, has not been studied or analyzed in great depth. Pratt claims it is

because women are never allowed the freedom for total self-realization, or perhaps it is because, for women, the consciousness of growing up has not been defined in as acutely sexual terms as can be found in books like *Catcher in the Rye* or *Portnoy's Complaint*.

For women, in the main, the traditional *Bildungsroman* was meant to prepare the young heroine for marriage. Annis Pratt points out that younger girls were given "tests in submission," while their older sisters were provided with "models of behavior appropriate for success in the marriage market" (Pratt, 14). While this may be typical of the writings of early Chicana writers, the contemporary growing-up story focuses around a general sense of loss, and around the realization that innocence is gone. It also centers around awareness of death and mortality, on the inability to retreat back into childhood, and on the necessity, at times, to conform to a life not freely chosen by them. Many of these stories find the woman in the child and represent the voice of reflection. Seeing the growing older of the child, they are the monitor of woman's going forth. They also chronicle the world in which the adolescent hero's expectations conflict with the dictates of the surrounding society. Chicana heroes wish freedom to come and go, to be accepted for meaningful work, to use their intelligence, and to understand their own sexual desires and capabilities: all these elements clash with the norms of a strongly traditional family and a male-oriented society. Thus the narrator is often the voice of guilt felt in the rebellion against established cultural institutions, a rebellion viewed as "sinning." This behavior is chronicled in rebellious thoughts or actions against the church and in secretive sexual actions, such as the exploration of body and sexuality ("In the Toolshed," by Patricia Santana-Béjar); and in emotional maturation stories, "Growing," by Helen María Viramontes).

Pratt images women's relationship to nature as "the green world," an archetype related to the "place from which she sets forth and a memory to which she returns for renewal" (Pratt, 22). This link to nature represents "something left behind or about to be left behind as one backs into the enclosure." In the Chicana literature contained here, one does not so much see the "green world" as nature, but as original innocence, and as (or) a state of freedom. In "Oooohh the Boogieman," and in the poem to her little sister Margarita Cota-Cárdenas clearly reflects the state of freedom, innocence and naturalness, vis-à-vis the "contained" persons the lyric speaker and her sister have become.

The stories and poems contained in this section are characterized by a child-narrator whose consciousness is filtered through that of the adult or "older" writer. Sandra Cisneros, for example, in "Velorio" presents the voice of a child remembering the death of a friend's babysister. The narrative voice remembers the event, not at the time it is occurring, but when the child is older and reminiscing. The speaker does not interpret the event for the reader, but it is rather a voice not fully conscious of the implication of what is happening: a child startled by the solemn, ritual starkness of death and the disruption of routine (kitchen chairs facing front in preparation for the wake), and how inappropriate the little girls feel as they enter with ankles raw from scratching mosquito bites, laughing.

In her short stories, Denise Chávez creates what could be called the "space" of childhood. The neighborhood, and that which is known to the child, is the yardstick against which the unfamiliar and mysterious is measured. For Chávez, the child's known world cushions her from stark reality: it represents comfort, substance, and permanence. Her child narrators accept the unknown, yet remain bewildered by the senselessness of death, violence, and destruction. These children protagonists of Chicana writers are often surrounded by fear of death, loss, and Anglo institutions such as the immigration patrol, which can turn childhood fantasies into terror. They also struggle to understand the prejudice against them (because they are girls/women) and the racism (because they are Mexicans). These fears and events, little understood by the child, are chronicled in poems and stories by Cota-Cárdenas, Chávez, Cisneros, and Rivera.

Nevertheless, sustained by strong female role models, these young adolescent heroines are told that there are worlds to explore. The influence of female forces in their lives (mothers, grandmothers, sisters, and other female role models) is very evident in their stories. For Chávez, for example, the links and roots to the community are seen through the women in the family. Often it is the rebel friend or family member who is seen as someone to be admired and respected in the eyes of the child ("Para Teresa," Hernández, or in poems by Cota-Cárdenas). Growing stubbornly, like thin weeds, linking themselves to the female forces in their lives, these heroines begin to make their own legends and their own realities. Past innocence, the "green world," the recognition of positive as well as negative forces surrounding them help these adolescents achieve self-realization, make accommodations and yet not lose the hope, vitality, and integration as they "steadily make" their way (Villanueva).

■ ■ ■

Growing

Helena María Viramontes

The two walked down First Street hand in reluctant hand. The smaller of one wore a thick, red sweater which had a desperately loose button that swung like a pendulum. She carried crayons, humming "Jesus loves little boys and girls" to the speeding echo of the Saturday morning traffic and was totally oblivious to her older sister's wrath.

"My eye!" Naomi ground out the words from between her teeth. She turned to her youngest sister who seemed unconcerned and quite delighted at the prospect of another adventure. "Chaperone," she said with great disdain. "My EYE!" Lucía was chosen by Apá to be Naomi's chaperone. Infuriated, Naomi dragged her along impatiently, pulling and jerking at almost every step. She was 14, almost 15, and the idea of having to be watched by a young snot like Lucía was insulting to her maturity. She flicked her hair over her shoulder. "Goddammit," she murmured, making sure that the words were soft enough so that both God and Lucía could not hear them.

There seemed to be no way out of the custom. Her arguments were always the same and always turned into pleas. This morning was no different. Amá, Naomi said, exasperated but determined not to cower out of this one, Amá, the United States is different. Here girls don't need chaperones. Parents trust their daughters. As usual Amá turned to the kitchen sink or the ice box, shrugged her shoulders and said: "You have to ask your father." Naomi's nostril's flexed in fury as she pleaded. But Amá, it's embarrassing. I'm too old for that. I am an adult. And as usual, Apá felt different, and in his house, she had absolutely no other choice but to drag Lucía to a sock hop or church carnival or anywhere Apá was sure a social interaction was inevitable, and Lucía came along as a spy, a gnat, a pain in the neck.

Well, Naomi debated with herself; it wasn't Lucía's fault, really. She suddenly felt sympathy for the humming little girl who scrambled to keep up with her as they crossed the freeway overpass. She stopped and tugged Lucía's shorts up, and although her shoelaces were tied, Naomi retied them. No, it wasn't her fault after all, Naomi thought, and she patted her sister's soft, light brown, and almost blondish hair, it was Apá's. She slowed her pace as they continued their journey to Jorge's house. It was Apá who refused to trust her, and she could not understand what she had done to make him so distrustful. TU ERES MUJER, he thundered, like a great voice above the heavens, and that was the end of any argument, any question, because he said those words not as a truth, but as a verdict, and she could almost see the clouds parting, the thunderbolts breaking the tranquility of her sex. Naomi tightened her grasp with the thought, shaking her head in disbelief.

"So what's wrong with being a mujer," she asked herself out loud.

"Wait up. Wait." Lucía said, rushing behind her.

"Well, would you hurry? Would you?" Naomi reconsidered: Lucía did have some fault in the matter after all, and she became irritated at once at Lucía's smile and the way her chaperone had of taking and holding her hand.

As they passed El Gallo, Lucía began fussing, hanging on to her older sister's waist for reassurance.

"Stop it. Would you stop it?" She unglued her sister's grasp and continued pulling her along. "What's wrong with you?" she asked Lucía. I'll tell you what's wrong with you, she thought, as they waited at the corner of an intersection for the light to change: You have a big mouth. That's it. If it wasn't for Lucía's willingness to tattle, she would not have been grounded for three months. Three months, twelve Saturday nights, and two church bazaars later, Naomi still hadn't forgiven her youngest sister. When they crossed the street, a homely young man with a face full of acne honked at her tight, purple petal pushers. The two were startled by the honk.

"Go to hell," she yelled at the man in the blue and white Chevy. She indignantly continued her walk.

"Don't be mad, my little baby," he said, his car crawling across the street, then speeding off leaving tracks on the pavement. "You make me ache," he yelled, and he was gone.

"GO TO HELL, goddamn you!" she screamed at the top of her lungs forgetting for a moment that Lucía told everything to Apá. What a big mouth her youngest sister had, for chrissakes. Three months.

Naomi stewed in anger when she thought of the Salesian Carnival and how she first met a Letterman Senior whose eyes, she remembered with a soft smile, sparkled like crystals of brown sugar. She sighed deeply as she recalled the excitement she experienced when she first became aware that he was following them from booth to booth. Joe's hair was greased back and his dimples were deep. When he finally handed her a stuffed rabbit he had won pitching dimes, she knew she wanted him.

As they continued walking, Lucía waved to the Fruit Man. He slipped off his teeth and again, she was bewildered.

"Would you hurry up!" Naomi told her as she told Lucía that same night at the Carnival. Joe walked beside them and he took out a whole roll of tickets, trying to convince her to leave her youngest sister on the ferris wheel. "You could watch her from behind the gym," he had told her, and his eyes smiled pleasure. "Come on," he said, "have a little fun." They waited in the ferris wheel line of people.

"Stay on the ride," she instructed Lucía, making sure her sweater was buttoned. "And when it stops again, just give the man another ticket, okay?" Lucía said Okay, excited at the prospect of heights and lows and her stomach wheezing in between. After Naomi saw her go up for the first time, she waved to her, then slipped away into the darkness and joined the other hungry couples behind the gym. Occasionally, she would open her eyes to see the lights of the ferris wheel spinning in the air with dizzy speed.

When Naomi returned to the ferris wheel, her hair undone, her lips still tingling from his newly stubbled cheeks, Lucía walked off and vomited. Lucía vomited the popcorn, a hot dog, some chocolate raisins, and a candied apple and all Naomi knew was that she was definitely in trouble.

"It was the ferris wheel," Lucía said to Apá. "The wheel going like this over and over again." She circled her arms in the air and vomited again at the thought of it.

"Where was your sister?" Apá had asked, his voice raising.

"I don't know." Lucía replied, and Naomi knew she had just committed a major offense, and Joe would never wait until her prison sentence was completed.

"Owwww." Lucía said. "You're pulling too hard."

"You're a slow poke, that's why," Naomi snarled back. They crossed the street and passed the rows of junk yards and the shells of cars which looked like abandoned skull heads. They passed Señora Núñez's neat, wooden house and Naomi saw her peeking through the curtains of her window. They passed the Tú y Yo, the one room dirt pit of a liquor store where the men bought their beers and sat outside on the curb drinking quietly. When they reached Fourth Street, Naomi spotted the neighborhood kids playing stickball with a broomstick and a ball. Naomi recognized them right away and Tina waved to her from the pitcher's mound.

"Wanna play?" Lourdes yelled from center field. "Come on, have some fun."

"Can't." Naomi replied. "I can't." Kids, kids, she thought. My, my. It wasn't more than a few years ago that she played baseball with Eloy and the rest of them. But she was in high school now, too old now, and it was unbecoming of her. She was an adult.

"I'm tired," Lucía said. "I wanna ice cream."

"You got money?"

"No."

"Then shut up." Lucía sat on the curb, hot and tired, and began removing her sweater. Naomi decided to sit down next to her for a few minutes and watch the game. Anyway, she wasn't really that much in a hurry to get to Jorge's. A few minutes wouldn't make much difference to someone who spent most of his time listening to the radio.

She counted them by names. They were all there. Fifteen of them and their ages varied just as much as their clothes. They dressed in an assortment of colors, looking like confetti thrown out in the street. Pants, skirts, shorts were always too big and had to be tugged up constantly, and shirt sleeves rolled and unrolled, or socks colorfully mismatched with shoes that did not fit. But the way they dressed presented no obstacle for scoring or yelling foul and she enjoyed the abandonment with which they played. She knew that the only decision these kids made was what to play next, and for a moment she wished to return to those days.

Chano's team was up. The teams were oddly numbered. Chano had nine on his team because everybody wanted to be on a winning team. It was a unwritten law of stickball that anyone who wanted to play joined in on whatever team they preferred. Tina's team had the family faithful 6. Of course numbers determined nothing. Naomi remembered once playing with Eloy and three of her cousins against ten kids, and still winning by three points.

Chano was at bat and everybody fanned out far and wide. He was a power hitter and Tina's team prepared themselves for him. They could not afford a homerun now because Piri was on second, legs apart, waiting to rush home and score. And Piri wanted to score it at all costs. It was important for him because his father sat outside a liquor store with a couple of his uncles and a couple of malt liquors watching the game.

"Steal the base," his father yelled. "Run, menso." But Piri hesitated. He was too afraid to take the risk. Tina pitched and Chano swung, missed, strike one.

"Batter, batter, swing," Naomi yelled from the curb. She stood up to watch the action better.

"I wannan ice cream," Lucía said.

"Come on, Chano," Piri yelled, bending his knees and resting his hands on them like a true baseball player. He spat, clapped his hands. "Come on."

"Ah, shut up, sissy." This came from Lourdes, Tina's younger sister. Naomi smiled at the rivals. "Can't you see you're making the pitcher nervous?" She pushed him hard between the shoulder blades, then returned to her position in the outfield, holding her hand over her eyes to shield them from the sun. "Strike the batter out," she screamed at the top of her lungs. "Come on, strike the menso out!" Tina delivered another pitch, but not before going through the motions of a professional pitcher preparing for the perfect pitch. Naomi knew she was a much better pitcher than Tina. Strike two. Maybe not. Lourdes let out such a cry of joy that Piri's father called her a dog.

Chano was angry now, nervous and upset. He put his bat down, spat in his hands and rubbed them together, wiped the sides of his jeans, kicked the dirt for perfect footing.

"Get on with the game," Naomi shouted impatiently. Chano tested his swing. He swung so hard that he caused Juan, Tina's brother and devoted catcher, to jump back.

"Hey, baboso, watch out," he said. "You almost hit my coco." And he pointed to his forehead.

"Well, don't be so stupid," Chano replied, positioning himself once again. "Next time back off when I come to bat."

"Baboso," Juan repeated.

"Say it to my face," Chano said, breaking his stand and turning to Juan. "Say it again so I can break this bat over your head."

"Ah, come on, Kiki," the shortstop yelled, "I gotta go home pretty soon."

"Let up," Tina demanded.

"Shut up, marrana," Piri said, turning to his father to make sure he heard. "Tinasana, cola de marrana, Tinasana, cola de marrana." Tina became so infuriated that she threw the ball directly to his stomach. Piri folded over in pain.

"No! No!' Sylvia yelled. "Don't get off the base or she'll tag out out."

"It's a trick," Miguel yelled from behind home plate.

"That's what you get!" This came from Lourdes. Piri did not move, and for a moment Naomi felt sorry for him, but giggled at the scene anyway.

"I heard the ice cream man," Lucía said.

"You're all right, Tina," Naomi yelled, laughing. "You're a-o-k." And with that compliment, Tina bowed her proud performance until everyone began shouting and booing. Tina was prepared. She pitched and Chano made the connection quick, hard, the ball rising high and flying over her head, Piri's, Lourdes, Naomi's, and Lucía's head and landed inside the Chinese Cemetery.

"DON'T JUST STAND THERE!!" Tina screamed to Lourdes. "Go get it, stupid." After Lourdes broke out of her trance, she ran to the tall, chain link fence, which surrounded the cemetery, jumped on the fence with great urgency, and crawled up like a scrambling spider. When she jumped over the top of the fence, her dress tore with a rip roar.

"We saw your calzones, we saw your calzones," Lucía sang.

"Go! Lourdes, go!" Naomi jumped up and down in excitement, feeling like a player who so much wanted to help her team win but was benched in the sidelines for good. The kids blended into one huge noise, like an untuned orchestra, screaming and shouting "Get the Ball; Run in, Piri; Go Lourdes, Go; Throw the ball; Chano pick up your feetthrowthe ballrunrunrunthrow the ball. "THROW the ball to me!!" Naomi waved and waved her arms. She was no longer concerned with her age, her menstruations, her breasts that bounced with glee. All she wanted was an out on home base. To hell with being benched. "Throw it to me," she yelled.

In the meantime, Lourdes searched frantically for the ball, tip-toeing across the graves, saying excuse me, please excuse me, excuse me, until she found the ball peacefully buried behind a huge gray marble stone, and she yelled to no one in particular, CATCH IT, SOMEONE CATCH IT. She threw the ball up and over the fence and it landed near Lucía. Lucía was about to reach for the ball when Naomi picked it off the ground and threw it straight to Tina. Tina caught the ball, dropped it, picked it up, and was about to throw the ball to Juan at homeplate when she realized that Juan had picked up the homeplate and ran, zig-zagging across the street while Piri and Chano ran after him. Chano was a much faster runner, but Piri insisted that he be the first to touch the base.

"I gotta touch it first," he kept repeating between pants, "I gotta."

The kids on both teams grew wild with anger and encouragement. Seeing an opportunity, Tina ran as fast as her stocky legs could take her. Because Chano slowed down to let Piri touch the base first, Tina was able to reach him, and with one quick blow, she thundered OUT! She threw one last desperate throw to Juan so that he could tag Piri out, but she threw it so hard that it struck Piri right in the back of his head, and the blow forced him to stumble just within reach of Juan and homeplate.

"You're out!!' Tina said, out of breath. "O-U-T, out."

"No fair!" Piri immediately screamed. "NO FAIR!!" He stomped his feet in rage like Rumplestilskin. "You marrana, you marrana."

"Don't be such a baby," Piri's father said. "Take it like a man," he said as he opened another malt liquor with a can opener. But Piri continued stomping and screaming until his shouts were buried by a honk of an oncoming car and the kids obediently opened up like a zipper to let the car pass.

Naomi felt like a victor. She had helped, once again. Delighted, she giggled, laughed, laughed harder, suppressed her laughter into chuckles, then laughed again. Lucía sat quietly, to her surprise, and her eyes were heavy with sleep. She wiped them, looked at Naomi. "Vamos," Naomi said, offering her hand. By the end of the block, she lifted Lucía and laid her head on her shoulder. As Lucía fell asleep, Naomi wondered why things were always so complicated once you became older. Funny how the old want to be young and the young want to be old. She was guilty of that. Now that she was older, her obligations became heavier both at home and at school. There were too many expectations, and no one instructed her on how to fulfill them, and wasn't it crazy? She cradled Lucía gently, kissed her cheek. They were almost at Jorge's now, and reading to him was just one more thing she dreaded to do, and one more thing she had no control over: it was another one of Apá's thunderous commands.

When she was Lucía's age, she hunted for lizards and played stickball with her cousins until her body began to bleed at twelve and Eloy saw her in a different light. Under the house, he sucked her swelling nipples and became jealous when she spoke to other boys. He no longer wanted to throw rocks at the cars on the freeway with her, and she began to act differently because everyone began treating her differently and wasn't it crazy? She could no longer be herself and her father could no longer trust her because she was a woman. Jorge's gate hung on a hinge and she was almost afraid it would fall off when she opened it. She felt Lucía's warm, deep, breath on her neck and it tickled her.

"Tomorrow," she whispered lovingly to her sister, as she entered the yard, "tomorrow I'll buy you all the ice creams you want."

Aay, Cucuy . . . !
"Ooooh! The Boogieman!"

Margarita Cota-Cárdenas

in Mesilla   New Mexico
in the summer
            when I was very young
we would go to play   in the old cemetery
            and I would chat very happily
              with my dead relatives
            and I would dance on top
                         of a big cement
                          tomb
            stepping on dancing, dancing
                a black painted skull
from delicious fright   my cousins would laugh
            and my little brother el Plonquito
            and my little sister la Billie
and among dust mesquite dried flowers and tombs
            they'd be nervously shouting and shouting
              and I'd be dancing and singing
                singing and dancing
but last night
            when the ghost of that poor soul buried
            in my former platform of cement
            came looking for me
I had to deny myself voice trembling
            three times

—No, I am not that daring young girl—
—No I am not the happy Plonquita—
—No I am not the same—

Nostalgia

Margarita Cota-Cárdenas

I thought then
that I would like to be a nun with
long white veil floating in the wind
mounted on horseback like the actress María Felix
riding riding off into
a lovely cinema type sunset
in the Convent of the Good Shepherd
we ate dark cornflakes
wheaties with coffee and not milk and thus
poor but pure we would get to be
instant nuns
the way I thought one could do everything
like in the movies of the 1940's
at the Motor-vu.

Pueblo, 1950

Bernice Zamora

I remember you, Fred Montoya.
You were the first *vato* to ever kiss me.
I was twelve years old.
My mother said shame on you,
my teacher said shame on you, and
I said shame on me, and nobody
        said a word to you

Elena at 5 Years

Demetria Martínez

Elena warms a brown egg
Between her palms, close to her lips,
Cold from a carton,
Chosen from the dozen.

It is the center now of a sphere
Of kitchen towels in a drawer,
Next to an Amish cookbook
Next to the oven's white side.

For three weeks at 3:15
Elena will breathe on that egg,
Held between her lifelines,
Against her grape stained lips.
She anticipates the birth
Although brown eggs, her mother says,
Can't hatch.

But at 5, Elena
Has a good ear for heartbeats.
Sidewalk cracks cry
When her tennis shoe touches them,
Lava chips that embroider
The yard have names,
And a brown egg is throbbing
In the cup of her hand.

Troublemaker (for all who ask what I plan to do with my degree)

Demetria Martínez

I want to be
a mango seed
that men trip over,

those innovators!
cradling print-outs
for the production
of pink liquid soap.

Once on a train
I complained to a man:
We should make bread
not pink liquid soap.
He said:
That's not the
American Way.
If we didn't innovate
those Mexicans
would be in worse shape
than what they are today.

I want to be a mango seed
in the street
grow into a tree
towering in the tar
to stop dead all trucks
full of pink
liquid soap.

Mother, father
there's no passing
the cup,
I'm going to be a troublemaker
when I grow up.

Excerpts from "Rosebud"

Erlinda Gonzales-Berry

You might say we were a wild bunch, especially for being girls. Though we spent part of our childhood on a ranch, Dad tried to keep us indoors, away from the corrals and animals. "Wasn't fit for ladies to be out in men's territory," he said. Our job was to learn to keep a good house, like our mother, and to make good tortillas. What Pop never knew is that when he and the hired hand had to make a trip out to pasture or into town, my sisters, Victoria, María, Luisita, and I headed straight for the corral, climbed the barn roof, and took turns jumping to the ground. The possibility of broken limbs was not out of the question. Not one of us, however, would ever admit to being a *gallina,* so jump we did.

High on the list of favorite pastimes was killing snakes. Red-racers were especially fun because we had to run all over chasing them, and it wasn't easy to make a good hit on the run. They often got away. Bull snakes were easier but no fun at all—they just laid there and let us blast stones at them until their tiny heads caved in. I remember an unusually long and fat one that kept squirming and wouldn't die. I finally got a great big rock, stood right over it, and delivered the death blow. I really felt kind of rotten about the whole thing but just shrugged my shoulders and said, "Heck, racers are more fun." We then headed for the pasture to look for horned toads.

II

True, we lived on a ranch, but we didn't have a lot of animals or money. In fact, it wasn't even our ranch. Pop had lost our ranch a long time ago. Actually, he sold it to his brother, and we moved to town. We hated town because we had to go to nuns' school. They were all mean, crotchety crones except for Sister Frances John. She was young and kind and she told us great stories about Saint Christopher who crossed the baby Jesus on his shoulders over the raging river and about the host that bled when dropped on the floor. Sister Anthony Marie, the seventh and eighth grade teacher was the worst. She pretty much ran the whole school and always threatened everyone with a good ear-boxing. I had never seen one, so I wasn't quite sure what that was all about. I found out, though, one Holy Thursday.

Monday and Tuesday of Holy Week we practiced for the Holy Thursday procession. I was to lead the third, fourth, and fifth graders. That meant I got to wear a flower wreath and carry a lit candle. I could hardly wait. Everyone would know I was the smartest girl in class. Actually, they already knew it because ever since I started school, I won the spelling bee. Truth is, we all won. Consuelo (the nuns tried to change her name to Consuela because *o* is masculine in Spanish they said, but Mom and Dad let them know in no uncertain terms that they did not approve and would send Consuelo to public school if they insisted) wiped out her class, and Victoria and María outspelled the younger wimps. The whole town admired the Martínez sisters, but I think they were a little jealous, too, because no one else ever stood a chance in the spelling bee.

Anyway, on Tuesday Sister Frances John said that right after the "Gloria," we should recite the "Pange Lingua." On Wednesday I was sick and didn't get to practice. What I didn't know is that the group was told that *if* the choir sang we should *not* recite. No one bothered to tell me about the change in game plans, so come Holy Thursday, right after the "Gloria," I led the little lambs of God in recitation of the "Pange Lingua" while Mrs. Oliva pounded the organ and the choir belted out a Latin hymn. The louder they sang, the louder we prayed. I was determined that we would prevail. After all, wasn't I a Spelling Bee Champ? When Mass was over, Sister Anthony Marie walked right over to me and BOXED MY EARS! Boy, was I embarrassed, and was I ever mad. At recess while Juanita, Suzy, and I were getting ready to play jacks, I said some real mean things about Sister Anthony Marie. I even called her a few bad words (if you must know they were: old cow, *pinche vieja,* and *cerote seco*) even though I knew I would have to go to confession after school if I wanted to receive Holy Communion on Good Friday. Juanita and Suzy threatened to tell on me, but I gave each one a Cracker Jacks prize, and they forgot about the bad words.

When we left town because Mom got a job teaching in Rosebud, we were happy to leave the ear-boxing nuns, and all the Catholic parents were happy because their kids would have a chance to win the Spelling Bee.

III

Rosebud was no rosebud. It was more like a rose thorn. There was a concrete schoolhouse with three rooms, a mailbox, an old abandoned building that was once a store, a house, and a corral with a barn. Actually, it was a pretty neat corral. It looked like those I had seen in story books. The corrals we knew from our old ranch had piñon posts lined unevenly side by side. This corral was made from lumber planks and was painted red. We could sit on the top plank like Dale Evans did in the movies and watch the cows. One was a milk cow. I always wanted to milk her, but Pop wouldn't hear of it. "That's men's work," he would say, and that was that. Although we talked about it a lot, we didn't dare approach her udders because Molly was not one of those dumb looking cows with soft bovine eyes. Quite the contrary, Molly had a mean streak in her and liked to bolt at anything in sight, aiming with her horns. I found that out the day I tried to bullfight her.

Summers were a bore in Rosebud. Only pleasant thing that happened was that Connie came home. During the winter she lived with Grandma in town and went to high school. Summers she spent in Rosebud helping dad take care of the wild bunch while mom went away to college. Since mom didn't have a degree, she had to take classes every summer in order to get her contract renewed.

So summers we read a lot and listened to Connie tell neat stories about high school. I could hardly wait to go there myself. I used to daydream about being the smartest and most popular girl in the freshman class, and at night, before going to sleep, I imagined myself kissing the basketball team captain. I would shiver just thinking how a kiss might feel. It was quite clear that I would have to wait til high school to find out because the oldest boy in Rosebud Grammar School was in the third grade. I was in the seventh. Kelly Marie and I were the oldest kids in school. That was good and also bad. The good part was that we could boss everyone else around. The bad part was that we had a lot of responsibilities. One day, for example, one of the first graders soiled his pants, and *we* had to tend to him because the teacher (Mom) was busy in the reading circle with the fourth grade Blue Birds. Sometimes Kelly and I got to lead the second grade Yellow Birds in their reading lesson because the teacher (Mom) was busy teaching Social Studies to the fifth graders. That's how things went at the Rosebud school. Everyone pitched in and helped each other learn. There were grades all right—first to seventh—but they weren't really all that important. What was important was fifteen cheerful kids who, every morning, sang "O Columbus the Gem of the Ocean" and "A Spanish Cavalier" and who tried, the rest of the day, to learn something about the marvelous world that lay beyond the wind-blown plains of Rosebud.

IV

Once a month on the last Friday of the month the older kids went with Mrs. Green to Amistad to 4-H Club. The idea of spending the afternoon with boys our age drove us gaga. We primped and giggled all the way on the bumpy gravel road. Deep down I had mixed feelings about Amistad. There were only white kids at that school. That was true about Rosebud, too. All the kids that were bused in from their ranches were white. We were the only brown kids. But we were one happy family, and color didn't matter. It did at Amistad. At least, I felt it did, and I got that feeling from the way kids stared at me and Vicky.

I found out just how much it mattered the day we baked biscuits. Mine turned out light and flaky like they were supposed to. Our group leader was kind, and said my biscuits were country fair prizewinners. That made me feel good. I wasn't even thinking about my brown skin when Tommy Bevins came up to me and said;

"Give me a biscuit."

"Gee, Tommy, I'd like to, but I only have one left, and I want to take it home to my Mom."

He looked at me real mean before he said it: "Dirty Mexican."

I ran to the bathroom and looked in the mirror. He lied. I wasn't dirty. Why did he say it? Why?

When we got home, I gave Mom her biscuit, and I told her about Tommy Bevins.

"AY, mi'ja," she said, "forget it. Just turn the other cheek." Mom always said, "Turn the other cheek." "That Tommy doesn't know anything. You're the cleanest and sweetest little Mexican I know." She held me in her arms and kissed away the tears.

V

Of course, Mom didn't know about the red racers and the bull snakes. She didn't know about the rock fights either, at least not until Connie told her about the day María came running in with blood gushing from her face.

It was summer, and we were specially bored. We decided to build a fort with crates and boxes we found in the garage. After it was built, we decided to tear it down and to build two small forts so we could have a war. María and I were the Huns, and Vicky and Luisita were the Goths. The stone shower began. When we ran out of ammunition we would wave a white hankie and take time-out to gather stones. When we were ready to resume the war, the side that took time-out blew a whistle and pelted the enemy fort with rocks.

Forts and war were forbidden the day María caught a rock in the nose. That was the same day our embroidery lessons began.

How I Changed the War and Won the Game
Mary Helen Ponce

During World War II I used to translate the English newspaper's war news for our adopted grandmother Doña Luisa and her friends. All were elderly ladies, señoras de edad, who could not read English, only their native Spanish. Every afternoon they would gather on Doña Luisa's front porch to await Doña Trinidad's son who delivered the paper to her promptly at five o'clock. There, among the geraniums and pots of yerbabuena[1] I would bring to them the news of the war.

At first I enjoyed this as the señoras welcomed me as a grownup. They would push their chairs in a semi-circle; the better to hear me. I sat in the middle on a banquito[2] that was once a milk crate. I don't remember how I

---

1. spearmint
2. little bench

began to be their translator but because I was an obedient child, and at eight a good reader, I was somehow coerced or selected.

I would sit down, adjust my dress, then slowly unwrap the paper, reading the headlines to myself in English, trying to decide which news were the most important, which to tell first. Then I would translate these into my best Spanish for Doña Luisa and her friends. The news of a battle would bring sighs of "Jesús, María, y José"[3] from the ladies. They would roll their eyes towards heaven as they implored the Lord to protect their loved ones from danger. In return they vowed to light candles or make a *manda,* a pilgrimage, to la Virgen de San Juan in the nearby town of Sunland. Once I had read the highlights of the war I was allowed to go play with my friends.

One day we had an important ballgame going. Our team was losing, it was my turn at bat. Just then Doña Luisa called me. It was time for las noticias![4] Furious at this interruption, yet not daring to disobey, I dropped the bat, ran to the porch, ripped open the paper, pointed to the headlines, and in a loud voice proclaimed: "Ya están los japoneses en San Francisco, . . . los esperan en Los Angeles muy pronto." The Japanese have landed in San Francisco, and should soon be in Los Angeles.

"Jesús María y José, la Sangre de Cristo, Ave María Purísima,"[5] chanted the ladies as I dashed off to resume my game. "Dios mío, ya vámonos, vamos a la iglesia a rezarle al Señor,"[6] they cried as chairs were pushed aside.

After this I was able to translate according to whim, . . . and depending on whether or not I was up to bat when the paper came.

Velorio

Sandra Cisneros

You laughing Lucy
and she calls us in
your mother

---

3. Jesus, Mary, and Joseph
4. the news
5. the Blood of Christ, Holy Mother Mary
6. Dear God, let's go already, let's go to church to pray to the Lord

Rachel me you I remember
and the living room dark
for our eyes to get used to

That was the summer Lucy remember
we played on the back
porch where rats hid under

And bad boys passed to look
and look at us and we look back
Lucy think how it was

Rachel me you
we fresh from sun and dirty
the living room pink

The paint chipped blue beneath
so bright for our eyes
to get used to and in rows and rows

The kitchen chairs facing front
where in a corner is a satin box
with a baby in it

Who is your sister Lucy
Your mama not crying
saying stay pray to Jesus

That baby in a box like a valentine
and I thinking it is wrong
us in our raw red ankles

And mosquito legs
Rachel wanting to go back out again
you sticking one dirty finger in

Said cold cold the living
room pink Lucy and your hair
smelling sharp like corn

Evening in Paris

Denise Chávez

Down the aisles of Woolworth's with my other self, Christmastime 1960, three shopping days left, a dollar for each day, and all I had was my awkward youth and one question, "What can I buy for you, Mother, this Christmas?"

The cellophane cannot conceal the rich colors of my dreams: The midnight blue bottles of *Evening in Paris,* the gift package I so long to receive myself. The deep pungent smell is sealed in silver and blue. Twinkling stars surround me as I ponder the inevitable. But first, "Just looking."

The lady at the counter has brows like a man's, fiercer than a man's. She is someone like Mrs. Limón who lives down the street, with her brown, fish eyebrows and her fleshy, large-pored smell.

I stand while the saleslady, Mrs. Limón Jr., slides a serpentine hand along those clear compartments of ice-cold adulthood, bringing into the light pale lipsticks in pink and white, and small compact circles of Angel Face powder, translucent as the sun. No salves, ointments, colors or cremes this time—"Just looking." My hungry lips and young girl's face contemplate an unclear view of potential self.

Please hurry, I haven't time to linger. My mother and sister are somewhere in this store, this circus of objects, searching for opiates, rickrack. I am wonderstruck by the colors behind the glass, by my image in the mirror, by the smell of this blue midnight time. It is as strong as scent of woman, faraway as Paris and full of lights.

The partitions in the case speak of care. "Now don't you touch," the eyebrows say. Color me Rosy Red, Angel Pink, Hot Rose, Dusty Brown and Heavenly Blue. My eyes are brown. But in the mirror they are Velvet Black, Torrid Blue and Nile Green.

I take out my Christmas gift list, crossing out Father. Mother takes care of him, house shoes and a tie, signs the card "We love you, Daddy." My sister? I don't know. Mother comes first. Perfume is what I want. Limón looks at me, probably thinks to herself: "What help is there?" I wonder myself. Young make-me-beautiful girl, fill my hanging darts with the fleshed-out dreams of a dark perfumed lady with loves. What help is there for three-dollar realities?

Mother gave me a wallet with Christ's picture on it to give to my sister. He is a Jesus anyone would love. He is so handsome with his long curly beard and deep-set eyes. He was painted by someone named Sallman, who perhaps saw him in a vision or a dream. It seems removed from me: Paris, Sallman, men become flesh. It is removed from me, my awkward limbs, uncertain dreams.

I am afraid to be seen looking at myself in the mirror, in my uniform of navy blue, with my white blouse and navy beanie, the center button of the beanie gone. Torn off. I look down to my bobby socks, the only pair I own. I wash them every morning, dry them on the heater, wear them dripping wet to school. I wore them then, in that after-school time of if only this and how to that.

I have decided to buy the gift package of *Evening in Paris Cologne and Bath Water* for my Mother. "I'll take this please," my voice falters. I don't remember how to speak, I am afraid, my clothes all wrong. Can't you cover me up? Shape my doubts, pluck the nervousness away, mask the fear and seal the lips with hope for self. Dynamite Red, of course.

The package lays heavily in my hands. I must not drop it. Oh, what a joyful treasure! This is the nicest gift I have ever given Mother. I know she'll like it, I know she will. Scent of Mother: those lilies she loves in our front yard. *Tabu* no longer her only recourse.

The Paris of my Mother's dreams momentarily fused with mine. They were one and the same, child's dreams of happiness, but more. Glory. We revel in it, rich and powdered queens, no worrying about money or any man who goes away, leaving us perfumed, alone.

I am on the edge of that vast, compartmentalized sea, looking across islands of objects, most of them man-made. I give the stranger waves of green. "Here's your change." Mother is the only one I can buy a gift for this year. I'm sorry, all of you, my friends. No one expects a gift from children, except other children. "Where's my gift?" they say, and so you look in your room, in your drawers, for something that is not used, *valuable*. I forgot about the Jesus wallet. And I can slip in a School Day's Picture. I don't know what happened to me that day. I thought I looked so good; I put the hair over my ears so they wouldn't stick out, but they did, and so did the hair.

There is a voice at the edge of this world. It is not the sour one's, she's turned away, shriveled up. The cash register has registered me. The voice calls: "Let's go, Mother's ready," and "What do you have in that package?"

Daylight darkens into dreams.

Most of the gifts under the tree are from Mother's students. We take turns passing them out—this is for you and this one and this one, too. Oh, and this is for *me*! The pile in front of Mother grows, her usual gifts are uncovered: a book of Lifesavers, Avon perfume in a white plastic vase, some green Thinking of You stationery, several cotton handkerchiefs flowered with roses, and a package of divinity, we'll all enjoy that. Most of these gifts will go into the gift box, so next year I'll have something to give to my teacher. But for now, they are relegated to a temporary space on the rug, to be covered by the falling needles of our dying tree.

That particular tree lasted into February. It was with great reluctance that it was dispatched into oblivion, which in this case was the irrigation ditch behind the house. The longest tree was flocked, we did it ourselves. The flocking hung from dried bushes and clung to the yellow winter grass, all the snow that would be seen *that* year.

Summer and Dust were the only real seasons. The dry brown grass bespoke winter and any other in-between time. Only farmers and the young, who live dependent upon change, would understand these small consistent movements toward growth. The rest of us are tucked into life's compartments, assigned worth, given shaded colors of illusion, with which to arm ourselves against changing mirrors. In days of childhood, our bright, eager faces stared from behind crystallized glass, reflected images tinted with prisms of available light, like the truncated boxes of fabricated well-being found at Woolworth's. All of us now see the edge of this material world, with its objects and playthings. But then, we were stuck! Heavenly Blue with a tinge of sweet cotton candy, little rosettes of illusion. And mine were the proudest, most sustained. They were founded upon hopes.

I recall the smell of our kitchen in those days of Christmas. There was a chicken in the oven, our Christmas "turkey." Empanadas de calabaza, indented and grooved into symmetry, lay in what might have been the "turkey tin," alongside bizcochos laid out by my Mother's holiday hands.

Most likely there was someone around to help us then: a maid from Mexico, a friend like Ninfa, who told us stories about the overly curious mouse who fell into the stew and was later eaten for his impudence. Or maybe Emilia, who showed me the round, not rectangular worlds of tortillas and how you turn-push-down-turn-keep-turning, the rolling pin her instrument of grace. There was a familiarity of shelves and counters where one perched along blue linoleum expanses and stared into the blocked universe of Emilia's cutting board. Her squat, heavy hands, her Saviour's hands, for once she saved me from sure death on the Tilt-A-Whirl, kneaded circular balls of inanimate masa into future life. Oftentimes Emilia would lean over, and with her flour covered hands, would search the airways for her favorite station, XELO. "Ay, qué lejos estoy del cielo donde he nacido," she sang, as from my Mother's room floated the sound of my favorite Christmas carol, "We Three Kings," sung so effortlessly by Perry Como.

It is enveloped in blue, this time of the past.

The shelf closest to me is one of Mother's miscellaneous shelves, her where-to-put-something-that-I-don't-know-what-to-do-with space. These four large areas contain many parts of my Mother's life. The first holds old dishes, cups and saucers, crystal plates with a thin, slightly greasy layer of moist dust, a bowl in the shape of a duck, its bright orange beak and blue eyes full of constant surprise. Near the back is a small statue of the Infant Jesus of Prague, in a long, red robe, his head awry and held in place with a wadded, previously chewed stick of old Juicy Fruit, his arms extended in benevolent greeting. This memento was the gift of some distressed Anglo woman who had spent several days with us, searching for her Filippino husband who was working in the cotton fields. She was one of the many who passed through our youthful lives, as servers or served. "Can I help you?" Mother said, and so she did, and they in turn left part of themselves with us. There was a constant stream of faces, but it is those few that I remember, like the lady with the unsteady Infant Jesus of Prague who stayed in my room and cried to herself while I slept on the couch.

The other shelves were duplicates of the first, with old dishes, broken wedding gifts, small bud vases and an occasional statuette. Amongst the clutter were other objects bespeaking personality: a twined and dried collection of palms from previous Palm Sundays, a small paper sack of cactus candy from Juárez, a stick of piloncillo, a half-empty box of Fig Newtons, a few votive candles left over from last year's luminarias, and in the corner, far from prying eyes, an ashtray filled with old cigarette butts left by my Father on his last visit. These inanimate objects assumed a banal ordinariness in full daylight, and yet their internal life danced in the darkness of significance and could never be understood by the casual observer.

Each object on those shelves had its smell and touch and taste. In those days of Sugar, it was the piloncillo that I gravitated toward, secretly chipping away rich amber edges and devouring them with delight. The cigarette butts I lifted, touched and pondered, and may have tried to smoke some in some long solitary afternoon in the backyard, near the garbage can, in that blind space that allowed concealment, freedom.

The dishes were tokens, and each plate was embossed with streams of invisible words, known only to my Mother. How I stared into the crystalline smoothness of those inaccessible and undecipherable emotions, as a small child stands in front of the new, the novel, and as I now stand, an adult, before the sublime fluctuations of an individual heart. My Mother's heart. And so it seemed to me this Christmas that at last I had found the perfect gift for her.

When the time came around for Mother to open the dark blue gift which I had so carefully wrapped in white tissue paper, the anticipation I felt uprooted any commonplace joy I might have felt upon receiving any gifts that stood before me in "my pile."

My sister's face fell as I handed the bright white package to Mother. I quickly gave my sister a smaller unboxed gift. The red Jesus wallet. Mother had signalled Ninfa to start gathering up wrapping paper and to put the bows in a plastic bag. I asked sheepishly, "Aren't you going to open your gift?" for as far as I was concerned, there was only one. "This one, it's from me." "Yes, oh, yes," she said, and stooped over to pick up several stray papers.

Later it seemed to me that perhaps Mother thought the *Evening in Paris* had been given to her by one of her students. I even imagined that she'd been disappointed in my gift. I couldn't understand why. Maybe she actually preferred *Tabu*.

The shimmering star-filled box ended up under the tree, along with the handkerchiefs and the Lifesavers. For a long time it stayed there, unopened, unused. The Avon somehow found its way into Mother's room.

Those nights it was my custom to sit in the darkness of the living room near the tree and watch the lights. The luminarias, as seen from the windows from where I sat, hazily burned their way into the black-blue night. As usual, I felt unfulfilled, empty, without the right words, gifts, feelings for those whose lives crowded around me and who called themselves my family. How removed I felt, far away as Paris, no longer glamorous or ageless or full of illusion. The streets outside were dark and long. Much later, when I was older and found myself in Paris, it was the lost little girl who understood so much about its reality. It was the person of the inappropriate gifts who followed hunchbacked old women on winding metal stairways into greyed, murky expanse of space with no stars. It was a Paris of balding, hennaed heads and odors of sausage exuded by men with polished, black umbrella handles that I knew, as intimately as the painted, illusionary worlds of the postcard Tour Eiffels that said, "Wish You Were Here" and "Sending Love Across the Miles."

That Paris of lights and magic exists, I have seen it, inside the haunting starless nights. And this is what I felt when I sat in the deep, embracing darkness of that special tree, the longest of all time.

Going back is going forward. It is better to give than to receive. All the familiar boring lessons are true.

The Infant Jesus of Prague with his gummed head eventually came to watch over those two ill-fated bottles of perfume. The candy changed shelves, was consumed, replaced, consumed. The wedding gifts were covered in plastic. Time was sectioned off, divided like the little boxes of painted worlds in Woolworth's. Previous intensity became a stale wash of growing up, without the standing back to choose.

I'll take this color here, that perfume there . . . that one. *Evening in Paris*. Dark blue bottle, liquid manifestation of so much hope, of long European nights, of voices mingling in the darkened streets, calling out: Remember me, Remember me.

The following Christmas Mother gave *me* the Jesus wallet. She'd forgotten that the year before I'd given it to my sister, who in turn had given it to her for the gift box.

What need had Mother of perfume on those dusty playgrounds?

What need had I of wallets?

That Sallman did a good job. You know the picture, don't you? He is a Christ that anyone could love, with his long brown curls and beard. His deep set eyes stare out.

Monarquía

Sylvia Lizárraga

Every year Regina Coeli High had a nobility contest. The main object was the gigantic task of collecting used paper to sell to the recycling company.

It started with a publicity campaign explaining the benefits of the winners. The girl who brought the most paper to the school would be crowned Queen of the Prom. Those who came close to the amount brought by the winner would be the princesses and first ladies of the Queen's Court.

It was very simple. All they had to do was pick up the papers from the whole neighborhood. That was the beginning of a frantic and chaotic race to overturn trash cans every morning before the garbage collector truck came by. For eight weeks there was not one magazine, one newspaper, not even one envelope left in the trash cans.

Every morning the paper was weighed and the new amounts of each participant were added on. The girls with the angora sweaters, those who ate at the cafeteria and came to school in private cars, always brought more papers. They knew where to get more magazines and newspapers. Already during the second week of the contest they strolled with royal airs around school.

But no one gave up. After all, weren't there signs all over the school which read, YOUR PERSEVERANCE WILL BE REWARDED? As time went by the paper struggle become more exciting. Since it was already impossible to find even a grocery list in the neighborhood, they had to go out farther. They would stop going to school or at least they would stay only long enough to find out their new score. Classrooms were almost empty. Only the girls with the angora sweaters continued to study during those last two months.

But the teachers were indulgent. They wanted every girl to win. There were no detentions, scoldings or notes sent to the transgressors' parents. All the students had the same opportunity to become queens and no one was about to endanger that noble opportunity.

Thus the contest went on. Each day they had to walk more and go farther. Block after block was cleaned. At the end of the eight weeks not only did the girls who owned cars end up crowned as your royal highness but they were also the ones with the highest grades. While the rest, with sore feet and holes in their soles joined the disenchanted world of the anonymous peasantry.

Para Teresa

Inés Hernández

A ti—Teresa
te dedico las palabras estas
que explotan de mi corazón[7]

That day during lunch hour
at Alamo which-had-to-be-its-name
Elementary
my dear raza
That day in the bathroom
Door guarded
Myself cornered
I was accused by you, Teresa
Tú y las demás de tus amigas
Pachucas todas
Eran Uds. cinco.[8]

Me gritaban que porqué me creía tan grande[9]
What was I trying to do, you growled
Show you up?
Make the teachers like me, pet me,
Tell me what a credit to my people
I was?

---

7. for you, I dedicate the words that explode from my heart
8. you and the rest of your friends, all Pachucas, there were five of you
9. they would scream at me and ask me why I thought I was so big

I was playing right into their hands,
    you challenged
And you would have none of it.
I was to stop.

I was to be like you
I was to play your game of deadly defiance
Arrogance, refusal to submit.
The game in which the winner takes nothing
Asks for nothing
Never lets his weaknesses show.

But I didn't understand.
My fear salted with confusion
Charged me to explain to you
I did nothing for the teachers.
I studied for my parents and for my
    grandparents
Who cut out honor roll lists
Whenever their nietos'[10] names appeared.
For my shy mother who mastered her terror
to demand her place in mothers' clubs
For my carpenter-father who helped me
    patiently with my math.
For my abuelos que me regalaron lápices
    en la Navidad[11]
And for myself.

Porque reconocí en aquel entonces
una verdad tremenda
que me hizo a mí un rebelde
Aunque tú no te habías dado cuenta[12]
We were not inferior
You and I, y las demás de tus amigas
Y los demás de nuestra gente[13]
I knew it the way I knew I was alive

_____

10. grandchildren's
11. for my grandparents who gave me pencils for Christmas
12. because I recognized even then a truth which made me a rebel although you didn't realize it
13. and the rest of your friends and the rest of our people

We were good, honorable, brave
Genuine, loyal, strong

And smart.
Mine was a deadly game of defiance,
    also.
My contest was to prove
beyond any doubt
that we were not only equal but
    superior to them
That was why I studied.
If I could do it, we all could.

You let me go then.
Your friends unblocked the way
I who-did-not-know-how-to-fight
was not made to engage with you
        who-grew-up-fighting
Tú y yo, Teresa
We went in different directions
Pero fuimos juntas.[14]

In sixth grade we did not understand
Uds. with the teased, dyed-black-but
        reddening hair,
full petticoats, red lipstick
And sweaters with the sleeves
pushed up
Y yo conformándome con lo que deseaba
    mi mamá[15]
Certainly never allowed to dye, to
        tease, to paint myself
I did not accept your way of anger,
Your judgements
You did not accept mine.

But now, in 1975, when I am twenty-eight
Teresa Compéan
I remember you
Y sabes—

----

14. But we went together
15. And I, conforming to what my mother wanted

Te comprendo
Es más
Te respeto
Y si me permites, te nombro hermana.[16]

I Was a Skinny Tomboy Kid

Alma Villanueva

I was a skinny tomboy kid
who walked down the streets
with my fists clenched into
            tight balls.
I knew all the roofs
and back yard fences,
      I liked travelling that way
            sometimes
         not touching
            the sidewalks
            for blocks and blocks
                  it made
                        me feel
            victorious
               somehow
over the streets.
I liked to fly
      from roof
            to roof
            the gravel
                  falling
                        away
beneath my feet,
            I liked
               the edge
            of almost

---

16. And you know I understand you. Moreover I respect you. If you'll allow me, I'll call you sister.

not making it.
     and the freedom
        of riding
       my bike
          to the ocean
and smelling it
      long before
I could see it,
       and I travelled disguised
          as a boy
       (I thought)
         in an old army jacket
          carrying my
            fishing tackle
             to the piers, and
              bumming bait
         and a couple of cokes
and catching crabs
             sometimes and
       selling them
to some chinese guys
        and i'd give
          the fish away,
I didn't like fish
       I just liked to fish
       and I vowed
         to never
           grow up
        to be a woman
       and be helpless
          like my mother
but then I didn't realize
       the kind of guts
       it often took
          for her to just keep
           standing
where she was.

I grew like a thin, stubborn weed
watering myself whatever way I could
believing in my own myth

transforming my reality
and creating a
legendary/self
every once in a while
late at night
in the deep
darkness of my sleep
I wake
with a tenseness
in my arms
and I follow
it from my elbow to
my wrist
and realize
my fists are tightly clenched
and the streets come grinning
and I forget who I'm protecting
and i coil up
in a self/mothering fashion
and tell myself
it's o.k.

In the Toolshed

Patricia Santana-Béjar

I can't be a nun anymore. And the more I think about it the more I just
want to cry and cry until I can't cry anymore. Maybe if my mother had let me
go to the convent now . . . but she said I had to wait until I was eighteen
years old. I wish I had gone to the convent last week. Then I wouldn't've committed a mortal sin. But I did. I committed a mortal sin and I'm going to
die soon. I'm too afraid to tell the priest. That's why I come into this toolshed
every day. I lock myself up in here and cry and pray. I say the Act of Contrition ten times—once I said it twenty times. But I know that God hasn't forgiven me because I still get scared after saying the Act of Contrition. I was
going to go to the priest the first time I did it but I knew what he'd say. He'd
tell me I couldn't go to heaven—ever—even if I went to purgatory first. I
should've listened to my good angel but I forgot to. I listened to my bad

angel. My bad angel stands on the left side of my head and my good angel stands on my right side. I hate my left side because that's the evil side. Everyone cleans themselves with the left hand. That's why the left side is the evil side. My mother told me that. And I'm always careful not to clean myself with my right hand. But sometimes I forget and I don't remember until after I've flushed the toilet. Then I wash my hands three times, one for the Father, then the Son, then the Holy Spirit. I know some people don't do it three times but I do because I want to be a nun and I want to do special things like that. Like I do the sign of the cross three times in a row. One time when I did it in mass a lady kneeling next to me saw me do it and smiled. I knew God was happy with me and would give me more grace, and the more grace I had the less time I would have to stay in purgatory. But now I won't even go to purgatory. God will send me straight down to the Devil. Because when you commit a mortal sin you can never be forgiven. And I committed a mortal sin. This whole week I've been doing it. It happens at night in bed when everyone's asleep. I touch myself. I don't know how I started doing it but after I smooth the little hairs growing around there, I can't keep my hand away from there. It makes me fall asleep real quick. I have a hard time going to sleep but when I touch myself I fall asleep real quick. That's why I do it. That's the only reason why I do it: because I fall asleep quicker. But some nights I don't smooth that hair. Sometimes I pull it until it hurts. I hate that hair. I wish I didn't have that hair. I think that's why my mother makes me take a bath with my underwear on: because she hates that hair, too. I once locked myself up in the bathroom and I was going to cut the hair all off but I felt sick just looking down at the hair. So I just laid the scissors on the sink and sat on the toilet and cried. But it wasn't my fault that I had that hair on me so I know I could've still gone to purgatory and maybe even heaven. But now I can't go to either place. I'm going to go to the Devil. Sometimes I wish God would kill me right now so I won't do it anymore. But then I get scared to die and I want to be punished in another way. One time I saw my father make my mother kneel down and pray the rosary. I was peeking through the door. They didn't see me. I heard him yelling at my mother and then he punished her. She had to kneel down and pray the rosary. I know my mother loves my father a lot because she obeys him. I once heard a lady say my mother was a "martyr." I asked my catechism teacher what that meant and she said it meant a "saint." I wish I could be a martyr. Maybe if my father made me get down on my knees and pray the rosary I would still have a chance to go to purgatory. . . .

Her Choice

Alma Villanueva

The way her whole body moves, the way she sits; the mood of sulky expectancy. The longing. She's barely sixteen, about the same age her mother was when she had her. The coincidence was too obvious.

I always wanted you to make love from your own choice the first time—not to be raped or forced in any way. I always wanted you to enjoy your own body, the mother thinks. She knows her daughter longs to be pregnant—she feels it like a magnet. She feels pulled by her daughter's longing, and her own—the body's strange urge to fill up warm and full and sexual. Only, her daughter's urge is to the boy, her first lover, and her own to the knowledge of baby weight. The smell, the feel, the urgent suckle, the silent language of mother-lust.

Tania heard her mother and friends talking, always, about the most intimate things. She loved to listen. It made her tremble. And when she heard her mother's voice lower, she felt cheated. There's *more*, she thought.

Tania had sat on her mother's lap, until her legs dangled quite comfortably on the floor. They had a game. When Tania would come home after school, she'd open the front door and shout, "I'm home!" Her mother, wherever she was, would sit down, and Tania would leap on her. They'd talk and smell each other, then Tania's mother would spank her on the panties and tell her to change and go play.

Little by little, as Tania grew older, she'd loiter by the older women. Then, once she sat down and they all looked at her, exchanged looks, and let her stay.

Tania liked her mother's friends better than her own. They really liked each other. She loved to go to the different women's houses and spend the night, being everyone's daughter. That's about when she stopped needing her mother to come during the night and lie next to her, talking, till the fear went away. That's about when she began to keep a secret or two from her mother.

"How are you feeling?" Vida asked.

"Okay, I guess, Mom—kind of sad," Tania replied.

"Do you want some coffee? I'm going to make some." That meant a talk.

Tania slowly sipped the coffee. It didn't even smell good, though she knew the coffee must be delicious. She and her mother had talked over pots of it, talking at faster pitches, till they realized they'd had enough—the ritual over. They'd go out to the bridge and sit and let the sun cook their faces, their tongues resting in their wet hollows. Or sometimes they'd separate in a burst—not one more word—to a task, to a separateness that each respected. Though, sometimes, Tania would shout, "Mom, can I have a ride to the bookstore?" where she worked. Implying she was late because they'd been talking. "Okay, but I don't want to pick you up tonight—so get a ride. If you really can't get a ride, call," Vida replied with studied irritation in her voice. You to your world, me to mine—I'm not a flunky, Vida thought. Balancing, always balancing, this growth—mother to daughter, daughter to mother.

There was no exchange, no flow between them today. Vida looked at her daughter and realized that to pry, would literally mean to pry a fury from Tania. She wasn't interested in doing that. It felt so heavy, sullen like clotted blood. A dam of blood needing to be released, Vida thought: a dam of dark anger where her child once was. There, she had been able to mirror herself once, quite clearly, in the pools of her daughter's eyes. Now, Tania locked her out with churned mud from a bottom that left her dazed.

They lived side by side like two women, some sympathy taking the place of words. Vida, herself, was planning to leave her second husband. *Planning* was the word: again? how? why? I must. She could think of having a child entirely separate from a man, except for the short tenderness of lovemaking. It was as though a man considered it a victory to make a woman pregnant. Then the victory lost its flavor, its appeal altogether; after all, the prize was won. It took her three children to realize this; three offerings to the male. Now she could envision having one for herself, if she chose. After all, these children *were* for herself—she hadn't blundered that far. They gave her a joy that seemed, at times, inexhaustible.

Tania's boyfriend stopped dropping by the house and waved quickly, looking away, in the street.

"How's Scott?" Vida would ask neutrally.

"He's all right," Tania would answer just as neutrally.

Oh, she's learned very well, Vida thought, letting it go. If she pressed, Tania looked trapped and the water would rise to her eyes. So Vida waited, the blood clotting thicker, it seemed. Something. A flesh, a membrane, a growth wouldn't let them reach or touch.

Tania remembered her father as charming and handsome and fun, when he wanted to be. Then, she remembered him gone for long periods (with terrible relief); then home, drunk (she remembered flying into the room, toward the end, just before her father left, when a fight seemed worse than the others—her mother yelling, "Don't you touch me!"). She remembered screaming, "You leave *my* mother alone!" He'd grabbed Tania by the arm, leading her back to bed, trying to say things like, "This is between your mother and I." Tania was struggling, still crying hysterically, and Vida ran in, pulling her daughter from him, shouting, "Leave us alone, goddamn you!" It was a moment of murder; they all knew it. He could kill her, it was his power—but Vida was so angry, so desperate she'd kill her husband if he touched either of them now. He left, Tania remembered.

Tania loved her mother's strength and worried about her mother's weakness. But, then, she knew her mother—a cup of coffee, a braided cinnamon roll, a special omelet, and there was her mother, full, again. At the center of her mother was a power she had never seen crushed.

Tania had been cutting school. They'd called with a list of days that were inexcusable. A day too beautiful to go to school, a day to stay home and read and hide: this Vida had condoned, always. But this new creature wanted to flaunt old trusts.

Tania walked in an hour late, with an off-handed apology and no offer to help with dinner.

"*Where* are you late from, Tania?" Vida spit.

Tania felt her mother open and close the door in an instant. She was in, whether she answered or not, and Tania knew it.

"Can I talk to you about it later?"

"I'll give you till tonight, and no later." And Tania knew she meant it. She'd heard everything in her mother's voice: anger, hurt, disappointment in a trust so long extended. The weapons of the gentle are harsher than the weapons of the cruel, Tania thought. The first seems inside of you and so hard to distinguish. The other can be fought like an outside pain.

Well, I can lie and be punished like everyone else. Tania comforted herself, and went to help with dinner in the guise of a sulky child.

Later, after dinner, the dishes were washed, the last log of the night in the fire toward morning—she came into her mother's room to lie:

"I'm pregnant. Tomorrow I'm going for an abortion. That's where I was all those days, trying to get an abortion." Her eyes were clear, the dam burst and nearly drowned Vida.

Vida choked, "My grandchild!" It slapped Tania's face. No anger, no shame—that would come later, Tania thought. She ran to her room and heard her mother begin to cry in a horrible hoarse voice, like something ancient being pulled from her belly. She'd never heard her mother cry like that before, and she was instantly frightened and sorry. She heard Vida slam and lock her door, and everytime Tania passed the room that night, she knew a candle was burning, which made her feel a little better. She knew her mother was thinking and taking comfort from that thin flame.

The fire was dying in the fireplace. Tania poured herself a glass of wine, taking it to her room. In the dark she drank it, lay on her stomach and cried her own tears. She didn't want this child: she knew that. She fell into her own sleep.

Tania woke up to the smell of coffee and remembered, instantly, the bus schedule. She ran to the bathroom, got dressed, ran to the kitchen trying not to look at Vida.

"How are you getting there?"

"By bus," Tania whispered.

Vida's eyes were huge in her head, "I'll take you."

Tania stumbled to her mother's arms, bending her head just a little, heaving her sorrow on the small shoulder. She had outgrown her mother this year, only in height.

Now they were both women.

EIGHT

Celebrations

I shall decide when to turn the
lights at the celebration of me, of
my womanness.
　　　SYLVIA CHACÓN

Let us never forget the dance
or lose the song
or cease to dream
　　　ALMA VILLANUEVA

I'm paralyzed by joy / and I forget how to act
　　　LORNA DEE CERVANTES

Chicanas' writings are full of nature, sensuousness, ceremonies, and rituals. Flowers, earth, wind, moon figure prominently in their creations. Rituals of womanhood—first love, marriage, childbirth—are present in the accounts of their femaleness. Even in the prose of urban narratives there is a richness of embroidered detail that appears among the thread of stories, telling about Chicanas' love of things, their passion for symbols. But it is their poetry that celebrates with joy; dancing naked by the road, rejoicing in motherhood, loving friends, and toasting their visits with apple cider ("Plumb," Zamora).

Chicana celebrations can go from the sublime to the ridiculous; a panoply of life about the *comadres* can be a showcase for scintillating humor when vignettes are drawn about a neighborhood (Valdés). The Chicanas' heritage is full of pride, and they write of their beautiful foremothers with musical verses ("San Antonio Rose era xicana," de Hoyos). Mostly, Chicanas sing of freedom and the glory of being *women*.

A whole chapter could be devoted to Chicana love poetry. It is not only the celebration of the flesh, but of feeling: the glowing blush of a bride, the lustful shyness of a bridegroom, the sweetness of remembering a lover's caresses on her body (Mora). In spite of what Chicanas have seen around them—women mistreated and abused by men—they still believe in the redeeming power of love and the hopeful healing of gentleness. Their blood sings and they dream on listening to wild bees: it is the buzzing of life's streams, flowing champagne ("bubbling, bubbling") in their veins. And even here humor creeps in: "sin ti la vida es / un taco sin tortilla" (Silva).[1]

Mostly, Chicana writers celebrate their joy of *being*. And this is best illustrated with the recurrent bird imagery that poets seem to relish. It is present in Villanueva and in Mora, but it is epitomized in the work of Cervantes: her book *Emplumada* (feathered, in plumage) is constructed around such symbolism. God is "a flock of crows" ("For All You Know"); the poetic persona of Cervantes herself is a bird of the same kind: "A crow flew . . . and I thought of the circle / my own life made" ("Como Lo Siento"). Her poems are full of mockingbirds, blue jays, sea gulls, geese, owls, sea birds, hawks, . . . and crows. Her images of writing are entwined with bird imagery:

> as pain sends seabirds south from the cold
> I come north
> to gather my feathers
> for quills
> (*"Visions of Mexico"*)

Poetic speakers in Cervantes' texts are women full of determination, ready to fight for life, such as the hummingbirds in the title poem: "These are warriors / distancing themselves from history." Seasons are celebrated by the coming and passing of birds and flowers; near the cannery, gulls walk over front lawns; snapdragons and peach blossoms attract winged creatures, who relish life. In her celebrated "Beneath the Shadow of the Freeway," her grandmother—role model and admired figure after which the poet will pattern her life—only believes in "myths and birds."

Poems and stories also tell of solidarity, fulfillment, growing, family ties, and affirmation of being. In this last respect, Chicana literature is very consistent. It defines its creator, it tells her story, it paints her life, and describes the forces that shape her world; but most of all, it reveals Chicanas in search of their own personhood.

We believe they have found it. The selections included in this chapter seem to prove it. The book ends on a positive note, chanting of and to life. In the final analysis, it is a celebration of womanness.

■ ■ ■

---

1. Without you, life is / like a taco without tortilla.

My Poetry

Sylvia Chacón

My poetry sings of warmth, of flowers, of poverty, of friendship, of endurance, of laughter, of anger, of growth, of fear, of pain, of children, of integrity, of rape, of innocence. My poetry is a struggle to share and convey a glow of warmth and also a bite of anger to a society that screws copper centered scented daisies in place with the sterile confines of an assembly line.

I celebrate the survival of our language, our customs, our people y nuestro gusto por vivir y saborear el momento. I celebrate the fruit, the strength, the integrity of my Mother—joya de mujer, Madre de nuestra cultura, who has cradled us in the tradition of dichos, cantos, cuentos, un jalón de orejas y la primera comunión. I am her celebration, her touch with eternity. I am a perpetuation of her struggle to survive in a world cold with men's paws and unthoughts.

I am a woman with fertile mind and body conceiving love for woman, man, and child. I find myself a woman struggling against a girl's fear of womanhood, a man's fear of fear, and a child's fear of night. I find myself in daily struggle to be strong, in constant struggle to BE.

I AM. But I cannot and will not be tradition's fiesta for I shall decide when to turn the lights at the celebration of me, of my womanness.

> and
> I must gentle into myself
> to fill the thirst
> that sand will knot
> and I must gentle
> in a firmness
> that will flower
> Springtime dawns
> in snow.

Fire

Barbara Brinson Curiel

I
It grew
from floorboards,
a rare orchid,

soft and grey,
ruffled,
white
at the edges.

Trellising,
it intertwined
with mimosas
in the wallpaper,

reached into the bed,
breathed a jungle
into the mouth
of the sleeper.

II
Hair
smokes
into a grey
vine.

Skin
shrinks,
fine cloth
in water.

Palms
sway
in
air.

III
It exhales,
consumes
the mimosas.

The jungle
blooms

red.

Hair
crackles:

flowering
vines.

Skin
blooms,

the darkest
of flowers.

IV
The body craves
heat.

The mouth
blooms,

welcomes
flames.

V
The smoke clears,
leaves
an odor
of carnations.

Movimiento / Movement

Lucha Corpi / Translated by Catherine Rodríguez-Nieto

Bailé desnuda
cabello suelto
sandalias a la
vera del camino

El primero ofreció
velos de seda
y esmeraldas
por mi desnudez

Otro llegó
guitarra en mano
y para mí tocó
Fuimos amigos

Un tercero exorcizó
demonios extraños
de mi cuerpo
Dios sonrió

El anciano
ojos semicerrados
cantó al viento
cuentos de amor

Pintor y poeta
en lienzo y palabra
diseñaron entradas secretas
a la inmortalidad

Llegó el último
y escuchó
giros de viento
ondular de alas

Pleno solsticio
en cada paso
despojados
bailamos juntos.

■

Naked
hair flowing
sandals left by the road
I danced.

The first who saw me offered
silken veils
and emeralds
for my nakedness.

Another approached
guitar in hand
and played for me.
We were friends.

A third exorcized
strange demons
from my body.
God smiled.

An old man
eyes half-closed
sang love stories
to the wind.

The painter and the poet
designed on canvas and paper
secret passages
to immortality.

One came at last who heard
the turnings
of the wind
the beating of wings.

With solstice
in every step
naked
we danced together.

Let Us Never Forget the Dance

Alma Villanueva

Let us never forget the dance
or lose the song
or cease to dream
or efface the mystery

zero in on life
myth

magic
mystery
revel in the extra ordinary
fill your
be
ing with it,

a bird is skimming the water
lands on a smooth surface,
the snow falls softly on a mountain
chilling the earth's crust,
a sapling smiles at the wind,
a cloud gathers and spills its rain
on a hungry field—

cock your head
and listen
it calls
 everyman
  not everyone
   hears

He was one of those special ones, she said

Inés Hernández

He has a way about him
that's for sure, she said
Can make you stop what you're doing
at a moment's notice

One time I remember
I even stopped the car
she said
pulled off the road
that is
to take the walk into the woods
where he was waiting
I knew he would be

I knew he would have me
find the curve of the hill
to fit my body into
reckless
strolling
motion

There were people up above
was one of those vista point
rest areas
but I didn't care
she said
everything else dissolved
in the rays of the sun warmth
moisture
and all I knew
was that I had to be there
He just knew how to call
to pull
she said

She could never tell anyone
but after they met that time
she felt like everyone knew

One of her past lovers knew
for sure
she saw him watching her
later
when she got back to town

He came over
kind of sad he hadn't been the one
to bathe her like that in radiance
knowing that this time
she looked like he had never seen
her before

And how could she tell him
anyway
about brilliance
he who lurked the nights
and days away

in clandestinity
This clouded-over-faced-one
knew he'd missed something
at least he knew that much

And she
she just smiled
and sang her heartstrings out
inside
and held that moment
until
forever.

The Ceremony of Orgasm

Alma Villanueva

Each time something broke in
me: I cried out beyond
my lips: how

many wounds we carry til
we release ourselves in
love, in
to the earth: this wounding

of the flesh: this making
into words of

small bloody cries
from birth (some
were tended like a
lovely hot house
   flower, some

defied the weather and grew
   tender
and wild): till love

passes you, an ordinary
stranger, and recognizes
your colors, your scent

from a dream and plucks
you brazenly, as love
does, imagining you grew
just for him, your
inarticulate greenery stretching

toward the sun, your
cries, stern roots in
the rotting earth, your
wounds the petals of
the body: the love

we dare imagine like
the sun on a cloudy day: the heat

in my body that healed
me, I break open and offer
you on a ceremonial platter,

the human heart.

Mielvirgen

Pat Mora

In the slow afternoon heat she sits
in the shade watching the bees,
remembering sweet evenings
of dipping her fingers into warm
honey, smoothing it on his lips,
licking it slowly with her tongue,
hearing him laugh
  then breathe harder
slowly unbuttoning her
blouse, rubbing his

tongue on her sweet skin,
  lips, honey, breasts
buzzing
like the bees she hears now,
her eyes closed, her tongue sliding
on her lips, remembering, remembering

Spring Tonic

Pat Mora

He had been her winter secret.
Her eyes had watched
how he folded his arms across his chest
at church,
how he wiped the sweat from his neck
in the cornfields,
how he drank beer slowly
at the village *fiestas*.
Tonight he had danced with her,
no words, but his arm around
her waist, pulling her,
and again when he walked her home,
pulling her, to kiss his lips.
When she entered her dark kitchen,
she lit a candle and saw
pink, yellow, white spring flowers
floating in a jar of cool water.
She poured some of her mother's
sweet-scented tonic into a clay mug,
sipped it slowly
listening to her blood sing.

Dream

Pat Mora

Village Women Say Orange Blossoms Melt on an Unclean Bride.

Today I wake slowly, scratching my scalp.
　I scratched you last night on that warm
　desert sand.

I wake feeling wax under my fingernails.
　Those nails stroked your lips, your frightening
　lips, dug into your back.

I wake wondering how to shampoo my black hair,
matted white, smelling sweet.
　You rubbed moonlight through that hair
　last night; you rubbed moonlight through me.

I wake blushing, a wax-capped bride.
　By day I laugh at our Mexican superstitions.
　At night they grab me. Draw blood. Like you.
I wake, fully wake. Smile.

Today is my wedding day, I kiss
the flowers for my hair and whisper,
"Don't tell, don't tell, don't tell."

The Body as Braille

Lorna Dee Cervantes

He tells me, "Your back
is so beautiful." He traces
my spine with his hand.

I'm burning like a white ring
around the moon. "A witch's moon,"
dijo mi abuela. The schools call it

"a reflection of ice crystals."
It's a storm brewing in the cauldron
of the sky. I'm in love

but won't tell him
if it's omens
or ice.

Como lo siento

Lorna Dee Cervantes

I heard an owl at midday.
A crow flew, spiraled, drifted,
and I thought of the circle
my own life made, and how
at heart I'm a hoverer
the way I've always drifted
toward you.
Another owl lifted from the palm.
She showed me how I rose, caught
in the wind by your skin and tongue.
I feel scooped from the banks like clay,
smoked and fired by your eyes
til I ring. I'm paralyzed by joy
and I forget how to act.
I'm a shell in the cliffs,
a thousand miles from sea.
You tide me and I rise,
and there's no truth
more simple.

Making Tortillas

Alicia Gaspar de Alba

My body remembers
what it means to love slowly,
what it means to start
from scratch:
to soak the maíz,
scatter bonedust in the limewater,
and let the seeds soften
overnight.

Sunrise is the best time
for grinding masa,
cornmeal rolling out
on the metate like a flannel sheet.
Smell of wet corn, lard, fresh
morning love and the light
sound of clapping.

                Pressed between the palms,
   clap-clap
                thin yellow moons—
   clap-clap
                still moist, heavy still
                from last night's soaking
   clap-clap
                slowly start finding their shape
   clap-clap.

My body remembers
the feel of the griddle,
beads of grease sizzling
under the skin, a cry gathering
like an air bubble in the belly
of the unleavened cake. Smell
of baked tortillas all over the house,
all over the hands still
hot from clapping, cooking.

Tortilleras, we are called,
grinders of maíz, makers, bakers,
slow lovers of women.
The secret is starting from scratch.

Bearded Lady

Bernice Zamora

I wanted to know about love
and was told to see the bearded lady.

As she stroked her treasure, she
told me of the melding wells of Julia,

Of the kissing stones shaped
like camels,

Of the hair like linen
found among the cloistered,

And she stroked, and stroked, and stroked

Two Brothers

Beverly Silva

One gives me kitchens
& kids
everyday phone calls
punctuality
fixes faucets & toilets
brings me coffee in bed.
          the other slips in late at night
not speaking
peels me like a banana
loves until dawn
leaves making no promises.

Plumb

Bernice Zamora

Before we ate
While I was putting
The snowshovel away,
I saw two robins.

The enchiladas and
Apple cider washed
Easily with our
Conversation down.

From the window
I studied the robins
Keeping each other warm
While you instructed
Me in Hemingway;

It was a fine day for learning.

Segments

Cordelia Candelaria

She peeled the orange tenderly
as if it were a letter from a lover.
Air became tangy citrus mist
caressing every fragrant breath she took.

She pulled the fruity wedge
from its vulnerable whole and sucked
it soft. Fingers of oily sweetness
clung to all she touched, orange prints

separate from the tender hand placing
peel and seed and stringy membrane
into another mass of parts.
Sweet grip on a segment of her life.

Emplumada

Lorna Dee Cervantes

When summer ended
the leaves of snapdragons withered
taking their shrill-colored mouths with them.
They were still, so quiet. They were
violet where umber now is. She hated
and she hated to see
them go. Flowers

born when the weather was good—this
she thinks of, watching the branch of peaches
daring their ways above the fence, and further,
two hummingbirds, hovering, stuck to each other,
arcing their bodies in grim determination
to find what is good, what is
given them to find. These are warriors

distancing themselves from history.
They find peace
in the way they contain the wind
and are gone.

'San Antonio Rose' Era Xicana

Angela de Hoyos

To Anita Morales

demure by day
under a canopy
of shy-blue lids

Tus ojos
     acerinas
     de noche[2]

---

2. Your eyes / night precious / stones

light their dazzling fires
to the melody
    of your voice
    guitarra xicana.

The night
    put to shame
quietly gathers its stars . . .

Sin Ti Yo No Soy Nada / Without You I Am Nothing

Beverly Silva

Tú eres
La salsa en mi enchilada
La carne en mi burrito
La oliva en mi tamal
El chocolate en mi mole
El chile en mis frijoles
La tequila en mi margarita.
    Seguramente yo puedo vivir sin ti, mi amor;
Pero sin ti la vida es
Un taco sin tortilla
El guacamole sin aguacate
La sal sin limón
Un pastel sin azúcar
El domingo sin baile
La cumbia sin música
Juan Gabriel sin Juárez
    Y todos los días sin el fin de semana.

■

You are
The salsa in my enchilada
The meat in my burrito
The olive in my tamal
The chocolate in my mole
The chile in my beans

The tequila in my margarita.
    Certainly I can live without you, my love;
But without you life is like
A taco without a tortilla
Guacamole without avocado
Salt without lemon
A cake without sugar
Sunday without a dance
A cumbia without music
Juan Gabriel without Juárez
    And every day without a weekend.

The Paris Gown

Estela Portillo Trambley

"Cognac with your coffee, Theresa?"

"No, thank you, Gran . . . Clo." Somehow the word "grandmother" did not fit Clotilde Romero de Traske, sophisticated, chic, and existentially fluent. Theresa had anticipated this after dinner *tête à tête*. In her mind there were so many things unclear about this woman who had left her home in Mexico so long ago. The traces of age in Clotilde were indistinguishable in the grace and youthful confidence exuded from her gestures, her eyes, her flexible body, and the quick discerning mind. Clotilde Romero de Traske, art dealer at the Rue Auber, was a legend back home. The stories about her numerous marriages, her travels, her artistic ventures, and the famous names that frequented her salon were many. But no one had ever discussed how she got to Paris in the first place when the women of her time had had small freedoms. Her life abroad had become scandal in epic to the clan of women in aristocratic circles back home. There was a daring in her grandmother's eyes.

"How do you like Paris, child?"

"I love it! It's like . . . like . . ."

"An opening up . . . as does a flower to the sun. That is the feel of Paris."

"Yes, that is the way I feel. I'm happy to be here."

"You should be. You are very lucky too. Everyone should see Paris before they are twenty-five . . . I heard that somewhere. It is true. It is like no place else in the world."

"You never went back home, Clo?"

"My dear girl, no one can truly ever go back home . . . for one changes and the home was a different you." The older woman spoke gently. "We journey; we find new tempests. These are good. This is the way beauty and trust are pieced."

Theresa sat silent. She had suddenly glimpsed into a beautiful clear depth in a human being. She felt sudden love and admiration for her grandmother. Clotilde's fragile, ember quality of spirit grew and filled the room. Theresa felt half-way beyond caprice into a giving. Theresa felt Clotilde had a deep and lasting comprehension of her place in the universe. How fresh and open was the world in this room. Theresa felt that the room itself was a composite of what Clotilde had become in the life process. Every piece of art and sculpture gave the impact of humanness. The colors were profuse and rich; they seemed to touch impulse and awaken still undefined passions. Yes, it was a room with a singular ferocity for life.

"I understand you are traveling with a university group?" Clotilde's expressive eyes searched her granddaughter's face.

"Yes . . . it is a way we are allowed to travel away from home; the old traditions still have strong ties. They teach us early that the world is too dangerous for innocent, young girls. I think it's silly!"

Clotilde smiled. "I agree with you one hundred percent." She put down her cup and walked to the mantlepiece over the fireplace as if she chose to observe her granddaughter from a new perspective. Theresa was somewhat startled by the impression Clotilde made with the room as background. A convex reflection of mood, the older woman was a human focal point against the subjectivity of artistic experience in meaningful arrangement around the room. Emotionally coded, Clotilde stood, a liberated form from civilized order. All this was a sensing to Theresa who knew little about art.

"The art in this room, Clo, it's so, . . . so . . ."

"What other artists call it . . . without doctrinaire implication. That says nothing, really, but it means that the artist makes his own rules for finding a strength out of the life experience.

There it goes again! thought Theresa . . . that flash of galvanic illumination . . . a look inside spirit again. Theresa asked: "You are an artist yourself?"

"A terrible one; it did not take me long to find that out when I first came to Paris."

"So you became a dealer in art."

"More of a lover of art . . . look!" Clotilde went up to a massive sculpture. She touched it reverently. "Have you ever heard the name Gaudier-Brzeska? This is his work. He has made out of stone and metal what I would like to make out of life, or have tried to make out of life."

Theresa leaned over in her chair; her eagerness to know was unmasked. "Explain it to me, Clo . . ."

"Gautier was a man of great passion; many consider him a primitive. He plunged into the instinctual and emotional to surface with an energy, a feeling, an ability free of barbarism."

Theresa was somewhat puzzled. "Isn't barbarism equated with the primitive?"

"Perhaps I look at the world as if I were standing on my head, Theresa, and many artists do. For that reason we define barbarism different from Civilization."

"I remember Clo, that history says that Civilization downed barbarism by making reason dominant over instinct."

"If you see it from a historical viewpoint. But look at it from a human viewpoint; barbarism is the subjugation of the instinctual for reason. I know that within the pretty works of the great Hellenes, reason is primary and instinct secondary. But man's reason is a boxed-in circumstance that has proved itself more violent against human beings than instinct. Instinct is part of survival law; it is also a part of what gathers a wholeness. Barbarism is a product of limited reason. And what reason is not, at least in part, limited? Instinct is an innate law without barrier . . . It is important to leave the field of invention open in art . . . as in life."

Theresa almost jumped up from her chair, her arms outstretched as if to encompass the room. "That's what I feel about this room! It is an open field! I see how this room is your beliefs, your history . . . how beautiful!"

"And isn't history, really, a personal thing, not belonging to nations, but to individuals?"

She was pleased by Theresa's natural discovery. Theresa, with extended hand, touched the Gautier figure as if savoring the meaning of a new part added to herself.

"I understand now, Clo, why you never went back. In a world still archaic, women suffer the barbarism of men. An injustice." Theresa looked at her grandmother with questioning eyes. Clotilde touched her cheek with the tips of her fingers and smiled at her granddaughter.

"I used to think so . . . when I was very young."

"Don't you feel that way anymore?"

"No . . . I don't think so. Maybe, because I know that the instinct that respects all life, the instinct that understands equality, survives in all of us in spite of overwhelming, unfair tradition. Men know this instinct, too, although thousands of years of conditioning made them blind to the equality of all life. The violence of man against woman is a traditional blindness whose wall can be broken. Isn't that the objective of love . . . to break walls?"

"But the unfairness is still there, Clo, even today. The woman has a secondary role to that of the man, and the brutish mind accepts it. I can imagine how it must have been in your time!"

Clotilde maintained the crystal of her world. "Men have attempted fairness since the beginning of time; it's just that sometimes they are overwhelmed . . . overwhelmed." She walked up to the window and looked out as if trying to gather a memory . . . pain and all. Theresa sensed it and went up to her and leaned her head on Clotilde's shoulder. Both looked out into a garden with its own kind of freedom. It had no symmetry, no pattern; the lawn and trailing vines, the cypress trees and profuse flowers had only been given a kind of order, only to free the life from complete chaos. Everything reached for the sun in its own way. Theresa caught a lovely fragrance.

"Mmmmm . . . what is that?"

"It is Italian jasmine; it is a beautiful part of my life brought into my garden."

"Tell me, Clo, how did you escape the blind tradition?"

Clotilde laughed her silvery laugh. "I thought you would never ask."

Theresa was intense about her question. "They never talk about that back home, only about the terrible things you do in Paris. Inside all our womenfolk, as they sit around the card table with their gossip, there is a wish, a wanting to be you . . . I felt it many times."

Clotilde hugged her granddaughter. "It is wonderful that you feel so much!" Theresa caught her grandmother's hands and led her to a settee.

"Come, tell me the story."

Clotilde did not resist. She sat back and cast off the years.

"How does one begin without condemnations, Theresa? When we are young, to condemn is simple and an easy way out for even our mistakes. I remember my indignant feeling of injustice! I felt like a victim from a very early age. but I would show them all! That was my battle-cry!"

Clotilde shook her head in memory and continued: "Yes, tradition was much heavier in my time. There was but a single fate for the gentlewoman . . . one variation of a cloister or another. To marry meant to become the lonely mistress of a household where husbands took unfair freedoms, unfair only because the freedoms belonged to them and were unthinkable for women! Children were the recompense, but children should not be a recompense; they are human beings belonging to themselves; and we should not need recompense. It can turn to bitterness, then we become the bitterness itself, a patterned, strict garden of dead things, poisoned things. If we did not marry, there was total dependency on the generosity of pitying relatives, with church and its rituals for comfort. The nunnery or running away with the stable boy offered many sacrifices and discomforts. No . . . no . . . There must be another solution, I would tell myself!"

"How did you turn to art, Clo?"

"I don't know whether you remember uncle Gaspar. He was considered the bohemian in the family. He had tried painting, writing, the theater, in his attempt to keep the gypsy spirit. I liked Uncle Gaspar. When he was around, I felt the gypsy spirit. He made me laugh and feel important. That was a lot to a girl. One Christmas he gave my brother an artist's palette. He brought him some books on design and color. My brother, Felix, became engrossed in his attempt to paint. In time, he discarded the palette and went on to other interests. I found it one day with the books, and began to awkwardly sketch and paint. This became an outlet, a hope. Felix had little talent. I think I had little talent too. But I stuck to the practice; I worked at it everyday . . . so naturally I acquired a certain proficiency and decided I had a talent and my brother did not. I had a compulsion to compare, to outdo him, because he was a boy with born privileges and I was a girl born into a kind of slavery. I poisoned my garden early in life, but to an extent, it was my nature to want freedom. I had a mind that craved and that weighed the inequalities as a gross injustice. I found ways of justifying my opinions, my martyrdom. My brother and I used to ride a lot. We had a pair of matched stallions, beautiful horses. Riding along the path of the high hills was an excitement that grew in the body and escaped in the wind. It was a taste of wild freedom. I was the better rider, or maybe it was my greater desire for the wildness that made me the better rider. It happens that way, sometimes, when you are fierce enough about things . . ."

Her voice trailed off in memory. There was a brief silence that caught the languid mood of afternoon. Then Clotilde continued her story:

"My father would say . . . A man must never allow a woman to outdo him. How typical of him! The way of the varón, and Felix was his varón . . . I was just a daughter, an afterthought, so I thought. My mother would whisper to me . . . Let your brother win when you race. It would please your father . . . I did not wish to please my father with the accomplishments of my brother. To outdo him became my constant form of revenge. My father resented the fact and overlooked my ability to outdo, as if it did not exist. This was adding salt to my wounds . . . I think I began to hate my father, poor father!" Clotilde caught Theresa's glance for a second. There was a slight sliver of anxiety in Clotilde's voice. "You must remember, Theresa, it was my poison."

"But it was unfair to you!"

"Yes, it was unfair . . . It was. Felix wanted to get out of going into the banking institute; he wanted to travel. My uncle Gaspar had painted glorious pictures of Europe, specially Paris. There were stories about the left bank, Montmartre, where one could buy delicious madness for a few francs . . . where people were alive. That was Gaspar's favorite expression. Felix told my father he wanted to go to Paris to study art. My father fumed and objected, but of course Felix got his way. My father excused it, saying the boy was sowing his wild oats! You know what I did? I decided to confront my father and ask him what he was going to do about my wild oats. Poor man! His reaction was violent. He accused me of insanity and willfulness. Perhaps, he said, what I needed was a nunnery. He meant it too!"

"You had no freedom, Clo?" Theresa's voice was full of sympathy.

"That was the price the female paid for being *bien gentil*! I began to argue with my father, to rationalize, to reason, to prove to him what a fine brain I had; I deserved better than the fate women had in the town. I drove him half-crazy with the potency of legitimate complaint. It was then that his natural instinct of survival prompted him to do what he did."

"What did he do?"

"He decided to marry me off to a neighboring widower old enough to be my father. Mind you, it was more than just desperation on his part; it was also a good business venture. Don Ignacio was the wealthiest man around. It was the usual contract marriage between parents of means. Daughters did not have a say in the matter. It was an excellent way of joining two fortunes by blood."

"How cruel, Clo. It must have been terrible for you."

"I thought at the time that it was the end of any kind of hope as a human being. I was repulsed by Don Ignacio. I began to show it. My father punished me and threatened the convent again. So then I tried to starve myself, lock myself up in my room forever. I even ran away on my horse and stayed out in the hills until my father sent out a searching party who found me half starved and with a bad case of pneumonia. For the first time in my life, I felt the full attention of my parents. While getting over my illness, I prayed my father would forget about the proposed marriage. One afternoon my father came into the bedroom. He was gentle and kind and truly concerned about my health. I took advantage of my illness and asked him to promise not to make me marry Don Ignacio." Clotilde paused and walked slowly to the window again. There was a stir of wind in her hair. She whispered almost in a child's cry. "You simply do not unpetal a flower for your advantage. You give it the chance of life!"

Theresa knew the answer. "He refused, didn't he?"

"Yes, he refused." Her eyes roamed the great expanse of horizon as if trying to forget, not the pain, but a loved one's shortcoming. "I remember a similar garden while I was getting well . . . no, now that I think of it, it was different. It was impressive and almost manicured to perfection. It was a showcase with swans in a pond and flowers arranged by species. There was hedge after hedge where children played hide-and-go-seek. One afternoon, during my illness, I watched some children bathing in the pond. They were three or four years old, no more. There was a little boy who decided to join the bathing children, so he took his clothes and waded in. His nurse caught sight of him and with great indignation caught him up in her arms and spanked his little bare back. It was a curious episode of innocence and the declaration of a truth. I remember going back into the house with the imprint in my mind. For the next few weeks, I felt a growing peace. I did not argue, or beg, or cajole. I simply enjoyed my time for contemplation. It was an attempt to accept. I tried, but I could not. One morning I awoke knowing the answer to my problem. I realized that my new-found calm was a part of the plan. So was my attempt to accept. I got well and offered no complaints about the proposed engagement. My father breathed a sigh of relief. I had come to my senses. I would obey him like a good daughter and marry the man that he had chosen for me."

Theresa's voice was somewhat incredulous. "You were giving up?"

"No . . . never. I simply had discovered a way out. But it took planning, calm and a feigned acceptance. I became docile and pretended a certain excitement over the plans for the engagement ball. The most difficult thing to accept was Don Ignacio's fawning over me. But I had to stand it; it was part of the plan. My father showed his generosity by telling me that expense was no object. I was to have the most exclusive, grandest ball anyone had ever had. He asked what my heart desired." Clotilde's voice broke momentarily. She quickly composed herself and continued. "I had devised a particular wish that would be part of the camouflage for my plan. I told my father I wanted a Paris gown. The most beautiful ever seen. I became very excited over the plans for designing the gown. I corresponded with French dress-shops and filled the dinner table conversation with detailed descriptions. My father was tremendously pleased I had finally fallen into the routine pattern of girls lost in their own frivolity. I had been saved. When the gown arrived, everybody was excited. It was a maze of tulle and lace and pearl insets. The ultimate of fashion. It was the most beautiful gown anyone had ever seen in that town. Every day was filled with the plans for the ball. There were gifts to put on display; there was the accounting and the usual courtesies before the engagement announcement. It was not a difficult thing to do. But, every night I would lock my room and put on the ball gown. For hours I would contemplate what I was going to do. I had to build the courage, for my plan included something completely against the grain of gentlewomen. It would scare me to even think of it. But I knew I had to do it. I would stare at my image in the Paris gown and tell myself that it was the price of freedom . . . there was no other way. That Paris gown was to become my final revenge against the injustice of men."

The afternoon sun had lost its full ardor. The pale coolness of early dusk melted gently in the sun. As the sun fell, the line of light chose among the garden freedoms pieces of shadow touching the world with a gentle sobriety. If there were a time in each day more suitable for sadness . . . or for finding gentle love . . . perhaps this time . . . . The modes of the now could not be forgotten for an old story. Nevertheless, the falling shadows upon light were a part of long ago as much as the story was a part of now.

Clotilde picked up the threads of her design of long ago: "I remember talking to my father about making an effective entrance. A champagne toast at the precise hour of nine after the guests had supped and drunk to their enjoyment, at a time when the music becomes a part of the breathing passion, at this particular time my father would offer a toast to the bride and groom. Not until then would I descend the staircase leading to the main ballroom where the guests were gathered. My father was impressed. Yes, it would be very effective; it would show off the Paris gown to its fullest. Don Ignacio approved. It would show off his new possession. Yes, everybody was in agreement.

"I stayed in my room the night of the ball listening to the rising talk and the sounds of the banquet. It was a foreign thing to me, for my thoughts were with the wind and a wide, wide freedom, soon, very soon. The gown was laid out on my bed in full glory. It was truly a beautiful thing. A few minutes before nine I began to put the final touches to the plan. I stood there before my mirror, full of an unknown terror at what I was about to do. I opened the door of my bedroom to meet the full force of happy voices awaiting my entrance. I heard the orchestra begin the music that was to signal my entrance. Then my father's voice, full of pride, was audible to me. He made a short, modest speech about the friendship between the two families about to be united. Finally I heard the words . . . May I present my daughter and the future bride of Don Ignacio Maez de Tulares. Let us toast the future of the ideal couple . . . The glasses were now raised. I swallowed hard and slipped silently down the hall leading to the staircase. My throat was tied and my hands trembled, but I knew I could not falter. Soon I was at the top of the staircase. Immediately, I heard the cries and horrified exclamations among the guests. I thought at the moment of closing my eyes, but I was certain to fall. Also, I did not wish to appear afraid or ashamed, so I tried to look down into their faces. All wore the same frozen, shocked look of disbelief. I saw my mother fall into a faint, and the choleric face of Don Ignacio was punctuated by a fallen jaw of disbelief and anger. He threw his champagne glass and it smashed on the floor, then he turned and left without ceremony. No one noticed his departure, for all eyes were upon me . . . All this I saw as I came down the stairs . . . *stark naked* . . ."

There was a sudden flurry of curtains and the light that gave life to the art in the room softened mysteriously to a promise. Clotilde touched the buttons of her blouse, still lost in that memory of what she had planned as a way of freedom. Theresa came up to her and kissed her cheek. "Oh, Clo . . . you were so brave, so brave!"

"I think now it was a kind of insanity finding its own method to fight what I considered a slavery. It was simple after that. My father could not abandon an insane daughter, but he knew that my presence meant constant reminder. He let me come to Paris with sufficient funds . . . and here I made my home . . . my home."

"Do you miss the other home?"

"Yes, I left part of myself there and the people of my blood . . . of course there is a certain nostalgia . . . but no regrets. That's what I hope you will learn in your journeys . . . never to have regrets."

"You have found . . . the freedom . . . the equality?"

"Yes, my child, I have known the depth of feeling in all its glorious aspects." Both women looked out the window and caught the full colors of life.

Weeping With Laughter

Gina Valdés

Slapping our thighs and weeping
with laughter at the worm
in Eve's apple, at Episcopalian
ladies with stiff clutch bags
at the red stains on our underwear
and more stains to come before
the predicted hot flashes have us
on the floor convulsing with
flaming laughter, at what silly
gooses we can be, at how many
mistakes we can make in one hour
at how smart we are, at that jerk

who outsmarted us, at our fathers
who didn't want baby girls, giggling
at the Pope with a rubber on
his nose, at Mother Teresa clutching
a red rose in her teeth, laughing
at our mothers' guilt pounding
our ovaries
a couple of giggling chicks
tickled babes
daffy ducklings
smirking broads
chuckling mother gooses
belly shaking mamas
cackling witches
crowing old hags
teetering old ladies
two females
shaking our butts
at a very serious world

Bibliography

Aguilar-Henson, Marcela. *The Multi-Faceted Poetic World of Angela de Hoyos*. Austin: Relámpago Books, 1982.

Alarcón, Norma. "Making 'Familia' from Scratch: Split Subjectivities in the Work of Helena María Viramontes and Cherríe Moraga." *The Americas Review* 15: 3–4 (Fall–Winter, 1987): 147–59.

———. "The Sardonic Powers of the Erotic in the Work of Ana Castillo." In *Breaking Boundaries: Latina Writing and Critical Readings*, Asunción Horno-Delgado et al., eds., pp. 94–107. Amherst: University of Massachusetts Press, 1989.

———. "The Theoretical Subject(s) in *This Bridge Called My Back* and Anglo-American Feminism." In *Making Face, Making Soul: Haciendo Caras*, Gloria Anzaldúa, ed., pp. 356–69. San Francisco: Aunt Lute, 1990.

———. "Traddutora, Traditora: A Paradigmatic Figure of Chicana Feminism." In *Changing Our Power: An Introduction to Women Studies*, eds. Jo Whitehorse Cochran, Donna Langston, and Carolyn Woodward. Dubuque, Ia.: Kendall-Hunt Publishing Co., 1988.

———. "What Kind of Lover Have You Made Me Mother?" In *Women of Color: Perspectives on Feminism and Identity*. Audrey T. McCluskey, ed. Occasional Papers Series, vol. 1, no. 1. Bloomington: Women's Studies Program, Indiana University, 1985.

Alarcón, Norma, Ana Castillo, and Cherríe Moraga, eds. *Third Woman: Sexuality of Latinas*. Berkeley: Third Woman Press, 1989.

Anaya, Rudolfo, ed. *Voces. An Anthology of Nuevo Mexicano Writers.* Albuquerque, El Norte Publications, 1987.

Anton, Ferdinand. *Women in Pre-Columbian America.* New York: Abner Schram, 1973.

Anzaldúa, Gloria. *Borderlands/La Frontera. The New Mestiza.* San Francisco: Spinsters/Aunt Lute, 1987.

———. *Making Face, Making Soul. Haciendo Caras.* San Francisco: Aunt Lute, 1990.

Arguelles, Lourdes. "Undocumented Female Labor in the United States Southwest: An Essay on Migration, Consciousness, Oppression and Struggle." In *Between Borders,* Adelaida R. Del Castillo, ed., pp. 299–312.

Baker, Houston A., Jr. *Three American Literatures.* New York: Modern Language Association, 1982.

Beltrán, Carmen Celia. *Remanso Lírico.* Published privately.

Blea, Irene. *Celebrating, Crying and Cursing.* Pueblo, Colo.: Pueblo Poetry Project, 1980.

Bornstein-Somoza, Miriam. *Bajo Cubierta.* Tucson: Scorpion Press, 1977.

Broyles Gonzáles, Yolanda. "Toward a Re-Vision of Chicano Theater History: The Women of El Teatro Campesino." In *Making a Spectacle" Feminist Essays on Contemporary Women's Theater,* Lynda Hart, ed., pp. 209–238. Ann Arbor: University of Michigan Press, 1989.

———. "Women in El Teatro Campesino: Apoco estaba molacha la Virgen de Guadalupe?" In *Chicana Voices,* pp. 162–87. The Austin Center for Mexican American Studies, 1990.

Cabeza de Baca Gilbert, Fabiola. *The Good Life.* Santa Fe: Museum of New Mexico Press, 1982.

———. *We Fed Them Cactus.* Albuquerque: University of New Mexico Press, 1954.

Calderón, Roberto R., and Emilio Zamora. "Manuela Solis Sager and Emma B. Tenayuca: A Tribute." In *Between Borders,* Adelaida R. Del Castillo, ed., pp. 269–80.

Camarillo, Albert. *Chicanos in a Changing Society.* Cambridge: Harvard University Press, 1979.

Candelaria, Cordelia. *Ojo de la Cueva/Cave Springs.* Colorado Springs: Maize Press, 1984.

Candelaria, Cordelia, ed. *The Wild Zone: Essays in Multi-Ethnic Literature.* Boulder: University of Colorado at Boulder, 1989.

Castañeda, Antonia. "The Political Economy of Nineteenth Century Stereotypes of Californianas." In *Between Borders,* Adelaida R. Del Castillo, ed., pp. 213–36.

Castillo, Ana. *My Father Was a Toltec.* Novato, Calif.: West End Press, 1988.

———. *The Mixquiahuala Letters*. Binghamton, N.Y.: Bilingual Press, 1986.

———. *Sapogonia*. Tempe: Bilingual Press, 1989.

———. *Women Are not Roses*. Houston: Arte Público Press, 1984.

Cervantes, Lorna Dee. *Emplumada*. Pittsburgh: University of Pittsburgh Press, 1981.

Chávez, Denise. *The Last of the Menu Girls*. Houston: Arte Público Press, 1986.

Chávez, John R. *The Lost Land. The Chicano Image of the Southwest*. Albuquerque: University of New Mexico Press, 1984.

———. *Chicana Voices: Intersections of Class, Race and Gender*. Austin, Tex.: Center for Mexican American Studies, 1986.

Cisneros, Sandra. *The House on Mango Street*. Houston: Arte Público Press, 1983.

———. *My Wicked, Wicked Ways*. Berkeley: Third Woman Press, 1987.

———. *Woman Hollering Creek and Other Stories*. New York: Random House, 1991.

Corpi, Lucha. *Delia's Song*. Houston, Arte Público Press, 1989.

———. *Palabras de mediodía: Noon Words*. Berkeley: El Fuego de Aztlán Publications, 1980.

———. *Variaciones sobre una tempestad/Variations on a Storm*. Berkeley: Third Woman Press, 1990.

Cota-Cárdenas, Margarita. *Marchitas de Mayo (Sones Pa'l Pueblo)*. Austin: Relámpago Press, 1989.

———. *Noches despertando inConciencias*. Tucson: Scorpion Press, 1977.

———. *Puppet*. Austin: Relámpago Press, 1986.

Crumm, Stella M., ed. *Down the Santa Fe Trail and into Mexico. The Diary of Susan Shelby Magoffin, 1846–1847*. New Haven: Yale University Press, 1926.

Curiel, Barbara Brinson. *Speak To Me From Dreams*. Berkeley: Third Woman Press, 1989.

de Hoyos, Angela. *Arise, Chicano! And Other Poems*. San Antonio: M & A Editions, 1975.

———. *Chicano Poems for the Barrio*. San Antonio: M & A Editions, 1975.

———. *Selected Poems/selecciones*. San Antonio: Dezkalzo Press, 1979.

———. *Woman, Woman*. Houston: Arte Público Press, 1985.

Del Castillo, Adelaida R., ed. *Between Borders: Essays on Mexicana/Chicana History*. Encino, Ca.: Floricanto Press, 1990.

Fisher, Dexter, ed. *The Third Woman. Minority Women Writers of the United States*. Boston: Houghton Mifflin, 1980.

Gaspar de Alba, Alicia, María Herrera-Sobek, and Demetria Martínez. *Three Times a Woman*. Tempe, Arizona, Bilingual Review Press, 1989.

Gómez, Alma, Cherríe Moraga and Mariana Romo-Carmona, eds. *Cuentos: Stories by Latinas*. New York: Kitchen Table Press, 1983.

Gonzales-Berry, Erlinda. *Paletitas de Guayaba*. Albuquerque: El Norte Publications, 1991.

Gonzales-Berry, Erlinda, and Tey Diana Rebolledo. "Growing Up Chicano: Tomás Rivera and Sandra Cisneros." *International Studies in Honor of Tomás Rivera*, Julián Olivares, ed. *Revista Chicano-Riqueña* 13 (3–4): 109–19.

Gregg, Josiah. *Commerce of the Prairies*, May L. Moorhead, ed. Norman: University of Oklahoma Press, 1954.

Griswold Del Castillo, Richard. *The Los Angeles Barrio, 1850–1890*. Berkeley: University of California Press, 1979.

Gutiérrez, Ramón A. "Marriage and Seduction in Colonial New Mexico." In *Between Borders: Essays on Mexicana/Chicana History,* Adelaida R. Del Castillo, ed., pp. 447–58. Encino, Calif.: Floricanto Press, 1990.

Hammond, George P., and Agapito Rey. *The Rediscovery of New Mexico, 1580–1594*. Albuquerque: University of New Mexico Press, 1987.

Hernández, Inés. *Con Razón, Corazón*. San Antonio: Caracol, 1977.

Hernández, Salomé. "The Present-day U.S. Southwest: Female Participation in Official Spanish Settlement Expeditions: Specific Case Studies in the Sixteenth, Seventeenth, and Eighteenth Centuries." Dissertation, University of New Mexico, 1987.

Herrera-Sobek, María, ed. *Beyond Stereotypes; The Critical Analysis of Chicana Literature*. Binghamton: Bilingual Press, 1985.

Herrera-Sobek, María, and Helena María Viramontes, eds. *Chicana Creativity and Criticism: Charting New Frontiers in American Literature. The Americas Review* 15 (3–4).

Jaramillo, Cleofas. *Romance of a Little Village Girl*. San Antonio: Naylor Co., 1955.

———. *Shadows of the Past*. np, 1941.

Johnson, Elizabeth A. "The Incomprehensibility of God and the Image of God Male and Female." In *Women's Spirituality: Resources for Christian Development*, edited by Joann Wolski Conn. New York: Paulist Press, 1986.

Lawhn, Juanita. "Women Publishing in La Prensa, 1913–1920." Unpublished paper, 1985.

Lecompte, Janet. "The Independent Women of Hispanic New Mexico, 1821–1846." In *New Mexico Women: Intercultural Perspectives,* Joan M. Jensen and Darlis A. Miller, eds. Albuquerque: University of New Mexico Press, 1986.

Lomas, Clara. "Mexican Precursors of Chicana Feminist Writing." In *Wild Zone: Essays on Multi-Ethnic American Literature,* Cordelia Candelaria, ed. Boulder: University of Colorado at Boulder, 1989.

Mazón, Mauricio. *The Zoot-Suit Riots. The Psychology of Symbolic Annihilation*. Austin: University of Texas Press, 1984.

Miller, Darlis A. "Cross-Cultural Marriages in the Southwest. The New Mexico

Experience, 1846–1900." In *New Mexico Women: Intercultural Perspectives,* Joan M. Jensen and Darlis A. Miller, eds. Albuquerque: University of New Mexico Press, 1986.

Mirandé, Alfredo, and Evangelina Enríquez. *La Chicana: The Mexican American Woman.* Chicago: University of Chicago Press, 1979.

Mora, Pat. *Borders.* Houston: Arte Público Press, 1986.

———. *Chants.* Houston: Arte Público Press, 1984.

———. *Communion.* Houston: Arte Público Press, 1991.

Moraga, Cherríe. *Giving Up the Ghost.* Los Angeles: West End Press, 1986.

———. *Loving in the War Years.* Boston: South End Press, 1983.

Moraga, Cherríe, and Gloria Anzaldúa, eds. *This Bridge Called My Back.* Watertown, Mass.: Persephone Press, 1981.

Niggli, Josephina. *Mexican Folk Plays.* Chapel Hill: University of North Carolina Press, 1938.

———. *Mexican Village.* Chapel Hill: University of North Carolina Press, 1945.

Olivares, Julián. "Seeing and Becoming: Evangelina Vigil, *Thirty an' Seen a Lot.*" In *The Chicano Struggle: Analyses of Past and Present Efforts.* Binghamton: Bilingual Press, 1984.

Ordóñez, Elizabeth. "Sexual Politics and the Theme of Sexuality in Chicana Poetry." In *Women in Hispanic Literature: Icons and Fallen Idols,* Beth Miller, ed., pp. 7–16. Berkeley: University of California Press, 1984.

Otero, Nina. *Old Spain in Our Southwest.* New York: Harcourt Brace and Co., 1936.

Padilla, Genaro M. "Imprisoned Narrative? Or Lies, Secrets and Silence in New Mexico Women's Autobiography." In *Criticism in the Borderlands,* Héctor Calderón and José David Saldívar, eds., pp. 43–60. Durham: Duke University Press, 1991.

———. "The Recovery of Chicano Nineteenth-Century Autobiography." *The American Quarterly* 42 (1988): 287–98.

Palomo Acosta, Teresa. *Passing Time.* Austin, Tex.: n.p., 1984.

Paredes, Raymond. "The Evolution of Chicano Literature." In *Three American Literatures,* ed. Houston A. Baker, Jr. New York: Modern Language Association, 1982.

Pérez, Emma. "A la Mujer: A Critique of the Partido Liberal Mexicano's Gender Ideology of Women." In *Between Borders,* Adelaida R. Del Castillo, ed., pp. 459–82.

———. "Sexuality and Discourse: Notes from a Chicana Survivor." In *Chicana Lesbians: The Girls Our Mothers Warned Us About,* Carla Trujillo, ed., pp. 159–84.

Pérez, Eulalia. "Una vieja y sus recuerdos." Manuscript in the Bancroft Library. Translated by Ruth Rodríguez. (C-D 139).

Phillips, Rachel. "Marina/Malinche: Masks and Shadows." In *Women in Hispanic Literature: Icons and Fallen Idols,* Beth Miller, ed., pp. 97–114. Berkeley: University of California Press, 1983.

Pico, María Inocenta. "Reminiscences of California." 1878. Manuscript in the Bancroft Library. (C-D 34).

Pineda, Cecile. *Face.* New York: Viking, 1985.

Ponce, Mary Helen. *Taking Control.* Houston: Arte Público Press, 1987.

———. *The Wedding.* Houston: Arte Público Press, 1990.

Portillo Trambley, Estela. *Rain of Scorpions.* Berkeley: Tonatiuh International, 1975.

———. *Sor Juana and Other Plays.* Ypsilanti, Mich.: Bilingual Press, 1983.

———. *Trini.* Binghamton: Bilingual Press, 1986.

Pratt, Annis. *Archetypal Patterns in Women's Fiction.* Bloomington: Indiana University Press, 1981.

Preciado Martin, Patricia. *Songs My Mother Sang to Me.* Tucson: University of Arizona Press, 1992.

Quintana, Alvina E. "Women: Prisoners of the Word. *Chicana Voices,* Teresa Córdova et al., eds., 208–19. Austin: Center for Mexican American Studies, 1986.

Rebolledo, Tey Diana. "Las Escritoras: Romances and Realities." In *Pasó por Aquí,* Erlinda Gonzalez-Berry, ed., pp. 199–214. Albuquerque: University of New Mexico Press, 1989.

———. "The Maturing of Chicana Poetry: The Quiet Revolution of the 1980s." In *For Alma Mater: Theory and Practice in Feminist Scholarship,* Paula A. Treichler, Cheris Kramarae, and Beth Stafford, eds., pp. 143–58. Chicago: University of Illinois Press, 1985.

———. "Narrative Strategies of Resistance in Hispana Writing." In *The Journal of Narrative Technique* 20 (2): 134–46.

———. "Tradition and Mythology: Signatures of Landscape in Chicana Literature." In *The Desert is No Lady,* Vera Norwood and Janice Monk, eds., pp. 98–124. New Haven: Yale University Press, 1987.

———. "Walking the Thin Line: Humor in Chicana Literature." In *Beyond Stereotypes: The Critical Analysis of Chicana Literature,* María Herrera-Sobek, ed., pp. 91–107. Binghamton: Bilingual Press, 1985.

———. "Witches, Bitches and Midwives: The Shaping of Poetic Consciousness in Chicana Literature." In *The Chicano Struggle,* pp. 166–77. Binghamton: Bilingual Press, 1984.

Rebolledo, Tey Diana, Erlinda Gonzales-Berry, and Teresa Márquez, eds. *Las Mujeres Hablan: An Anthology of Nuevo Mexicana Writers.* Albuquerque: El Norte Publications, 1988.

Ríos-Bustamante, Antonio, and Pedro Castillo. *An Illustrated History of Mexi-*

can *Los Angeles, 1781–1985*. Los Angeles: Chicano Studies Research Center Publications, 1986.

Rivera, Marina. *Mestiza*. Tucson: Grilled Flowers, 1977.

———. *Sobra*. San Francisco: Casa Editorial, 1977.

Rivero, Eliana. "Escritoras chicanas: Fronteras de la lengua y la cultura." *Anales del Pacífico* (forthcoming).

———. "Escritura chicana: Introducción y contexto." *Areíto* 5 (18): 38–52.

———. "Escritura chicana: La mujer." *La Palabra* 2 (2): 2–9.

———. "La mujer y la raza: Latinas y chicanas." *Areíto* 5 (19–20): 339.

———. "Poesía en Arizona: Las voces de *Mestiza*." *La Palabra* 1 (1): 26–33.

———. "*The House on Mango Street*: Tales of Growing Up Female and Hispanic." SIROW Working Paper Series, no. 21 (University of Arizona-Southwest Institute for Research on Women, 1986), pp. 2–19.

Rocha, Rina García. *Eluder*. Chicago: Alexander Books, 1980.

Romano-V., Octavio Ignacio, and Herminio Ríos. C., eds. *El Espejo-The Mirror. Selected Chicano Literature*. Berkeley: Quinto Sol Publications, Inc., 1969.

Ruiz, Vicki. *Cannery Women, Cannery Lives: Mexican Women, Unionization, and the California Food Processing Industry, 1930–1950*. Albuquerque: University of New Mexico Press, 1987.

Saldívar, Ramón. *Chicano Narrative. The Dialectics of Difference*. Madison: University of Wisconsin Press, 1990.

Sánchez, Marta. *Contemporary Chicana Poetry: A Critical Approach to an Emerging Literature*. Berkeley: University of California Press, 1984.

———. "Chicana Prose Writers: The Case of Gina Valdés and Sylvia Lizárraga." In *Beyond Stereotypes*, María Herrera-Sobek, ed., pp. 61–70. Binghamton: Bilingual Press, 1985.

Sánchez, Rosaura. *Requisa Treinta y Dos*. La Jolla, Calif.: Chicano Research Publications, 1979.

Sánchez, Rosaura, and Rosa Martínez Cruz. *Essays of La Mujer*. Los Angeles: Chicano Studies Center Publications, 1977.

Silva, Beverly. *The Cat and Other Stories*. Tempe, Ariz: Bilingual Press, 1986.

———. *The Second St. Poems*. Ypsilanti: Bilingual Press, 1983.

Stephens, Sandra L. "The Women of the Amador Family, 1860–1940." In *New Mexico Women: Intercultural Perspectives*, Joan Jensen and Darlis Miller, eds., pp. 257–78. Albuquerque: University of New Mexico Press, 1986.

Tafolla, Carmen. *Curandera*. San Antonio: M & A Editions, 1983.

———. *Get Your Tortillas Together*. n.p., 1976.

Tinajero, Sara G. "The Role of a Mexican American Woman Poet in the Southwestern United States." M.A. thesis, Laredo State University, Laredo, Texas, 1988.

Trujillo, Carla, ed. *Chicana Lesbians. The Girls Our Mothers Warned Us About*. Berkeley: Third Woman Press, 1991.

Valdés, Gina. *Comiendo lumbre/Eating Fire*. Colorado Springs: Maize Press, 1986.

———. *Puentes y Fronteras*. Los Angeles: Castle Lithograph, 1982.

———. *There Are No Madmen Here*. San Diego: Maize Press, 1981.

Vigil, Evangelina. *The Computer is Down*. Houston: Arte Público Press, 1987.

———. *Thirty an' Seen a Lot*. Houston: Arte Público Press, 1982.

Vigil, Evangelina, ed. *Woman of Her Word: Hispanic Women Write*. Houston: Arte Público Press, 1984.

Villanueva, Alma Luz. *Bloodroot*. Austin: Place of Herons Press, 1982.

———. *Life Span*. Austin: Place of Herons Press, 1985.

———. *Mother, May I?* Pittsburgh: Motheroot, 1978.

———. *The Ultraviolet Sky*. Tempe: Bilingual Press, 1988.

Viramontes, Helena María. *The Moths and Other Stories*. Houston: Arte Público Press, 1985.

Wilbur-Cruce, Eva Antonia. *A Beautiful, Cruel Country*. Tucson: University of Arizona Press, 1987.

Xelina. *KU*. San Antonio: Caracol, 1977.

Zamora, Bernice. *Restless Serpents*. Menlo Park, Calif.: Diseños Literarios, 1974.

Acknowledgments and Sources

THE ORAL TRADITION

"Eufemia's Sopapillas," told by Catalina Gurulé and Patricia Gallegos. Compiled by Lou Sage Batchen. New Mexico Federal Writers' Project, September 17, 1938.

"An Old Native Custom: La Curandera." New Mexico Federal Writers' Project, 5-5-49, #45.

"Quiteria Outwits the Witch Nurse," told by Rumaldita Gurulé. Compiled by Lou Sage Batchen. New Mexico Federal Writers' Project, September 17, 1938.

"Las Tres Gangozas" (The Three Sisters), told by Guadalupe Gallegos. Compiled by Bright Lynn. New Mexico Federal Writers' Project, 5-57-4.

CREATIVE WRITING

Anzaldúa, Gloria. "By Your True Faces We Will Know You / El día de la chicana," "El retorno," "Linguistic Terrorism"; and "To Live in the Borderlands means you" from *Borderlands / La Frontera: The New Mestiza* (San Francisco: Aunt Lute, 1987). Reprinted by permission of Aunt Lute Press.

Beltrán, Carmen Celia. "Flores secas"; Quinceañera" from *Remanso Lírico* (Tucson, 1980). Reprinted by permission of the author.

Blea, Irene. "Creations"; "Mourning A Sister's Death"; "Spaces Like the Barrio" from *Celebrating Crying and Cursing* (Pueblo, Colorado: Pueblo Poetry Project, 1980). Reprinted by permission of the author.

Bornstein, Miriam. "Para el consumidor"; "Toma de nombre" from *Siete Poetas* (Tucson: Scorpion Press, 1978). Reprinted by permission of the author.

Brinson Curiel, Barbara. "Drought" in *Grito del Sol* 2:3, 1977; and "Roads" *Prisma* (Spring, 1977). Reprinted by permission of the author. "Fire" from *Revista Chicana Riqueña* 10:3, 1981. Reprinted by permission of Arte Público Press.

Cabeza de Baca Gilbert, Fabiola. "The Herb Woman" from *The Good Earth* (Santa Fe: The Museum of New Mexico Press, 1982).

Calvillo-Craig, Lorenza. "soy hija de mis padres" from *El Grito* 7:1, 1973. Reprinted by permission of the author.

Camarillo, Lydia. "Mi reflejo" from *La Palabra* 2:2, 1980.

Candelaria, Cordelia. "Go 'Way from My Window, La Llorona" (1); "Haciendo tamales"; "Segments" from *Ojo de la cueva* (Colorado Springs: Maize Press, 1984). Reprinted by permission of the author. "La Llorona at Sixteen" and "Portrait by the River," printed by permission of the author.

Castillo, Ana. "From 'A Letter to Alicia,'" "Paradox," "Whole," "Women Are Not Roses" from *Women Are Not Roses,* copyright by Ana Castillo 1984. Originally published by Arte Público Press. "The Toltec" from *My Father Was a Toltec,* copyright by Ana Castillo 1988. Originally published by West End Press. Reprinted by permission of Susan Bergholz Literary Services, New York.

Cervantes, Lorna Dee. "Crow," "Emplumada," "For Virginia Chávez," and "Poem for the Young White Man Who Asked Me How I, an Intelligent, Well-Read Person Could Believe in the War Between Races" reprinted from *Emplumada,* by Lorna Dee Cervantes, by permission of the University of Pittsburgh Press, copyright 1981 by Lorna Dee Cervantes. "Como lo siento," "Oaxaca 1974," "Para un revolucionario," "The Body as Braille," "Refugee Ship," all reprinted by permission of Arte Público Press. "Beneath the Shadow of the Freeway" reprinted by permission of *The Latin American Literary Review* 15:30. "Declaration on a Day of Little Inspiration" and "El Sueño de Las Flores" from *Mango* 1:1, 1976.

Chacón, Sylvia. "My Poetry," *Capirotada*. Los Angeles: Fronteras, 1976.

Chávez, Denise. "Evening in Paris" from *The Last of the Menu Girls* (Houston: Arte Público Press, 1976) reprinted by permission of Arte Público Press. "On Meeting You in Dream": copyright by Denise Chávez 1977. First published in *The Indian Rio Grande,* eds. Gene Frumkin and Stanley Noyes. San Marcos Press. Reprinted by permission of Susan Bergholz Literary Services, New York.

Cisneros, Sandra. "Mango Says Goodbye Sometimes," "My Name," "The Three Sisters" from *The House On Mango Street*. Copyright by Sandra Cisneros 1989. Published in the United States by Vintage Books, a division of Random House, Inc., New York, and distributed in Canada by Random House of Canada Limited, Toronto. Originally published in somewhat different form by Arte Público Press in 1984 and revised in 1989. "Little Miracles, Kept Promises" from *Woman Hollering Creek*. Copyright by Sandra Cisneros 1991. Published in the United States by Vintage Books, a division of Random House, Inc., New

York, and simultaneously in Canada by Random House of Canada Limited, Toronto. Originally published in hardcover by Random House, Inc., New York in 1991. Reprinted by permission of Susan Bergholz Literary Services, New York. "Arturo Burro," "His Story," "South Sangamon," "Velorio" from *My Wicked Wicked Ways* (Bloomington, Ind.: Third Woman Press, 1987). Reprinted by permission of Third Woman Press.

Corpi, Lucha. "Como la semilla / Like the Seed," the English version of the "Marina Poems," "Movimiento / Movement," "Nuestros mundos / Our Worlds" from *Fireflight* (Oakland: Oyez, 1975). "Protocolo de verduras / The Protocol of Vegetables" *Prisma* (Spring, 1979). Spanish versions of the poems reprinted by permission of the author. English translations of the poems reprinted by permission of the translator, Catherine Rodríguez-Nieto.

Cota-Cárdenas, Margarita. "Crisis de identidad," "Desveladas inútiles," "Gullible," "Lírica fanática," "To a Little Blond Girl of Heber, Califas" from *Noches despertando inConciencias* (Tucson: Scorpion Press, 1975). "Malinche's Discourse," "Wimpy's Wake," from *Puppet* (Austin: Relámpago Books Press, 1985). "Nostalgia" from *Siete Poetas* (Tucson: Scorpion Press, 1978). "Aay Cucuy" from *La Palabra* 2:2, 1980. "Dedicated to American Atomics, 11," from *Marchitas de mayo* (Austin: Relámpago Books Press, 1989). Reprinted by permission of the author. Original translations printed by permission of the author.

Cunningham, Veronica. "a woman was raped . . . ," "ever since" from *Capirotada* (Los Angeles: Fronteras, 1976).

de Hoyos, Angela. "Fairy Tale / Cuento de Hadas," "La Malinche a Cortez y Vice Versa," "'San Antonio Rose' era Xicana" from *Woman, Woman* (Houston: Arte Público Press, 1985). Reprinted by permission of Arte Público Press. "La gran ciudad" from *Chicano Poems for the Barrio*. Reprinted by permission of the author.

Gaspar de Alba, Alicia. "Literary Wetback" *The Massachusetts Review* 29:2, Summer 1988. Reprinted by permission of the author. "Making Tortillas," "Malinchista, A Myth Revised" from *Beggar on the Córdoba Bridge* in *Three Times a Woman: Chicana Poetry* (Tempe: Bilingual Review/Press, 1989). Reprinted by permission of Bilingual Review/Press.

Gonzales-Berry, Erlinda. "Malinche Past" (translation) in *Paletitas de guayaba* (Albuquerque: El Norte Publications, 1991). "Rosebud" from *Las Mujeres Hablan* (Albuquerque: El Norte Publications, 1988). Reprinted by permission of the author.

Gonzales-Flores, Judy. "Julieta's Muses" from *De colores* 4:30, 1978.

Hernández, Inés. "After the Name-Giving" from *Ceremony of Brotherhood* (Albuquerque: Academia, 1981); "Guerrillera soy" and translation from *Con Razón, Corazón* (San Antonio: Caracol Publications, 1977); "Para Teresa" from *Siete Poetas* (Tucson: Scorpion Press, 1978); "To Other Women Who Were Ugly

Once" from *Encuentro Artístico Femenil* (Austin, 1978). Reprinted by permission of the author. "He Was One of Those Special Ones, She Said," printed by permission of the author.

Herrera-Sobek, María. "Mi poesía" from *Chasqui* (9 February–May 1980). Reprinted by permission of the author. "La casa" and "Poema inédito," printed by permission of the author.

Jaramillo, Cleofas M. "VI. Memorias." *Shadows of the Past* (Santa Fe: Ancient City Press, 1987).

La Chrisx. "La Loca de la Raza Cósmica," in *Comadre* 2, 1978.

Lizárraga, Sylvia S. "The Gift?" *Caracol* (1973); "Monarquía" from *Requisa Treinta y Dos,* ed. Rosaura Sánchez (La Jolla: Chicano Research Publications, University of California, San Diego, 1979). Reprinted by permission of the author and Rosaura Sánchez.

López de Padilla, María Esperanza. "Drama en Mañanitas," "María Esperanza," "Simplicidades" from Anselmo F. Arellano, *Los Pobladores Nuevo Mexicanos y su Poesía, 1889–1950* (Albuquerque: Pajarito Press, 1976). Reprinted by permission of the author.

Martínez, Demetria. "Elena at 5 Years," "Troublemaker" from *Turning* in *Three Times a Woman* (Tempe: Bilingual Review/Press, 1989). Reprinted by permission of Bilingual/Review Press.

Montes, Ana. "Adelita" from *Comadre* 2:2. Reprinted by permission of the author.

Mora, Pat. "Cheap Trick," "Cuentista / Story Teller." Printed by permission of the author. "Aztec Princess," "Dream," "Legal Alien," "Mielvirgen," "1910," "Plot," and "Sola" from *Chants* (Houston: Arte Público Press, 1984). Reprinted by permission of Arte Público Press. "Desert Women," "Maybe a Nun After All" from *Borders* (Houston: Arte Público, 1986). Reprinted by permission of Arte Público Press. "Hands" *Revista Chicana-Riqueña* x:33, 1982. Reprinted by permission of Arte Público Press.

Moraga, Cherríe. "For the Color of My Mother" from *This Bridge Called My Back* (Persephone Press, 1981). 2nd Edition. (Kitchen Table: Women of Color Press, 1983). Reprinted by permission of the author.

Otero-Warren, Nina. "Asking for the Bride" and "The Field Crosses of the Farmers": Excerpts from *Old Spain In Our Southwest,* copyright 1936 by Harcourt Brace Jovanovich, Inc. and renewed 1964 by Nina Otero-Warren. Reprinted by permission of the publisher.

Palomo Acosta, Teresa. "My Mother Pieced Quilts" from *Fiesta in Aztlán* (Santa Barbara: Capra Press, 1982); "They Are Laying Plans For Me . . . Those Curanderas," from *Passing Time* (1984). Reprinted by permission of the author.

Pérez, Eulalia. "Una vieja y sus recuerdos dictado . . . ," San Gabriel, Calif., 1877, translated by Ruth Rodríguez (C-D 139), The Bancroft Library, University of California, Berkeley. Reprinted by permission of the Bancroft Library.

Ponce, Mary Helen. "How I Changed the War and Won the Game" from *Corazón de Aztlán* (Los Angeles, Dec. 1981). Reprinted by permission of the author. "The Jewelry Collection of 'la Güera,' Marta M." Printed by permission of the author.

Portillo Trambley, Estella. "Sor Juana," Act II, from *Sor Juana and Other Plays* (Ypsilanti: Bilingual Review/Press, 1983). Reprinted by permission of Bilingual Review/Press. "The Paris Gown" from *Rain of Scorpions* (Berkeley: Tonatiuh, 1975). Reprinted by permission of the author.

Preciado Martin, Patricia. "The Journey," *La Confluencia* 3:3–4, 1980. Reprinted by permission of the author.

Quintana Pigno, Antonia. "The Album," *La Confluencia* 3:3–4, 1980. Reprinted by permission of the author.

Quiñonez, Naomi. "The Confession," "La Llorona" from *Sueño de Colibrí / Hummingbird Dream* (Los Angeles: West End Press, 1985). Reprinted by permission of the author and West End Press.

Rivera, Marina. "Chon," "Mestiza" from *Mestiza* (Tucson: Grilled Flowers, 1977). "Mama Toña" from *Sobra* (San Francisco: Casa Editorial, 1977). Reprinted by permission of the author.

Rocha, Rina García. "Baby Doll," "Chicana Studies," "New Year's Eve," "The Truth in My Eyes" from *Eluder* (Chicago: Alexander Books, 1980).

Sánchez-Padilla, Beverly. "Somos la tierra" from *De Colores* 2:3, 1975.

Santana-Béjar, Patricia. "In The Toolshed" from *Maize* 4:1–2, 1981. Reprinted by permission of the author.

Silva, Beverly. "Sin ti," "Two Brothers" from *Second St. Poems* (Ypsilanti: Bilingual Review/Press, 1983). Reprinted by permission of Bilingual Review/Press.

Sosa Riddell, Adaljiza. "Como ducle" from *Chicanas en el Arte / El Grito* 7:1, 1973. Reprinted by permission of the author.

Tafolla, Carmen. "Caminitos," "La Malinche," "444 Years After" from *La Isabela de Guadalupe y otras chucas, Five Poets of Aztlán,* ed. Santiago Daydí-Tolson. (Binghamton, N.Y.: Bilingual Review/Press, 1985). Reprinted by permission of Bilingual Review/Press.

Valdés, Gina. "The Valley of the Sun" (new version). Original version in *Requisa Treinta y Dos,* ed. Rosaura Sánchez (La Jolla: Chicano Studies Research Publications, 1979). Printed by permission of the author. "Josefina's Chickens" from *Caracol* (March 1979). Reprinted by permission of the author. "The Border," "Weeping with Laughter." Printed by permission of the author.

Vernon Galindo, Esther. "School" printed by permission of her daughter Tey Diana Rebolledo.

Vigil-Piñón, Evangelina. "kitchen talk," "mente jóven," "ser conforme," "tavern taboo," "was fun running 'round descalza" from *Thirty An' Seen a Lot*

(Houston: Arte Público Press, 1982). Reprinted by permission of Arte Público Press. "como embrujada" from *nade y nade* (San Antonio: M and A Editions, 1978). Reprinted by permission of the author.

Villanueva, Alma Luz. "A poet's job," "I sing to myself," "It is my nature," "Let us never forget the dance," "To My Daughter," "I Was a Skinny Tomboy Kid," "Witches' Blood," from *Bloodroot* (Austin: Place of Herons Press, 1982). Reprinted by permission of the author. "School," "Selection" from *Mother, May I?* (Motheroot Publications, 1978). Reprinted by permission of the author.

"The Ceremony of Orgasm" from *Hispanics in the United States* (Ypsilanti: Bilingual Review/Press, 1982). "Her Choice" from *Maize* 4:3–4, 1981. Reprinted by permission of the author.

Viramontes, María Helena. "Growing," "The Moths" from *The Moths and Other Stories* (Houston: Arte Público Press, 1985). Reprinted by permission of Arte Público Press.

Xelina. "mi mamá se sentaba," "tía Juana U glisten" from *Maize* 3:1–2, 1979–1980. Reprinted by permission of the author.

Zamora, Bernice. "Bearded Lady," "Plumb," "Progenitor," "Pueblo, 1950" "Restless Serpents," "So Not to be Mottled" from *Restless Serpents* (Menlo Park, Calif.: Diseños Literarios, 1976). "Do you take" from *El Fuego de Aztlán* (Summer, 1977); "Fecundating" from *Mango* 1:3–4, 1978. Reprinted by permission of the author.

About the Contributors

Gloria E. Anzaldúa is a Chicana, tejana, lesbian-feminist, poet-writer-critic, the author of *Borderlands/la frontera: The New Mestiza*; editor of *Making Face/Making Soul: Haciendo caras: Creative and Critical Perspectives by Women of Color*; and co-editor of *This Bridge Called My Back*.

Celia Carmen Beltrán was born in 1905 in Durango, Mexico. She has been the author of poetry, radio plays, articles, and dramas. She has also been an actress. She has won seven awards and five medals during her career. She was given a Cesar Award by Pan American Theatrical Association in Los Angeles for her work on press, radio, and theater. She also received an Outstanding Citizen Award from the city of Tucson for her contributions to art and literature, and has published a book of poetry, *Remanso Lírico*.

Irene I. Blea has returned to New Mexico, the land of her birth, after a thirty-five-year absence. Currently, she is Director of Hispanic Student Services at The University of New Mexico. Her poetry is rooted in the Chicano experience and the Civil Rights Movement of the sixties. Blea was chair of the Department of Chicano Studies at the University of Denver. She was the first female National Coordinator of the National Association for Chicano Studies and has served as Chair of the Chicana Caucus of NACS. Blea has won several awards for poetry including the Golden Globe Award and first place in the Martin Luther King Jr. Essay contest for "The Day I Discovered I Was Mexican." Her other publications include: *Toward a Chicano Social Science,* Praeger, 1988; *Bessemer,* AMS Press, 1988, and *Race, Class and Gender in the Life of La Chicana,* 1991.

Miriam Bornstein is Assistant Professor of Latin American Literature at the University of Denver. She is the author of studies on Chicano and Chicana literature and Latin American socio-political poetry and poetic history. Her publications of poetry include *Bajo Cubierta* as well as poems in journals and anthologies. She has completed *Donde Empieza la Historia,* her most recent collection of poetry.

Barbara Brinson Curiel is the author of *Speak To Me From Dreams,* a collection of poetry published by Third Woman Press (1989). She lives in Southern California and is a lecturer in Womens Studies and English at San Diego State University. She is the mother of two children, María Allegra and Alejandro.

Fabiola Cabeza de Baca was born in La Liendre, New Mexico, in 1895. She was a rural schoolteacher, home economist, writer, historian, cultural and civil leader, linguist, and pioneer educator. Her books include *The Good Life,* (1949), *We Fed Them Cactus* (1954), and *Historic Cookery* (1954).

Lorenza Calvillo-Craig is one of nine children born to a farmworker family. She was a teacher and administrator for fifteen years and has been practicing law for three years.

Cordelia Candelaria, a native of New Mexico, is the author of *Ojo de la Cueva/Cave Springs* (1984); *Chicano Poetry, A Critical Introduction* (1986); *Seeking the Perfect Game: Baseball in American Literature* (1989); and over six dozen other titles. She is also the co-editor of *Frontiers: A Journal of Women Studies*; *Multiethnic Literature of the United States: Critical Introductions and Classroom Resources* (1989); *American Book Review* (1989).

Ana Castillo is well known for both her prose and poetry. Her publications include two collections of poems, *Women Are Not Roses* and *My Father Was a Toltec*; two poetry chapbooks, *Otro Canto, The Invitation*; and two novels, *The Mixquiahuala Letters* and *Sapagonia*. She is the recipient of the Women of Words Awards in San Francisco and an NEA Fellowship. She is widely published throughout the country, and she has taught at many universities. Currently, she is living in Albuquerque, New Mexico.

Lorna Dee Cervantes is the author of *Emplumada* and *From the Cables of Genocide: Poems on Love and Hunger.* She teaches in the Creative Writing Program at the University of Colorado.

Denise Chávez is a native of New Mexico. She holds a Master's Degree in Creative writing from the University of New Mexico. She is a playwright, poet, and storyteller. Author of *The Last of the Menu Girls,* she has taught at the University of Houston.

Sandra Cisneros was born and raised in Chicago but currently lives in San Antonio, Texas. She is the author of two books of poetry, *Bad Boys* and *My Wicked Wicked Ways,* as well as two books of fiction, *The House on Mango Street* and *Woman Hollering Creek.* She has taught at several universities throughout the country and is the recipient of various writing awards including two NEA grants for fiction and poetry. She is presently at work on a novel.

Lucha Corpi was born in México in 1945 and moved to California in 1964. She is the author of two collections of poetry: *Palabras de Mediodía/Noon Words* and *Variaciones sobre una tempestad/Variations on a Storm,* and two novels *Delia's Song* and *Eulogy for a Brown Angel.* She is a teacher with the Neighborhood Centers Program in the Oakland Unified School District.

Margarita Cota-Cárdenas was born in 1941 in Heber, Imperial Country, California. She has published two books of her own poetry, short stories, critical essays, and a novel, *Puppet* (1985). She is cofounder of Scorpion Press, which published works by bilingual/bicultural women. She teaches Mexican and Chicano literature at Arizona State University, and is working on a second novel. She says: "I consider myself a *Chicana* feminist; we had to invent ourselves, back in 1975."

Angela de Hoyos has published five books of poetry, including *Woman, Woman,* Arte Público Press. "Widely acclaimed, her poetry has been recognized for its insight into the feminist concerns of Chicanas, and women everywhere" (Bryce Milligan). She is co-publisher and general editor of M and A Publications.

Alicia Gaspar de Alba is the author of a book of poems, *Beggar on the Cordoba Bridge,* and a collection of short fiction, *The Mystery of Survival and Other Stories.* She won a Massachusetts Artists Fellowship in Poetry in 1989, and currently is completing her Ph.D. in American Studies and a novel on Sor Juana Inés de la Cruz.

Erlinda Gonzales-Berry teaches Chicano Literature at the University of New Mexico. She is the author of a novel, *Paletitas de Guayaba,* El Norte Publications, 1991. She has also published many articles on Chicano literature and is the editor of *Pasó por aquí* for the University of New Mexico Press, 1989.

Inés Hernández is of Chicana and Nimpu (Nez Perce) descent. She is presently Assistant Professor of Native American Studies at the University of California at Davis. Her poetry has appeared in *Third Woman, Ceremony of*

Brotherhood, Frontiers, Calyx, Quarry West, Wicazo Sa, and *Americas Review,* among others.

María Herrera-Sobek obtained her Ph.D. from UCLA. She is a Full Professor in the Spanish and Portuguese Department at U.C. Irvine. Her books include: *The Bracero Experience: Elitelore Versus Folklore* (1979); *The Mexican Corrido: A Feminist Analysis* (1990); *Northward Bound: The Mexican Immigrant Experience in Corridos and Canciones* (forthcoming). She has edited *Beyond Stereotypes* (1985); *Chicana Creativity and Criticism* (1987) with María Helena Viramontes; and *Saga de México* (1991) with Seymour Menton. She has also published numerous articles and was featured in the poetry anthology, *Three Times A Woman* (1989).

Cleofas Jaramillo was born in 1895, and she lived as a child in Arroyo Hondo, New Mexico. She was a folklorist, business woman, and community leader. She founded the The New Mexico Folklore Society. Her books include *Shadows of the Past, Romance of a Little Village Girl,* and *The Genuine Tasty New Mexico Recipes.*

Sylvia S. Lizárraga was born in Mazatlán, Mexico, in 1925, but has lived in the United States for a long time. She obtained her Ph.D. in Literature at the University of California, San Diego in 1979. Later she occupied the position of Professor at the University of California, Berkeley, where she taught Chicano Studies. She moved to San Diego in 1987, where she currently resides. Lizárraga has written for many literary magazines such as *FEM* from Mexico. In the United States she has been published in *Revista Chicano-Riqueña, Maiz, Metamorphosis, La Opinión.* In Lizárraga's narrative, the condition of being both a Chicana and a woman is forcefully and, many times, ironically presented. She is working to publish a collection of her stories in the near future.

María Esperanza López de Padilla was born on April 5, 1918, in Pueblo, Colorado. Her parents were from Rio Arriba County in New Mexico, and were among the first settlers there. She graduated from high school in La Jara, Colorado, in 1937, having attended many schools because her family moved often. Her mother and father taught her to read Spanish and English before she started school. Her father composed poetry, but he never wrote it down. Her mother recited verses and stories from memory. María Esperanza López de Padilla is the first member of her family to put down on paper her creative writings. Nature fascinated her and inspired her first poetry. She has a husband, Manuel, and five sons. She has always been attracted to study and has taken many courses. She decided to attend the University when she was 53. She graduated from the University of New Mexico in 1975 with a major in Spanish and minors in science and American studies.

Demetria Martínez writes about Hispanic and women's issues for the *National Catholic Reporter,* based in Kansas City, Missouri. She is the author of *Turning,* a collection of poetry published in *Three Times a Woman* (Tempe: Arizona: Bilingual Review/Press). Her new manuscript, *The Darkness and the Light* will be published next year.

Ana Montes was raised in Stockton, California, and resides in San Francisco. She is currently involved in her own Desktop Publishing business. She hopes to return to San Francisco State University and complete an Ethnic Studies Masters degree.

Pat Mora's three poetry collections, *Communion, Borders,* and *Chants* are published by Arte Público Press. Two children's books are in press with Knopf and Macmillan. She is currently completing a collection of essays "Nepantla, The Land Between" to be published by the University of New Mexico Press.

Cherríe Moraga is a poet, playwright and essayist. She is co-editor of *This Bridge Called My Back: Writing by Radical Women of Color* and author of *Loving in the War Years: Lo Que Nunca Pasó por sus Labios,* among other titles. In 1990 her play, *Shadow of a Man,* was produced in San Francisco and received The Fund for New American Plays Award.

Adelina "Nina" Otero-Warren was an educator, politician, and writer. She ran for Congress on the Republican ticket in the 1930s. She is the author of *Old Spain in Our Southwest.*

Teresa Palomo Acosta has published her poetry since 1976. A Chicana born in Central Texas "aislada" from her pueblo, her own large and extended familia kept her connected to "la raza." She had added the short story and play writing to her repertoire. Acosta is a research associate at the Texas State Historical Association and teaches a course on Chicanas at the University of Texas at Austin.

Eulalia Pérez is one of the early pioneers in California, first arriving around 1801. She was a nurse and midwife. At Mission San Gabriel she was the housekeeper, bookkeeper, and treasurer. It is thought she was born in 1768. She died in 1878.

Mary Helen Ponce has taught "Chicana Literature from a Socio-Historical Perspective" at the University of New Mexico, where she is completing her doctorate in American studies. She is writing an official biography of Fabiola Cabeza de Baca. Her book, *Hoyt Street: Autobiography,* will be published in 1993. Her next book is "Mujeres Solas/ Women Alone."

Estela Portillo Trambley was born in El Paso, Texas. She is a playwright and novelist. Her books include *Sor Juana and Other Plays, Trini,* and *Rain of*

Scorpions. She has won many awards for her plays. She was one of the first Chicanas whose work was published during the early days of the Chicano Renaissance.

Patricia Preciado Martin graduated from Salpointe High School, Tucson, in 1956, and the University of Arizona with honors in 1960. She served as a teacher in the Peace Corps from 1962 to 1964. She is married to Jim Martin and has two children, Elena and Jim. Her publications include *Images and Conversations* (University of Arizona Press, 1983); *Days of Plenty, Days of Want* (Bilingual/Review Press, 1988); and *Songs My Mother Sang To Me* (University of Arizona Press, 1992).

Antonia Quintana Pigno is a native of Albuquerque and a 1991 finalist in the Barnard New Women Poetry Series. Her poems have appeared recently in *Kenyon Review, 13th Moon, Puerto del Sol,* and *Writers Forum.* She has two fine press publications by Zauberberg Press: *Old Town Bridge* and *La Jornada.*

Naomí Helena Quiñonez was born in Los Angeles. She is the author of *Sueños de Colibrí/Hummingbird Dream.* She has taught at the University of California at Santa Cruz, California State College at Northridge, and at California State College at Long Beach. She has been the director of the adult literacy program in the Los Angeles area and has been an advocate of Chicano culture. Her poems have appeared in many reviews and journals.

Marina Rivera has published two chapbooks, *Mestiza* and *Sobra,* both in 1977. She has two unpublished manuscripts, "The Celia Poems" and "Half a Caramel and a Cluster of Chile Pequín" on which she has based many readings. She recently completed a chapbook manuscript. Ms. Rivera lives near Tucson.

Catherine Rodríguez-Nieto's translations have appeared in numerous reviews and anthologies. She compiled and translated the poems in *Fireflight: Three Latin American Poets,* and translated two volumes of poetry by Lucha Corpi, *Palabras de mediodía/Noon Words* and *Variaciones sobre una tempestad/Variations on a Storm.* She and her husband own and operate Other Words . . . Inc., a translation service in the San Francisco Bay Area.

Beverly Sánchez-Padilla, a native of New Mexico, considers her work over the last twenty years as cultural. She has written and produced her first full length play, "La Guadalupe Que Camina," performed at the Guadalupe Theater in San Antonio, Texas, on December 14, 1990. "La Guadalupe . . ." is based on the true story and life of Hermana Rosa Marta Zarate Macías. Also in 1989 and 1990 she wrote and produced five television stories on Mexican American Women for national PBS out of KLRN in San Antonio, Texas. Trained in film, she has worked as an independent media producer for many years. She is working on a music-documentary video called "El Corrido de Juan Chacón."

Patricia Santana-Béjar was born and raised in San Diego where she lives with her husband and two children. She teaches Spanish at the community college and is currently working on a collection of short stories.

Beverly Silva graduated from San Jose State University in 1976 with an M.A. in English. She is the author of *The Second St. Poems*, 1983, and *The Cat and Other Stories*, 1986, and co-editor of *Nosotras: Latina Literature Today*, 1985. She is a native Californian relocated to Arizona, where she is presently employed at Mesa Community College teaching English.

Adaljiza Sosa Riddell was born and raised in Colton, California. Her parents were from León, Guanajuato, Mexico. She attended the University of California, Berkeley and Riverside. She has been teaching at UC Davis since 1971 when she joined the Political Science Department. She joined the Chicano Studies Program full-time in 1978 and was director from 1978 to 1989. She is a founding member of Mujeres Activas en Letras y Cambio Social, MALCS, and was awarded the National Association for Chicano Studies Scholar of the year Award in 1989. She derives her greatest satisfaction from working with her communities, the Chicano/Latino community of workers, the mujeres, and the scholarly community who are workers in their own right.

Carmen Tafolla, a native San Antonian, is the author of three books of poetry. A fourth, *Sonata to Human Beings* (First Place Poetry Winner of the U.C. Irvine National Chicano Literature Contest in 1987) is in press in bilingual edition in Germany. A noted speaker and educational consultant, with a wide variety of publications including a book on Chicanos, racism, and sexism (*To Split a Human: Mitos, Machos y la Mujer Chicana*), she is presently at work on a novel and TV mini-series, "La Gente."

Gina Valdés was born in Los Angeles, California, and grew up on both sides of the U.S.-Mexico border. She has published three books, *There Are No Madmen Here,* a novel, Maize Press, 1981; *Eating Fire,* a bilingual book of poetry, Maize Press, 1986; and *Puentes y fronteras,* a self-published book of coplas, 1982. Her work has also been published in journals and anthologies in the United States, Mexico, and Europe.

Esther Vernon Galindo was born in Jalapa, Veracruz, Mexico, in 1906. She lived in the United States for many years. Mother of four children, she wrote a novel which is to be found in a trunk at her daughter's house.

Evangelina Vigil-Piñón has been a Fellow of the National Endowment for the Arts and winner of many literary awards. She is widely published in literary magazines and is the author of *Nade y Nade,* 1978; *Thirty an' Seen a Lot,* 1982; *The Computer is Down,* 1987; and editor of *Woman of Her Word: Hispanic Women Write,* 1983. Currently, she works for *The Americas Review* as an editor.

Alma Luz Villanueva is the author of four volumes of poetry: *Bloodroot; Mother, May I?; Life Span;* and *La Chingada. The Ultraviolet Sky* (1989), a novel, won the American Book Award. Her second novel, *Naked Ladies,* is scheduled for publication in 1993 (Bilingual Press), as is a book of poetry entitled "Planet." She received a MFA in writing from Vermont College, Norwich University, 1984. She is the mother of four children.

Helena María Viramontes was born in East Los Angeles. She has been coordinator of the Los Angeles Writers Association, literary editor of *Xhisme Arte Magazine,* and an organizer of community and university poetry and fiction readings, as well as a Fellow of the National Endowment for the Arts. She is the author of *The Moths and Other Stories* and coeditor of *Chicana Creativity and Criticism: Charting New Frontiers in American Literature*.

Xelina served as an editor of Maize Press, a publications house for Chicano and Third World literature for ten years. She is the author of *KU* and has had her poetry published in anthologies and journals.

Bernice Zamora teaches Chicano literature, Native American literature, and Third World Women Writers in the United States at Santa Clara University. She is the author of *Restless Serpents* and has published many poems and essays.

About the Editors

TEY DIANA REBOLLEDO is an Associate Professor of Spanish at the University of New Mexico. She is the author of many articles on Chicana literature. She has been named a New Mexico Eminent Scholar and a Faculty Scholar at UNM. She has served as Chair of the National Association for Chicano Studies, as well as a Commissioner on the MLA Commission on the Status of Women. Born in Las Vegas, New Mexico in 1937, she now lives in Albuquerque with her husband Michael Passi and two spaniels. Currently she is working on a cultural history of Chicana literature as well as on a cultural history of Spanish/Mexicanas in the Southwest.

ELIANA S. RIVERO is a Professor of Spanish at the University of Arizona. She is the author of *El gran amor de Pablo Neruda: estudio crítico de su poesía* (1971), *De cal y arena* (1975), *Cuerpos breves* (1977), and coeditor of *Siete poetas* (1978). She has published numerous articles on contemporary Latin American literature and U.S. Hispanic literatures (especially on women authors), as well as poems in collections, magazines, and anthologies. A native of Cuba, she has lived in Tucson since 1967. Her most recent studies include "The 'Other's Other': Chicana Identity and Its Textual Expressions," in Gisela Brinker-Gabler, ed., *The Question of the Other/s* (Albany: SUNY Press, 1992), and "Cuban American Writing," in *The Oxford Companion to Women's Writing in the United States* (Oxford University Press, 1993). She is now working on a collection of essays about Latinos in the U.S.A.